PHILOSOPHY OF
HUMAN
RIGHTS

PHILOSOPHY OF HUMAN RIGHTS

Theory and Practice

DAVID BOERSEMA

PACIFIC UNIVERSITY

WESTVIEW PRESS

A Member of the Perseus Books Group

Westview Press was founded in 1975 in Boulder, Colorado, by notable publisher and intellectual Fred Praeger. Westview Press continues to publish scholarly titles and high-quality undergraduate- and graduate-level textbooks in core social science disciplines. With books developed, written, and edited with the needs of serious nonfiction readers, professors, and students in mind, Westview Press honors its long history of publishing books that matter.

Published by Westview Press,
A Member of the Perseus Books Group

Find us on the World Wide Web at www.westviewpress.com.

Westview Press books are available at special discounts for bulk purchases in the United States by corporations, institutions, and other organizations. For more information, please contact the Special Markets Department at the Perseus Books Group, 2300 Chestnut Street, Suite 200, Philadelphia, PA 19103, or call (800) 810-4145, ext. 5000, or e-mail special.markets@perseusbooks.com.

Designed by Trish Wilkinson
Set in 11 point Adobe Garamond Pro

Library of Congress Cataloging-in-Publication Data

Boersema, David.
    Philosophy of human rights : theory and practice / David Boersema.
        p.   cm.
    Includes bibliographical references and index.
    ISBN 978-0-8133-4492-8 (alk. paper)
    1. Human rights—Philosophy. I. Title.
JC571.B572 2011
323.01—dc22   2010040980

E-book ISBN: 978-0-8133-4493-5

Contents

v

PART III
SELECTED RIGHTS DOCUMENTS   367

Preface

Having taught philosophy courses (including those on rights) for many years, and having used a variety of types of texts over those years, I wanted this book to reflect, both in content and in style, what I believe works well pedagogically. For good reasons, philosophers often use anthologies of previously published (classic) papers as their primary class textbooks. These papers have usually been influential in the field and are noted for having advanced our understanding of the relevant issues. They provide a spectrum of voices on the topic at hand and let the authors speak for themselves, providing students with models of good (and sometimes not-so-good) philosophical work. However, as anyone who has taught with such books knows, the papers are often tough going for students first encountering them. They were, after all, often written by professional philosophers for an audience of other professional philosophers. As a result, these papers can be daunting for students, and quite a bit of class time must be devoted to "translating" them so that some genuine philosophical work can be done in the classroom.

On the other hand, a single-authored text, frequently more accessible to the student, is only a single voice. In an effort to capture the virtues of an anthology of papers while avoiding what can be their pitfalls, I chose to make this book a hybrid of selections from various authors and my own writing. I hope to present issues and views in an accessible manner by speaking directly to the reader and by laying the groundwork for weaving together selections from various philosophers. The reprinted selections from other philosophers are brief but (I believe) substantive and are integrated into each chapter with my own introduction and discussion. Each chapter includes not only a general analysis of some basic issue connected to rights or of some particular right but also at least two reprinted selections by authors who take different stands with respect to that issue or right. In addition, each chapter includes discussion questions at the end, which I hope will generate useful conversations and thought both in and out of the classroom. The questions are also intended to relate matters raised in earlier chapters to those in subsequent chapters—for example, to connect issues and views regarding what justifies rights generally with what justifies rights to privacy or to intellectual property in particular. Likewise, I hope the suggested materials in each chapter's "Further Reading" section will prove fruitful for the teacher as well as the student. Given the vast literature on rights, these suggested materials are, of course, very selective but (I believe) tried and true.

My assumption is that anyone reading this book assumes that he or she has a multitude of rights but has not questioned or analyzed that assumption. I intend this book as an introduction to the philosophical analysis of rights—as a way to look at that assumption. So, what exactly are rights? What makes us think that we "have" them? Just exactly who or what does have them? As will become apparent, I base the structure of the book on the notion that the claim to "have a right" is really shorthand for the following form or schema:

S has a right to x against o in virtue of j.

In this schema, s signifies rights holders (who or what has rights), x signifies the content and scope of rights (what we have rights to), o signifies the "others," or addressees, of our rights (those against whom rights holders hold rights), and j is the justification of rights, or at least our claims to rights.

I have divided the book into three main parts. Part I (Chapters 1 through 5) provides an in-depth look at the various components of rights just discussed. These address basic theoretical issues about rights. Chapter 1 focuses on the nature of rights: What exactly are rights, and how do they relate to other sorts of social features about agents (e.g., privileges). For example, are rights truly "inalienable"; that is, can they not be lost or separated from a rights holder? Are rights truly a social relation between persons or agents such that the relation is or is not optional between those persons or agents? As we will see, there are many fundamental questions about just what rights are. Chapter 2 looks at attempts to provide justification for rights, to provide some legitimacy for why we have rights at all and why we have particular rights (and why there are things to which we do not have rights). As Chapter 2 explains, this issue is connected to, though not the same as, the question of the source of rights, or where rights come from. Chapter 3 emphasizes concerns related to the content and scope of rights, that is, what we have rights to and what sorts of rights we have. For example, while many people claim that they have a right to education or to employment, do they really? Also, some have argued that people have a right to employment, whereas others have said they have, at best, a right to pursue employment but not a right to any actual job. In addition, many people claim that there are not only civil rights (i.e., rights they have as citizens of some legal system) but also human rights (i.e., rights they have as humans, independent of any legal system). As in the previous chapters, we investigate the complexities of these sorts of issues. Chapter 4 considers the issue of rights holders, the *s* in our schema above. This includes a consideration of the rights of the addressee, the *o* above. We look at what sorts of things can reasonably be said to have rights (the *s*) or to be bound by rights (the *o*). For instance, is the environment itself something that can legitimately be considered a rights holder? Or can future generations of humans, who do not yet exist, legitimately be considered rights holders? Then, in Chapter 5, we survey various criticisms that have been made about rights, both those that speak to the very concept and nature of rights and more specific criticisms about particular features of rights and particular rights claims.

Moving past this coverage of some fundamental conceptual and theoretical issues about rights, the remaining chapters of the book (Chapters 6 through 13) focus on the practice and application of rights, both broadly socially and with respect to specific rights. Following some of the criticisms about rights from Chapter 5, Chapter 6 examines how an emphasis on rights has played out and affected political discourse and social interaction in the United States today. Some theorists and commentators have argued that addressing our collective social concerns via an emphasis on rights has had negative consequences, while other theorists and commentators have insisted that this emphasis has led to positive consequences. Chapter 7 extends the focus on the practice of rights beyond the United States to consider global concerns, including the examination of rights as enunciated in the constitutions of various nations.

The remaining chapters of the book zero in on specific rights or claims for kinds of rights. Chapters 8 through 11 deal with specific rights: the right to free expression, the right to employment, the right to privacy, and intellectual property rights. A great many specific rights could be discussed. I chose these four because, I believe, they are especially relevant to the day-to-day lives of many people. For example, with the changes and advances in technology, personal information—what one takes as a matter of personal privacy—is becoming more and more public. The means for accessing, storing, and distributing information about individuals are growing more prevalent every day, making the issue of a right to privacy increasingly salient. Likewise, although intellectual property rights might seem a matter of business law, changing technology has made this issue of such rights a matter of increasing concern. It is very likely that you, dear reader, have downloaded music without paying for it—and that you would recoil if you were told that you had to pay for it! Because information is so readily available and easy to duplicate today, many people assume that it should be free, on demand, and not treated as private property. So, again, the topics covered in these chapters represent but a few of a great many that could be covered, yet they seem particularly relevant to daily life today. Finally, Chapters 12 and 13 focus not on specific rights content (such as the right to privacy) but rather on specific groups of rights holders. These chapters deal with victims' rights and children's rights, that is, rights claimed by persons or agents in their capacity as victims or as children. The primary focus of these two chapters is on their philosophical and conceptual content, not simply their historical and political content. We will see how the basic theoretical discussion in Part I of the book relates to and informs discussions of these specific practices and applications. In addition, by looking at our practices and applications of rights, we will reflect back on and examine the theoretical perspectives made in the book's early chapters.

Finally, Part III consists of various important rights documents. They are discussed at various times throughout the earlier chapters, and I hope it will be helpful to have them available for reference and fuller analysis, should that be desired. For instance, having them compiled together, one can see how, say, the Universal Declaration of Human Rights is both like and different from earlier and later rights documents.

Because the various features and aspects of rights intertwine and overlap, many of the issues covered here return and repeat throughout the different chapters. For example, in discussing the very nature of rights—just what they are—one inevitably speaks to what justifies claims to rights. Or when speaking of what justifies claims to rights or of who or what can properly be deemed a rights holder, it is inevitable that one speaks to the content of rights. For instance, those who advocate for nonhuman animals as rights holders certainly do not claim that cats have the right to vote or to political participation, but they do have a right to freedom from abuse. As a result, the various issues addressed in a particular chapter inevitably refer to aspects of rights further addressed in other chapters. This is not a problem of vagueness or lack of precision regarding rights (or regarding the book's chapters!); rather, it illustrates the complexity of focusing on one aspect of rights while keeping other related aspects in the wings.

Finally, this book would not have been possible without the help, assistance, and guidance of a number of people. In particular, I want to thank Karl Yambert and Kelsey Mitchell at Westview Press for their support and patience, as well as several reviewers of the manuscript, all of whom gave thoughtful, substantive, and good-spirited suggestions and advice. Thanks also to Melissa Veronesi and Jennifer Kelland for their gracious suggestions to make the book more readable and accessible. Any flaws and faults that remain here are in spite of the fine work of all these good people. Lastly, I want to thank Kari Middleton for her thoughtful commentary and assistance with this project.

INTRODUCTION

Modern social life seems inconceivable without the notion of rights. Today, we all take it for granted that we have a multitude of rights, and if asked, we could enumerate many of them without any difficulty: the right to vote, the right not to vote if we so choose, the right to freedom of expression, the right to the pursuit of happiness, the right to bear arms, the right to privacy, the right to fair wages, the right to drive, the right to get married, and so on. We are also aware of the social and political conflicts and controversies that often get framed in the language of rights. For example, many people characterize the issue of abortion as entailing the right of a human fetus to be born (right to life) versus the right of the mother to decide whether to bear the child (right to choose). Likewise, we are all aware of the controversy concerning the right, or purported right, of same-sex couples to marry. We hear about, and often are asked to vote on, "new" rights or rights extending to people who did not have certain rights before: the right to physician-assisted suicide, victims' rights, animal rights, the right to a clean environment, economic rights, smokers' rights, rights to be free from smoke, prisoners' rights, employee rights, and employer rights, among many others.

Despite the overwhelming presence and prevalence of rights in our lives, all too often we do not reflect either on just what we mean when we claim that we have rights or on just what rights are. But doing this—examining and analyzing rights—is what this book is all about. For instance, we look at various arguments for and against the importance of privacy rights or victims' rights, as well as the general role and value of addressing social conflicts by appealing to rights at all.

There are many approaches to examining rights. There is a historical approach, and, indeed, there are a number of excellent works on the history of rights, such as Gary Herbert's *A Philosophical History of Rights*, Micheline Ishay's *The History of Human Rights: From Ancient Times to the Globalization Era*, and Richard Tuck's *Natural Rights Theories: Their Origin and Development*, to name just a few. There is also a religious approach, in the sense of connecting notions of human identity, and its relation to divine origins or destiny, with notions of obligation toward and permission from other moral agents as part of a divine creation. Here, the focus is often on how rights relate to, say, divinely ordained responsibilities or how rights relate to promoting a divinely sponsored sense of human community. Some works in this religious approach include Leroy Rouner's *Human Rights and the World's Religions*, Elizabeth Bucar and Barbra Barnett's *Does Human Rights Need God?*, and Joseph Runzo's *Human Rights and Responsibilities in World Religions*.

Even more prolific are works on rights that are primarily political and/or social in nature. These works often emphasize and investigate the development and kinds of civil rights and how those rights relate to legal systems and legal traditions. For example, many works have been written on the interpretations of the right to bear arms in the United States, given the language of the U.S. Constitution's Second Amendment. Or, there are many works on the meaning and interpretations of the right to habeas corpus (i.e., laws requiring the bringing to court of a legal party). Or, there are many works on the development and interpretations of the enforcement of rights legislation both within a given legal system and also across international borders (e.g., international rights treaties or agreements). Likewise, there are numerous works on the social and legal aspects of particular rights and rights legislation, for example, with respect to same-sex marriage or physician-assisted suicide, as well as a multitude of works on particular legal rights connected to contract law, property law, and so forth.

This book, however, is about the philosophy of rights; it is a philosophical examination of rights; that is to say that it emphasizes the basic concept of rights as well as the implications and presuppositions of rights. Such an approach, of course, overlaps with historical, religious, and political/social approaches, but the emphasis is more immediately and directly conceptual. For example, nearly all these other approaches take as given that rights are something held by humans (and some human extensions, such as corporations) and do not discuss or treat nonhumans, but a philosophical question is just what makes something (human or otherwise) the kind of thing that has rights. Historically, the kinds of things generally acknowledged as rights holders have expanded over time; at one time women and minorities in the United States were not acknowledged as having the right to vote, and now they are. Today, some people, but not all, claim that many nonhuman animals and even the environment itself are legitimate rights holders. What kinds of things, then, are properly said to be rights holders and why? This is a philosophical question, not just a historical or political one.

In some respects, then, this philosophical approach is theoretical—or at least conceptual. This book addresses what rights are, what features they have, how claims to them can be justified, and the like. But such a philosophical approach is not "merely" theoretical or conceptual. Practical issues and applications to specific issues arise, and they are also philosophical. For example, does an unborn human fetus have rights? As we know, this is a very practical social question, and the answers to it are in large part philosophical; not only do we answer this question by taking a position on what sort of things are legitimately rights holders, but at the same time we also address the issue of the relative importance of the right of an unborn human fetus to be born against the right of an adult human (i.e., the mother, regardless of her age) to self-determination and freedom of choice. For both issues we are asking for justification for answers to the question about abortion. These are philosophical matters, though they overlap with social and political concerns. So, again, while the topics and issues raised in this book are philosophical, they are by no means impractical or "merely" theoretical. Indeed, as we will see, more than half of the chapters focus on the practice of rights in our daily lives and on applications of conceptual matters to particular, specific rights. After all, it is how rights play out in our day-to-day lives that makes them a concern for us.

A PHILOSOPHICAL APPROACH TO RIGHTS

Before we look at the various issues concerning rights in the following chapters, a few words are in order about a philosophical approach to examining rights. First, like law, rights are a mode of regulating our behavior. This is not the only way that rights have been understood, but it is a (if not the) primary way they are understood today. They are a means by which today we legitimately determine and regulate what people do and do not get to do. For example, we claim that our right to freedom of expression both permits us to express ourselves, even in ways that other people sometimes do not like or endorse, and prevents others from censoring us. In a word, our rights regulate our behavior. Of course, it is not quite that simple. As we know with the right to freedom of expression, there are limits to the regulation as well as the practice of that behavior. There are limits to how, where, and when we can express ourselves. The upcoming chapters of this book will take up these sorts of issues. Right now, the point is that when we speak of rights as a mode of regulating behavior, we are speaking both descriptively and prescriptively. That is to say, we are both describing what behaviors actually do get regulated and making value claims about what behaviors should be regulated (and why). A philosophical approach, then, is not simply one that is descriptive, that discusses what the current laws are regarding, say, a right to freedom of expression. To philosophy it is certainly relevant just what the facts are, but describing and analyzing those facts is not the only, or even the main, issue. In addition, we want to go beyond the current facts and ask what legitimates, or could legitimate, such regulation of behavior. Rights, then, like law, are not simply a matter of what is the case; they are also a matter of what ought to be the case. As a result, a philosophical approach to rights will include a discussion of what facts are relevant to the issue and also what values and goals, even if they are not currently realized, are relevant to the issue. When we turn, for instance, to the issue of who or what are legitimate rights holders, we will not merely look to see who or what kinds of things "have" rights that are recognized today in our legal system; we will also look at what arguments are and can be offered to justify why some things are and ought to be considered proper rights holders, while other things are not and ought not be considered proper rights holders. It is this reflective moving back and forth between description and prescription in an effort to analyze and critique arguments that will constitute the following chapters as philosophy of rights. Lest we think that this is "merely" philosophizing, keep in mind that this is what we all do at some level—explicitly or implicitly, in a focused or vague manner—when we take a stand on some particular issue—for example, when we vote for or against, say, abortion on demand or same-sex marriage. The decisions we make about these sorts of issues reflect underlying answers to the theoretical, conceptual, philosophical questions. This book is written with the commitment that there is genuine value in addressing these underlying questions directly, not only for gaining clarity of thought but also for promoting rightness of action.

Rights have been understood in a variety of ways over the years in a variety of contexts and from a variety of philosophical and social perspectives. In this book, I approach rights as I think most people do today, at the beginning of the twenty-first century. We take rights as a mode of social interaction, as a way of engaging with one another, especially in a world of increased globalization and diversity. I am also approaching rights, at least to begin with, using assumptions that I think many people today use. For instance, at times I interchange the terms *human rights* and *natural rights*. I use both to refer to those rights that people understand today as being held by humans simply due to their status as humans, not their status as citizens. So, I use those two terms interchangeably to distinguish certain rights from legal or civil rights, that is, rights that are held by people because they are part of some legal or social system (i.e., they are citizens) and that come from those systems. This, I think, is how most people today think of these notions, when they in fact do think of them. However, historically and conceptually, *human rights* and *natural rights* are not equivalent terms. (This point is made very clearly and substantively in Herbert's excellent *A Philosophical History of Rights*.) What people today mean by "human rights," namely, rights related to just treatment and pertaining to humans in terms of their well-being as persons, is not what the important rights theorists in the seventeenth and eighteenth centuries (such as Thomas Hobbes, John Locke, and Jean-Jacques Rousseau) meant by "natural rights." They took natural rights more as liberties that all living beings have and that clash when different interests clash. Or, as rights theorist Kenneth Minogue has noted, earlier thinkers understood natural rights to be derived from the operation of natural reason, while today human rights are understood to be derived from what it is to be human, particularly what is needed to thrive as a human. Today, most people understand rights as claims (or what Herbert calls "usages"), but rights have not always been understood in this way. Even the notion that rights impose duties or obligations on others (e.g., my right to free expression entails that you have a duty not to suppress that expression) is not something that, say, Hobbes would have believed; however, that is how rights are understood today. This book, then, is written on the assumption of how (I think) most people today understand rights and, therefore, address rights issues. Whether such an understanding is especially fruitful or rigorous is an important question and worthy of a sustained analysis—but it is not this book.

RIGHTS SCHEMA

So, how do people address rights issues today? When we claim to "have a right," we are saying something much more complex than when we claim to "have a car" or even to "have a wish." To begin with, we never simply have a right. Rather, when we make such a claim, we are actually saying that we have a right to something or other. We never merely have a right; we have a right to vote or to worship as we please or to own a home or to not own a home, and so forth. So, to have a right is always to have a right to x, where x might be to own some object (such as a home), to receive some good or service (such as a public education), or to behave in some way (such as voting).

In addition, when we claim to have a right to x, this right is said to be held against some other person or moral agent (I use the term *moral agent* to include not only individual humans but also other entities, such as corporations or governments). If you and I sign a contract saying that you will perform certain work for me by a certain date—so I have a right to x, where x is the work to be performed—then I have that right with respect to you, but not with respect to some other person. In this case, you (not your mother!) are the person against whom I hold this right. If you fail to perform the contracted work, then you are the person who has violated my right to have that work performed. Some rights, at least some applications of rights, are such that they relate specific persons or agents to each other. Other times we speak of having rights that relate an individual (the rights holder) to everyone else. For example, if I have a right to worship as I please, then I have that right with respect not only to specific persons and agents but to all persons and agents. So, if I have such a right, not only do you not get to interfere with my worshipping behavior, but neither does your mother or the government or anybody else. Broadly speaking then, when we have a right, we have a right to x, and we hold this right against o (some other person or agent).

Furthermore, when we claim to have a right to x against o, we need to offer some justification for that claim. A claim to have a right is just that—a claim. But what makes me think that I have a right to x? Clearly, I do not have a right to something simply because I want it. I might want your car, but that does not mean that I have a right to it. There must be some grounds or justification for the rights that we have. So, the simple beginning remark that we "have a right" has now expanded to the claim that we "have a right to *x* against *o* in virtue of some *j* (justification)."

Finally, although I have so far remarked that we claim to have a right, there is a question of exactly who "we" are. With respect to the actual social practices all around us, the rights-holding "we" includes not just individual people or humans but other agents, such as nations, states, corporations, and (some) nonhumans. For example, we often speak of the right of a country to defend itself or the right of some business entity (such as Microsoft) to take over some other company. Likewise, those sorts of agents or entities can be the others against whom we hold rights (e.g., we can sue a business, so we treat it as the kind of thing against which we have rights). Noting who or what has rights entails the issue of who or what is a rights holder (or rights bearer).

These preceding remarks can be summarized by saying that a claim to "have a right" is really shorthand for the following form or schema:

S has a right to *x* against *o* in virtue of *j*.

In this schema, *s* signifies rights holders (who or what has rights), *x* signifies the content and scope of rights (what we have rights to), *o* signifies the "others," or addressees, of our rights (those against whom rights holders hold rights), and *j* is the justification of rights, or at least our claims to rights. The structure of this book, particularly Part I, is based on this schema, with chapters focusing on its various components (i.e., what are legitimate rights holders, in virtue of why do some agents have rights, and so forth). After setting out basic theoretical and conceptual aspects of rights in Part I, I shift the emphasis in Part II to the practice and application of rights, with Chapters 6 and 7 devoted to broad social and cultural questions. How we "use" rights today is the focus of these chapters, which are then followed by a number of chapters that stress the application of rights theory to specific rights, such as the right to free expression or the right to privacy or children's rights. Finally, Part III provides some of the important rights documents that have been instrumental in how people in the twenty-first century understand rights.

PART I

THEORY

The chapters that form Part I all focus on basic conceptual issues related to rights. These include various conceptions of what exactly rights are, what justifies the claim that people in fact have rights, what it is, broadly speaking, that people (or moral agents) have rights to, who or what is seen as a legitimate holder or subject of rights, and various criticisms that have been leveled against rights. For example, what is meant when someone says that education is a right or that education is a privilege, not a right? How could someone make the case that education is a right and not (merely) a privilege? On what grounds might someone criticize such a view? If the U.S. Constitution does not explicitly state that citizens have a right to privacy, does that mean that they, in fact, do not?

These are basic questions about the nature, justification, and range of rights. They are, simply put, about the theory of rights. The emphasis here is on the deep, underlying aspects of rights. Chapter 1 looks at what rights are (as opposed to, say, privileges), that is, at conceptions regarding their very nature. Chapter 2 considers several views of what justifies claims to rights. What makes us think that we have rights, anyway? What grounds are there for saying that we have (or do not have) a right to education? Chapter 3 deals with very broad aspects of the content and scope of rights, focusing not on specific content, such as the right to education, but rather on what kinds of obligations are put on others in terms of what they may or must do if we have rights. In addition, this chapter deals with whether the content and scope of the rights we have is a matter of what our legal systems say or of our nature as moral agents. Chapter 4 takes this last issue one step further and looks at some basic questions about what kinds of things can legitimately be said to have rights. Can animals have rights? Can groups of people, as opposed to the individuals who make up those groups, have rights? Why can certain things hold rights and not other things? Finally, Chapter 5 focuses on basic criticisms of rights—not of specific rights, such as to education or to assisted suicide, but of human rights and rights in general. In all, these chapters are concerned with broad conceptual matters about rights.

CHAPTER 1

THE NATURE OF RIGHTS

Imagine if some stranger said to you that she most liked about her native country that she enjoyed so many *glubs* there. No doubt you would have no idea what she was talking about. Naturally, you would ask, "What are glubs?" Furthermore, imagine that this was not just a translation issue—for example, that *glubs* was merely her native word for "turnips"—but that the word itself was vague or unclear. So, if it turned out that the closest translation of the word *glubs* was "happinesses," you would still be puzzled by exactly what she meant when she said that she enjoyed so many happinesses in her native country. This is also true of the notion of rights. Although we use that term all the time and insist that we have numerous rights, if asked to say exactly what rights are, we find it difficult to answer. What rights are—the nature of rights—is the focus of this chapter.

WHAT RIGHTS ARE NOT

When we claim that we have rights, or even that we have some particular right, such as the right to vote or the right to think whatever we want, what exactly are we talking about? It is fairly easy to say what rights are not. For example, it is obvious that rights are not the same thing as abilities, since you have the ability to kill me or steal my property, but you do not, thereby, have the right to do either of those things. It is also obvious that rights are not the same thing as desires or wishes or wants; again, you might want to kill me or steal my property, but that does not mean that you have such a right. Rights

11

are also not the same thing as deserts, or what you deserve; you might very well deserve some honor or reward for your wonderful behavior (or, for that matter, you might deserve some rebuke or punishment for your wicked behavior), but that is not the same thing as having a right to the honor or reward (or rebuke or punishment).

So, it is fairly intuitive that rights are not the same thing as abilities, desires, or deserts. Less intuitive or obvious is that rights are not the same as liberties or freedoms. Liberties are actions that we engage in, or may engage in, that are not required of or forbidden to us. So, I am at liberty to wear ugly clothes or to talk in annoyingly cutesy ways to my cat. I do not have to do those things; there is no duty, legal or moral, for me either to do them or not to do them. These actions might be related to rights in the sense that you do not get to prevent me from doing them, so you do not have the right to prevent me from doing them, but their nature as *liberties* is that they are actions I can and may perform but have no duty to perform.

Likewise, the word "freedom(s)" does not denote exactly the same thing as liberties or rights. I might be at liberty to do something, in the sense of having no duty to do or not do it, but I might not be free to do that action for various reasons. If the action is to talk in cute, annoying ways to my cat, I might not be free to do so because you have taped my mouth shut! Or if my action is to wear ugly clothes, I might not be free to do so because you have burned all of them, or you have had me thrown in jail, where I cannot access them.

So, although rights are related to liberties and freedoms, they are not exactly identical to them. The same situation holds—although it is less intuitive or obvious and, indeed, somewhat controversial—that rights are not the same thing as needs. We cover this issue in greater detail later in this chapter, as well as in Chapter 2, but for now suffice it to say that needing something is not the same thing as having a right to that thing. Of course, an important issue with respect to this point is what constitutes a need. Part of the complexity herein is that needs are relative. For example, as a biological organism, I need food to survive but not a computer. However, as a writer of textbooks I need a computer (or some other medium to write with). Where many people claim that because I need food to survive, I therefore have a right to food—many others disagree that I have a right to food just because I need it—very few people, if any, claim that I have a right to a computer, even if, as a writer, I need one. In addition, I have some rights that seem unrelated to some of my needs. As a biological organism, I do not need to be able to worship as I please, but, at least legally speaking, I do have the right to worship as I please. Again, we return to this issue of rights and needs later on, but for now let us say that rights are not the same thing as needs.

RIGHTS AS RELATIONS

Notice that above I keep remarking that rights are not the same *thing* as abilities, liberties, needs, and so forth. Clearly, rights are not things in the sense of objects, like tables or cats; they are instead relations between (some) things. Some philosophers have claimed that rights are properties of persons (or moral agents, if we include, say, animals or nations as having rights). These two notions of properties and relations need to be explained: An object such as my cat, Mycroft, is a thing; he is a physical object. But we can speak of his properties or characteristics. For example, he is a certain color, he weighs a certain amount, and he has reached a certain age. His color, weight, age, and so forth, are all properties of him. In addition, he is smaller than I am and younger than I am, and he sleeps more than I do. These features of being *smaller than* and *younger than* and *sleeping more than* are all relations that hold between Mycroft and me. They are not exactly the same thing as properties of him because "being smaller than" only makes sense when two things are being talked about or compared, so it is a relation between two things, not a property of one thing.

As mentioned above, some philosophers have said that rights are properties of certain objects. So, having a right is like having an arm or having a car; it is a property of something independent of anything else. Most philosophers do not say that rights are properties in this sense, but many assert that the justification for something having rights stems from some property or properties it has. So, one might say that something has rights because it has certain capabilities—for instance, to suffer or to make life plans. This is really a claim about what justifies something as having rights, not exactly about what rights are, and we turn to that issue later in this chapter as well as in the next one.

Most philosophers speak of rights as a relation because most of them see rights in the context of social interaction. When we normally speak of rights, we speak of them as regulating people's behavior *with respect to each other* not simply as regulating any behavior, such as my making sure that I sit up straight or walk without slumping. Imagine that you were the only person in the world: Would you have rights? If rights are properties, then you might very well say that you would have rights even if no one else existed. However, if rights are relations, then it is difficult to comprehend that someone could have rights if no one else existed. You might have liberties, freedoms, needs, desires, and the like, but it is much less plausible to speak of having rights.

If rights are relations, then various questions emerge: what kind of relation (since rights are not a physical relation like "smaller than") and relation between what (what things or kinds of things are related by rights)? A further question—how and why are things related by rights?—is really about justifying rights, and, again, we turn to that issue in Chapter 2.

So, what kind of relation is a rights relation? First, it is a relation between moral or legal agents. Moral agents are those things that can behave in moral (or immoral) ways and are part of some sort of moral system or community. Legal agents are those things that can behave in legal (or illegal) ways and are part of some sort of legal system or community. I use the term *moral agent* here rather than "person" because the latter is generally associated with human individuals. Some rights theorists include some nonhumans, or at least nonindividual humans, as moral agents and certainly as legal agents. For example, corporations are treated as entities that can function legally; they can own property, pay taxes, sue or be sued, and so forth. Likewise, nations or governments are often spoken of as having both legal and moral status. Chapter 4 focuses directly on the issue of just what kinds of things are said to be rights holders, so to avoid those issues here, I use the terms *moral agent* and *legal agent*, and, again, the present point is that rights are a relation between moral or legal agents. The following scenario, offered by philosopher Heather Gert, makes obvious that rights are fundamentally a relation between moral (or legal) agents: Suppose you are attacked by *x* (let's call *x* Bertha) and injured. Would we say that your right (to bodily security) has been violated? For Gert, it depends on who or what attacked you. If a "normal" person attacked you, then, yes, we would no doubt say your rights had been violated, but if a wild bear attacked you, then, no, we would not say that your rights had been violated, even though your bodily well-being was. Or, to give another example, being struck by a person is one thing, but being struck by lightning is quite another! In the first case, perhaps your rights have been violated, but in the second case, they have not. The point, of course, is that not only what counts as an infringement on a right but also what counts as a right is not simply a matter of identifying some wrong that has occurred or some particular action or event.

In addition, rights are said to be both a descriptive and a prescriptive relation. That is, when we speak of rights, we sometimes speak in purely descriptive ways. For example, in the United States at the beginning of the twenty-first century there *is*, with some restrictions, a (legal) right for a woman to have an abortion on demand. One might think women should or should not have this right, but speaking descriptively, in the legal system there is such a right. However, sometimes when we speak of rights, we speak in prescriptive ways, that is, about what ought to be the case. So, some people claim that there *should be* a right for same-sex couples to marry. Or laws have recently been passed in various states to legalize certain victims' rights because supporters of such rights lobbied that victims *should* have them recognized and established by law. Chapter 3 focuses more directly on issues related to these matters of how to understand the prescriptive aspects of rights.

The primary nature of the rights relation is, as noted earlier, to regulate behavior. When we speak of rights, we do so in order to say what we get to do ("I have the right to think what I want!") or in order to say what others do not get to do ("You don't have the right to make me do that!"). In the early 1900s, legal theorist Wesley Hohfeld enumerated four elements of rights, or perhaps four ways that we use the notion of rights. The first way he called a *liberty*. Liberties, for Hohfeld, are statements of how I may behave. I have mentioned liberties above, in the sense of actions that I have no duty to perform or not to perform; they are permitted but not required. Sometimes when people speak of rights, this is the sort of notion they have in mind ("It's my right to wear ugly clothes if I want to!"). A second way, said Hohfeld, that we use the notion of rights has to do with how others must behave toward us and other moral agents. This sense he called a *claim*. For example, if you owe me money, then I have a claim on you with respect to that money, and you must behave in certain ways because of that claim; namely, you must pay me back ("I have a right to that money that you owe me!"). Hohfeld called a third way that we use the notion of rights a *power*. A power refers to ways that I can bring about change. This is a way of speaking of rights in the sense that, if I have a certain right, then I am empowered to do certain things, and I have that power over others. In other words, with certain property rights, I might have the power (meaning legal or moral legitimacy, not physical strength) to prevent you from walking in certain places (i.e., trespassing on my property). Finally, Hohfeld called a fourth way we use the notion of rights an *immunity*. An immunity refers to ways that I can resist change or your power over me. So, in a legal or moral sense, my right to worship as I please makes me immune to your attempts to force me to behave in certain ways. These four Hohfeldian notions of rights reflect two broad ways that we understand and use rights: (1) as empowerments or signs of what I get to do, and (2) as protective securities against what you (meaning any agent) might want to do to me. In an even broader sense, these two ways are meant to emphasize rights as a means of securing and preserving the well-being of whoever has those rights.

CORRELATIVITY THESIS

One final introductory word before we look at specific philosophical views of the nature of rights. That word is "duties." Philosophers have long spoken of various kinds of legal and moral relations that agents have with respect to one another. So far, we have briefly touched on rights as one such relation, and of course, this entire book is about that. But two other important types of relations between agents with respect to regulating behavior must be mentioned, as they relate to our understanding and practice of rights as well as to our justification of them. One of these relations is the notion of duties. "Duty" probably sounds rather old-fashioned, and it is not exactly the same as obligation or responsibility, but it is the word that has stuck with philosophers. The notion of a duty connects to rights because of what some philosophers have termed the *correlativity thesis*, which is as follows: Rights and duties are relative to each other, meaning that they imply each other. One agent's right implies another agent's duty and vice versa. Now, there are two parts to this thesis: (1) every right implies some duty, and (2) every duty implies some right. Most rights theorists agree with the first part, but many do not accept the second part. Here is why:

Whenever one person has a right, that right (or at least its exercise) imposes a duty on other agents. Sometimes that duty is simply for those other agents not to interfere with the agent who has the right. For example, if I have a right to vote, then my right—or at least my ability to exercise that right—imposes a duty on you not to interfere with my voting; all you have to do is leave me alone, but the point is that you *do have* to leave me alone and not interfere with me (i.e., prevent me from voting). Other times, my right might impose a duty on some agent to do more than simply not interfere and actually to perform some positive act. For example, if I have a right to an attorney, then someone (i.e., the state) must provide me with an attorney; my right imposes a duty on the state to do something. Chapter 3 discusses these matters in detail. The point for now is that if one agent has a right, then that implies a duty on some other agent(s). However, as just mentioned, many rights theorists deny that every duty implies some right. I might have a duty that has nothing at all to do with any rights that you have. So, I might have a duty to pick up some litter that I find in the street or to shovel snow off the sidewalk in front of my house, but even if I do have these duties (shoveling snow off my sidewalk is, in fact, a legal duty that I do have!), it is not because someone has the right to have litter picked up or to have my sidewalk cleared of snow. Now, some rights theorists do think that these duties follow from someone else's rights; that someone else, however, is not any particular person but all moral or legal agents treated collectively. Whether that is so or not is beyond the present concern, which is simply to point out that rights are related to duties as another means of regulating behavior. In the readings upcoming in this chapter, various philosophers speak directly to the correlativity thesis.

The other important relation between agents that involves regulating behavior and is also connected to rights is the notion of goals. In the context of rights, goals are almost always spoken of collectively. That is, collective social goals are said to be one ground for regulating behavior. For example, if we collectively decide via the ballot box that our local city will increase people's taxes in order to pay for some city service—say, a new city library—then we have collectively identified some goal (building the library), and we will regulate behavior (collect taxes or penalize those who do not pay those taxes) in order to achieve that goal. Goals are sometimes said to relate to rights by (1) conflicting with rights, and (2) serving as the ground for rights. Goals can conflict with rights by running counter to the protective nature of the rights of agents. For example, suppose a local government wants to build a road on my property in order for more people to have easy access to a hospital on the other side of it, but I do not want that road built on my property. Here the goal of providing access to the hospital runs counter to my claim to property rights. Contrarily, goals can also provide the grounding of rights by serving as the impetus for granting new rights. For example, some people have argued that the goal of promoting an educated citizenry was the impetus for establishing a right to public education. (Not everyone agrees with this, but the point is clear.) The readings below speak to the issue of goals and their relations to rights, especially in the context of utilitarian concerns. For now, it is important to remember that the three relational notions of rights, duties, and goals often are seen as being in tension with each other, though not necessarily. For example, in the controversy over whether people have a legitimate right to die (or a related right to physician-assisted suicide), those who oppose such a right often do so from the perspective of duties—namely, we have a basic duty to respect the sanctity of life, and this duty overrides any claim to a right to die—or from the perspective of goals—namely, there is an important social goal to preserve and protect life, and this overrides any claim to a right to die. However, there is not a necessary tension between or among these three relational notions. In the example just given, the duty to respect the sanctity of life and the goal to protect life are certainly in harmony with each other, and for that matter, both are in harmony with at least some conceptions of a right to life, if not a right to die. Likewise, some goals or duties might be the very basis for justifying and embracing certain rights. This matter of balancing rights, duties, and goals, as well as of determining the relative weight and importance of each, is taken up throughout the chapters in this book.

PARTICULAR MODELS OF THE NATURE OF RIGHTS

Up to this point, the discussion has centered on some broad aspects of rights. Rights are a social relation between legal/moral agents that serve to regulate behavior primarily as empowerments or as protections. In effect, they are a condition of existence for some agent to have some object or be in some state of being. We are now in the position to consider in detail several philosophical models or views of the nature of rights. All of these views focus on what exactly rights are. They are a relation, yes, but what kind of relation are they? Another way of thinking of this is that they all are defining, or at least characterizing, rights in terms of something else. For example, as the readings below illustrate, Joseph Raz argues that rights really are significant interests, while Joel Feinberg says rights really are valid claims. So, it is to these various conceptions of the nature of rights that we now turn.

The first reading is by Joseph Raz, who argues that rights are essentially significant interests. At first glance this statement might not seem very profound or informative, but there is more here than meets the eye. For one thing, Raz recognizes that rights are not merely some feature that agents have but are normative and purposive. Rights have to do with one's well-being. In addition, only those things (agents) that can have interests can have rights. So, it makes no sense to speak of inanimate things as having rights, because they cannot have any interests to protect or promote. Furthermore, the fact that some agent can have interests is sufficient for then claiming that this holds other agents under some kind of duty with respect to this agent. Simply having interests is not the primary issue with respect to rights; the primary issue is that having interests is the legitimate ground for entailing duties on others. So, my rights come about because of my interests (at least some of them) and your duties (at least some of them) come about because of my rights. Notice that Raz does not embrace the other half of the correlativity thesis; he is not saying that all duties entail some right(s). Also, by "interests" Raz does not mean simply what we are interested in but rather what is in our interest. So, I might be interested in eating lots and lots of chocolate, but eating vegetables might actually be more in my interest. In any case, as he remarks below, rights are "intermediate conclusions" from ultimate values (interests) to duties. He does not say here what those interests or values are, but we can assume that he means things like life, liberty, and whatever kinds of *significant interests* for which we place others under some duty. Clearly, we have some interests (meaning values and not simply what we are interested in) that are not particularly significant, and those interests are not rights and do not entail duties on others. Again, he does not enunciate specifically what those are; he takes it that collectively we will recognize and determine what interests are truly significant such that they will impose duties on others. So, here is Raz:

JOSEPH RAZ, "ON THE NATURE OF RIGHTS"*

The Outline of an Account of Rights

Philosophical definitions of rights attempt to capture the way the term is used in legal, political, and moral writing and discourse. They both explain the existing tradition of moral and political debate and declare the author's intention to carry on the debate within the boundaries of that tradition. At the same time they further that debate by singling out certain features of rights, as traditionally understood, for special attention, on the grounds that they are the features which best explain the role of rights in moral, political, and legal discourse. It follows that while a philosophical definition may well be based on a particular moral or political theory (the theory dictates which features of rights, traditionally understood, best explain their role in political, legal, and moral discourse), it should not make the theory the only one which recognizes rights. To do so is to try to win by verbal legislation. A successful philosophical definition of rights illuminates a tradition of moral and political

---

*Mind 93 (1984): 194–214.

discourse in which different theories offer incompatible views as to what rights there are and why. The definition may advance the case of one such theory, but if successful it explains and illuminates all. In this spirit, I shall first propose a definition of rights and then explain various features of the definition and criticize alternative definitions.

Definition: "x has a right" if and only if x can have rights, and other
　　things being equal, an aspect of x's well-being (his interest) is a suffi-
　　cient reason for holding some other person(s) to be under a duty.
The Principle of Capacity to Have Rights: An individual is capable of
　　having rights if and only if either his well-being is of ultimate value
　　or he is an "artificial person" (e.g., a corporation).

Note that since "a right" is a very general term, one rarely asserts that someone has a right without specifying what rights he has, just as one does not normally mention that a person is subject to a duty without saying something more about what duty it is. Sometimes one may state of another that he has rights in order to indicate that he is the kind of creature who is capable of having rights. For example, one may say that slaves have (legal or moral) rights, or that partnerships have rights, or that fetuses have them. (Similarly one may say that the monarch has duties, etc.) The fact that assertions of rights *tout court* are rare does not invalidate the definition, nor does it detract from its value as the key to the explanation of all rights. It is true that there is much about statements of rights which cannot be learned from my definition alone. One needs to distinguish a right to act from a right in an object, and that from a right to an object, and that from a right to a service or a facility, and that again from "a right to . . . " where the dots stand for an abstract noun. A right to use the highway, for example, is a liberty right to use the highway or a right to have that liberty. A right in a car may be a right of ownership in a car, or some other right in it. Detailed explanations of rights are in part linguistic explanations (a right to a car differs from a right in a car), but in part they depend on political, legal, or moral argument. (Does a right to free speech include access to the mass media or to private premises?) The proposed definition is meant to be neutral concerning all such detailed questions. At the same time, it aims to encapsulate the common core of all rights, and thus to help to explain their special role in practical thought.

The definition is of rights *simpliciter*. Some discourse of rights is of rights as viewed from the point of view of a certain system of thought, as when one compares Kantian rights with Utilitarian rights. Prefixing an adjective to "rights" is one way to indicate that the speaker does not necessarily accept the existence of the right and is merely considering the implications of a system of thought. (On other occasions such adjectives identify the contents of the rights, e.g., economic rights, or their source, e.g., promissory rights, or both.)

Rights are grounds of duties in others. The duties grounded in a right may be conditional. Consider the duty of an employee to obey his employer's instructions concerning the execution of his job. It is grounded in the employer's right to instruct his employees. But it is a conditional duty, i.e., a duty (in matters connected with one's employment) to perform an action if instructed by the employer to do so. When the condition which activates the duty is an action of some person, and when the duty is conditional on it because it is in the right-holder's interest to make that person able to activate the duty at will, then the right confers a power on the person on whose behavior the duty depends. Thus the employer's right over the employees is a ground for his power to instruct them. This power is one aspect or one consequence of his right. But the very same right also endows him with a power to delegate his authority to others. It can, if he chooses to delegate authority, become the source of a power in one of his subordinates. In that case the employee will have a duty to obey the person in whom power was vested, and that duty as well as the power of the delegated authority are grounded in the right of the employer. To simplify I shall not dwell specifically on rights as the grounds of powers.

Capacity for Rights

The definition of rights itself does not settle the issue of who is capable of having rights beyond requiring that right-holders are creatures who have interests. What other features qualify a creature to be a potential right-holder is a question bound up with substantive moral issues. It cannot be fully debated here. But the special role of statements of rights in practical thought cannot be elucidated and the significance of the definition cannot be evaluated without a brief explanation of the conditions for the capacity for having rights.

There is little that needs to be said here of the capacity of corporations and other "artificial persons" to have rights. Whatever explains and accounts for the existence of such persons, who can act, be subject to duties, etc., also accounts for their capacity to have rights. Whether certain groups, such as families or nations, are artificial or natural persons is important for determining the conditions under which they may have rights. But we need not settle such matters here.

There is a view, which I shall call the reciprocity thesis, that only members of "the same moral community" can have rights. This is narrowly interpreted when the same moral community is a community of interacting individuals whose obligations to each other are thought to derive from a social contract or to represent the outcome of a fair bargaining process or if morality is conceived of in some other way to be a system for the mutual advantage of all members of the community. Wider conceptions of the moral community extend it to all moral agents and regard anyone who is subject to duties as being capable of rights.

The principle of capacity for rights stated above is not committed to the reciprocity thesis but is consistent with it. Since by definition rights are nothing but grounds of duties, if duties observe a reciprocity condition and can be had only toward members of the (same) moral community, then the same is true of rights. Alternatively, the reciprocity thesis obtains even if one can have duties toward non-members of the (same) moral community, provided those are not based on the interests of the beneficiaries of those duties. For example, if my duties to animals are based on considerations of my own character (I should not be a person who can tolerate causing pain, etc.) and not on the interests of animals, then animals do not have rights despite the fact that I have duties regarding them.

The merits of the reciprocity thesis will not be examined here. The problem to which the principle of capacity for rights is addressed is different. Often we ought or even have duties to act in ways that benefit certain things, and often we ought so to act because of the benefit our action will bring those things. For example, I have a duty to preserve certain plants because I promised their owners to do so while they are away on holiday. My gardener has a duty to look after my garden because his contract of employment says so. Some scientists have a duty to preserve certain rare species of plants because they are the only source of medicine for a rare and fatal disease. In all these cases the people who have duties to act in certain ways have them because [to have them] benefits plants. Yet in none of these cases is it true that the plants have a right to those benefits. The reason is that in all these cases the benefit is to be conferred on a thing whose existence and prosperity are not of ultimate value. . . .

It seems plausible to suppose that just as only those whose well-being is of ultimate value can have rights so only interests which are considered of ultimate value can be the basis of rights. But there are plenty of counter-examples demonstrating that some rights protect interests which are considered as of merely instrumental value. All the rights of corporations are justified by the need to protect the interests of these corporations, but these are merely of instrumental value. But the counter-instances are not confined to the rights of "artificial persons." Consider the rights (however qualified) of journalists to protect their sources (i.e., not to disclose their sources). Those who believe that journalists have such a right base it on the interest of journalists in being able to collect information which is valued because of its usefulness to members of the public at large. The rights of priests, doctors, and lawyers to preserve the confidentiality of their professional contacts are likewise justified ultimately by their value to members of the community at large.

Rights and Interests

The proposed definition of rights identified the interest on which the right is based as the reason for holding that some persons have certain duties. Later on I referred to the rights themselves as being the ground for those duties. The explanation is simple: The interests are part of the justification of the rights which are part of the justification of the duties. Rights are intermediate conclusions in arguments from ultimate values to duties. They are, so to speak, points in the argument where many considerations intersect and where their results are summarized to be used with additional premises when need be. Such intermediate conclusions are used and referred to as if they are themselves complete reasons. The fact that practical arguments proceed through the mediation of intermediate stages so that not every time a practical question arises does one refer to ultimate values for an answer is of crucial importance in making social life possible, not only because they save time and tediousness, but primarily because they enable a common culture to be formed around shared intermediate conclusions, in spite of a great degree of haziness and disagreement concerning ultimate values. . . .

The Importance of Rights

The main purpose of this article was to state and explain a coherent account of rights. . . . I will conclude by commenting briefly on the main feature of my account, its view of rights as intermediate between individual interests and people's duties.

Rights ground duties. To say this is not to endorse the thesis that all duties derive from rights or that morality is right-based. It merely highlights the precedence of rights over some duties and the dynamic aspect of rights, their capacity to generate new duties with changing circumstances. Notice that precisely because duties can be based on considerations other than someone's rights the statement (1) "Children have a right to education" does not mean the same as the statement (2) "There is a duty to provide education for children." (1) entails (2) but not the other way round. (1) informs us that the duty stated in (2) is based on the interests of the children. This information is not included in (2) by itself. . . . By definition rights are not fundamental but derive from interests. ▲

A second conception of the nature of rights comes from Joel Feinberg. In a nutshell, Feinberg argues that rights are valid claims. As will be seen in the reading below, Feinberg spells out in great detail what is meant by a claim, or having a claim, but the emphasis is on the relational nature of rights and that relation is one of (1) placing others under a duty and (2) embracing the inherent dignity of agents. He gets at these points by considering an imaginary place that he calls Nowheresville. Nowheresville is a place where the concept of rights is nonexistent. People still interact with each other and have goals and duties, but no rights. Feinberg says that in such a community something very important is missing, something that recognizes and reinforces the worth and dignity of those community members. Rights, for Feinberg, do something; they are the "force" that carry out and, so to speak, enforce moral worth. They render others subject to one's claims for dignity and worth. This is what he means in the reading below by the "performative" sense of claiming (and of rights). Rights actually perform a function; they do not simply passively state that something or other is the case. Rights-claims do something beyond simply being words; they impose regulations on the behavior of others and empower the one claiming. Finally, for Feinberg, rights as *valid* claims reflect the fact that rights are always part of some system or other. People can make all sorts of claims, but what gives those claims genuine performative power is that they are backed by some justification (laws if they are legal claims/rights, morality if they are moral claims/rights). Being a claim is not sufficient for something being a right; in addition, what is needed is the justificatory grounding or backing of those claims. Here, then, is Feinberg:

JOEL FEINBERG, "THE NATURE AND VALUE OF RIGHTS"*

I would like to begin by conducting a thought experiment. Try to imagine Nowheresville—a world very much like our own except that no one, or hardly anyone (the qualification is not important), has *rights*. If this flaw makes Nowheresville too ugly to hold very long in contemplation, we can make it as pretty as we wish in other moral respects. We can, for example, make the human beings in it as attractive and virtuous as possible without taxing our conceptions of the limits of human nature. In particular, let the virtues of moral sensibility flourish. Fill this imagined world with as much benevolence, compassion, sympathy, and pity as it will conveniently hold without strain. Now we can imagine men helping one another from compassionate motives merely, quite as much or even more than they do in our actual world from a variety of more complicated motives.

This picture, pleasant as it is in some respects, would hardly have satisfied Immanuel Kant. Benevolently motivated actions do good, Kant admitted, and therefore are better, *ceteris paribus*, than malevolently motivated actions, but no action can have supreme kind of worth—what Kant called "moral worth"—unless its whole motivating power derives from the thought that it is *required by duty*. Accordingly, let us try to make Nowheresville more appealing to Kant by introducing the

---

*Journal of Value Inquiry 4 (1970): 243–251.

idea of duty into it and letting the sense of duty be a sufficient motive for many beneficent and honorable actions. But doesn't this bring our original thought experiment to an abortive conclusion? If duties are permitted entry into Nowheresville, are not rights necessarily smuggled in along with them?

The question is well-asked and requires here a brief digression so that we might consider the so-called "doctrine of the logical correlativity of rights and duties." This is the doctrine that (1) all duties entail other people's rights and (2) all rights entail other people's duties. Only the first part of the doctrine, the alleged entailment from duties to rights, need concern us here. Is this part of the doctrine correct? It should not be surprising that my answer is: "In a sense yes and in a sense no." Etymologically, the word *duty* is associated with actions that are *due* someone else, the payments of debts *to* creditors, the keeping of agreements with promises, the payment of club dues, or legal fees, or tariff levies to appropriate authorities or their representatives. In this original sense of "duty," all duties are correlated with the rights of those *to* whom the duty is owed. On the other hand, there seem to be numerous classes of duties, both of a legal and non-legal kind, that are *not* logically correlated with the rights of other persons. This seems to be a consequence of the fact that the word "duty" has come to be used for *any* action understood to be *required*, whether by the rights of others, or by law, or by higher authority, or by conscience, or whatever. When the notion of requirement is in clear focus it is likely to seem the only element in the idea of duty that is essential, and the other component notion—that a duty is something *due* someone else—drops off. Thus, in this widespread by derivative usage, "duty" tends to be used for any action we feel we *must* (for whatever reason) do. It comes, in short, to be a term of moral modality merely; and it is no wonder that the first thesis of the logical correlativity doctrine often fails.

Let us then introduce duties into Nowheresville, but only in the sense of actions that are, or are believed to be, morally mandatory, but not in the older sense of actions that are due others and can be claimed by others as their right. Nowheresville now can have duties of the sort imposed by positive law. A legal duty is not something we are implored or advised to do merely; it is something the law, or an authority under the law, *requires* us to do whether we want to or not, under pain of penalty. When traffic lights turn red, however, there is no determinate person who can plausibly be said to claim our stopping as his due, so that the motorist owes it to *him* to stop, in the way a debtor owes it to his creditor to pay. . . .

The remainder of this paper will be devoted to an analysis of what precisely a world is missing when it does not contain rights and why that absence is morally important.

The most conspicuous difference, I think, between the Nowheresvillians and ourselves has something to do with the activity of *claiming*. Nowheresvillians, even when they are discriminated against invidiously, or left without the things they need, or otherwise badly treated, do not think to leap to their feet and make righteous demands against one another though they may not hesitate to resort to force and trickery to get what they want. They have no notion of rights, so they do not have a notion of what is their due; hence they do not claim before they take. The conceptual linkage between personal rights and claiming has long been noticed by legal writers and is reflected in the standard usage in which "claim-rights" are distinguished from other mere liberties, immunities, and powers, also sometimes called "rights," with which they are easily confused. When a person has a legal claim-right to X, it must be the case (1) that he is at liberty in respect to X, i.e., that he has no duty to refrain from or relinquish X, and also (2) that his liberty is the ground of other people's *duties* to grant him X or not to interfere with him with respect to X. Thus, in the sense of claim-rights, it is true by definition that rights logically entail other people's duties. The paradigmatic examples of such rights are the creditor's right to be paid a debt by his debtor, and the landowners' right not to be interfered with by anyone in the exclusive occupancy of his land. The creditor's right against his debtor, for example, and the debtor's duty to his creditor, are precisely the same relation seen from two different vantage points, as inextricably linked as the two sides of the same coin. . . .

Many philosophical writers have simply identified rights with claims. The dictionaries tend to define "claims," in turn, as "assertions of right," a dizzying piece of circularity that led [H. B. Acton] to complain—"We go in search of rights and are directed to claims, and then back again to rights in bureaucratic futility." What then is the relation between a claim and a right? . . .

Let us begin by distinguishing between: (1) making claim to . . . , (2) claiming that . . . , and (3) having a claim. One sort of thing we may be doing when we claim is to *make claim to something*. This is "to petition or seek by virtue of supposed right; to demand as due." Sometimes this is done by an acknowledged right-holder when he serves notice that he now wants turned over to him that which has already been acknowledged to be his, something borrowed, say, or improperly taken from him. . . .

Generally speaking, only the person who has a title or who has qualified for it, or someone speaking in his name, can make claim to something as a matter of right. It is an important fact about rights (or claims), then, that they can be claimed only by those who have them. Anyone can claim, of course, *that* this umbrella is yours, but only you or your representative can actually claim the umbrella. If Smith owes Jones five dollars, only Jones can claim the five dollars as his own, though any bystander can *claim that* it belongs to Jones. One important difference then between *making legal claim to* and *claiming that* is that the former is a legal performance with direct legal consequences whereas the latter is often a mere piece of descriptive commentary with no legal force. Legally speaking, *making claim to* can itself make things happen. This sense of "claiming," then, might well be called "the performative sense." The legal power to claim (performatively) one's right or the things to which one has a right seems to be essential to the very notion of a right. A right to which one could not make claim (i.e., not even for recognition) would be a very "imperfect" right indeed!

Claiming that one has a right (what we can call "propositional claiming" as opposed to "performative claiming") is another sort of thing one can do with language, but it is not the sort of doing that characteristically has legal consequences. . . . What is essential to *claiming that* is the manner of assertion. One can assert without even caring very much whether anyone is listening, but part of the point of propositional claiming is to *make sure* people listen. . . .

Even if there are conceivable circumstances in which one would admit rights diffidently, there is no doubt that their characteristic use and that for which they are distinctively well suited, is to be claimed, demanded, affirmed, insisted upon. They are especially sturdy objects to "stand upon," a most useful sort of moral furniture. Having rights, of course, makes claiming possible; but it is claiming that gives rights their special moral significance. This feature of rights is connected in a way with the customary rhetoric about what it is to be a human being. Having rights enables us to "stand up like men," to look others in the eye, and to feel in some fundamental way the equal of anyone. To think of oneself as the holder of rights is not to be unduly but properly proud, to have that minimal self-respect that is necessary to be worthy of the love and esteem of others. Indeed, respect for persons (this is an intriguing idea) may simply be respect for their rights, so that there cannot be the one without the other; and what is called "human dignity" may simply be the recognizable capacity to assert claims. To respect a person then, or to think of him as possessed of human dignity, simply *is* to think of him as a potential maker of claims. Not all of this can be packed into a definition of "rights"; but these are *facts* about the possession of rights that argue well their supreme moral importance. More than anything else I am going to say, these facts explain what is wrong with Nowheresville.

We now come to the third interesting employment of the claiming vocabulary, that involving not the verb "to claim" but the substantive "a claim." What is to *have a claim* and how is this related to rights? I would like to suggest that *having a claim consists in being in a position to claim, that is, to make claim to or claim that.* . . . On this analysis, one might have a claim without ever claiming that to which one is entitled, or without even knowing that one has the claim; for one might simply be ignorant of the fact that one is in a position to claim; or one might be unwilling to exploit that position for one reason or another, including fear that the legal machinery is broken down or corrupt and will not enforce one's claim despite its validity.

Nearly all writers maintain that there is some intimate connection between having a claim and having a right. Some identify right and claim without qualification, some define "right" as justified or justifiable claim, others as recognized claim, still others as valid claim. My own preference is for the latter definition. . . . All claims, to be sure, are *put forward* as justified, whether they are justified in fact or not. A claim conceded even by its maker to have no validity is not a claim at all, but a mere demand. The highwayman, for example, *demands* his victim's money; but he hardly makes claim to it as rightfully his own. . . . [It] remains true that not all claims put forward as valid really are valid; and only the valid ones can be acknowledged as rights. . . .

"Validity," as I understand it, is justification of a peculiar and narrow kind, namely justification within a system of rules. A man has a legal right when the official recognition of his claim (as valid) is called for by the governing rules. . . . A man has a moral right when he has a claim the recognition of which is called for—not (necessarily) by legal rules—but by moral principles, or the principles of an enlightened conscience. . . .

In brief conclusion: To have a right is to have a claim against someone whose recognition as valid is called for by some set of governing rules or moral principles. To have a *claim* in turn, is to have a case meriting consideration, that is, to have reasons or grounds that put one in a position to engage in performative and propositional claiming. The activity of claiming, finally, as much as any other thing, makes for self-respect and respect for others, gives a sense to the notion of personal dignity, and distinguishes this otherwise morally flawed world from the even worse world of Nowheresville. ◣

Yet another conception of rights comes from legal philosopher Ronald Dworkin. Below Dworkin argues that rights are trumps. This notion of trump is a convenient way to pack in quite a bit of information. First, trumps, as usually understood in the context of card games, are part of a system of rules. So, within the game of hearts, cards of the hearts suit are trumps and have power over other cards; outside of the game of hearts, however, those cards do not have such power. So, by calling rights trumps, Dworkin acknowledges, or at least states, that rights are part of a rule-governed context and set of processes. In addition, as trumps, rights have a special power over other concerns in this rule-governed context and set of processes. So, in a conflict, say, between rights and goals, rights trump goals. This trumping ability of hearts in some card games is not the result of some inherent property or feature of hearts but of the rules of the game agreed on by its players. Likewise, the trumping ability of rights results not from some inherent property or feature of rights but from the "rules of the game" (i.e., social decisions in the context of regulating behavior) agreed upon by the "players" of the "game" (i.e., by members of some social or collective structure). So, as Dworkin says at the outset, he seeks to develop a theory of rights that is relative to the other elements of a political theory (e.g., justice, fairness, efficiency). Rights, for Dworkin, can be understood and enacted only within the context of political theory and political practice, but rights are only one element among others in such a context.

In the reading below, Dworkin speaks of utilitarianism and how his conception of rights relates to that doctrine. This is because he is particularly concerned with addressing the issue of how to balance rights with these other elements of political theory and practice. Not every social regulation of behavior is a matter of invoking and recognizing rights; we can and do use duties and goals to settle many conflicts and disputes. Where rights are particularly important—and where they serve as trumps—is where the well-being of an individual comes up against the well-being of the collective, and some grounds are needed for determining the best or appropriate balance between the parties involved. So, while there are some similarities and overlaps between what Dworkin says here and the conceptions of rights articulated above by Raz and Feinberg, Dworkin stresses the understanding of rights always in the context of collective decision making as well as goals and duties. It is only in the context of balancing multiple elements of social and political life that rights make any sense, and they serve as trumps in this balancing process only because the players of the game agree to this balance and the trumping ability of rights. In Chapter 2, we look more explicitly at the connection between utilitarianism and rights in terms of the justification of rights. Here, Dworkin speaks of how rights are to be understood:

RONALD DWORKIN, "RIGHTS AS TRUMPS"*

Rights are best understood as trumps over some background justification for political decisions that states a goal for the community as a whole. . . .

My aim is to develop a theory of rights that is relative to the other elements of a political theory, and to explore how far that theory might be constructed from the exceedingly abstract (but far from empty) idea that government must treat people as equals. Of course that theory makes rights relative in only one way. I am anxious to show how rights fit into different packages, so that I want to see, for example, which rights should be accepted as trumps over utility if utility is accepted, as many people think it should be accepted, as the proper background justification. That is an important question because, as I said, at least an informal

---

*In *Theories of Rights*, ed. Jeremy Waldron (Oxford: Oxford University Press, 1984), 153–167. Also Ronald Dworkin, *Taking Rights Seriously* (Cambridge, MA: Harvard University Press, 1977), xi, 204–207, 268–269, 277.

kind of utilitarianism has for some time been accepted in practical politics. It has supplied, for example, the working justification of most of the constraints on our liberty through law that we accept as proper. But it does not follow from this investigation that I must endorse (as I am sometimes said to endorse) the package of utilitarianism together with the rights that utilitarianism requires as the best package that can be constructed. In fact I do not. Though rights are relative to packages, one package might still be chosen over others as better, and I doubt that in the end any package based on any familiar form of utilitarianism will turn out to be best. Nor does it follow from my argument that there are no rights that any defensible package must contain—no rights that are in this sense natural rights—though the argument that there are such rights, and the explanation of what these are, must obviously proceed in a rather different way from the route I followed in arguing for the right to moral independence as a trump over utilitarian justification.

But if rights figure in complex packages of political theory, it is both unnecessary and too crude to look to rights for the only defense against either stupid or wicked political decisions. No doubt Hitler and Nero violated whatever rights any plausible political theory would provide; but it is also true that the evil these monsters caused could find no support even in the background justification of any such theory. Suppose some tyrant . . . did forbid sex altogether on penalty of death, or banned all religious practice in a community whose members were all devout. We should say that what he did (or tried to do) was insane or wicked or that he was wholly lacking in concern for his subjects which is the most basic requirement that political morality imposes on those who govern. Perhaps we do not need the idea of equality to explain that last requirement. (I am deliberately cautious here.) But neither do we need the idea of rights.

We need rights, as a distinct element in political theory, only when some decision that injures some people nevertheless finds some prima facie support in the claim that it will make the community as a whole better off on some plausible account of where the community's general welfare lies. But the most natural source of any objection we might have to such a decision is that, in its concern with the welfare or prosperity or flourishing of people on the whole, or in the fulfillment of some interest, widespread within the community, the decision pays insufficient attention to its impact on the minority; and some appeal to equality seems a natural expression of an objection from that source.

We want to say that the decision is wrong, in spite of its apparent merit, because it does not take the damage it causes to some into account in the right way and therefore does not treat these people as equals entitled to the same concern as others.

Of course, that charge is never self-validating. It must be developed through some theory about what equal concern requires, or, as in the case of the argument I offered, about what the background justification itself supposes that equal concern requires. Others will inevitably reject any such theory. Someone may claim, for example, that equal concern requires only that people be given what they are entitled to have when their preferences are weighed in the scales with the preferences, including the political and moral preferences, of others. In that case (if I am correct that the right to sexual freedom is based in equality), he would no longer support that right. But how could he? Suppose the decision to ban homosexuality even in private is the decision that is reached by the balance of preferences that he thinks respects equality. He could not say that, though the decision treats homosexuals as equals, by giving them all that equal concern for their situation requires, the decision is nevertheless wrong because it invades their liberty. If some constraints on liberty can be justified by the balance of preferences, why not this one? Suppose he falls back on the idea that sexual freedom is a fundamental interest. But does it treat people as equals to invade their fundamental interests for the sake of minor gains to a very large number of other citizens? Perhaps he will say that it does, because the fundamental character of the interests invaded have been taken into account in the balancing process, so that if these are outweighed the gains to others, at least in the aggregate, were shown to be too large in all fairness to be ignored. But if this is so, then deferring to the interests of the outweighed minority would be giving the minority more attention than equality allows, which is favoritism. How can he then object to the decision the balancing process reached? So if anyone really does think that banning homosexual relationships treats homosexuals as equals, when this is the decision reached by an unrestricted utilitarian balance, he seems to have no very persuasive grounds left to say that that decision nevertheless invades their rights. My hypothesis, that the rights which have traditionally been described as consequences of a general right to liberty are in fact the consequences of equality instead, may in the end prove to be wrong. But it is not, as [H. L. A.] Hart says it is, "fantastic."

Individual rights are trumps held by individuals. Individuals have rights when, for some reason, a collective goal is not a sufficient justification for denying them what they wish, as individuals, to have or to do, or not a sufficient justification for imposing some loss or injury upon them. That characteristic of a right is, of course, formal in the sense that it does not indicate what rights people have or guarantee, indeed, that they have any. But it does not suppose that rights have some special metaphysical character, and the theory defended [here] therefore departs from older theories of rights that do rely on that supposition.

I said at the beginning . . . that I wanted to show what a government must do that professes to recognize individual rights. It must dispose with the claim that citizens never have a right to break its law, and it must not define citizens' rights so that they are cut off from supposed reasons of the general good. Any Government's harsh treatment of civil disobedience, or campaign against vocal protest, may therefore be thought to count against its sincerity.

One might well ask, however, whether it is wise to take rights all that seriously after all. America's genius, at least in her own legend, lies in not taking any abstract doctrine to its logical extreme. It may be time to ignore abstractions, and concentrate instead on giving the majority of our citizens a new sense of their Government's concern for their welfare, and of their title to rule.

That, in any event, is what former Vice-President [Spiro] Agnew seems to believe. In a policy statement on the issue of "weirdos" and social misfits, he said that the liberals' concern for individual rights was a headwind blowing in the face of the ship of state. That is a poor metaphor, but the philosophical point it expresses is very well taken. He recognized, as many liberals do not, that the majority cannot travel as fast or as far as it would like if it recognizes the rights of individuals to do what, in the majority's terms, is the wrong thing to do. . . .

The bulk of the law—that part which defines and implements social, economic, and foreign policy—cannot be neutral. It must state, in its greatest part, the majority's view of the common good. The institution of rights is therefore crucial, because it represents the majority's promise to the minorities that their dignity and equality will be respected. When the divisions among the groups are most violent, then this gesture, if law is to work, must be most sincere. . . .

A successful claim of right . . . has this consequence. If someone has a right to something, then it is wrong for the government to deny it to him even though it would be in the general interest to do so. This sense of right (which might be called the anti-utilitarian concept of a right) seems to me very close to the sense of right principally used in political and legal writing and argument in recent years. It marks the distinctive concept of an individual right against the State which is the heart, for example, of constitutional theory in the United States. . . .

I wish now to propose the following general theory of rights. The concept of an individual political right, in the strong anti-utilitarian sense I distinguished earlier, is a response to the philosophical defects of a utilitarianism that counts external preferences and the practical impositions of political democracy, which enforce overall or unrefined utilitarianism, and yet protect the fundamental right of citizens to equal concern and respect by prohibiting decisions that seem, antecedently, likely to have been reached by virtue of the external components of the preferences democracy reveals. ◣

A number of social and political theorists have recently articulated another very influential conception of rights. This conception focuses on the exhortative nature of rights—that is, on what rights do and how they function rather than on what they are. To some extent, all rights theorists are concerned with this issue, but some theorists emphasize it and develop that feature of rights as fundamental. The point is that when speaking of or invoking rights, we are not so much describing aspects of moral agents (i.e., that in fact they have certain features, one of which is rights); rather, we are exhorting or urging certain kinds of actions. Rights, under this emphasis, are not so much a matter of saying what is the case but of prompting behavior; rights claims are not so much descriptive as they are prescriptive. Among the rights theorists who have emphasized this approach is Martha Nussbaum. In various works, she has argued for what she calls a "capabilities" conception of rights. This conception underscores the role of rights as a means to promoting and securing the flourishing and well-being of moral agents. Moral agents need to be able to function fully so as to realize their capabilities as moral agents. Rights are a means by which we realize such functioning and capabilities.

In the reading below, Nussbaum points out many complexities and concerns about the nature and role of rights. Basic to her argument is that the important thing is what moral agents are capable of: What can they actually do and be? Enhancing capability is the political goal, and rights are a means to accomplish that goal. As she claims, given a variety of functions that seem to be important for a fully realized moral agent (she speaks of a human life here rather than of a moral agent and its life), the fundamental question is, Is the agent capable of those functions or not? Rights are a means to make sure, or at least attempt to make sure, that the answer is yes.

Nussbaum identifies a number of what she calls "central human capabilities," which one can convincingly argue to be of fundamental importance to the functioning of any human life, regardless of context. Among those central capabilities (and Nussbaum stresses that her list is not exhaustive or closed) are life, bodily health and integrity, affiliations with and attachments to others (both human and nonhuman), some level of control over one's political and material environments, and recreation and personal enjoyment. Nussbaum claims that these capabilities do not simply form a "wish list" that she has come up with but reflect empirical and normative findings of broad and ongoing cross-cultural inquiry. Of course, each of these items needs fleshing out, as do the particularities of how they play out in various contexts. For instance, the specific material environment obviously will differ in the Australian outback and in the Canadian Arctic, as well as in a small nomadic clan versus a large metropolitan city. Nevertheless, all humans have a fundamental need to have some control over their respective environments. Just as all humans, regardless of where they live, need food to survive, so do they all need affiliations with and attachments to others. Of course, they can choose not to fulfill some function, but they need to be able to fulfill it and to make the choice. Here, then, is Nussbaum:

MARTHA NUSSBAUM, "CAPABILITIES AND HUMAN RIGHTS"*

When governments and international agencies talk about people's basic political and economic entitlements, they regularly use the language of rights. When constitutions are written in the modern era, and their

---

*Fordham Law Review 66 (1997): 273–300.

framers wish to identify a group of particularly urgent interests that deserve special protection, once again it is the language of rights that is regularly preferred.

The language of rights has a moral resonance that makes it hard to avoid in contemporary political discourse. But it is certainly not on account of its theoretical and conceptual clarity that it has been preferred. There are many different ways of thinking about what a right is, and many different definitions of "human rights." For example, rights are often spoken of as entitlements that belong to all human beings simply because they are human, or as especially urgent interests of human beings *as human beings* that deserve protection regardless of where people are situated. Within this tradition there are differences. The dominant tradition has typically grounded rights in the possession of rationality and language, thus implying that non-human animals do not have them, and that mentally impaired humans may not have them. Some philosophers have maintained that sentience, instead, should be the basis of rights; thus, all animals would be rights-bearers. In contrast to this entire group of natural-rights theorists, there are also thinkers who treat all rights as artifacts of state action. The latter position would seem to imply that there are no human rights where there is no state to recognize them. Such an approach appears to the holders of the former view to do away with the very point of rights language, which is to point to the fact that human beings are entitled to certain types of treatment *whether or not* the state in which they happen to live recognizes this fact.

There are many other complex unresolved theoretical questions about rights. One of them is the question of whether the individual is the only bearer of rights, or whether rights belong, as well, to other entities, such as families, ethnic, religious, and linguistic groups, and nations. Another is whether rights are to be regarded as side-constraints on goal-seeking action, or as parts of a goal that is to be promoted. Still another unresolved question is whether rights—thought of as justified entitlements—are correlated with duties. If *A* has a right to *S*, then it would appear there must be someone who has a duty to provide *S* to *A*. But it is not always clear who has these duties—especially when we think of rights in the international context. Again, it is also unclear whether all duties are correlated with rights. One might hold, for example, that we have a duty not to cause pain to animals without holding that animals have rights—if, for example, one accepted one of the classic accounts of the basis of rights that makes reference to the abilities of speech and reason as the foundation, and yet still believed that we have other strong reasons not to cause animals pain.

Finally, there are difficult theoretical questions about what rights are to be understood as rights *to*. When we speak of human rights, do we mean, primarily, a right to be treated in certain ways? A right to a certain level of achieved well-being? A right to certain resources with which one may pursue one's life plan? . . .

Thus, one might conclude that the language of rights is not especially informative, despite its uplifting character, unless its users link their references to rights to a theory that answers at least some of these questions. It is for this reason, among others, that a different language has begun to take hold in talk about people's basic entitlements. This is the language of capabilities and human functioning. . . .

Instead of asking "How satisfied is a person *A*," or "How much in the way of resources does *A* command," we ask the question: "What is *A* actually able to do and to be?" In other words, about a variety of functions that would seem to be of central importance to a human life, we ask: Is the person capable of this, or not? This focus on capabilities, unlike the focus on GNP, or on aggregate utility, looks at people one by one, insisting on locating empowerment in *this* life and in *that* life, rather than in the nation as a whole. Unlike the utilitarian focus on satisfactions, it looks not at what people feel about what they do, but about what they are actually able to do. Nor does it make any assumptions about the commensurability of the different pursuits. Indeed, this view denies that the most important functions are all commensurable in terms of a single metric and it treats the diverse functions as all important, and all irreducibly plural. Finally, unlike the focus on resources, it is concerned with what is actually going on in the life in question: not how many resources are sitting around, but how they are actually going to work in enabling people to function in fully human ways.

I have spoken of both functioning and capability. How are they related? Understanding this relationship is crucial to defining the relation of the "capabilities approach" to both liberalism and views of human rights. For if we were to take functioning itself as the goal of public policy, the liberal would rightly judge that we were precluding many choices that citizens may make in accordance with their own conceptions of the good, and perhaps violating their rights. A deeply religious person may prefer not to be well-nourished, but instead prefer to engage in strenuous fasting. Whether for religious or other reasons, a person may prefer a celibate life to one containing sexual expression. A person may prefer to work with an intense dedication that precludes recreation and play. Am I declaring, by my very use of the list, that these are not fully human or flourishing lives? And am I instructing government to nudge or push people into functioning of the requisite sort, no matter what they prefer?

It is important that the answer to these questions is no. Capability, not functioning, is the political goal. Capability must be the goal because of the great importance the capabilities approach attaches to practical reason, as a good that both suffuses all the other functions, making them human rather than animal, and figures itself as a central function on the list. It is perfectly true that functionings, not simply capabilities, are what render a life fully human: If there were no functioning of any kind in a life, we could hardly applaud it, no matter what opportunities it contained. Nonetheless, for political purposes it is appropriate for us to strive for capabilities, and those alone. Citizens must be left free to determine their course after they have the capabilities. The person with plenty of food may always choose to fast, but there is a great difference between fasting and starving, and it is this difference that we wish to capture. . . .

How, then, are capabilities related to human rights? We can see, by this time, that there are two rather different relations that capabilities have to the human rights traditionally recognized by international human rights instruments. In what follows, I shall understand a human right to involve an especially urgent and morally justified claim that a person has, simply by virtue of being a human adult, and independently of membership in a particular nation, or class, or sex, or ethnic or religious or sexual group.

First, there are some areas in which the best way of thinking about rights is to see them as, what I have called, *combined capabilities* to function in various ways. The right to political participation, the right to religious free exercise, the freedom of speech, the freedom to seek employment outside the home, and the freedom from unwanted search and seizure are all best thought of as human capacities to function in ways that we then go on to specify. The further specification will usually involve both an internal component and an external component: a citizen who is systematically deprived of information about religion does not really have religious liberty, even if the state imposes no barrier to religious choice.

On the other hand, internal conditions are not enough: women who can think about work outside the home, but who are going to be systematically denied employment on account of sex, or beaten if they try to go outside, do not have the right to seek employment. In short, to secure a right to a citizen in these areas is to put them in a position of capability to go ahead with choosing that function if they should so desire.

Of course, there is another way in which we use the term "right" in which it could not be identified with a capability. We say that A has "a right to" seek employment outside the home, even when her circumstances obviously do not secure such a right to her. When we use the term "human right" this way, we are saying that just by virtue of being human, a person has a justified claim to have the capability secured to her: so a right in that sense would be prior to capability, and a ground for the securing of a capability. "Human rights" used in this sense lie very close to what I have called "basic capabilities," since typically human rights are thought to derive from some actual feature of human persons, some untrained power in them that demands or calls for support from the world. Rights theories differ about which basic capabilities of the person are relevant to rights, but the ones most commonly chosen are the power of reasoning, generally understood to be moral reasoning, and the power of moral choice.

On the other hand, when we say, as we frequently do, that citizens in country C "have the right of free religious exercise," what we typically mean is that this urgent and justified claim is being answered, that the state responds to the claim that they have just by virtue of being human. It is in this sense that capabilities and rights should be seen to be equivalent. For I have said, combined capabilities are the *goals* of public planning.

Why is it a good idea to understand rights, so understood, in terms of capabilities? I think this approach is a good idea because we then understand that what is involved in securing a right to people is usually a lot more than simply putting it down on paper. We see this very fully in India, for example, where the Constitution is full of guarantees of Fundamental Rights that are not backed up by effective state action. Thus, since ratification women have had rights of sex equality—but in real life they are unequal not only *de facto*, but also *de jure*. This inequality results from the fact that most of the religious legal systems that constitute the entire Indian system of civil law have unequal provisions for the sexes, very few of which have been declared unconstitutional. So we should not say that women have equal rights, since they do not have the capabilities to function as equals. Again, women in many nations have a nominal right of political participation without really having this right in the sense of capability; for they are secluded and threatened with violence should they leave the home. This is not what it is to have a right. In short, thinking in terms of capability gives us a benchmark in thinking about what it is really to secure a right to someone. . . .

If we have the language of capabilities, do we still need, as well, the language of rights? The language of rights still plays, I believe, four important roles in public discourse, despite its unsatisfactory features. When used in the first way, as in the sentence "*A* has a right to have the basic political liberties secured to her by her government," rights language reminds us that people have justified and urgent claims to certain types of urgent treatment, no matter what the world around them has done about that. I have suggested that this role of rights language lies very close to what I have called "basic capabilities," in the sense that the justification for saying that people have such natural rights usually proceeds by pointing to some capability-like feature of persons that they actually have, on at least a rudimentary level, no matter what the world around them has done about that. And I actually think that without such a justification the appeal to rights is quite mysterious. On the other hand, there is no doubt that one might recognize the basic capabilities of people and yet still deny that this entails that they have rights, in the sense of justified claims, to certain types of treatment. We know that this inference has not been made through a great deal of the world's history, though it is false to suppose that it only was made in the West, or that it only began in the Enlightenment. So, appealing to rights communicates more than appealing to basic capabilities: it says what normative conclusions we draw from the fact of the basic capabilities.

Even at the second level, when we are talking about rights guaranteed by the state, the language of rights places great emphasis on the importance and the basic role of these things. To say, "Here's a list of things that people ought to be able to do and to be," has only a vague normative resonance. To say, "Here is a list of fundamental rights," means considerably more. It tells people right away that we are dealing with an especially urgent set of functions, backed up by a sense of justified claims that all humans have to such things, by virtue of being human.

Third, rights language has value because of the emphasis it places on people's choice and autonomy. The language of capabilities, as I have said, was designed to leave room for choice, and to communicate the idea that there is a big difference between pushing people into function-ing in ways you consider valuable and leaving the choice up to them. At the same time, if we have the language of rights in play as well, I think it helps us to lay extra emphasis on this very important fact: that what one ought to think of as the benchmark are people's autonomous choices to avail themselves of certain opportunities, and not simply their actual functionings.

Finally, in the areas where there is disagreement about the proper analysis of rights talk—where the claims of utility, resources, and capa-bilities are still being worked out—the language of rights preserves a sense of the terrain of agreement, while we continue to deliberate about the proper type of analysis at the more specific level. ▙

Questions for Discussion

1. Raz sees rights as protecting and enforcing significant interests. Who or what determines what counts as significant? Is this lack of specificity a problem for his project of trying to give a general statement of the nature of rights?

2. Does Feinberg adequately support his contention that something crucial is missing in Nowheresville, even though people there seem to function very well together? Are rights necessary for genuinely embracing the dig-nity of moral agents?

3. For Dworkin, rights are trumps. What exactly do they trump? Following the analogy of trumps, what functions as a trump varies from one game to another and even from one play within a game to another play. So, could some other social or moral concern also function as a trump, even some-times trumping rights? Who or what determines what counts as a trump?

4. Are there objective capabilities or features of capabilities that adequately characterize well-being, hence rights? Is a capabilities approach to rights like Nussbaum's compatible with nonhumans, or at least nonindividuals, as rights holders? For example, what are the "central" capabilities of other species or of corporations or nation-states?

5. Is it correct to say that rights are a relation between agents? Why could the notion of rights not apply to someone even if that person were the only agent?

Further Reading

Campbell, Tom. *The Left and Rights: A Conceptual Analysis of the Idea of Socialist Rights*. London: Routledge & Kegan Paul, 1983. A socialist perspective on the nature of rights, both conceptual foundations and specific rights.

Edmundson, William A. *An Introduction to Rights*. Cambridge: Cambridge University Press, 2004. A fine, historically focused introduction to the nature of rights.

Freeden, Michael. *Rights*. Minneapolis: University of Minnesota Press, 1991. A brief, accessible work emphasizing liberal, communitarian, and utilitarian issues and perspectives.

Hayden, Patrick, ed. *The Philosophy of Human Rights*. Saint Paul, MN: Paragon House, 2001. A very fine and comprehensive collection of essays on human rights, including important political rights documents.

Herbert, Gary B. *A Philosophical History of Rights*. New Brunswick, NJ: Transaction Publishers, 2002. A comprehensive historical survey of the evolution of conceptions of rights.

Singer, Beth J. *Operative Rights*. Albany: State University of New York Press, 1993. A pragmatist conception of the nature of rights as related to how we operate in social and political settings.

Thomson, Judith Jarvis. *The Realm of Rights*. Cambridge, MA: Harvard University Press, 1990. A sustained analysis of the nature and content of rights, with an emphasis on relating rights and morality.

Waldron, Jeremy, ed. *Theories of Rights*. Oxford: Oxford University Press, 1984. A collection of classic essays on the nature of rights.

Werhane, Patricia, A. R. Gini, and David T. Ozar, eds. *Philosophical Issues in Human Rights: Theories and Applications*. New York: Random House, 1986. A thorough collection of essays on the nature of rights as well as their relation to specific rights.

Winston, Morton E., ed. *The Philosophy of Human Rights*. Belmont, CA: Wadsworth, 1989. A fine collection of essays on the various aspects of rights, such as the nature of rights, the scope and content of rights, and criticisms of rights.

CHAPTER 2

THE JUSTIFICATION
OF RIGHTS

In Chapter 1 we saw a variety of conceptions of the nature of rights and that one difficult issue, both philosophically and socially, has been to come up with any broad consensus on just what rights are. But even if there were general agreement on the nature of rights, another important question is, What justifies rights? This question of justification applies both to particular rights, such as a right to bear arms or to health care, and to rights broadly speaking, in the sense of what justifies rights, rather than some other mode, as a means of regulating behavior.

The issue of justification is really a matter of addressing a why question: Why do I have some particular right, or any rights at all, for that matter? This chapter addresses this question and focuses on several kinds of answers to it. Before considering those answers directly, however, there are two preliminary points to make. First, when we ask about justification for rights, we are always asking about some content. That is, as noted in the introduction to this book, we never simply have a right but always have a right *to* something; there is always some content to a right (whether it is a right to life or property or free association or education or whatever). Chapter 3 focuses on the issue of the content and scope of rights, while this chapter focuses more directly on the broader conceptual issue of what justifies rights at all. It is somewhat difficult to address the latter issue without specifying some content, but in order to make things manageable, that is what we will do. It is somewhat like considering the shape of, say, a rug without caring about its color. No rug has just shape and no color, but for some purposes, we might ignore the color (whatever it happens to be) and focus just on the shape. This is not a perfect analogy, but the point is that here the emphasis is on what justification can be, and has been, given for identifying and acknowledging rights per se as legitimate regulations of behavior rather than on the specific content of particular rights.

SOURCE VERSUS JUSTIFICATION

A second preliminary point has to do with the issue of the source versus the justification of rights. These are related issues—for some theorists they are the same—but here, at the outset, we need to separate them. This comes up because the question "Why?" sometimes calls for a descriptive answer and sometimes for a prescriptive one. For example, if we ask, "Why is the sky blue?" we want an answer that provides a description or explanation of, say, physical laws concerning light refraction in the atmosphere. But if we ask, "Why is hate speech subject to prosecution?" we are not merely asking for some description or explanation of legal practice. Many people might initially answer this question about hate speech by giving a descriptive answer: "It is subject to prosecution because we have certain laws on the books." That, however, only moves the real question back: What justifies those particular laws?

Consider this example: Suppose I make a blatantly racist or sexist claim: "White males are obviously superior to everyone else!" You are amazed to hear me say this and ask, "Why do you think that?" I reply, "That's what my dad told me, and I believe him." Now, I have given a descriptive explanation of the source of my belief, but I certainly have not given a prescriptive justification of my belief. My racism or sexism is not justified just because it comes from somewhere! The point is that asking for the justification for something—for our purposes, the justification of rights—is not the same thing as asking for the source of it. These issues may very well be related—indeed, it might turn out that the justification for some claim really is inherently connected to its source—but at the outset we need to separate them. I raise this point here especially because the justification of rights often gets framed along the lines of the question, Where do our rights come from? Asking the question in this way could easily lead us to look to the source of rights as their justification. Again, these might be closely related, but it is clearer to phrase the question as why we have rights not where they come from.

This issue of the source versus justification of rights connects with a basic issue of legal (or civil) rights on the one hand and natural (or human) rights on the other. Another way to characterize this is to think of one's rights as a citizen versus as a moral agent. So, at the level of asking where our rights come from, one view holds that they come from the particular legal, social context(s) in which we find ourselves. In this view, we have whatever rights we have because they are granted by the legal system within which we function. So, I have the right to freedom of speech because the First Amendment of the Bill of Rights says I do or the right to be free of cruel and unusual punishment because the Eighth Amendment of the Bill of Rights says I do. Again, the essential point is that I have the rights I have because the legal system in which I function grants and acknowledges (and enforces) those rights. Outside of that legal system, under this view, I do not have such rights. As an analogy, in the game of baseball, I have the right to (attempt to) steal second base. However, outside of the game of baseball, the right to (attempt to) steal second base does not exist; indeed, it does not even make sense. Just as my right to (attempt to) steal second base exists only within the context of the rules of baseball, so my right to freedom of speech exists only within the context of the rules of the legal system within which I function. If I do not have some particular right, say, to health care, then, under this view, I need to change the rules of the legal system to acquire such a right (i.e., have it become law). But I cannot claim that my right to health care has been violated if such a right is not part of the "rules of the game" any more than I could claim that my right to steal first base has been violated. (In case you do not know, in baseball you can [attempt to] steal second base, but not first base.) Such a right simply does not exist until and unless the legal system says it does.

A separate view is associated with natural rights or human rights. (As an aside, these two terms, *natural rights* and *human rights*, do not mean exactly the same thing, but for our purposes we can treat them as interchangeable.) The notion of natural or human rights is that moral agents have at least some rights because of their very nature as humans (or moral agents). It is irrelevant whether or not a legal system acknowledges those rights; we have them not as citizens but as persons. Not only do our rights not come from legal systems, but legal systems themselves might very well violate our natural rights. For example, in 1800 slaves in the United States were not acknowledged within the legal system as having a right to vote. The natural rights view would say that this was a violation of their human right to self-determination. In a nutshell, they had such a right, and it was violated by the legal system. The other view noted above would hold that they did not have such a right because it was not part of the legal system, even if we think they should have had such a right.

So, was their right to vote being violated? Under one view, yes, because as persons they had natural rights; under the other, no, because rights come from the legal system, which did not recognize such a right at that time.

This discussion of rights as pertaining to agents as part of some system of rules (e.g., as citizens) versus rights pertaining to agents as agents has had a long and controversial history. We return to it in Chapter 4, where we consider what counts as a rights holder (e.g., do nonhuman animals have rights?), as well as in Chapter 5, where we look at various criticisms of rights, including the notion of human or natural rights. Also, we return to this topic in Chapter 7, where we cover rights in international and global contexts.

For now, we need to return directly to the issue of justification. The discussion above about where rights come from—the legal system (e.g., the Bill of Rights, statutes) or our nature as moral agents—really was phrased as an issue of the source of rights. Another way to understand the issue, however, is as the justification of rights. That is, what justifies the right to (attempt to) steal second base? In this case, the justification simply is the source, namely, the rules of baseball. But what justifies the right to free speech? Here, one view holds, as in the baseball case, that the legal rules within which we function provide the justification, while the other view holds that this justification lies outside the particular legal rules. After all, says this latter view, those legal rules do not come from nowhere. There were moral and social reasons for why some regulations of behavior got codified into law, such as the rights enunciated in the Bill of Rights, while others did not. So, the justification question really is not answered by pointing to what the legal system says; the issue of justification lies beyond and beneath that system's specifics. A clear example has to do with the issue of abortion on demand. For those who favor a right to such abortion, it is not the legal system that justifies the behavior; that system merely acknowledges and guarantees a right to engage in it. For those who oppose abortion, the current law does not justify the behavior; it merely acknowledges and guarantees a right to engage in it, even though it should not!

JUSTIFICATORY SCHEMES

If appealing to actual legal rules does not justify rights, what does? Throughout the rest of this chapter, we look at four different justificatory schemes. Broadly speaking, we can say that some attempts to justify rights are, or at least are said to be, objective, while other attempts are said to be subjective. For example, one broad justificatory scheme is that moral agents have some definite, specific needs that must be met in order for the agent to survive. There are objective needs, such as for food and shelter. Without those, organisms—including moral agents—cannot survive, and this is an objective fact about the world, not a subjective opinion. Having rights and having specific rights, under such a view, would be justified ultimately in terms of meeting those objective needs. Another view—we see an example of this in the reading by Gilbert Harman below—holds that the only "fact" that justifies rights is moral relativism; in other words, there is no objective grounding for rights.

This way of framing justificatory schemes as objective or subjective is not intended to suggest that one must choose between one or the other. In fact, there is more of a continuum of justifications, some of which rely more on social factors and others that rely on them less. For example, as just mentioned, the reading by Harman attempts to justify rights on the basis of moral relativism, while the reading by John Hospers attempts to justify rights on the basis of what he takes to be an objective feature of humans, namely, that they must be free to choose because they are not equipped with noncognitive instincts that will allow them to flourish. Another view, John Stuart Mill's utilitarian perspective, certainly emphasizes social factors, such as what regulations of behavior promote the greatest good, and so is "subjective"; at the same time, however, it provides a means of going beyond simple subjective preferences and decisions by having a clear, "objective" means (namely, greater utility) to determine whether rights are justified. As an example, voting is based on the subjective preferences of each individual voter, but objectively determining the outcome of a fair vote can simply be a matter of counting up the total votes. So, the objective/subjective split here is not intended to establish explicit pigeonholes into which to put different justificatory schemes; rather, it is a way of characterizing a greater or lesser emphasis on conventional social features and factors.

A final word before looking at the specific readings and views: One approach to addressing why some moral agent has rights is to consider why some other thing would not have rights. For instance, just about everyone would agree that adult humans have a right to self-determination (at least within some limits), but that no chair has such a right. Why? The answer is usually along the lines that chairs are inanimate; rights simply do not make sense for them. But, then, what about horses? They are animate, so do they have a right to self-determination (at least within some limits)? For those who say no, the reason is usually to the effect that they lack some trait or feature that is relevant for something to be a rights holder. So, one might claim that horses lack moral awareness or some level of cognition or, perhaps, a soul. The point here is that it is not uncommon for this question of justification to be framed in terms of the status of what are already taken to be rights holders because they either have or lack some trait, such as a soul or interests or cognition or even the ability to suffer pain and injury. Because this sort of issue overlaps so strongly with the notion of rights holders, we take up such matters in Chapter 4, where we focus on the issue of rights holders. In the readings in this chapter, the justificatory schemes will instead center on utility (John Stuart Mill), human nature and moral agency (John Hospers), moral relativism (Gilbert Harman), and wrongs suffered (Alan Dershowitz).

PARTICULAR VIEWS ON JUSTIFYING RIGHTS

Chapter 1 notes that rights are sometimes seen as one social value often in opposition to goals as another social value. Or, as the reading by Ronald Dworkin shows, there can be tension between individual rights and social utilitarian goals. For example, an individual's right to open a business such as an adult bookstore (i.e., selling pornography) might be opposed by many members of the local community. It is precisely one's rights that are often seen as the protective bubble for individuals against the "tyranny of the majority." Nonetheless, many theorists have argued that rights and utilitarian concerns are not at all necessarily in conflict. One such theorist is John Stuart Mill, the famous utilitarian thinker of the nineteenth century. Not only does Mill think that rights and utility are not in conflict, but at the end of the reading below he claims that utility is the very justification for rights! Utility is the justification for rights because, as we have noted already, rights are a means of regulating behavior and, indeed, of achieving justice. After all, we can regulate behavior in lots of ways—for example, by sheer force. In addition, we want to regulate behavior for certain reasons; the regulation of behavior is not an end in itself. Rights, then, for Mill, are a means to an end, namely, justice. As a means to attaining and preserving justice, rights have great utility and are socially important. They are so important, for Mill, that they can override particular, specific utilitarian goals. For instance, the right to free expression is so important for the general welfare of a community (not to mention of an individual) that it should be protected against censure and oppression, even if the expression creates discord in the short run. But the force of the "should" in saying the right should be protected is, for Mill, the result of there being greater utility in allowing people free expression generally speaking than in not allowing it. Mill wrote at great length in defense of individual liberty against the power of the community, but always against a background of claiming that allowing greater liberty (and rights) enhanced overall welfare and justice.

In the reading below, Mill speaks of both legal and moral rights in the context of justice. Note that he speaks of rights, like Joel Feinberg in the previous chapter, as valid claims against society, though Feinberg does not offer a utilitarian justification for rights.

JOHN STUART MILL, "ON THE CONNECTION BETWEEN JUSTICE AND UTILITY"*

In all ages of speculation one of the strongest obstacles to the reception of the doctrine that utility or happiness is the criterion of right and wrong has been drawn from the idea of justice. The powerful sentiment and apparently clear perception which that word recalls with a rapidity and certainty resembling an instinct have seemed to the majority of thinkers to point to an inherent quality in things; to show that the just must have an existence in nature as something absolute, generically distinct from every variety of the expedient and, in idea, opposed to it, though (as is commonly acknowledged) never, in the long run, disjoined from it in fact.

In the case of this, as of our other moral sentiments, there is no necessary connection between the question of its origin and that of its binding force. That a feeling is bestowed on us by nature does not necessarily legitimate all its promptings. The feeling of justice might be a peculiar instinct, and might yet require, like our other instincts, to be controlled and enlightened by a higher reason. If we have intellectual instincts leading us to judge in a particular way, as well as animal instincts that prompt us to act in a particular way, there is no necessity that the former should be more infallible in their sphere than the latter in theirs; it may as well happen that wrong judgments are occasionally suggested by those, as wrong actions by these. But though it is one thing to believe that we have natural feelings of justice, and another to

---

*In *Utilitarianism* (Indianapolis: Hackett, 1979), 41–53.

acknowledge them as an ultimate criterion of conduct, those two opinions are very closely connected in point of fact. Mankind are always predisposed to believe that any subjective feeling, not otherwise accounted for, is a revelation of some objective reality. Our present object is to determine whether the reality to which the feeling of justice corresponds is one which needs any special revelation, whether the justice or injustice of an action is a thing intrinsically peculiar and distinct from all its other qualities or only a combination of certain of those qualities presented under a peculiar aspect. . . .

To throw light upon this question, it is necessary to attempt to ascertain what is the distinguishing character of justice, or of injustice; what is the quality, or whether there is any quality, attributed in common to all modes of conduct designated as unjust (for justice, like many other moral attributes, is best defined by its opposite), and distinguishing them from such modes of conduct as are disapproved, but without having the particular epithet of disapprobation applied to them. . . .

To find the common attributes of a variety of objects, it is necessary to begin by surveying the objects themselves in the concrete. Let us therefore advert successively to the various modes of action and arrangements of human affairs which are classed, by universal or widely spread opinion, as just or as unjust. The things well known to excite the sentiments associated with those names are of a very multifarious character. I shall pass them rapidly in review, without studying any particular arrangement.

In the first place, it is mostly considered unjust to deprive anyone of his personal liberty, his property, or any other thing which belongs to him by law. Here, therefore, is one instance of the application of the term "just" and "unjust" in a perfectly definite sense, namely, that it is just to respect, unjust to violate, the *legal rights* of anyone. But this judgment admits of several exceptions, arising from the other forms in which the notions of justice and injustice present themselves. For example, the person who suffers the deprivation may (as the phrase is) have *forfeited* the rights which he is so deprived of—a case to which we shall return presently. . . .

Secondly, the legal rights of which he is deprived may be rights which *ought* not to have belonged to him; in other words, the law which confers on him these rights may be a bad law. When it is so or when (which is the same thing for our purpose) it is supposed to be so, opinions will differ as to the justice or injustice of infringing it. Some maintain that no law, however bad, ought to be disobeyed by an individual citizen; that his opposition to it, if shown at all, should only be shown in endeavoring to get it altered by competent authority. This opinion (which condemns many of the most illustrious benefactors of mankind, and would often protect pernicious institutions against the only weapons which, in the state of things existing at the time, have any chance of succeeding against them) is defended by those who hold it on grounds of expediency, principally on that of the importance to the common interest of mankind, of maintaining inviolate the sentiment of submission to law. Other persons, again, hold the directly contrary opinion that any law, judged to be bad, may blamelessly be disobeyed, even though it be not judged to be unjust but only inexpedient, while others would confine the license of disobedience to the case of unjust laws; but, again, some say that all laws which are inexpedient are unjust, since every law imposes some restriction on the natural liberty of mankind, which restriction is an injustice unless legitimated by tending to their good. Among these diversities of opinion it seems to be universally admitted that there may be unjust laws, and that law, consequently, is not the ultimate criterion of justice, but may give to one person a benefit, or impose on another an evil, which justice condemns. When, however, a law is thought to be unjust, it seems always to be regarded as being so in the same way in which a breach of law is unjust, namely, by infringing somebody's right, which, as it cannot in this case be a legal right, receives a different appellation and is called a moral right. We may say, therefore, that a second case of injustice consists in taking or withholding from any person that to which he has a *moral right*. . . .

Justice implies something which it is not only right to do, and wrong not to do, but which some individual person can claim from us as his moral right. No one has a moral right to our generosity or beneficence because we are not morally bound to practice those virtues toward any given individual. And it will be found with respect to this as to every correct definition that the instances which seem to conflict with it are those which most confirm it. For if a moralist attempts, as some have done, to make out that mankind generally, though not any given individual, has a right to all the good we can do them, he at once, by that thesis, includes generosity and beneficence within the category of justice. He is obliged to say that our utmost exertions are *due* to our fellow creatures, thus assimilating them to a debt; or that nothing less can be a sufficient *return* for what society does for us, thus classing the case as one of gratitude; both of which are acknowledged cases of justice, and not of the virtue of beneficence; and whoever does not place the distinction between justice and morality in general, where we have now placed it, will be found to make no distinction between them at all, but to merge all morality in justice. . . .

To recapitulate: the idea of justice supposes two things—a rule of conduct and a sentiment which sanctions the rule. The first must be supposed common to all mankind and intended for their good. The other (the sentiment) is a desire that punishment may be suffered by those who infringe the rule. There is involved, in addition, the conception of some definite person who suffers by the infringement, whose rights (to use the expression appropriated to the case) are violated by it. And the sentiment of justice appears to me to be the animal desire to repel or retaliate a hurt or damage to oneself or to those with whom one has sympathies, widened so as to include all persons, by the human capacity of enlarged sympathy and the human conception of intelligent self-interest. From the latter elements the feeling derives its morality; from the former, its peculiar impressiveness and energy of self-assertion.

I have, throughout, treated the idea of a *right* residing in the injured person and violated by the injury, not as a separate element in the composition of the idea and sentiment, but as one of the forms in which the other two elements clothe themselves. These elements are a hurt to some assignable person or persons, on the one hand, and a demand for punishment, on the other. An examination of our own minds, I think, will show that those two things include all that we mean when we speak of a violation of a right. When we call anything a person's right, we mean he has a valid claim on society to protect him in the possession of it, either by the force of law or by that of education and opinion. If he has what we consider a sufficient claim, on whatever account, to have something guaranteed to him by society, we say that he has a right to it. If we desire to prove that anything does not belong to him by right, we think this done as soon as it is admitted that society ought not to take measure for securing it to him, but should leave him to chance or to his own exertions. Thus a person is said to have a right to what he can earn in fair professional competition, because society ought not to allow any other person to hinder him from endeavoring to earn in that manner as much as he can. But he has not a right to three hundred a year, though he may happen to be earning it; because society is not called on to provide that he shall earn that sum. On the contrary, if he owns ten thousand pounds three-per-cent stock, he *has* a right to three hundred a year because society has come under an obligation to provide him with an income of that amount.

To have a right, then, is, I conceive, to have something which society ought to defend me in the possession of. If the objector goes on to ask why it ought, I can give him no other reason than general utility. ◣

Without question, rights are intimately related to the issue of justice, as Mill argues. Of course, one does not need to endorse utilitarianism or a utilitarian justification of rights in order to embrace this relationship between rights and justice. A very different view that does embrace this relationship is associated with the political philosophy known as libertarianism. As the reading below by John Hospers makes clear, for libertarianism, individual liberty to make choices is a necessary condition for humans to exist and survive. Liberty, being free to make one's choices, is primary; hence the label "libertarianism." Liberty is fundamental because of what libertarians take as human nature. Humans, they claim, are not equipped by nature with inborn instincts sufficient for survival. Rather, humans by their very nature function via conceptual awareness. That is, they must reason about the world, not merely respond instinctively to stimuli. Of course, like many other kinds of organisms, humans do respond to stimuli, but they are distinctive in that they use concepts; indeed, for libertarians, they must. Because humans must make judgments (i.e., think in conceptual ways), they must make choices and, indeed, must be in the position of being able to make choices, which is simply to say that they must be at liberty to do so. This is the very nature of human life and existence.

Rights are the expression of this fundamental human condition. With respect to social and political life, all individuals must be free to make choices, so rights must be understood as the means for this. Human associations, such as societies and governments, are legitimate only to the extent that they do not run counter to this fact of human nature. In a word, they exist to preserve and protect individuals. As a result, most libertarians identify three basic rights: life, liberty, and property. Rights pertain to actions (choices), not goods or services. Rights are the expression of our need to choose. The right to property is basic because property is the result of our choices; it is the manifestation of the actions we (must) take. As Hospers puts it, unlike other species, humans must produce their livelihoods. Property is, in a sense, the extension of our actions and choices in the world; it is the result of our productivity. In Chapter 3, we look at how this view plays out in terms of the content and scope of rights—what kinds of rights we have—but for now the point is that libertarians (and Hospers in particular) claim that there is an objective justification for rights, namely, human nature itself. Here, then, is what Hospers says:

JOHN HOSPERS, *LIBERTARIANISM**

The libertarian account of rights can be stated simply: "Every man has the right to be free." What this means was stated by Herbert Spencer: "Every man may claim the fullest liberty to exercise his faculties compatible with the possession of like liberty by every other man." And again, "Every man has freedom to do all that he wills, provided he infringes not on the equal freedom of every other man." . . . How you should run your life or dispose of your property (as conditions of living by your own judgment) is a matter for you to decide; it is not for me to preempt that decision by taking it from you.

Why is the ability to act on one's own judgment a matter of such importance? Because man is a volitional being who, to survive and prosper, must live and plan in accordance with his own decisions—or those of others only if they are voluntarily accepted by him, in which case they become his. Let us note some facts about man's nature and the world in which he lives, which are relevant to the concept of man's rights:

What are the conditions of man's existence? Under what conditions can he live and prosper? Let us note some facts:

1. Each form of organic life populating this planet has its own distinctive kind of existence and survives in its own distinctive way. Plants, incapable of locomotion, do not survive by the same means as animals do; and among the animals, fish do not survive as worms do, or

---

*(Santa Barbara, CA: Reason Press, 1971), 50–58.

either of them as lions do. In every one of these cases, however, the means of survival of the organism depends on features which are "built in," in which the creature has no choice, but acts for its survival by means implanted in it by nature.

2. Man too has a distinctive means of survival, and that is the use of his mind. He is not as fully equipped with instincts as are the other animals, which "program" his response to most life-situations; if left to these alone, he would long since have vanished form the scene. But alone among the animals, what happens in man's life is the result of *choices*, choices which he consciously makes. Man alone can promote his life through thought, and man alone can act so as to destroy himself. But whichever he does, he does it by virtue of his distinctive nature as a rational animal, that is, an animal capable of reason. Virtually everything that distinguishes man's life from that of the animals is a result of his ability to think: he has learned to grow crops and harvest them, to build fires and harness rivers, to find cures for diseases, and to read books and write them—and most important of all, since books allow the knowledge laboriously gained by one man to be transmitted from one generation to another, with each generation being able to stand on the shoulders of the one before. In this way man has been able to master virtually the entire animal creation, and to acquire knowledge extending back aeons in time and millions of light-years in space.

3. One of the very first lessons that reality teaches man is that to live he must produce and that to produce he must work. He can't sit by and do nothing and yet live.

4. The effects of his acts are largely *on himself*. If a person drinks poison, it is his digestive tract, not his neighbor's that absorbs the effect. If he is to support himself, it is he who must work—except in unusual cases, another's work will not help him. He is himself the principle beneficiary or the maleficiary of his own actions.

5. To live he must plan long-range. He cannot rely on instincts to store nuts for the winter, and if he fails to make the conscious choice of doing so, he will place his life in jeopardy. He who is caught without preparation by each successive winter will probably not survive many winters.

6. In working and planning long-range, he cannot place upon his own shoulders the survival of a large group of others, else he will find

himself borne down in the process. He may keep himself and his family going, but if he undertakes much more, he will not be able to succeed. He may want to but he cannot. Reality makes it impossible.

7. One of the things that makes human survival possible—not merely his biological survival, but his survival as a civilized being—is the possibility of *transmission* of knowledge and technique (art, applied science, medicine) from one generation to the next. If each generation had to start from zero, then the vicissitudes of a single generation could wipe man out. But man's knowledge is a cumulative thing; in one generation he discovers an herb that will cure a certain disease; in another generation he discovers still more, and applies the knowledge to wider areas; in another generation he delves into chemistry and discovers the physical explanation underlying the cure—such as the germ theory of transmission of disease; and this permits him in a still later generation to devise complex medication, anesthetics, surgery, and the taking of precautions against the communication of disease. The non-human animals, relying chiefly on instincts, do not have this power, and their lives, except insofar as affected by human beings, are pretty much the same from one generation to another. Man's survival *qua* man—that is, as a being of intelligence, volition, and feeling—depends upon this accumulation of knowledge from generation to generation. . . .

I can violate the rights of others only by the use of force—to take his life, to deprive him of some aspect of his liberty of speech or action. If he voluntarily stops speaking or voluntarily parts with his [property], there is no violation of rights; the violation occurs when force is used to keep him from doing what he would have done through his own free decisions. . . .

Since a man must determine the course of his life by means of his own free decisions, the use of force against him represents the ultimate negation of his status as a human being. . . .

When I claim a right, I carve out a niche, as it were, in my life, saying in effect, "This activity I must be able to perform without interference from others. For you and everyone else, this is off limits." And so I put up a "no trespassing" sign, which marks off the area of my right. Each individual's right is his "no trespassing" sign in relation to me and others. I may not encroach upon his domain any more than he upon mine, without my consent. Every right entails a duty, true—but the duty is only that of *forbearance*—that is, of *refraining* from violating the other person's right. If you have a right to life, I have no right to take that life; if you have a right to the products of your labor (property), I have no right to take it from you without your consent. The non-violation of these rights will not guarantee your protection against natural catastrophes such as floods or earthquakes, but it will protect you against the aggressive activities *of other men*. And rights, after all, have to do with one's relations to other human beings, not with one's relations to physical nature. ◣

In stark contrast to libertarians like Hospers, philosopher Gilbert Harman claims that "moral relativism provides the only plausible foundation for a theory of natural rights." Although Harman agrees with Hospers (and others) about what natural rights are—rights held by moral agents simply by virtue of their nature as moral agents—he disagrees about what justifies them. Since rights are a moral concept relating to our actions, Harman claims that they must be understood along the lines of any moral concept, which is "the result of implicit bargaining and adjustments among people of varying powers and resources." But, for Harman, there is no agreed-upon set of values or goals that all (or enough) moral agents share; that is, there is moral relativism. Instead, this implicit bargaining and adjustment continually takes place. For example, broadly speaking, people's attitudes about the rightness or wrongness of interracial marriage have changed over the years. The rightness or wrongness of this is not, for Harman, a matter of discovering the truth about something but simply the result of whatever psychological and sociological factors influence people's values and goals.

Much of Harman's reading focuses on the issue of a moral duty not to harm others versus a moral duty to assist others. While that issue is not immediately and explicitly about rights, it is closely related to rights in two ways. First, it connects up with the question of whether moral agents have a right to be assisted, not to mention whether they have a right not to be harmed. This issue takes center stage in Chapter 3 on the content and scope of rights, and we consider it in much greater detail there. Second, this issue connects up with rights in Harman's approach to addressing the issue—namely, his sociological approach. For Harman, it is simply a sociological fact that moral agents do not share a common morality, at least not in great detail. As a result, we appeal to various moral notions in order to be able to function together. We might appeal to some common goals that we would like to achieve or to others to recognize some common duty or obligation. Or, what is important here, we might appeal to regulations of behavior that we identify as rights. But it is really only because of the fact of moral relativism that we need to make such an appeal to rights. Implicit in Harman's claims here is the notion that if we all agreed on questions of justice, fairness, and appropriate regulations of behavior, we would not need to enlist rights. To look for a justification of rights, then, we need to acknowledge this moral relativism and not insist on some descriptive ("objective") feature of moral agents as some sort of supra-sociological ground for rights.

GILBERT HARMAN, "MORAL RELATIVISM AS A FOUNDATION FOR NATURAL RIGHTS"*

The theory of natural rights is often put forward as competition of moral relativism, most recently in an article in this journal by Loren Lomasky ["Harman's Moral Relativism," *Journal of Libertarian Studies* 3 (1979): 279–291]. I want to suggest, on the contrary, that the two positions are compatible and, indeed, that moral relativism provides the only plausible foundation for a theory of natural rights.

Natural rights are rights people have simply by virtue of being people, for example, the right not to be harmed by others, and to say that people have the right not to be harmed is to say more than that it is bad to harm them or that one ought not to harm them. People have the right not to be harmed even if this will prevent more harm to others. A doctor may not kill one patient and distribute his healthy organs among his other patients even if the result is to save five people who would otherwise have died, because that would violate the murdered patient's right not to be killed. Rights are also stronger than oughts. One ought to be charitable, but it is doubtful anyone has a right to one's charity.

A foundation for the theory of natural rights must explain why there should be a strong duty not to harm others but not an equally strong symmetrical duty to help others avoid harm. If there were an equally

Journal of Libertarian Studies 4 (1980): 367–371.

strong symmetrical duty to help others, people would not have the natural right not to be harmed, since they could be, and indeed should be, harmed in order to prevent more harm to others. The doctor could kill and cut up one patient and then distribute his organs to the others.

Why is there a strong duty not to harm others but not an equally strong symmetrical duty to prevent harm to others? The answer, I suggest, is that morality is the result of implicit bargaining and adjustments among people of varying powers and resources and, although it is in everyone's interest that there should be a strong duty not to harm others, it is not in everyone's interest that there should be an equally strong symmetrical duty to help others avoid harm. A duty to prevent harm to others favors the interests of the poorer and weaker members of society over the richer and more powerful members. The richer and more powerful members of society have less need of outside help in order to avoid being harmed than the poorer and would end up doing most of the helping, given a strong symmetrical duty to help others avoid harm. The rich and powerful would do best with a strong duty not to harm others and no duty to help others. The poor and weak would do best with equally strong duties of both sorts. Implicit bargaining should therefore yield as a compromise a strong duty not to harm others and a weaker duty to help others avoid harm; it should in other words yield a natural right not to be harmed, which is what we have.

It might be objected that such a sociological explanation cannot account for the right not to be harmed but can account only for our beliefs that there is such a right. Indeed, it might be thought that such a sociological explanation of our belief in this right casts doubt on the truth of the belief, since the explanation would appear to show we would have the belief whether or not it were true. But that would be to assume moral relativism is false. If moral relativism is true and morality has its source in convention, then a sociological account of our moral conventions can explain why we have the rights we have. That is why I suggest moral relativism provides a more adequate foundation for natural rights, such as the right not to be harmed, than moral absolutism does.

Of course, moral relativism needs to be formulated carefully. To say that morality has its source in convention is not to say that what is right is what people say is right or that the moral conventions of a group are beyond criticism. A set of conventions is subject to internal criticism if some of the conventions do not cohere well with others, given the facts.

And one group's moral conventions might be evaluated in the light of another group's values.

In his article, Lomasky raises several questions about the sociological explanation of the right not to be harmed and then offers a nonrelativistic explanation instead. I will say something about his own account in a moment. First let me take up the objection he raises to the claim that a strong duty not to harm others and a weaker duty to help others arises from a compromise between the richer and stronger on the one hand and the poorer and weaker on the other.

He begins by asking why the richer stronger people should agree to any duty to help others at all, given that such a duty is not in their interest. The answer, of course, is that they have to agree for the sake of social stability, so that the poorer and weaker people will accept the duty not to harm others. Otherwise there is the threat of a breakdown in law and order, even revolution.

Next, he commends Christopher New's observation that the sociological explanation talks only about people who are richer and stronger or poorer and weaker, ignoring people who are richer but weaker or stronger but poorer. The reason for this is that the richer tend to be the stronger and the poorer tend to be the weaker. The strong can take from the weak. The rich can afford armies.

Lomasky goes on to note Robert Coburn's suggestion that there might be an evolutionary explanation of why we acknowledge a stronger duty not to harm others and only a weaker duty to help them avoid harm. That would indeed undermine the sociological explanation, but (as Lomasky acknowledges) neither Coburn nor anyone else has offered a plausible evolutionary explanation of this sort.

Lomasky ultimately opts for a different explanation of why the duty to help others is not as strong as the duty not to harm them. His own explanation is that accepting a strong duty to help others would involve taking others' ends as one's own in a way that would actually undermine the distinction between one person's goals and another's. But at best that explains why we do not have a strong duty to help others in the sense of benefiting them, of doing whatever will promote their interests. What has to be explained is why there is not a strong duty to help others in a stricter sense, to help them when they really need help to avoid harm. Such a duty would be symmetrical with the strong duty not to harm others oneself. The duty to avoid harming others is not a duty to refrain from anything that is against another person's interest. If one raises one's prices, that makes things more expensive for others without harming them in the relevant sense. Similarly, a symmetrical duty to help others would not be an all-encompassing duty to do anything and everything that would advance another person's interest. The duty to avoid harming others is a duty to avoid certain specific harms to others (where in my view exactly what counts as such a harm is itself partly determined by convention), so a symmetrical duty to help others avoid harm would be a duty to help them in situations of real need when they are threatened with the sort of harm specified by the duty not to harm others. Lomasky's account does not explain why there is no such symmetrical duty to help others.

It might be suggested that so many people are threatened with harm from disease, famine, ruffians, and bullies that a strong symmetrical duty to help others avoid harm would after all require one to spend almost all one's time helping others, with little time for projects of one's own, so that Lomasky's argument is basically correct even for such a symmetrical duty. And it is true that, as things are now, one could probably help save many people's lives if, instead of pursuing one's narrow goals, one were to devote one's energies to famine relief or to helping people escape from totalitarian regimes. But things are as they are now because a strong duty to help others avoid harm is not widely accepted. If it were widely accepted, one could rely for the most part on others who were better placed to help out; one would be called upon oneself to help only rarely where one was in the best position to help. It would indeed be foolish or saintly to accept for oneself a strong duty to help others if no one else was going to do so, but that does not show such a duty to be unworkable. It would be similarly foolish or saintly to accept for oneself the strong duty not to harm others if no one else accepted that duty. Either duty is acceptable only if generally accepted. In this respect then there seems no reason to prefer the duty not to harm others to the duty to help them avoid harm, so there is no explanation of the natural right to be free from harm. We are left with moral relativism as the only plausible foundation for that natural right.

I conclude with a remark about "inner judgments." A moral relativist does not suppose that there is a single set of basic moral demands which everyone accepts or has reason to accept, as demands on everyone, from which derive all moral reasons to do things. The moral relativist supposes that different people accept different moralities which can give them different moral reasons. So there can be, and no doubt are, people who have no reason to act in accordance with the basic principles of one's own morality. If a moral judgment based on one's own principles implies that an agent has reasons deriving from those principles to do something, then that judgment cannot be made truly about "outsiders" who do not accept the relevant principles and therefore do not have those reasons. I call such judgments "inner" since they can be truly made only about insiders who have reasons to follow the relevant principles. Judgments about what someone ought morally to do and judgments about what it would be morally wrong of someone to do are inner judgments in this sense since they imply the agent has certain reasons. Moral relativists will distinguish inner moral judgments ("it was wrong of him to do that") from other moral judgments, not implying the agent had certain moral reasons, which can be made of outsiders ("it was evil of him to do that"). Nonrelativists who think there is a single true morality that gives everyone reasons will not distinguish insiders and outsiders in this way and will not need to distinguish inner moral judgments from others. Lomasky therefore misrepresents the notion of inner judgment in saying that such judgments are "motivating" and are odd if made in certain situations or made to certain people. And the fact (if it is a fact) that *he* takes *his* principles to apply to everyone, including those who do not accept those principles, shows only that *he* is not a moral relativist. Many other people are moral relativists and clearly do restrict their inner judgments in the relevant way. And anyone who believes in natural rights had better be a moral relativist if that belief is to receive an adequate foundation. ◣

Following on the heels of Harman's emphasis on social and historical justification for rights, in the final justificatory scheme for rights covered here, Harvard law professor Alan Dershowitz argues that it is not some trait or moral theory or external agent that justifies rights; it is, rather, actual wrongs that agents have suffered, at least some wrongs. In effect, rights are justified because they are our responses to what get acknowledged as clear and serious wrongs done to agents. Regardless of one's political theoretical views, he says, we all recognize great injustices, such as slavery or torture, and rights are our means of trying to make sure that those injustices are prevented or at least lessened in the future. As he puts it, there is an ongoing "righting process," which is the history of our responses to injustices. As he remarks near the end of the reading below, "Where the majority does justice to the minority, there is little need for rights. But where injustice prevails, rights become essential."

Because rights arise from, and are finally justified because of, our responses to righting gross wrongs that agents have suffered, Dershowitz suggests that "nurtural rights" might be a better term and concept than "natural rights." This is because the notion of natural rights rests on the view that agents have rights simply because of their nature (e.g., as Hospers argues above). Dershowitz, however, suggests that a more accurate and fruitful view is that agents have rights because they (or other agents like them) have suffered wrongs, and we want those wrongs stopped. In a sense, then, rights are a means to help nurture the well-being of agents, not some property they "have" naturally. In addition, because rights are responses to wrongs, the specific (kinds of) rights moral agents hold will depend on the specific (kinds of) wrongs they suffer. For example, if no one had ever endured slavery, there would be no need to invoke or recognize a right to be free from it. So, for Dershowitz, there is no timeless set of rights but instead a changing and evolving set of rights. Here is what he says:

▌ ALAN DERSHOWITZ, *RIGHTS FROM WRONGS**

. . . [R]ights are those fundamental preferences that experience and history—especially of great injustices—have taught are so essential that the citizenry should be persuaded to entrench them and not make them subject to easy change by shifting majorities.

In one important respect, therefore, this theory of rights is a theory of wrongs. It begins with the worst injustices: the Crusades, the Inquisition, slavery, the Stalinist starvation and purges, the Holocaust, the Cambodian slaughter, and other abuses that reasonable people now recognize to have been wrongs.

The ongoing nature of the righting process—and the fact that there is no consensus with regard to perfect justice—does not require that we ignore the wrongs of obvious injustice or allow those who advocate or inflict them to fall back on moral relativism as a justification for immorality.

---

*(New York: Basic Books, 2004), 81–96.

There is no moral justification for genocide, as evidenced by the fact that no reasoned argument has ever been attempted on its behalf—certainly none that has succeeded in the marketplace of ideas over time. . . .

My approach to rights first identifies the most grievous wrongs whose recurrence we seek to prevent, and then asks whether the absence of certain rights contributed to these wrongs. If so, that experience provides a powerful argument for why such rights should become entrenched. This bottom-up approach builds on the reality that there is far more consensus about what constitutes gross injustice than about what constitutes perfect justice. If there can be agreement that certain rights are essential to reduce injustice, such agreement constitutes the beginning of a solid theory of rights. We can continue to debate about the definition of, and conditions for, perfect justice. That debate will never end because perfect justice is far too theoretical and utopian a concept. But in the meantime, we can learn a considerable amount about rights from the world's entirely untheoretical experiences of injustice. Building on this negative experience, we can advocate and implement basic rights that have been shown (or can be shown) to serve as a check on tyranny and injustice. Perhaps someday we will be able to construct a complete theory of rights designed to lead to perfect justice. But since we have had far more experience with palpable injustice than with abstractly perfect justice, the bottom-up approach seems more grounded in reality than any top-down approach. It is more modest in its scope, but if it can contribute to a slowing down of the kind of injustice we have experienced in the twentieth and other centuries, it will have accomplished a great deal.

Aristotle [in *The Politics*] had it upside-down when he argued that before we can define people's rights or investigate "the nature of the ideal constitution . . . it is necessary for us first to determine the nature of the most desirable way of life. As long as that remains obscure, the nature of the ideal constitution must also remain obscure." In my view, it is sufficient to agree upon the *least* desirable ways of life and seek to protect against those evils. Such a minimalist conception of rights may not be "ideal," but it may be the best we can ever hope for. . . . But in seeking to prevent recurrence of grievous wrongs, we need not limit ourselves to combating perfect injustice. It is enough to recognize serious injustices that are down-to-earth, real, and generally produced by imperfect human beings. Moreover, the need to reduce it is practical and immediate. We need not agree on what constitutes "perfect injustice" in order to build a pragmatic theory of rights (which does not itself claim perfection). It is enough to agree on what constitutes the kinds of injustices that are sufficiently wrong to occasion a system of rights designed to prevent their recurrence. Seeking to achieve the perfect is the enemy of trying to prevent the very bad.

Building a theory of rights on the history of wrongs has another important virtue. It is a call to immediate action. We need not await the arrival of the Aristotelian Messiah—agreement on "the most desirable way of life"—before we can begin to confront the wrongs we all seek to prevent. While we wait for this Messiah (along with others), many horrible wrongs will be committed, some in his name. As soon as we see such wrongs, and decide to prevent their recurrence, our mission becomes clear: Invent and advocate rights designed to stop (or slow down) these wrongs. The Aristotelian approach is an invitation to inaction. An approach that bases rights on wrongs is a demand for immediate action. . . .

If rights grow out of the experiences and histories of human beings, then they are more a function of nurture than nature. The term "nurtural rights," though a bit clumsy, is closer to the truth than natural rights. In this respect, rights—like morals—are somewhat situational, not in the sense that there is no commonality in their application to differing situations, but in the sense that they reflect the differing histories and conditions in which people have found themselves when they have invented, articulated, and ranked rights. . . .

Building a system of rights from the bottom up, based on the experiences of injustice, is consistent with the common-law approach to the development of legal doctrines. Injustice provides the occasion for change. The history of the common law has been a history of adapting legal doctrine to avoid or minimize injustice. When all parties to a dispute believe that justice has been done, there is no occasion for litigation, no need for dispute resolution, and hence no stimulus to change the law. The case reports are not about instances of perceived justice, but about injustices in search of remedies. Even Aristotle's theory of corrective justice recognized the close relationship between wrongs and the need for corrective laws to restore equilibrium.

The same is true of the history of rights. Where the majority does justice to the minority, there is little need for rights. But where injustice prevails, rights become essential. Wrongs provoke rights, as our checkered history confirms. . . .

Perhaps it is impossible to come up with a completely unassailable theory of rights. If that were so, it would be an argument in favor of, not against, a process-oriented, advocacy approach to rights. Doing right, while advocating a continuous process of righting—of exploring the possible sources of rights outside of natural and positive law and inventing and implementing new rights as a work in progress—is entirely consistent with an acceptance of this possibility, indeed the likelihood, that we will never devise a perfect theory of rights. Advocating rights without a perfect theory is far better than silently accepting wrongs until a theory can be perfected.

The development of rights is an ongoing human process, because changing experiences demonstrate the need for changing rights. Rights once "discovered" or "revealed" do not remain immutable. The process of "righting" must always adapt to the human capacity to do wrong. . . .

The righting process is always in flux. Its pace will change with the human capacity to inflict wrongs. It is a never-ending process that rarely produces a static result or a perfect set of eternal rights. We must strive not for perfection but for pragmatic rights that are capable of keeping up with the human capacity to generate new and more horrible wrongs. ◤

Questions for Discussion

1. Mill claims that although people often think utility runs counter to justice and rights, in fact, only utility can justify rights. For him, if the practice of rights did not actually bring about (greater) justice—that is, if this practice were not useful for promoting (greater) justice—then the practice would not be justified. To support this claim, he argues that a legal right would not be justified if it were the result of a bad (unjust) law. Is Mill correct that utility justifies rights? Is he correct that only utility justifies rights?

2. Hospers states that rights are justified on the basis of an objective account of human nature. Is there, in fact, some essence to human nature, and if so, is that essence truly unique among living organisms? Humans must eat to survive, but that is true for other species as well; so, for Hospers, that is not crucial to understanding essential human nature. If there is an essential human nature, is Hospers correct that this is what justifies rights? Under Hospers's conception of rights, what would justice be?

3. Whereas Hospers claims that there is an objective human nature, hence an objective basis for rights, Harman explicitly rejects that view and insists that only the fact of moral relativism can justify rights. Harman says that morality—including issues of justice—is a matter of bargaining and negotiating between moral agents, with identified rights as an outcome of such actions. To what extent and in what ways is this similar to or different from Mill's utilitarian view?

4. Dershowitz argues that we simply do not have a theory or justice upon which to base rights. We do have clearly and (almost) universally recognized violations of justice, such as genocide and torture. Hence, for him, we have not only a source of rights—namely, clear and obvious wrongs done to moral agents—but also a justification for rights. Does this view, then, embrace the notion that there are objective criteria for what is wrong or unjust? If so, does this view more closely relate to the notion that there is an objective basis for rights (as Mill and Hospers seem to claim) or that there is not an objective basis for rights (as Harman seems to claim)?

5. With which fundamental conception of the nature of rights from Chapter 1 do these various justifications for rights best cohere?

Further Reading

Fried, Charles. *Right and Wrong*. Cambridge, MA: Harvard University Press, 1978. An analysis of the basic moral concepts of right and wrong, with a focus on negative and positive rights.

Gewirth, Alan. *Human Rights: Essays on Justification and Applications*. Chicago: University of Chicago Press, 1982. A sustained analysis of the justification and applications of rights.

Held, Virginia. *Rights and Goods: Justifying Social Action*. New York: Free Press, 1984. An analysis of social justice with a treatment of rights and law in the context of justice.

Hunt, Lynn. *Inventing Human Rights: A History*. New York: W. W. Norton, 2007. An analysis of the social contexts for the emergence of natural and human rights in the West.

Machan, Tibor. *Individuals and Their Rights*. LaSalle, IL: Open Court, 1989. A classic statement of a libertarian perspective on rights.

Melden, A. I. *Rights and Persons*. Berkeley: University of California Press, 1977. An analysis of rights, emphasizing their relations to morality and the nature of persons.

Meyers, Diana. *Inalienable Rights: A Defense*. New York: Columbia University Press, 1987. A sustained analysis of rights and their inherent nature to persons.

Nickel, James W. *Making Sense of Human Rights*. Berkeley: University of California Press, 1987. An analysis of rights, centered on the Universal Declaration of Human Rights.

Orend, Brian. *Human Rights: Concept and Context*. Toronto: Broadview Press, 2002. A fine introductory analysis of rights also with a brief history of the development of rights.

Simmons, A. John. *Justification and Legitimacy: Essays on Rights and Obligations*. Cambridge: Cambridge University Press, 2000. An analysis of obligation in social and political contexts, with an emphasis on its relation to human rights.

CHAPTER 3

THE CONTENT AND SCOPE OF RIGHTS

In the introduction to this book, I noted that we never merely "have a right"; we always have a right to something or other. That is to say, there is always some content to a right (claim). That content involves some opportunities or goods or services. For example, if you have a right to the pursuit of happiness, it is understood that you have the right not to be happy but to the opportunity to be happy. Or to say that you have the right to be president of the United States someday really means that you have the right to try to become president. On the other hand, when we say that you have the right to an attorney, we do not simply mean that you have the right to try to get an attorney; rather, we mean that you have the right to the services (at least some) of an attorney. Likewise, if you have a right to an education, we do not simply mean that you have the right to try to get an education; rather, you have the right to have some goods and services provided for you (such as books and teachers). At least, this is what most people mean when they make these claims. As we will see below, not everyone agrees with these remarks, but most people and rights theorists do. Of course, agreeing with what a statement means is not the same as agreeing that the statement is true or accurate. As we will see below, it is definitely not the case that everyone agrees that you have a right to an education, if that right means that you have a right to goods and services. We will get to these points and arguments soon, but first there are some more preliminary points to make.

As we saw in the previous two chapters, what rights are (the nature of rights) and how to justify (claims to) rights are separate but closely related issues. For instance, if rights are relations involving interactions, then what would seem to justify them depends on the nature of relevant interactions. But it is not obvious if the nature of relevant interactions is best understood by, say, Gilbert Harman's view that moral relativism is the only justification for rights or by John Hospers's view that the essence of human nature is the only justification for rights. Likewise, John Stuart Mill's view that rights can only be justified, in the final analysis, by their utility in bringing about the happiness of rights holders seems to rest on some conception of just what rights are. But which conception best captures this: Martha Nussbaum's capabilities view or Ronald Dworkin's trump view or some other? The point here is that, of course, the issue of what rights are is closely related to the issue of how they are justified.

The further point is that this also holds for the content of rights, that is, what we think we have rights to. Indeed, more often than not, when the issue of justification of rights comes up, it is in the context of some particular right, or the content of some purported right. While few people (other than political philosophers and rights theorists) ask what justifies rights generally speaking, many ask what justifies some particular right, such as the right to bear arms or the right to remain silent or the right to government-sponsored health care. As we consider the issue of the content and scope of rights in this chapter, we need to keep in mind the questions of justification, not only regarding some particular right at issue but in terms of how the justification for that particular right coheres with or follows from the broad conceptions of justification discussed earlier.

NEGATIVE RIGHTS VERSUS POSITIVE RIGHTS

One of the most cited and influential rights documents ever written is the Universal Declaration of Human Rights (UDHR) (see Part III), ratified by the UN General Assembly in 1948. Article 23 of the UDHR states, "Everyone has the right to work, to free choice of employment, to just and favorable conditions of work and to protection against unemployment." Several claims are being made here, but we can simplify them by saying that this article states that people have a right to employment. Now, what exactly does that mean? One interpretation is that people have the right to seek employment; they have the right to the opportunity to be employed. A second interpretation is that people have the right to actual employment, that is, a right to some good or service, in this case, a job.

Remember, from Chapter 1, that a right is not the same thing as a liberty or privilege. Rights entail duties for other agents; they regulate other agents' behavior. When your rights place a duty on other agents (or regulate their behavior) in the sense of requiring those other agents not to interfere with you, this is usually referred to as a "negative right." This simply means that other agents have the duty not to interfere with you; they just need to leave you alone. So, if you have the right to worship as you please, then the duty placed on others is not to do anything to interfere with you with respect to that. This is called a negative right because, in effect, the duty on others is negative in that they have to do nothing (except leave you alone).

On the other hand, sometimes people claim that one agent's rights place duties on others that require some positive action by those others in order for that right to be realized. For example, earlier we noted that having a right to an attorney requires that others (in this case the state) provide the right holder with the services of an attorney. In this case, it is not enough simply to leave the right holder alone and do nothing. Doing nothing is not the same thing as providing an attorney. This sort of right, in which something must be provided to the right holder, is usually said to be a "positive right" because some positive action, not mere noninterference, is required in order for the right to be realized.

Returning to the example above of a right to employment, the interpretation holding that this really just means that agents have a right to seek employment sees this as a negative right. It is a negative right because, under this interpretation, others are merely required not to interfere with the agent who is seeking employment. Under the second interpretation, however, in which a right to employment means a right to a job, this is a positive right because, in order to realize that right, the agent must receive a job, not merely the opportunity to find a job.

This distinction between negative and positive rights is crucial and has generated an enormous amount of attention among political philosophers and rights theorists, not to mention among everyday people. Indeed, the history of rights theory and rights legislation and practice has often been characterized—not always favorably—as a movement toward acknowledging and enunciating positive rights. Usually, in fact, rights theorists speak of first-generation and second-generation rights. First-generation rights, also sometimes called "political rights," are essentially negative rights. The specific rights under this label emphasize personal liberty. For example, the U.S. Bill of Rights speaks of rights to free speech, peaceful assembly, bearing arms, freedom from cruel and unusual punishment, due process, and so forth. All of these rights focus on the liberty of individual agents not to be restrained or constrained by others (usually the government). But the U.S. Bill of Rights makes no mention of a right to employment or education or health care or any other sort of good or service that requires others to provide someone with something.

While first-generation rights are negative rights focused on political liberty, second-generation rights, often spoken of as economic and social rights, are (at least predominantly) positive rights. They are also often called "welfare rights." The specific rights usually identified here include, for instance, a right to employment, education, or health care (yes, just the sort of rights not included in the U.S. Bill of Rights). Again, these are positive rights because, in order to be realized, they require some positive action beyond noninterference from others.

Since the very end of the twentieth century and into the twenty-first, there has also been a movement to speak of a third generation of rights, called "solidarity rights." These purported rights include a right to cultural heritage, environmental sustainability, economic development, world peace, and so forth. These sorts of rights emphasize "fraternity," or the notion of moral collectives as the fundamental holders of rights and global unity as necessary for rights to be meaningful. Such a movement harkens back to the rallying cry of the French Revolution in the eighteenth century: liberty, equality, fraternity. First-generation rights are said to be concerned with liberty, second-generation rights with equality, and third-generation rights with fraternity. While there is a growing body of work on third-generation rights, the readings in this chapter focus instead on controversy about second-generation, or positive, rights. As we will see, although many people see positive rights as not only unproblematic but obviously reasonable and important, many other people see them as controversial and destructive.

The first two readings below focus on the appropriateness of positive rights. The first reading, by Henry Shue, speaks in favor of them, while the second reading, by Tibor Machan, speaks against them. The primary focus of Shue's reading is that there are some "basic rights." By that phrase, he means that some rights are fundamental and necessary in order for other rights to be meaningful and even possible. For example, I have the right to vote, but that right presupposes and relies upon other rights, such as the right to self-determination and freedom of movement. But even those rights presuppose the more basic right, for Shue, of physical security. I cannot really exercise my right to vote if my personal security is at risk, or, as Shue puts it, I can talk about having a right, but enjoying that right is something else and requires physical security. Having argued for physical security as a basic right—and seeing physical security as a negative right since the duty on you is simply to leave me alone—Shue then goes on to say that subsistence, or some minimum level of food, shelter, and the like, is also a basic right. Subsistence rights are basic, for Shue, for exactly the same reasons that physical security rights are basic: No other rights are possible without them. As he says, "No one can fully, if at all, enjoy any right that is supposedly protected by society if he or she lacks the essentials for a reasonably healthy and active life. Deficiencies in the means of subsistence can be just as fatal, incapacitating, or painful as violations of physical security." Subsistence rights, of course, are positive rights. Something (beyond noninterference) must be provided to an agent in order for those rights to be realized. Here, then, is what Shue says:

HENRY SHUE, *BASIC RIGHTS: SUBSISTENCE, AFFLUENCE, AND U.S. FOREIGN POLICY**

Security and Subsistence

Basic Rights

. . . [O]ne of the chief purposes of morality in general, and certainly of conceptions of rights, and of basic rights above all, is indeed to provide some minimal protection against utter helplessness to those too weak to protect themselves. Basic rights are a shield for the defenseless against at least some of the more devastating and more common of life's threats, which include, as we shall see, loss of security and loss of subsistence. Basic rights are a restraint upon the economic and political forces that would otherwise be too strong to be resisted. They are social guarantees against actual and threatened deprivations of at least some basic needs. Basic rights are an attempt to give to the powerless a veto over some of the forces that would otherwise harm them the most. . . .

*(Princeton, NJ: Princeton University Press, 1980), 13–34.

And it is not surprising that what is in an important respect the essentially negative goal of preventing or alleviating helplessness is a central purpose of something as important as conceptions of basic rights. For everyone healthy adulthood is bordered on each side by helplessness, and it is vulnerable to interruption by helplessness, temporary or permanent, at any time. And many of the people in the world now have very little control over their fates, even over such urgent matters as whether their own children live through infancy. Nor is it surprising that although the goal is negative, the duties correlative to rights will turn out to include positive actions. The infant and the aged do not need to be assaulted in order to be deprived of health, life, or the capacity to enjoy active rights. The classic liberal's main prescription for the good life—do not interfere with thy neighbor—is the only poison they need. To be helpless they need only to be left alone. This is why avoiding the infliction of deprivation will turn out . . . not to be the only kind of duty correlative to basic rights.

Basic rights, then, are everyone's minimum reasonable demands upon the rest of humanity. They are the rational basis for justified demands the denial of which no self-respecting person can reasonably be expected to accept. Why should anything be so important? The reason is that rights are basic in the sense used here only if enjoyment of them is essential to the enjoyment of all other rights. That is what is distinctive about a basic right. When a right is genuinely basic, any attempt to enjoy any other right by sacrificing the basic right would be quite literally self-defeating, cutting the ground from beneath itself. Therefore, if a right is basic, other, non-basic rights may be sacrificed, if necessary, in order to secure the basic right. But the protection of a basic right may not be sacrificed in order to secure the enjoyment of a non-basic right. It may not be sacrificed because it cannot be sacrificed successfully. . . .

In practice, what this priority for basic rights usually means is that basic rights need to be established securely before other rights can be secured. The point is that people should be able to *enjoy*, or *exercise*, their other rights. . . . For example, if people have rights to free association, they ought not merely to "have" the rights to free association but also to enjoy their free association itself. Their freedom of association ought to be provided for by the relevant social institutions. This distinction between merely having a right and actually enjoying a right may seem a fine point, but it turns out later to be critical. . . .

Security Rights

. . . If we had to justify our belief that people have a basic right to physical security to someone who challenged this fundamental conviction, we
could in fact give a strong argument that shows that if there are any rights
(basic or not basic) at all, there are basic rights to physical security:

> No one can fully enjoy any right that is supposedly protected by society if
> someone can credibly threaten him or her with murder, rape, beating, etc.,
> when he or she tries to enjoy the alleged right. Such threats to physical secu-
> rity are among the most serious and—in much of the world—the most wide-
> spread hindrances to the enjoyment of any right. If any right is to be exercised
> except at great risk, physical security must be protected. In the absence of
> physical security people are unable to use any other rights that society may
> be said to be protecting without being liable to encounter many of the worst
> dangers they would encounter if society were not protecting the rights.
>
> A right to full physical security belongs, then, among the basic rights—
> not because the enjoyment of it would be more satisfying to someone who
> was also enjoying a full range of other rights, but because its absence would
> leave available extremely effective means for others, including the govern-
> ment, to interfere with or prevent the actual exercise of any other rights that
> were supposedly protected. Regardless of whether the enjoyment of physical
> security is also desirable for its own sake, it is desirable as part of the enjoy-
> ment of every other right. No rights other than a right to physical security
> can in fact be enjoyed if a right to physical security is not protected. Being
> physically secure is a necessary condition for the existence of any other
> right, and guaranteeing physical security must be part of guaranteeing any-
> thing else as a right. . . .

Subsistence Rights

The main reason for discussing security rights, which are not very controversial, was to make explicit the basic assumptions that support the
usual judgment that security rights are basic rights. Now that we have
available an argument that supports them, we are in a position to consider whether matters other than physical security should, according to
the same argument, also be basic rights. It will emerge that subsistence,
or minimal economic security, which is more controversial than physical security, can also be shown to be as well justified for treatment as a
basic right as physical security is—and for the same reasons.

By minimal economic security, or subsistence, I mean unpolluted air, unpolluted water, adequate food, adequate clothing, adequate shelter, and minimal preventive public health care. Many complications about exactly how to specify the boundaries of what is necessary for subsistence would be interesting to explore. But the basic idea is to have available for consumption what is needed for a decent chance at a reasonably healthy and active life of more or less normal length, barring tragic interventions. The central idea is clear enough to work with, even though disputes can occur over exactly where to draw its outer boundaries. A right to subsistence would not mean, at one extreme, that every baby born with a need for open-heart surgery has a right to have it, but it also would not count as adequate food a diet that produces a life expectancy of 35 years of fever-laden, parasite-ridden listlessness.

By a "right to subsistence" I shall always mean a right to at least subsistence. People may or may not have economic rights that go beyond subsistence rights, and I do not want to prejudge that question here. But people may have rights to subsistence even if they do not have any strict rights to economic well-being extending beyond subsistence. Subsistence rights and broader economic rights are separate questions, and I want to focus here on subsistence.

I also do not want to prejudice the issue of whether healthy adults are entitled to be provided with subsistence *only* if they cannot provide subsistence for themselves. Most of the world's malnourished, for example, are probably also diseased, since malnutrition lowers resistance to disease, and hunger and infestation normally form a tight vicious circle. Hundreds of millions of the malnourished are very young children. A large percentage of the adults, besides being ill and hungry, are also chronically unemployed, so the issue of policy toward healthy adults who refuse to work is largely irrelevant. By a "right to subsistence," then, I shall mean a right to subsistence that includes the provision of subsistence at least to those who cannot provide for themselves. . . .

The same considerations that support the conclusion that physical security is a basic right support the conclusion that subsistence is a basic right. Since the argument is now familiar, it can be given fairly briefly.

It is quite obvious why, if we still assume that there are some rights that society ought to protect and still mean by this the removal of the most serious and general hindrances to the actual enjoyment of the rights, subsistence ought to be protected as a basic right:

No one can fully, if at all, enjoy any right that is supposedly protected by society if he or she lacks the essentials for a reasonably healthy and active life. Deficiencies in the means of subsistence can be just as fatal, incapacitating, or painful as violations of physical security. The resulting damage or death can at least as decisively prevent the enjoyment of any right as can the effects of security violations. Any form of malnutrition, or fever due to exposure, that causes severe and irreversible brain damage, for example, can effectively prevent the exercise of any right requiring clear thought and may, like brain injuries caused by assault, profoundly disturb personality. And, obviously, any fatal deficiencies end all possibility of the enjoyment of rights as firmly as an arbitrary execution.

Indeed, prevention of deficiencies in the essentials for survival is, if anything, more basic than prevention of violations of physical security. People who lack protection against violations of their physical security can, if they are free, fight back against their attackers or flee, but people who lack essentials, such as food, because of forces beyond their control, often can do nothing and are on their own utterly helpless. . . .

It is not enough that people merely happen to be secure or happen to be subsisting. They must have a right to security and a right to subsistence—the continued enjoyment of the security and the subsistence must be socially guaranteed. Otherwise a person is readily open to coercion and intimidation through threats of the deprivation of one or the other, and credible threats can paralyze a person and prevent the exercise of any other rights as surely as actual beatings and actual protein/calorie deficiencies can. Credible threats can be reduced only by the actual establishment of social arrangements that will bring assistance to those confronted by forces that they themselves cannot handle. . . .

Why . . . are security and subsistence basic rights? Each is essential to a normal healthy life. Because the actual deprivation of either can be so very serious—potentially incapacitating, crippling, or fatal—even the threatened deprivation of either can be a powerful weapon against anyone whose security or subsistence is not in fact socially guaranteed. People who cannot provide for their own security and subsistence and who lack social guarantees for both are very weak, and possibly helpless, against any individual or institution in a position to deprive them of anything else they value by means of threatening their security or subsistence. A fundamental purpose of acknowledging any basic rights at all is to prevent, or to eliminate, insofar as possible the degree of vulnerability that leaves people at the mercy of others. Social guarantees of security and subsistence go a long way toward accomplishing this purpose. ▲

While a great many people find Shue's view that there are positive subsistence rights correct, many others are also critical of it. One of the most fundamental criticisms of positive rights in general (with a few exceptions to be noted below) is that one agent's positive rights entail an infringement on other agents' negative rights. Quite simply, for the critics, if someone has a right to, say, health care, that means that others have a duty to provide that agent with health care even if they do not want to. Consequently, the liberty and freedoms of those agents are violated. For example, if x has a right to health care, and this is a positive right, then y must provide that health care. This is almost surely done via y paying taxes that the government collects and then uses to pay for x's health care. In effect, then, via the use of governmental power, y is forced to provide for x's health care, so y's basic negative rights are violated by x's supposed positive right. In addition, say the critics, it does not matter that in such a system y also has a positive right to health care. All that means is that some other agent (whether it is x or someone else, z) has negative rights violated in order to pay for y's health care. The principle is that (again, with a few exceptions) any and every positive right entails the infringement of someone else's negative rights, and for these critics, those negative rights are more fundamental and, indeed, are truly the basic rights.

One instance of such criticism comes from Tibor Machan, who explicitly criticizes Shue by claiming that not only do positive rights infringe upon the negative rights of others, but Shue's own view of physical security is actually itself a positive right. This is because in order to enjoy the right of physical security (as opposed to merely having it), one's physical security must be protected by the government. But that would entail having a variety of goods and services provided in order to genuinely protect one's physical security. For instance, since I could easily be killed or harmed by a hurricane, then for me to truly enjoy my right to physical security, would Shue's view not entail that the government must provide me with certain things (minimally, say, home insurance or some form of safe shelter)? So, says Machan, when it really comes down to it, Shue's view advocates only for positive rights, and positive rights always infringe on someone else's negative rights.

Several times above, I have noted that critics of positive rights allow a few exceptions. Machan speaks of these: Some positive rights are legitimate, but only if and when they are necessary for the protection of negative rights. For example, the negative right to vote (which is an instance of a more basic right to liberty) requires some things to be provided, such as voting machines and places to vote. Another case of legitimate positive rights results from voluntary contracts. If I order some delightful toys for my cat Mycroft from Amazon.com, then Amazon is under a duty to provide me with those toys. In effect, I have a positive right to them, but only because we entered a voluntary contract (i.e., we both exercised our own negative rights). Such cases of positive rights are legitimate for Machan and like critics, but, again, only because they are needed in order for negative rights to be realized. However, the main point is that, with these few exceptions, positive rights are illegitimate. Machan makes his points here:

TIBOR MACHAN, "BETWEEN POSITIVE AND NEGATIVE RIGHTS"*

One philosopher who has dealt with whether positive and negative rights are capable of being distinguished directly is Henry Shue. In essence Shue holds that all basic rights are really positive rights. This is because he believes that we do not so much have a basic right to life or liberty but to having our life or liberty (or as he calls it, "security and subsistence") protected by the government. To accomplish this task, Shue states the position of those who uphold the positive/negative rights distinction and defend negative rights as dominant:

> Since subsistence rights are positive and require other people to do more than negative rights require—perhaps more than people can actually do— negative rights, such as those to security, should be fully guaranteed first.

But to this understanding of the situation (framed here without benefit of the terminology of actual proponents of the distinction) Shue objects as follows:

---

*In *Individuals and Their Rights* (LaSalle, IL: Open Court, 1989), 123–134.

> . . . neither rights to physical security nor rights to subsistence fit neatly into
> their assigned sides of the simplistic positive/negative dichotomy. . . . In an
> organized society . . . no one would have much interest in the bare rights to
> physical security. . . .

Shue holds that people have an interest in what "might be called rights-to-be-protected-against-assault-upon-physical-security," which is a positive right in that government must produce protection. Thus, Shue believes, the so-called negative rights, the existence of which even many advocates of positive rights accept, are in fact positive rights.

Shue appears to take his thesis back when he explains that "in any imperfect society enjoyment of a right will depend to some extent upon protection against those who do not choose not to violate it." Here Shue speaks of the *enjoyment of a right* depending upon its protection. That suggests that the right in question exists prior to its protection or any "right-to-be-protected-against-assault-upon-[e.g.-]physical-security." That leaves open the possibility that the right that may or may not be protected is a negative right after all. Of course, talk about "enjoyment of a right" is murky from the start, so Shue might reformulate his claim to read: "My right that you protect me depends upon your actually protecting me." But I am not sure this will help. The language Shue employs suggests that there is some (negative?) right and that could be violated, which generates the further (positive) right to be provided with protection.

Shue . . . fails to notice that the existence of the government or state—which is supposed to fulfill the duty which is the correlative of the positive right to being protected he believes we all have—is morally problematic. For example, where did the state derive its authority to restrain those who would violate our rights, ones we might enjoy without this violation? And how does its right to use the resources needed to provide protection arise? Furthermore, if, as Shue . . . seems to suggest, we have no basic negative rights which we may justifiably protect, how does the government get its authority to deliver the protection Shue agrees it must deliver? The negative-rights theorist has an answer: the government is voluntarily created to protect negative rights and our positive right to receive its protection is derivative from our compact to have those negative rights protected by someone. Thus the positive right is not basic.

But Shue's case has additional weaknesses. For one, it is not the right to "physical security" that most negative-rights theorists regard as a basic negative right. Rather it is the right to life and, derivatively, the rights to liberty and property. Physical security *per se* is not something anyone has a negative right to because physical security can be threatened and destroyed by other than human agents. Negative-rights theories spell out only such rights as could be violated by persons. They have caused confusion when they have failed to make themselves clear enough, as when they speak of the "right to life" or the "right to property," which has been misread to mean "the right to be provided with life" or "the right to be given property."

But perhaps Shue has in mind, when he speaks of the basic right to physical security, the basic rights to life and liberty. These imply, among other things, not only that none may destroy or threaten to destroy one's physical security, but that one may resist any attempt by others to do so. And then a basic right to physical security would amount to a negative right.

Still, the possibility of an ambiguity in Shue's choice of terms needs to be considered because if indeed we have a right to physical security *per se*, whatever the source of threats against it, then this suggests that we possess more than a negative right from the very outset. If one had a right to physical security against, say, the San Andreas Fault or Mount Saint Helens, then to have this right respected, some people may have to engage in some positive actions—such as building earthquake-proof dwellings or lava barriers for everyone. In short, one could read Shue as suggesting that we all have a claim against others to make them do what they can to protect us from such dangers to our physical security. . . .

So the positive "rights-to-be-protected-against-assault-upon" one's autonomy and independence from other people really is not a basic right at all. It is a special political right which, if it developed without the violation of anyone's basic rights—for example, "with the consent of the governed"—may be enforced, just as terms of other voluntarily created contracts may be. The rights Shue so readily collapses are, in fact, morally distinct and necessarily so. The authority of government to act in behalf of someone—for example, as police, prosecutor, and prison warden—rests on the prior justifiability of hiring such an organization in the first place. And this hiring is justified because we possess the basic (negative) rights we do.

No one who upholds the doctrine of negative basic rights and duties need deny the existence of special positive rights and duties—e.g., those arising from contract or special relationships voluntarily created (parents vis-à-vis children). The point negative-rights theorists stress is that basic rights are negative and subsequent positive rights must square with them—for example, rights arising out of contract must never contradict basic rights to life, liberty, or property. Which means that contracts must rest on consent. That is why involuntary servitude—not, however, voluntary service—would be prohibited in a society which regarded the negative right to liberty as basic.

Among the positive rights and duties viewed as important by negative-rights theorists, we may find all of the civil and political rights of citizens in a free society. Once the Declaration of Independence of the new American republic had asserted the existence of basic negative rights, the rest of the detailed work had to be done under the rubric of the U.S. Constitution, which, ideally, should have spelled out the various positive rights which emerged from the compact that established the government. Citizens, upon having established and/or consented to live under a government which exists to protect their basic rights, owe their government certain (agreed upon) duties—payments for services, participation in administration, cooperation in crime detection and prevention, offering testimony in the pursuit of justice, and so on. This is not negligible by any means, but it fails to usher in the whole slew of positive duties that Shue and others wish to uphold with their doctrine of the inherent positive nature of all rights. In any case, the positive rights and duties so grounded would not be "basic." . . .

[With respect to a negative-rights theory of government], quite outside of politics, it can invoke considerations of moral virtue and vice in any area of human action and institution. All this tradition insists upon is that in a just society the scope of rights and duties (as here understood, namely, enforceable moral imperatives) is limited to preserving the "moral space" of all individuals. That is, everyone has the basic right to his or her own life, liberty, and property and the duty not to violate others' similar rights, so that everyone can be in charge of his or her moral life. None of this makes it impossible to morally criticize governments which mistreat civil servants, squander resources, implement irresponsible hiring and firing practices, and so on. Government, as other human agencies, can act wrongly in several ways, some involving the violation of rights, which they are prohibited from doing (so that at some point doing such wrongs can lead to the loss of its moral authority), and some involving the breach of various moral principles—courage, prudence, generosity, and so forth.

Since advocates of negative rights are not usually intuitionists, they are usually not that impressed when philosophers have strong feelings about equality of opportunity, racial prejudice, frivolity, waste, obscenity, irreverence, sexual indiscretion, and so forth. These may be valid moral concerns but not ones which justify violating basic negative rights. It can be morally callous to ignore other people's needs or to exhibit pictures of women in degrading poses. But what is to be done about such things is a matter of personal moral responsibility, not of enforceable duty. It does not follow from negative-rights theory that public opinion, social pressure, or even ostracism would always be ruled out. . . . There are other than political means by which charity can be practiced or soulcraft administered. . . .

[As for any basic right to subsistence—better termed "welfare rights"—such as Shue advocates, the enjoyment of which requires that things be provided to persons:] This outlook sees persons as we do trees or flowers that grow not from their own determination but spurred on by the natural environment. And if there are deficiencies in that environment, there will be impediments standing in the way of growth. . . .

In this perspective the primary task of good government—of those who understand and have the power to upgrade the species—is to free them from such impediments to growth. This is clearly not accomplished simply by protecting people against the aggressive intrusion of other human beings. No, they need total "liberation"—the prevention of all intrusions such as poverty, disease, ignorance, illness, even sin. Thus [such a view] holds that "physical force need not always be either morally objectionable or a denial of freedom. Efforts physically to restrain drug addicts from gaining access to drugs may be done for moral reasons and in the interest of freedom—to enhance the addicts' ability to make deliberate choices." It is but a short distance from here to the view that forcing people not to advocate revolutionary policies, or the wrong religion, or censoring trashy movies and bad literature is morally proper because it enhances people's ability to live properly. ◣

LEGAL RIGHTS VERSUS MORAL RIGHTS

One way to focus on the content and scope of rights is to look closely at specific rights. For example, one could look at the right to bear arms and consider what exactly that covers. The content "bear arms" has two words: "bear" and "arms." Does *bear* arms mean "own," "carry," "sell," "produce," and so forth? Does bear *arms* mean "knives," "handguns," "torpedoes," "battleships," "biological weapons," and so forth? Obviously, there are plenty of questions about the content and scope of particular rights; indeed, a great deal of legal activity goes into just that issue. It is pretty much standard fare for the U.S. Supreme Court to wrestle with the content and scope of particular rights (e.g., is water boarding included in the scope of cruel and unusual punishment?).

In this chapter, however, we look not so much at the content and scope of particular rights (though we do in later chapters) but rather at broad issues of content and scope. We just looked at one broad issue, namely, negative and positive rights. Should positive rights, generally speaking, be included within the scope of legitimate rights? We saw that Shue said yes and Machan said no.

A second broad issue here is that of legal versus moral rights. We touched on this issue in the previous chapter when we considered the topic of the source versus the justification of rights. There we said that although these two notions of source and justification are related, they are not equivalent. Where our rights come from, and certainly where we think they come from, does not in itself provide a justification for those rights. Nonetheless, when we speak of the content and scope of rights, we do often, and appropriately, look at their source. (When I say "appropriately" here, that does not mean it is without controversy!) For example, I live in the state of Oregon. If I claim to have the right to post bail (and not be held in jail) for specific offenses (except murder and treason), I might very well claim to have that right because it is spelled out in Section 14 of the Constitution of the State of Oregon. Or if I claim I have the right to wear a shirt that displays profanity in public, I might claim to have this right because it is spelled out in Section 8 of the Constitution of the State of Oregon (as well as in the First Amendment of the U.S. Constitution). Clearly, a great many specific rights that we claim to have and enjoy are spelled out in legal statues. Likewise, there are statues that regulate behavior by prohibiting it (e.g., Section 23 of the Constitution of the State of Hawaii prohibits same-sex marriage) and, so, declare that agents do not have such a right.

Broadly speaking, this is the view of *legal rights*, which are rights that have their legitimacy because they are acknowledged within some legal system. The legal system not only acknowledges those rights but also—according to many people—grants them. If it were not for the legal system, those rights would not exist, at least for citizens governed by that legal system. Under a legal-rights view, black slaves in antebellum Southern states did not have the right to vote, and they did not have it *because* the legal system said so. Likewise, under the legal-rights view, ever since 1973 women in the United States (with some exceptions) have had the right to abortion on demand, and they have it *because* the legal system says so.

A great many people certainly hold this legal-rights view. It is almost a knee-jerk reaction for people to say that they have some right because "it's in the Constitution!" As we all know, there are constant attempts via the ballot box and the courts to guarantee or prevent some right's enactment into law (e.g., same-sex marriage). Under this legal-rights view, the only rights that exist are those codified into the legal system.

An alternative view of legal rights is that the legal system merely acknowledges and guarantees the protection of rights; it does not create those rights and cannot negate them. Rather than positing a legal system as the source of rights, many people argue that there are *moral rights*, which come from, and are justified by, moral principles, independently of whether any legal system codifies them. As the previous chapter demonstrates, the view of natural and human rights takes this stance. Without such legal protection, we might not be in a position to enjoy and exercise our moral rights, but those rights exist nonetheless. For advocates of this view, the fact that a (moral) right is violated, even by a legal system, is no more evidence that the right does not exist than the fact that civil laws are violated is evidence that those laws do not exist. Indeed, their violation presupposes their existence, since they could not be violated if they were not there! Ideally, under this view, moral and legal rights would be identical, with laws acknowledging and protecting all our moral rights and with no laws violating them.

At the beginning of this chapter, we considered different interpretations of the claim to a right to employment. There was the question not only of whether this purported right is a negative or positive right but also of whether this is a moral right or not. These two pairs of distinctions—negative/positive and legal/moral—are not the same and, indeed, do not necessarily match up at all. For instance, someone like Shue advocates positive rights and could very easily (and probably would) see a positive right to employment as a moral right, since employment is most likely a necessary condition for subsistence. On the other hand, as we saw, Machan is critical of positive rights, but under a negative-rights view could (and probably would) very much support the notion that a negative right to employment (i.e., to seek employment) is a moral right, since, for him, the government is not the source or justification but the guarantor of rights (if it is acting properly). So, one can—and many do—advocate for moral rights as distinguished from legal rights, whether or not one advocates for positive rights as distinguished from negative rights. Likewise, one could, and many do, advocate for only negative legal rights, while others also advocate for positive legal rights, but in both cases against the notion of "real" nonlegal moral rights.

Not all rights theorists embrace the legal/moral rights distinction. As we will see soon, for example, R. G. Frey does not embrace it because he denies that there are any moral rights. At best, then, he might embrace or accept a conceptual distinction but not an important practical one. Another rights theorist, whom we will not read here, Judith Jarvis Thomson, rejects the legal/moral rights distinction because she believes that legal rights themselves have moral sources and justifications, so to draw a distinction between legal and moral rights really has no important consequences. It is, she argues, a distinction that makes no distinction. It is better to drop the adjectives and simply speak of rights.

Notwithstanding Thomson's view, most rights theorists, and certainly many others, speak of legal rights as opposed to moral rights. That leaves us with the question, Are there nonlegal moral rights? The final two readings in this chapter provide different answers. The next reading, by H. L. A. Hart, says yes; the final reading, by R. G. Frey, says no. Hart claims that although rights form one among many moral concepts (which regulate behavior), they are unique because they focus specifically on the legitimate limitation of agents' liberties. Because rights entail duties on others, says Hart, their real weight has to do with how they regulate others' behavior, and this is a normative, moral matter. Law is our way of codifying moral values and decisions, not of creating them. To speak only, or even primarily, about legal rights, then, is to put the cart before the horse. As he puts it at the end of this reading, rights and wrongs, as opposed to right and wrong actions, make sense only when related to the moral aspects of agents. For Hart, just as law and government derive duties and goals only from the duties and goals of agents, so law and government have rights only so derivatively. The real source and justification of rights lie at the level of moral principles.

H. L. A. HART, "ARE THERE ANY NATURAL RIGHTS?"*

A. Lawyers have for their own purposes carried the dissection of the notion of a "legal right" some distance, and some of their results are of value in the elucidation of statements of the form "X has a right to . . . " outside legal contexts. There is of course no simple identification to be made between moral and legal rights, but there is an intimate connection between the two, and this itself is one feature which distinguishes a moral right from other fundamental moral concepts. It is not merely that as a matter of fact men speak of their moral rights mainly when advocating their incorporation in a legal system, but that the concept of a right belongs to that branch of morality which is specifically concerned to determine when one person's freedom may be limited by another's and so to determine what actions may appropriately be made subject of coercive legal rules. The words *"droit," "dritto,"* and *"Recht,"* used by continental jurists, have no simple English translation and seem to English jurists to hover uncertainly between law and morals, but they do in fact mark off an area of morality (the morality of law) which has special characteristics. It is occupied by the concepts of justice, fairness, rights, and obligation (if this last is not used as it is by many moral philosophers as an obscuring general label to cover every action that morally we ought to do or forbear from doing). The most important common characteristic of this group of moral concepts is that there is no incongruity, but a special congruity in the use of force or the threat of force to secure that what is just or fair or someone's right to have done shall in fact be done; for it is in just these circumstances that coercion of another human being is legitimate. . . . [W]e must distinguish from the rest of morality those principles regulating the proper distribution of human freedom which alone make it morally

---

Philosophical Review 64, no. 2 (1955): 175–191.

legitimate for one human being to determine by his choice how another should act; and a certain specific moral value is secured (to be distinguished from moral virtue in which the goodwill is manifested) if human relationships are conducted in accordance with these principles even though coercion has to be used to secure this, for only if these principles are regarded will freedom be distributed among human beings as it should be. And it is, I think, a very important feature of a moral right that the possessor of it is conceived as having a moral justification for limiting the freedom of another and that he has this justification not because the action he is entitled to require of another has some moral quality but simply because in the circumstances a certain distribution of human freedom will be maintained if he by his choice is allowed to determine how that other shall act.

B. I can best exhibit this feature of a moral right by reconsidering the question whether moral rights and "duties" are correlative. The contention that they are means, presumably, that every statement of the form "X has a right to . . . " entails and is entailed by "Y has a duty (not) to . . . ," and at this stage we must not assume that the values of the name-variables "X" and "Y" must be different persons. Now there is certainly one sense of "a right" . . . such that it does not follow from X's having a right that X or someone else has any duty. Jurists have isolated rights in this sense and have referred to them as "liberties" just to distinguish them from rights in the centrally important sense of "right" which has "duty" as a correlative. The former sense of "right" is needed to describe those areas of social life where competition is at least morally unobjectionable. Two people walking along both see a ten-dollar bill in the road twenty yards away, and there is no clue as to the owner. Neither of the two are under a "duty" to allow the other to pick it up; each has in a sense a right to pick it up. Of course there may be many things which each has a "duty" not to do in the course of the race to the spot—neither may kill or wound the other—and corresponding to these "duties" there are rights of forbearances. The moral propriety of all economic competition implies this minimum sense of "a right" in which to say that "X has a right to" means merely that X is under no "duty" not to. . . .

C. More important for our purpose is the question whether for all moral "duties" there are correlative moral rights, because those who have given an affirmative answer to this question have usually assumed without adequate scrutiny that to have a right is simply to be capable of benefiting by the performance of a "duty"; whereas in fact this is not a sufficient condition (and probably not a necessary condition) of having a right. Thus animals and babies who stand to benefit by our performance of our "duty" not to ill-treat them are said *therefore* to have rights to proper treatment. The full consequence of this reasoning is not usually followed out; most have shrunk from saying that we have rights against ourselves because we stand to benefit from our performance of our "duty" to keep ourselves alive or develop our talents. But the moral situation which arises from a promise (where the legal-sounding terminology of rights and obligations is most appropriate) illustrates most clearly that the notion of having a right and that of benefiting by the performance of a "duty" are not identical. *X* promises *Y* in return for some favor that he will look after *X*'s aged mother in his absence. Rights arise out of this transaction, but it is surely *Y* to whom the promise has been made and not his mother who *has* or *possesses* these rights. Certainly *Y*'s mother is the person concerning whom *X* has an obligation and a person who will benefit by its performance, but the person *to whom* he has an obligation to look after her is *Y*. This is something *due to* or *owed to Y*, so it is *Y*, not his mother, whose right *X* will disregard and to whom *X* will have done *wrong* if he fails to keep his promise, though the mother may be physically injured. And it is *Y* who has a moral *claim* upon *X*, is *entitled* to have his mother looked after, and who can *waive* the claim and *release X* from the obligation. *Y* is, in other words, morally in a position to determine by his choice how *X* shall act and in this way to limit *X*'s freedom of choice; and it is this fact, not the fact that he stands to benefit, that makes it appropriate to say that he has a *right*. Of course often the person to whom a promise has been made will be the only person who stands to benefit by its performance, but this does not justify the identification of "having a right" with "benefiting by the performance of a duty." It is important for the whole logic of rights that, while the person who stands to benefit by the performance of a duty is discovered by considering what will happen if the duty is not performed, the person who has a right (to whom performance is *owed* or *due*) is discovered by examining the transaction or antecedent situation or relations of the parties out of which the "duty" arises. These considerations should incline us not to extend to animals and babies whom it is wrong to ill-treat the notion of a right to proper treatment, for the moral situation can be simply and adequately described here by saying that it is wrong or that we ought not to ill-treat them or, in the philosopher's generalized sense of "duty," that we have a duty not to ill-treat them. If common usage sanctions talk of the rights of animals or babies, it makes an idle use of the expression "a right," which will confuse the situation with other different moral situations where the expression "a right" has a specific force and cannot be replaced by the other moral expressions which I have mentioned. Perhaps some clarity on this matter is to be gained by considering the force of the preposition "to" in the expression "having a duty to Y" or "being under an obligation to Y" (where "Y" is the name of a person); for it is significantly different from the meaning of "to" in "doing something to Y" or "doing harm to Y," where it indicates the person affected by some action. In the first pair of expressions, "to" obviously does not have this force, but indicates the person to whom the person morally bound is bound. This is an intelligible development of the figure of a bond (*vinculum juris: obligare*); the precise figure is not that of two persons bound by a chain, but of *one* person bound, the other end of the chain lying in the hands of another to use if he chooses. So it appears absurd to speak of having duties or owing obligations to ourselves—of course we may have "duties" not to do harm to ourselves, but what could be meant (once the distinction between these different meanings of "to" has been grasped) by insisting that we have duties or obligations *to* ourselves not to do harm to ourselves.

D. The essential connection between the notion of a right and the justified limitation of one person's freedom by another may be thrown into relief if we consider codes of behavior which do not purport to confer rights but only to prescribe what shall be done. Most natural law thinkers down to [Richard] Hooker conceived of natural law in this way: there were natural duties compliance with which would certainly benefit man—things to be done to achieve man's natural end—but not natural rights. And there are of course many types of codes of behavior which only prescribe what is to be done, e.g. those regulating certain ceremonies. It would be absurd to regard these codes as conferring rights, but illuminating to contrast them with rules of games, which often create rights, though not, of course, moral rights. But even a code which is plainly a moral code need not establish rights; the Decalogue [Ten Commandments] is perhaps the most important example. Of course, quite apart from heavenly rewards human beings stand to benefit by general obedience to the Ten Commandments: disobedience is wrong and will certainly harm individuals. But it would be a surprising interpretation of them that treated them as conferring rights. In such an interpretation obedience to the Ten Commandments would have to be conceived as not merely wrong but as a *wrong to* (as well as harm to) individuals. The Commandments would cease to read like penal statutes designed only to rule out certain types of behavior and would have to be thought of as rules placed at the disposal of individuals and regulating the extent to which *they* may demand certain behavior from others. Rights are typically conceived of as *possessed* or *owned by* or *belonging to* individuals, and these expressions reflect the conception of moral rules as not only prescribing conduct but as forming a kind of moral property of individuals to which they are as individuals entitled; only when rules are conceived in this way can we speak of *rights* and *wrongs* as well as right and wrong actions. ◤

While Hart argues for the existence (and priority) of moral rights, in the following reading, R. G. Frey casts doubt on their legitimacy. Indeed, he rejects the nature and value of moral rights. That is to say, he argues not only that there are no moral rights but also that the concept of them is of no value; it does no important work in regulating behavior or enhancing and protecting the well-being of moral agents. Contrary to Hart, Frey claims that our other moral concepts, such as utility, justice, and fairness, accomplish just what advocates of moral rights want. As he puts it, claiming that there are moral rights without offering some sort of justification for them is simply empty verbiage. While he draws on Joel Feinberg's conception of rights as valid claims, he could make his point without relying on Feinberg (so, even if Feinberg's views were in question, it does not follow that Frey is therefore mistaken). But given Frey's acceptance that rights are valid claims against others, the assertion of a right requires some ground or justification. So, disputes about rights, says Frey, really happen at the level of the justification. If that is so, he says, then the real questions occur regarding the existence not of (moral) rights but of a nonrights ground or justification for those purported rights. And if that is so, he says, then the real issue with respect to appropriate regulation of behavior has nothing to do with moral rights but with their grounding. To put it another way, for Frey, (moral) rights do not ground or justify regulation of behavior but are themselves grounded or justified by some other moral basis for the regulation of behavior. In addition, contrary to Harman's claim that moral relativism justifies rights, Frey argues that the sociological fact of moral relativism shows that there are no moral rights but at best a basis for legal rights. To support such a claim, Frey claims that when we advocate for some moral right, we try to get that right enacted into law—in effect, acknowledging that what really matters are legal rights. The concept of moral rights, then, is superfluous at best and, indeed, mistaken.

R. G. FREY, "MORAL RIGHTS: SOME DOUBTS"*

My reason for doubting that there are any moral rights is perfectly straightforward and can be briefly put.

What is it to have a right? Doubtless the most prominent answer to this question today is Joel Feinberg's, as set out in his papers "Duties, Rights and Claims" and "The Nature and Value of Rights." To have a right, according to Feinberg, whose answer is drawn up around the notion of a legal right, is to have a claim to something or against others. To have a legal right to the collection of rent is to have a claim of prompt payment from one's tenants; to have a legal right to privacy in one's home is to have a claim against others not to invade one's privacy through trespass, and so on. Thus, to have a legal right is to be able to make claims, claims which can be enforced, which one can properly insist upon having enforced, and which the courts, properly petitioned, will see are enforced. In this way, being able to make claims, enforced and backed by sanctions, forms an important part of what it is for a person to function in society, which is why the deprivation of one's legal rights, as in the case, for instance, of some Soviet dissidents, is such a severe loss, even though one remains at liberty in society.

---

*In *Interests and Rights: The Case Against Animals* (Oxford: Clarendon Press, 1980), 4–17.

But what if one lacks the ability to make claims at all? This problem, obviously of concern, for example, to animal and environmental rightists, since neither dogs nor trees can make or insist upon or petition the courts on behalf of their claims, is held to be solved by appealing to the cases of small children, the very seriously infirm, and the mentally subnormal, all of whom are conceded legal rights but in respect of whom the courts, if necessary, appoint persons to make and exercise claims and to petition for legal proceedings on their behalf. It is arguable that nothing prevents a similar treatment of dogs and trees.

Though Feinberg's analysis of rights is drawn up with legal rights in mind, it is widely extended to morals, and Feinberg himself so extends it in "The Nature and Value of Rights." . . . I want to explore . . . the conclusion that claims to moral rights do not play the serious and decisive role that claims to rights play in law. There are two ways of showing this, though, as will be seen, they are connected; the first leads to the view that moral rights are superfluous, and the second, issuing out of the first, leads to the view that we cannot affirm that there are any moral rights.

To have a legal right to the collection of rent is to have a claim to prompt payment from one's tenants; but it is not only this. It is also, as Feinberg is aware, to have a claim that is justified. What justifies one's claim to the collection of rent are the terms of the lease, contract, or certificate of agreement which has been agreed between one's tenants or their agents and oneself and which is legally enforceable, except in certain specifiable circumstances, in the courts. Suppose, then, that a feminist claims that women have a moral right to abortion on demand: what must confer this right upon women, since there is no agreed contractual agreement (either implicit or explicit) between society and individual women which does, must be some moral principle or other which is alleged by the feminist to be the ground of this right. A principle to the effect that it is wrong to interfere with a woman's control or power over her own body is, for example, one possibility sometimes suggested in this regard; and what the feminist is ultimately claiming is that this principle justifies her claim to an abortion on demand.

Thus, if we challenge the claim that women have such a right, what we find ourselves arguing about with the feminist is the moral principle which is alleged by her to be the ground of this right; and what ends up being in dispute between us is the acceptability of this principle. Its acceptability is everything: you are only going to accept that women have a moral right to abortion on demand if you accept the moral principle which is alleged to confer this right upon them. There are five aspects to this argument between the feminist and ourselves to which attention must be drawn.

1. What we are arguing about is not the right but the ground of the right, the particular moral principle appealed to; and the point at issue between us is the acceptability of this principle. Not to accept it, given it is the ground of the right, is effectively to deny that women have the right in question.
2. It is a plain fact that there is widespread disagreement over moral principles, whether or not they are cited as the alleged ground of some moral right. It is not at all obvious that women have a moral right to an abortion on demand, and anyone who thought that the moral principle (or that interpretations of it) which is alleged to confer this right upon women commanded widespread assent would be deceiving themselves. . . .
3. Worse yet, there is widespread disagreement among us even about the very canons of acceptability in moral principles. . . . The feminist will not be allowed merely to suppose that some moral principle is acceptable, she must show that it is; but then she faces the difficulty that the criteria of acceptability in moral principles are not settled and agreed among us, as anyone who places a principle of utility among these criteria and anyone who does not easily attest. . . .
4. Argument can and does proceed about moral principles and their acceptability *whether or not* there are rights alleged grounded upon them. Indeed, even in a world devoid of moral rights, argument of this sort can easily occur. Thus, we can argue about the acceptability of a principle which gives a woman absolute control or power over her own body, even when a fetus is present in it, whether or not we posit some moral right to an abortion on demand grounded upon it. . . . The point, then, is an important one vis-à-vis claims to moral rights; if such claims are made, then we have to argue about the principles cited as their ground; if such claims are not made, we can still argue about these and other moral principles of rightness and justifi-

cation of treatment. It is not as if the making of such claims is what opens up the possibility of argument about the moral principles in which they are allegedly grounded.

On the basis of these four aspects of our argument with the feminist, a fifth can now be seen in the form of a conclusion.

5. If we do reach agreement on canons of acceptability in moral principles, and if we do then reach agreement in moral principles, what is the point of going on to posit this or that moral right? For if we take morality seriously and try to put our principles into action, we shall change our behavior to accord with our principles. To posit a moral right in addition seems a superfluous gesture. If we cannot reach agreement of the sorts described, we are not going to agree about whether there is such a right in the first place; and if we do reach agreement of the sorts described, there no longer is a need to postulate the existence of a right, since my moral principles will not direct me to act in ways perhaps different from those in which I have been acting. So far as I can see, not even a practical advantage is gained by positing some moral right based upon agreed moral principles, since I as a moral man, implementing and following my principles, will behave the way you want me to *even without the right.* . . .

Interestingly, feminists widely use as a way of rallying their supporters the cry "Women ought to have the right to abortion on demand" (or, less commonly, "Women should be able to have an abortion when they want one"); but this way of putting the matter makes it quite clear, I think, that women are not being credited with "having the right" to an abortion on demand. In fact the cry "Women ought to have the right to abortion on demand" strikes me as pointing away from morals and moral rights, and towards the law and legal rights; it is maintaining, I think, that legislation ought to be enacted—among other reasons, because it is thought morally wrong (at the very least, by the feminist) to deprive a woman of an abortion when she wants one—so that women come to enjoy the *legal right* to abortion on demand.

Now though the feminist thinks it morally wrong to deprive a woman of an abortion on demand, a good many other people do not;

and this is the point from which my second argument to show that claims to rights in morals do not play the serious and decisive role they play in law begins. *Per se*, such clashes in moral judgments are common and, philosophically, rather uninteresting; where they become interesting, as should be clear from my first argument, is when we attempt to arbitrate them by trying to come up with theses or standards of rightness, wrongness, and justification. For what we find when we try to do this is that these theses and standards are themselves in dispute; and since they are dependent upon the normative ethical theory we embrace, it follows that it is *the adequacy* of such theories which is really in dispute between us and which we find it difficult to deal with. . . .

Since my normative ethical views depend upon my normative ethical theory, to query me on the worth of the one without querying me on the adequacy of the other is pointless. But how do we tell whether a normative theory is adequate? Or whether it is perhaps more adequate than certain rival theories? These are by no means easy questions; certainly, as is well known and long bemoaned in the literature, there are no agreed answers to them, which explains the otherwise curious fact that act-utilitarians and their critics, in spite of numerous differences in theory and practice, each continue to flourish. Yet such questions must be addressed and answered, I think, if one's own or one's group's moral convictions about the rightness or wrongness or justification of this or that are to be given or considered to have pre-eminent weight. . . .

In short, it must simply be said that, in morals, not only are the theories in doubt but also (and, in my view, more importantly) even the test(s) of adequacy by which we might evaluate them; and to go on about moral rights under these conditions is not to argue the pertinent issues at all. Here, too, therefore, claims to rights do not play the serious and decisive role in morals which they play in Feinberg's paradigm, the law. For the quest for theses, standards, or principles of rightness, wrongness, and justification by which to ground, support, and justify claims to moral rights leads directly to a quest for agreed criteria of adequacy by which to adjudicate the conflicting normative ethics in which theses, standards, and principles find a home; and the derivation of these criteria remains a task, both crucial and fundamental, yet to be satisfactorily concluded. Thus, far from ever resolving anything in morals, claims to rights merely reemphasize the unsatisfactory state in which the issues surrounding this question of adequacy remain; it is difficult, therefore, to see how these pertinent issues are or could be either argued or advanced by continually making such claims. Accordingly, until these issues are resolved, always assuming they can be, I do not see how it can be affirmed that women have a moral right to abortion on demand or that animals have a moral right to life.

To my mind, then, either moral rights are superfluous or we are not yet in a position to affirm that there are any; whichever it is, I cannot see that anything is lost by giving up claims to moral rights altogether. ◢

Questions for Discussion

1. Shue remarks, in effect, that deprivation has the same moral weight as assault, in the sense that agents who are deprived of the requirements for subsistence are on a par with agents who are assaulted. Another way of stating this is, Violation of economic security has the same moral weight as violation of physical security. Is this correct? Shue also claims that there is a difference between having a right and enjoying a right, with the latter being what is actually important. For example, saying that an agent has the right to vote, though he or she has no means of voting is, in effect, to say that the agent has the right but does not truly enjoy the right. Is Shue correct about this distinction? If so, does this entail that purported rights not codified into a legal system are insignificant? If not, why not?

2. Machan remarks that Shue's notion of enjoying a right presupposes the existence of that very right (since to enjoy it, there must already be something there to enjoy); hence, his conception of basic rights actually must not depend upon the significance of enjoying a right nearly so much as Shue claims. Is Machan correct? In addition, Machan claims that legitimizing positive rights—at least, such rights as Shue embraces—leads to the infringement of genuine negative rights and unjustifiable governmental intervention into people's lives. Is he correct? Machan also states that the government has legitimacy only via the voluntary creation of it by individuals with (prior) rights. Is this correct?

3. Hart argues that moral rights capture an important regulation of behavior that other moral concepts do not, in large part because moral rights focus on determining when one agent's freedoms may legitimately limit another's.

Is it correct that moral rights are unique and distinct in this way? In addition, Hart holds that because of this unique feature, moral rights indeed exist and are distinct from legal rights as much as they are from other moral concepts. Is this view correct?

4. Contrary to Hart, Frey argues that there are no moral rights, or, at best, they are superfluous. To support this conclusion, he claims that other moral concepts actually do the work that moral rights are said to do, namely, justifying certain regulations of behavior. What is his argument for this claim, and is it correct? Frey also remarks that when people claim to have a moral right, they really are lobbying for the creation of a legal right, and this is an implicit acknowledgement that there really are no moral rights. In what ways is this like and unlike Shue's distinction between having a right and enjoying a right?

5. How do the various views and arguments concerning positive and moral rights contained in this chapter relate to the various conceptions of the nature of rights outlined in Chapter 1?

6. How do the various views and arguments concerning positive and moral rights contained in this chapter relate to the various justifications of rights outlined in Chapter 2?

Further Reading

Brettschneider, Corey. *Democratic Rights: The Substance of Self-Government*. Princeton, NJ: Princeton University Press, 2007. An analysis of core democratic values, with an emphasis on particular rights and their meaning and role in a democracy.

Campbell, Tom, David Goldberg, Sheila McLean, and Tom Mullen, eds. *Human Rights: From Rhetoric to Reality*. New York: Basil Blackwell, 1986. A collection of essays emphasizing specific rights and their implementation.

Dershowitz, Alan. *Rights from Wrongs*. New York: Basic Books, 2004. A lawyer's perspective on the nature of rights as responses to wrongs suffered by people.

Domino, John C. *Civil Rights and Liberties: Toward the 21st Century*. New York: Harper Collins, 1994. An analysis of American legal rulings on particular civil rights.

Machan, Tibor R., ed. *The Libertarian Reader*. Totawa, NJ: Rowman and Allanheld, 1982. A classic collection of essays on rights from a libertarian perspective.

Moon, J. Donald, ed. *Responsibility, Rights, and Welfare: The Theory of the Welfare State*. Boulder, CO: Westview Press, 1988. A collection of essays for and against (mostly for) positive rights.

Paul, Ellen Frankel, Fred Miller Jr., and Jeffrey Paul, eds. *Human Rights*. New York: Basil Blackwell, 1984. A collection of essays debating different features of rights as well as specific rights.

Perry, Michael J. *The Idea of Human Rights: Four Inquiries*. New York: Oxford University Press, 1998. Four short essays analyzing different features of rights.

Reed, Esther D. *The Ethics of Human Rights: Contested Doctrinal and Moral Issues*. Waco, TX: Baylor University Press, 2007. An analysis of rights and their relation to Christian theology.

Sunstein, Cass. *The Second Bill of Rights: FDR's Unfinished Revolution—and Why We Need It More Than Ever*. New York: Basic Books, 2006. A legal philosopher's perspective on rights from a modern liberal point of view.

CHAPTER 4

RIGHTS HOLDERS

In the mid-1990s a public transportation system (called a light-rail train) was being put in place in the suburbs just west of Portland, Oregon. As part of the installation of the track's rails, workers needed to tunnel through some hills. On top of one of these hills was a cemetery, and a group of citizens objected to the plan (which included dynamiting) to bore the tunnel under the cemetery. One concern some of these citizens raised was that the process would violate the rights of those buried there in their final resting place. Other citizens, who favored the light-rail system and the boring of the tunnel, responded that the dead do not have rights. In reply, some members of the original group changed their claim to assert the rights of surviving family members and their property rights to the cemetery plots, while other members of the original group insisted that, yes, the dead do have rights—that rights apply as much to past and future generations as to present ones. Although this particular case was settled without having the courts decide on any relevant rights, and the tunnel was bored, it nonetheless points to the issue of who or what is a rights holder.

We take it for granted that individual humans are rights holders. If anything has rights, they do. Very commonly, however, we speak of other entities as having rights. For example, we speak of corporations such as Microsoft as having rights, and we speak of whole nations or states such as New Zealand as having rights. A very broad and basic question connected to rights generally entails exactly who or what has rights, or who or what is a rights holder? Besides the kinds of things just mentioned (individual humans, corporations, nations), many people speak of future generations as having rights (as in the right of future generations to have a clean environment). As noted above, some people argue that past generations are rights holders. There has also been a great deal of argumentation for and against considering at least some nonhumans as legitimate rights holders. We have all heard of the animal rights movement (and we look at it more explicitly in the second half of this chapter). In addition, many people have come to speak of the environment or Earth itself as having rights. Of particular importance over the last century especially has been the question of group rights.

GROUP RIGHTS

In 1984 the Detroit Tigers baseball team won the World Series, its first such victory since 1968 and only the fourth in its history (the other two times being in 1935 and 1945). No players on the 1984 team had even been alive when the Tigers won the 1935 series. Despite the fact that the team roster had changed completely over those five decades, it is still said that the Detroit Tigers have won four World Series titles. The team as a collective is credited with those four wins, not the individual players who played in the games. In 1973 the U.S. Supreme Court ruled 7–2 in the case of *Roe v. Wade* that a human fetus is not a legal person with constitutional rights. Although the Court's decision comprised the decisions of individual justices, the Court as a collective made the ruling. These two examples, and countless others, demonstrate how commonly we think of groups as agents; teams win, and courts make rulings.

The significance of such thinking relates to the topic of rights when we turn to the issue of group rights, which centers, first and foremost, on the question of whether groups *as groups* are rights holders. Other questions immediately follow. For instance, if they are rights holders, what justifies them as such, and if they are not, why not? If they are rights holders, what is the content of their rights? Against whom or what do they hold them (or, who or what has the correlative duties that result from their rights)? And if they are rights holders, are they also rights addressees (and duty holders)?

In addressing these various questions, most rights theorists first speak to what is meant by a "group." Uniformly, these rights theorists do not mean simply any collection of individuals. Indeed, we recognize that there are all sorts of groups; some stem from nature (e.g., women) or from social relations (e.g., Oregonians) or from interests (e.g., smokers), and so forth. Although all of these specific examples have been championed as rights holders (i.e., people speak of women's rights or smoker's rights), the word "group" in the notion of group rights does not refer to just any set of individuals. No unambiguous set of criteria has been agreed upon with respect to what constitutes a group, especially a group with the status of rights holder. However, various sorts of features are usually identified: some level of unity and identity among the members of the group, perhaps even a sense of being bound together by common interests or common history or common treatment (i.e., members of group *x* being treated by others outside the group "as an *x*"). With respect to rights, such groups are often identified, at least in legal contexts, as "suspect classifications." For example, we identify race, ethnicity, religious affiliation, or sexual orientation as classifications by which some people are discriminated against; hence, we say they functionally constitute a group that needs protection and so has rights. As we know, not everyone agrees with this—for instance, some people claim that the concept of gay rights is appropriate since it is *as being gay* (not as being male or white or having some other trait) that some people are discriminated against, while other people see gay rights as inappropriate special rights not equally shared by other citizens or rights holders. The present point is only that a group is sometimes said to be constituted based on some property (or set of properties) or some relation (or set of relations). This raises the issue of whether those properties or relations provide a morally relevant basis for establishing rights for a group. So, is being gay (or black or female or a Jehovah's Witness) relevant to having certain rights—and this is the important point—not as an individual or as a citizen but as a member of that group?

Now, a number of interrelated questions have been raised very quickly here, so it is worth restating them. First, what constitutes a group such that we would appropriately recognize it as a rights holder? Second, what is the relation between a group and its members? Third, what about a group legitimizes it as a rights holder? Other questions arise, which we consider shortly. For now, the first reading below by Carol Gould addresses the question of the status of a group as a kind of entity that has rights. Gould argues that, yes, some groups have an ontological status that is not reducible to the status of the members who comprise it, even though the group exists only because of its members. In a sense, it is a way of saying that the whole is greater than the sum of its parts, although in this case, Gould is speaking of whether the whole (the group) has moral standing, hence rights, beyond the moral standing and rights of the individuals who constitute the group. In this reading she focuses on groups that happen to be minorities within larger contexts (e.g., Latinos in the United States), but her view would be relevant to the consideration of groups in general. She claims that some groups, at least, are "constituted entities" and consist not merely of individuals but of "individuals-in-relations." The very identity of the members of such groups lies in the network of relations that constitute who these people are. So, these individuals are not people who just happen to be members of some group; rather, being members of the group, thus being part of these networks of relations, is part of the very nature of who the individuals are (she speaks of such relations as "internal relations"). There is one small point to note about her remarks: She speaks of "prima facie" equal rights. "Prima facie" means "at first glance" or "to start with." The point is that we take something to be the case *to start with*, but we might be persuaded otherwise; the burden of proof, however, is to show that this prima facie assumption is mistaken. So, if there are prima facie equal rights, we assume, or take as given, that there indeed are such rights, but we might accept an argument that would reject this assumption. So, again, Gould argues that the notion of group rights makes sense, that is, that some groups are rights holders; she focuses on addressing the status of groups over and above the status of the individual members of groups.

CAROL C. GOULD, "GROUP RIGHTS AND SOCIAL ONTOLOGY"*

The increasing globalization and universalization of culture worldwide has paradoxically been matched at the same time by increasing cultural particularism and separatism. The two conflicting trends are reflected in cosmopolitanism or the homogenization of cultures, on the one hand, and in claims to cultural autonomy or to ethnic and nationalist chauvinism, on the other. At the same time that sixteen-year-olds all over the world are drinking their Cokes while listening to MTV and wearing their Levis (many sizes too large), their parents and siblings are often reviving ancient ethnic feuds, rediscovering their distinctive cultural identities, and attempting to exclude alien others from their midst. Against

---

*In *Groups and Group Rights*, ed. Christine Sistare, Larry May, and Leslie Francis, 43–57. Lawrence: University of Kansas Press, 2001.

the background of an increasing awareness of the value of cultural difference, but also in the context of the alternative claims of equal and universal freedom and global interconnectedness, the question of group rights has recently emerged with particular force and has been developed in newly sophisticated ways in social and political philosophy. What are group rights? Do we need to recognize them as a condition for preserving and enhancing cultural diversity? Are they fundamental rights, or do they instead derive from individual rights? And indeed, what do we mean when we speak of a "group" in this connection?

In my discussion, I will draw upon what I have called *social ontology*, as a theory of social reality . . . and will use it as a framework for considering what constitutes a group and what normative claim there can be for group rights. [Here] the focus will be on the rights of cultural minorities in liberal democratic societies and the problems that arise when a democratic majority takes its dominant culture and language to be obligatory and adopts assimilationist or integrationist policies that deny rights of cultural self-expression and development to such minority ethnic groups. . . .

Groups As Constituted Entities

In the discussion that has developed on group rights, there has been no little confusion about what the term *group* should be taken to refer to. It is commonly agreed that it is not simply an accidental aggregation of individuals, nor even one where the individuals share some common characteristic. That is far too abstract for a social group of the sort intended. It is also commonly agreed that it is not a reified entity, a collectivity that exists over and above its individual members, on the model of a Platonic class or a Durkheimian structure. Instead, a number of theorists have characterized a group as made up of individuals who stand in certain relations to each other, for example, as sharing a common purpose or having a common intentionality, or acting together, or at least having a common interest. . . . In the social ontology developed in [my works], I characterized a social group as an entity constituted by "individuals-in-relations," eschewing both aggregative and holistic readings. Further, I argued that while individuals as agents are ontologically prior to the groups that they constitute, they stand in internal relations to each other such that they become the individuals they are in and through such social relations and may therefore be described as social individuals. By internal relations we mean relations among entities; a change in these relations would therefore effect a change in the character of the entity itself. In external relations, by contrast, the identity of individuals is independent of these relations. Thus, where such internal relations are social relations among persons, for example, in those between teacher and students or between parents and children, the characters of the individuals are transformed by the interactions between them. The ontological priority of the individuals is retained, however, in virtue of their agency, as a capacity to change these relations and to choose new ones (either by themselves or together with others).

The sociality of individuals consists not only in their interactions, which may take reciprocal or nonreciprocal forms, but also in what I have called *common* or *joint activity*. I argue that participation in such activity is one of the main conditions for individual self-development. In this framework, groups are defined by such joint activity or common purposes, whether explicitly recognized or not. On my view, groups are constituted entities, that is, they come into being by virtue of actual relations among their constituent individual members, but are not reducible to the individuals distributively, taken apart from these relations. We may observe that constituted entities are not the less real for being constituted; but they do not exist independently as Platonic universals. Rather, they exist only in and through the individuals related to each other in the group and cease to exist when these relations no longer hold.

How to Derive Group Rights from Individual Rights

We begin from the principle of justice as equal positive freedom, which . . . is the normative conception that goes along with such a social ontology of individuals-in-relations and constituted social groups. This principle entails a (prima facie) equal right of individuals to the conditions of their self-development or to the exercise of their freedom over time. Since participation in common activity is one of the main conditions for such development, it follows that individuals as agents have prima facie equally valid claims or rights to such opportunities for participation in joint activity. Among the modes of such activity involving a shared understanding of common interests and a mutual recognition as participants in it are work, political life, culture, and also various forms of voluntary association and face-to-face interactions. If we focus on culture here, it is because it is a pervasive source of social identity, providing a context for thought and action that involves language, values, modes of behavior, education, socialization, practices, traditions, and shared history. Cultural life, in these terms, essentially involves common or joint activity with others, as members of the cultural group. Common activity is taken here in the generic sense to include not only joint participation in explicit and organized or institutionally defined practices, such as the celebration of holidays or historical events, but also the more tacit forms of activities expressing shared beliefs or values, such as modes of social behavior, styles of dress or speech, and so forth. It is evident from this pervasiveness of culture, then, that an individual's participation in some mode of cultural life as a form of common activity is a condition for self-development. It therefore follows that if individuals have equal rights to the conditions of their self-development, they have equal rights to have the opportunity to participate in a culture. We may say that there is an equal right to access to the conditions of cultural self-development. . . .

But what exactly is a group right as against the rights that individual members of a culture have to their own cultural expression and development? And how would such group rights be derived from the cultural rights of individuals? Part of the confusion in talking about group rights derives from an ontological error, specifically, to consciously or unconsciously reify the conception of a group as something independent of or abstractable from its constitution by individuals, in the specific relations that characterize them as members of that group. Such a group as an abstract entity cannot have rights. Even if one were to identify a culture with such institutional or social facts as language or a system of values, or structures of belief, these entities would themselves be constituted by their actions, beliefs, and linguistic practices of individuals-in-relations. On the other hand, individual members of a culture, whether majority or minority, cannot develop their cultural activity except with respect to the existence of a culture to which they belong, namely, to a relatively persisting and emergent form of cultural life, which they in turn appropriate in the course of their interaction with others.

Group rights therefore pertain to groups as constituted entities and thus are rights derived from the rights of the constituent individuals who are members of the group and who have these group rights insofar as they are members of the group and not apart from these relations to each other. The group rights that a cultural minority can bear are therefore rights to the cultural conditions for the self-development of its members. Since it is not the group that has the equal right to cultural self-development but the individual members of the culture, these group rights are derivative from and instrumental to the equal rights to self-development of the members. They are not rights of the group sui generis. Yet group rights are not reducible to or identifiable with the distributive rights of each individual to the conditions for his or her own cultural development, but rather are rights of the constituency of the culture in the literal sense of those who constitute the group collectively. As a necessary condition for the exercise of individual rights, the group can make a valid claim against the majority culture to provide the individuals with these conditions. Thus, a minority culture that may be expressed in a language other than a dominant language of the majority would have a group right to provide the means for the perpetuation of that linguistic community through its educational system and other means. This does not entail, however, that the cultural minority could insist that all of its members were required to be educated only in that language, but rather that the choice to be educated in this way would be available to its members. . . .

Constraints on Group Rights for Cultural Minorities

An interesting and not uncommon problem arises with respect to group rights for some cultural minorities. When the practices of a cultural minority, which are to be supported by group rights, themselves violate the human rights of individual members of the culture, does the autonomy of the cultural group permit the violation of human rights? I would argue that any of the rights of a minority cultural group would have to be compatible with the human rights, for otherwise the justification of the group rights on the basis that they provide conditions for the equal freedom of self-development of the individuals who are members of that group would be undermined. Since the human rights are the fundamental conditions for the exercise of agency and hence are given priority in the application of the principle of equal positive freedom, they cannot be abrogated by group rights applied or interpreted in such a way as to violate them.

This has particularly important bearing for the difficult question of the pervasive oppression of women within many cultural minorities (and majorities as well!). Thus, for example, a traditional practice of female genital mutilation is still condoned within certain cultural groups. The claim has been made that the autonomy of a culture demands non-interference or nonintervention even with such practices. Without addressing the difficult issue of intervention here, we may say that cultural group rights would not justify such practices, since such practices entail a violation of human rights. Further, insofar as women's equality is formally protected by the human rights, it can be appealed to as a ground for eliminating other cultural practices that oppress women. ▰

Before looking at Gould's argument, we noted various questions related to the issue of group rights, such as whether groups have rights in and of themselves, separate from the rights of individuals who are members of the group. We also mentioned but delayed discussing other important questions about group rights. The remarks at the end of Gould's reading raise one of those questions—namely, if a group has rights, can they conflict with the rights of its members, and if so, whose rights have priority? Gould uses the example of an individual female member of a social group, who does not want to undergo an expected surgical procedure (female genital mutilation). Gould claims that the individual's right not to have such a surgery trumps the right of the group to require her to do so. This example points to the broad issue of the relation between group rights and the rights of individual members of a group.

One philosopher who has written extensively on this issue, Will Kymlicka, has claimed that when we speak of group rights, we need to do so in terms of both intragroup rights (i.e., rights within groups, or between the group in question and its members) and intergroup rights (i.e., rights between groups, or between the group in question and other relevant moral agents). Intragroup rights focus on internal restrictions vis-à-vis the group—for example, rights pertaining to the group as a group that involve protecting the group from the destabilizing impact of internal dissent. Intergroup rights focus on external protections, that is, protecting a group from the destabilizing impact of external decisions. In the case of intragroup rights, the rights holder is the group, and the rights addressee is its members, while in the case of intergroup rights, the rights holder is the group, and the rights addressee is other relevant external agents (such as other groups or nations or the world community).

In either case, says Kymlicka, there can be both good and bad group rights. Group rights are good when they supplement or strengthen efforts to combat injustices that "traditional" rights do not or cannot combat, while they are bad when the result of intentions to restrict the liberties of the group's members. In the latter case, it cannot be enough, for Kymlicka, to say that whatever practice the group engages in is legitimate and that regulating such practice would violate that group's rights. After all, says Kymlicka, "tradition is not self-validating." So, depending upon the content of the behavior, for Kymlicka, there are indeed group rights, which can supersede the rights of the individual members of the group. Nonetheless, for Kymlicka as for Gould, it is appropriate to say that some groups—as groups—are rights holders. In the reading below, Edmund Wall disagrees. He explicitly challenges and rejects Gould's views, arguing that her efforts to strike a balance between the rights of groups as groups and the rights of individuals who are members of groups fail. He posits that the capacity for moral agency applies only to individuals, not to groups. In addition, he claims that Gould's notions of "constituted entities" and "individuals-in-relations" are neither helpful nor functional and that when scrutinized carefully, her view is either mistaken or falls back to the rights of individuals after all. In either event, the case for group rights is not, and for Wall cannot be, made.

EDMUND WALL, "PROBLEMS WITH THE GROUP RIGHTS THESIS"*

This paper attempts to answer the conceptual question whether social groups can be the subjects of moral rights (i.e., whether social groups can be moral rights bearers). An argument will be developed that social groups cannot be subjects of moral rights. This investigation examines not only questions pertaining to value and the grounding of moral rights, but also questions centering on the ontological status of social groups. . . .

[One] attempt to establish the derivative moral rights of groups has been offered by Carol Gould. In her paper, "Group Rights and Social Ontology," Gould . . . has attempted to steer a middle course between

*American Philosophical Quarterly 40 (2003): 269–285.

the reification of social groups and the view that social groups are re-ducible to individual human beings. According to Gould, a social group is not a collective unity above its individual members, but neither, in her estimation, is it a mere aggregate of individuals sharing some common characteristic. Gould sides with those theorists who maintain that a given social group consists of "individuals who stand in certain relations to each other." She believes that these relations make possible the notion of a common interest as well as joint activity. . . .

Let us examine Gould's ontology. She tells us that social groups are real (i.e., that they are entities), but we are also told that when a group's relations no longer hold, the group ceases to exist. A social group is, in her view, a "constituted entity." But this leads one to believe that social groups *are* reducible to the individuals who are said to be members of the group. After all, relations themselves are not entities, but individual human beings are. Indeed, according to Gould, it is the "interactions" between individuals, and not the relations *per se*, that are said to trans-form individual character. . . .

There has been a long-standing rift between metaphysical holists who believe that social groups are metaphysical entities existing above and beyond individual group members and methodological individualists who believe that, in principle, social groups can be reduced to their in-dividual members. But even those methodological individualists who believe that all talk of social groups is reducible to individuals and the actions of individuals acknowledge, like Gould, that individuals *interact* with other individuals. Like Gould, they acknowledge that individuals can influence each other within a network of social relations. This leads me to believe that Gould is actually a methodological individualist who has incorrectly ascribed a discrete ontological status to "individuals-in-relations."

The "interactions" between individuals, referred to by Gould, can ulti-mately be reduced to individual actions. Her formulation of "individuals-in-relations" does not alter this ontological fact. It is certainly true, as Gould . . . and others point out, that one individual's actions can greatly influence another individual's actions, and even, over time, influence the other individual's character. And surely individuals can work together to produce something of enormous significance. Joint activity enables group members to accomplish what they could not dream of accomplishing by themselves. (Consider, for instance, five individuals lifting up a car, as opposed to one individual trying to lift up the car.) Such extraordinary accomplishments are surely important aspects of "joint" activity, and surely joint activity can strongly affect the lives of many individuals. But *none of this entitles Gould to assume that these mutually reinforcing and coordinated individual actions can be viewed as one overall entity with ontological status (i.e., as "individuals-in-relations").* In attempting to steer a middle course, Gould's analysis attempts to make its way between the view that social groups are entities *per se,* and the view that they are ultimately reducible to individuals. However, her proposal that social groups are "constituted entities" in which we find "individuals-in-relations" does nothing to alter the discrete ontological status of individuals.

Someone defending Gould's position might respond by saying that Gould does not have to say that social relations and interactions are entities, that perhaps she got a bit carried away when she said that schools, law courts, etc., are objectified social relations. Gould's important point, as this defense goes, is that, even though social relations and interactions are not entities, that does not mean that they lack reality. They contribute to the ontological make-up of the constituted entities that we refer to as social groups. One could further this argument by examining a successful conversation between a few individuals. Surely we would not describe the communication merely in terms of individuals reacting to external stimuli. Instead, we would find that each individual is internalizing the perspective of the other. Each individual's contribution to the conversation is partially based on their own understanding of what others have said.

I think we can, and should, grant this point about successful conversations. Surely there is more to conversation than individual reactions to external stimuli. But this observation is perfectly compatible with an account couched exclusively in terms of individual actions and reactions. Each participant in the conversation can interpret what another participant has said and react to it based on that interpretation. Such individuals would be relating to each other. They are, as it were, "individuals in relations." No reasonable methodological individualist would deny any of this. What they *would* deny is the more conspicuous claim made by Gould that "individuals in relations" have some ontological status distinct from individual persons or human beings. Gould refers to this, of course, as "individuals-in-relations." If Gould's point is that, even though relations are not entities, that does not entail that relations lack reality, let us then inquire as to the ontological status of these realities. Just what is a "relation" and "interaction" on Gould's account? Just what does it contribute to the make-up of "individuals-in-relations" and "constituted entities" such as social groups? We do not appear to need such "realities" to adequately describe conversations, joint projects, and other interactions between individual human beings.

After describing her ontology, Gould attempts to establish that a cultural minority group can have "rights to the cultural conditions for the self-development of its members." Like [some others], she attempts to derive group moral rights from individual rights. She begins with a principle of justice couched in terms of equal positive freedom. This principle of justice implies that each individual has a *prima facie* equal moral right to exercise his or her own freedom and to have access to the conditions of his or her own development. Given that joint activity is one very significant condition for self-development, individuals, as agents, have *prima facie* equally valid rights to participate in joint activities. Activities within a cultural group will include distinctive joint activities. Indeed, culture, for Gould, is a "pervasive source of social identity." Thus Gould finds that individuals have *prima facie* equal moral rights to the conditions of cultural development. She characterizes the group rights of a given cultural minority in terms of *members'* moral rights to the cultural conditions of self-development.

Gould makes clear that only individual members can have this *prima facie* equal moral right to cultural self-development. She states that group rights "are not rights of the group *sui generis*." On the other hand, she contends that group rights are not reducible to the distributive rights of each individual to the conditions of his or her cultural self-development. Rather they are rights held by group members, or rights held by the "constituency of the culture."

Gould's position is that social groups, if construed as overarching metaphysical entities, cannot have any rights because they do not exist. The brunt of her argument for group rights seems to be that the rights enjoyed by individual agents who are members of a given group are enjoyed within a network of distinctive human relations. In other words, a rights-protected individual from a social group, such as an individual from a cultural minority group, does not merely enjoy a right to the cultural conditions of self-development. The individual actually enjoys that right *as* a member of his or her cultural group.

Christine Sistare makes a similar point in her attempt to justify the existence of group interests or common interests. She introduces the example of a sports team enjoying a victory. Such enjoyment, she argues, cannot be experienced, or at least fully experienced, on an individual basis. The individuals experience the enjoyment as members of the sports team. After all, she reasons, it is the *team* that wins or loses, not some individual. . . . The problem with this line of thought is that Sistare as well as Gould have conceded that only individuals can experience pleasure or act as agents. This is a fundamental ontological point. When an individual enjoys a team victory or acts in concern with others to achieve a set of objectives, she or he can only do so as an individual.

No matter how mutually reinforcing a network of social relations can get, the capacity for rational agency, the capacity to experience pleasure and pain, the capacity to make choices, or any other capacity rich enough to ground moral rights, are all limited to individuals. Moral rights are aspects of *persons*. That is why even middle-of-the-road justifications for group moral rights, however interesting they may be, are unlikely to succeed. It may be true that, in some sense, moral rights are collective guarantees against harms. Indeed, nothing in the analysis proposed in this paper precludes the possibility that mutual or joint guarantees can be made by members of a given social group to each other to protect themselves against harm. What is not possible, if the proposed arguments have been successful, is for social groups to provide the guaranteed protection. Social groups cannot protect anyone. Neither can they make guarantees. Social groups cannot *do* anything. If group rights theorists choose to avoid the problem of grounding group rights in agency by focusing on the alleged interests of social groups, they must make their case that there truly are such things as common interests attributable to social groups. There is good reason to believe that a social group cannot act through a representative to protect the interests of its members. Rather, representatives can act on behalf of social groups in an attempt to protect their individual members from harm. The conclusion of this paper is that attempts to ground group rights on common interests are unlikely to be successful. And such attempts are made that much more difficult by the fact that social groups cannot exercise their own alleged rights. Social groups are not agents, let alone persons. ▲

ANIMAL RIGHTS

In 1792 Mary Wollstonecraft wrote a book titled *A Vindication of the Rights of Women*. This book responded, in part, to an earlier book by Thomas Paine titled *A Vindication of the Rights of Man*, itself, in part, an endorsement of the 1789 French Declaration of the Rights of Man and Citizen (see Part III). Paine claimed that matters such as social class and standing were irrelevant to possessing fundamental rights. For Paine, all men, or at least all citizens, possessed natural rights (the rights of man) equally. Wollstonecraft argued that the concept of natural rights should have been extended to women as well as to men. In today's terminology, Wollstonecraft claimed that fundamental rights applied to humans regardless of gender.

Also in 1792, Thomas Taylor wrote a book satirizing Paine's and Wollstonecraft's works. He titled his book *A Vindication of the Rights of Brutes*, where "brutes" referred to nonhuman animals. In effect, Taylor argued that if one were to take Paine's and Wollstonecraft's views seriously, then one might as well extend the concept of rights to animals, based on the principle of "the equality of all things, with respect to their intrinsic and real dignity and worth." Taylor, along with many others, thought this notion of fundamental natural equality—and subsequently equality of rights—was ridiculous, and if one were really to believe it, then one should extend rights even to animals (since they, too, are part of God's creation and have fundamental equal value).

Although Taylor intended this "vindication" of animals as rights holders as a mockery, a growing number of people have put forth and strongly endorsed this very same argument ever since. Indeed, as the next reading shows, two centuries after Taylor's satire, Tom Regan and many others have offered much the same reasoning in favor of animal rights—and offered it sincerely.

Many people credit today's serious consideration of animals as legitimate rights holders to the 1975 publication of philosopher Peter Singer's *Animal Liberation*. Singer's book generated a huge response, some positive and some negative, over broad social, political, and moral issues related to the treatment of animals by humans. One issue to receive a great deal of attention was the question of whether nonhuman animals are rights holders, particularly holders of moral rights and not "merely" legal protections.

Many arguments have been put forth with respect to animal rights. One such argument—and this is Regan's primary one—is that just noted above:

All living beings have a fundamental inherent value and therefore have some fundamental rights. Before looking more closely at this argument, I mention here two other sorts of arguments that have been advanced and then arguments opposing animal rights.

Besides the inherent value argument, some people have offered a utilitarian argument in favor of animal rights. At the same time that Paine and Wollstonecraft argued for the natural rights of humans and Taylor ridiculed their views, utilitarian philosopher Jeremy Bentham suggested that the key criterion to consider with respect to an entity's being a rights holder was whether it suffered mistreatment. Since animals clearly do, they should be considered as appropriate holders of rights. Bentham claimed that just as the color of a person's skin is no reason to deny him or her rights, so, too, "the number of legs, the villosity of the skin [i.e., having fur], or the termination of the *os sacrum* [i.e., basically, having a tail]" is morally irrelevant to possessing rights. For Bentham, we would generate greater overall happiness by ignoring morally irrelevant features such as agents' skin color or number of legs in our determination of who or what has rights.

This emphasis on ignoring morally irrelevant features of agents is the primary gist of the other major argument in favor of animal rights: No criterion appropriately rules animals out as rights holders. What about humans distinguishes them from nonhuman animals and is relevant to possessing rights, they ask? The following sorts of answers are common: Humans have a certain level of awareness; humans have self-awareness and recognize themselves (and others) as moral agents; humans have a soul; and so forth. Defenders of animal rights argue that none of these features suffice to account for who or what has rights. For instance, it will be arbitrary to say what level of awareness, or even self-awareness, is appropriate for having rights, since some humans will not meet that level (say, newborn infants or people in comas), and as we learn more about the cognitive abilities of nonhuman species, we are discovering that some animals do meet that level of (self-)awareness. Further, the notion of having a soul depends heavily on particular religious beliefs and does not have the warrant on which to base social and political decisions. In addition, the metaphysical concept of souls would not apply to human collectives, such as groups noted earlier in this chapter, as being rights holders. We look later at other arguments against animal rights, but for the moment the point is that one argument in favor of animal rights is that the arguments against them do not suffice.

So, as stated earlier, probably the major argument given in favor of animal rights—and the one that Regan offers below—is that of inherent value. This argument basically states that every living being has a fundamental value that is not grounded in anything other than itself. As Regan puts it, inherent value is not reducible to any other kind of value. For example, some things, such as money, have value, but money is not valuable in itself. Its value lies in how it functions; namely, it allows me to acquire other things of value. So, wealth is not valuable in itself, though we might claim that health is. (It is much easier to answer, and seems more reasonable to ask, "Why would I want to be wealthy?" than to ask, "Why would I want to be healthy?") This difference between the values of wealth and health is often put this way: Wealth has extrinsic value (because its value really is that it is a means to attain something else of value), while health has intrinsic value (because its value lies in itself, not as a means toward some other value).

Now, Regan claims that inherent value, like intrinsic value, is not a means toward something else, but inherent value is not the same thing as intrinsic value. Intrinsic value applies to things or features as they relate to agents (so health is an intrinsic value for people, but not for rocks), whereas inherent value applies to living beings simply as living beings. And, as already mentioned, Regan claims that all living beings have inherent value.

Regan also distinguishes between moral agents and moral patients. Throughout this book we have already been using the term *moral agent* to include individual humans and possibly any other entity that might engage in moral behavior (such as groups of people or nation-states or perhaps nonhuman animals). A moral agent is an entity than can act in moral ways. A moral patient is something that can be acted upon in moral ways. So, we assume there is a moral difference between kicking a rock and kicking a dog. We assume that the rock cannot be harmed or suffer as a result of being kicked, while a dog can. Of course, a rock might shatter if we kick it, but it is not alive and cannot feel pain or suffer. In this view then, dogs, but not rocks, are moral patients. This point is especially important for animal rights advocates because, Regan recognizes, rights are a relation involving the regulation of behavior, and they are a moral concept. Yet, we do not see animals as moral agents. When a lion kills a zebra, we do not think that it has acted immorally or violated the zebra's rights. Those moral concepts seem simply irrelevant to the behavior of lions and zebras. As a result, many opponents of animal rights claim that the concept of moral behavior and rights is irrelevant to animals;

they are not moral agents. (We see this argument below when we look at Carl Cohen's response to Regan.) Regan agrees that animals are not moral agents, but he claims that they are moral patients and, as such, have inherent value that moral agents (i.e., humans) must respect. (Some rights theorists phrase this by saying that we might not have duties *to* animals, but we have duties *regarding* animals.)

One final comment before we turn to Regan's own words: Regan and other animal rights advocates recognize that the content of rights will vary depending on the rights holder. No one, no animal rights advocate, suggests that sea turtles should have the right to vote! That would, of course, be ridiculous. They should, in this view, have rights to equal respect for their inherent value and their well-being. This would have implications—indeed, perhaps wide-ranging implications—regarding the treatment of animals by humans, including in such areas as food production and consumption, farming, experimentation, hunting, and entertainment (e.g., circuses, zoos, racing, and so forth). Depending on how the content of animal rights is fully considered— for example, would animals, or at least some of them, have positive rights?— this could relate to issues such as habitat preservation or conservation. These topics go beyond the scope of our discussion here but are taken up in the fuller discussions of animal rights in the works noted in the "Further Reading" at the end of this chapter. For now, here is Regan's case for animal rights:

TOM REGAN, *THE CASE FOR ANIMAL RIGHTS**

Individuals As Equal in Value

The interpretation of formal justice favored here, which will be referred to as *equality of individuals*, involves viewing certain individuals as having value in themselves. I shall refer to this kind of value as *inherent value* and begin the discussion of it by first concentrating on the inherent value attributed to moral agents.

The inherent value of individual moral agents is to be understood as being conceptually distinct from the intrinsic value that attaches to the

---

*(Berkeley: University of California Press, 1983), 235–248, 279, 295–296, 328–329.

experiences they have (e.g., their pleasures or preference satisfactions), as not being reducible to values of this latter kind, and as being incommensurate with these values. To say that inherent value is not reducible to the intrinsic value of an individual's experiences means that we cannot determine the inherent value of individual moral agents by totaling the intrinsic values of their experiences. Those who have a more pleasant or happier life do not therefore have greater inherent value than those whose lives are less pleasant or happy. Nor do those who have more "cultivated" preferences (say, for arts and letters) therefore have greater inherent value. To say that the inherent value of individual moral agents is incommensurate with the intrinsic value of their (or anyone else's) experiences means that the two kinds of value are not comparable and cannot be exchanged one for the other. Like proverbial apples and oranges, the two kinds of value do not fall within the same scale of comparison. One cannot ask, How much intrinsic value is the inherent value of this individual worth—how much is it equal to? The inherent value of any given moral agent isn't equal to any sum of intrinsic values, neither the intrinsic value of that individual's experiences nor the total of the intrinsic value of the experiences of all other moral agents. To view moral agents as having inherent value is thus to view them as something different from, and something more than, mere receptacles of what has intrinsic value. They have value in their own right, a value that is distinct from, not reducible to, and incommensurate with the values of those experiences which, as receptacles, they have or undergo. . . .

Three corollaries . . . are worth noting. First, the inherent value of moral agents cannot be viewed as something they can earn by dint of their efforts or as something they can lose by what they do or fail to do. A criminal is no less inherently valuable than a saint, if both are moral agents and if moral agents have inherent value. Second, the inherent value of moral agents cannot wax or wane depending upon the degree to which they have utility with respect to the interests of others. The most beneficent philanthropist is neither more nor less inherently valuable than, say, an unscrupulous used-car salesman. Third, the inherent value of moral agents is independent of their being the object of anyone else's interests. When it comes to inherent value, it matters not whether one is liked, admired, respected, or in other ways valued by others. The lonely, forsaken, unwanted, and unloved are no more nor less inherently valuable than those who enjoy a more hospitable relationship with others. To view all moral agents as equal in inherent value is thus decidedly egalitarian and nonperfectionist. . . .

"All Animals Are Equal"

Some might concede that moral patients must be viewed as having *some* inherent value, if we postulate inherent value in the case of moral agents, but deny that the inherent value of moral patients is equal to that possessed by moral agents. But the grounds on which this could be argued will inevitably confuse the inherent value of individuals with (a) the comparative value of their experiences, (b) their possession of certain favored virtues (e.g., intellectual or artistic excellences), (c) their utility relative to the interests of others, or (d) their being the object of another's interests. And this confusion will prove fatal to any attempt to defend the view that moral patients have less inherent value than moral agents. Since the inherent value of moral agents does not wax or wane depending on *their* comparative happiness or *their* total of pleasures-over-pains, it would be arbitrary to maintain that moral patients have less inherent value than moral agents because *they* (i.e., moral patients) have less happy lives or because *their* total of pleasures-over-pains is less than that of moral agents—even if this were true, which it may not be in some cases. . . . If we postulate inherent value in the case of moral agents and recognize the need to view *their* possession of it as being equal, then we will be rationally obliged to do the same in the case of moral patients. *All* who have inherent value thus have it equally, whether they be moral agents or moral patients. All animals *are* equal, when the notions of "animal" and "equality" are properly understood, "animal" referring to all (terrestrial, at least) moral agents and patients, and "equality" referring to their equal possession of inherent value. Inherent value is thus a *categorical* concept. One either has it, or one does not. There are no in-betweens. Moreover, all those who have it, have it equally. It does not come in degrees. . . .

Justice: The Principle of Respect for Individuals

The view that moral agents and moral patients have equal inherent value is not itself a moral principle since it does not itself enjoin us to treat these individuals in one way or another. In particular, the postulate of inherent value does not itself provide us with an interpretation of the formal principle of justice, the principle . . . that requires that we give each individual his or her due. Still, that postulate does provide us with a basis for offering such an interpretation. If individuals have equal inherent value, then any principle that declares what treatment is due them as a matter of justice must take their equal value into account. The following principle (*the respect principle*) does this: *We are to treat those individuals who have inherent value in ways that respect their inherent value*. . . . The principle does not apply only to how we are to treat some individuals having inherent value (e.g., those with artistic or intellectual virtues). It enjoins us to treat *all* those individuals having inherent value in ways that respect their value, and thus it requires respectful treatment of all who satisfy the subject-of-a-life criterion. Whether they are moral agents or moral patients, we must treat them in ways that respect their equal inherent value. . . .

The Rights of Moral Patients

The case for recognizing the moral right of moral patients to respectful treatment parallels the argument given [for moral agents]. The validity of the claim to respectful treatment, and thus the case for recognition of the right to such treatment, cannot be any stronger or weaker in the case of moral patients than it is in the case of moral agents. Both have inherent value, and both have it equally; thus, both are owed respectful treatment, as a matter of justice. . . . Because moral patients have inherent value and have neither more nor less inherent value than that possessed by moral agents, they have the same right to respectful treatment. . . .

The Moral Status of Animals

[One argument against animal rights holds that because] they are not moral agents, they can neither do what is right nor what is wrong; like human moral patients [e.g., newborn infants or people in comas], therefore, animals can do nothing that merits treatment that is prima facie violative of their rights. But because the case has been made for the recognition of animal rights, their inability to do what is wrong does not entail that they are not to be protected by principles that specify how the innocent are to be treated. On the contrary, as in the case of human moral patients, the inability of animals in this regard shows that they cannot be anything but innocent. The principle that it is prima facie wrong to harm the innocent demonstrably applies to our dealings with animals.

Now, reasons have been advanced [concerning the] dispute regarding prohibitions against harming innocents as absolute, allowing of no justified exceptions, and it would be arbitrary to suppose that the status of animals somehow differs from other innocents in this regard. Since there are circumstances that justify harming human beings, despite their innocence, it would be perverse to deny this possibility in the case of animals. In particular, if human moral patients may be justifiably harmed because they pose innocent threats or because they are made to serve as innocent shields, there is no reason why animals might not also be justifiably harmed in such cases—though, as in the case of justifying harm done to human moral patients, we shall be unable to justify harming animals on the grounds of punishing, or defending against the guilty. . . . [For example,] a rabid dog is guilty of no moral offense when he attacks us in our backyard; yet he poses a distinct threat, and we do no wrong if we harm the animal in the course of defending ourselves. . . .

A final objection to viewing moral patients as innocent holds that, on this view of things, *anything* that cannot do what is either right or wrong is innocent and must be included in the scope of principles concerning how the innocent should be treated. Thus do we have, so this objection urges, duties to mud, hair, and dirt, which is absurd. This objection misses the mark. Moral patients are intelligibly viewed as innocent because they may be treated in ways that are prima facie violative of *their moral rights* and because they cannot do anything that merits treatment that violates them. The case of mud, hair, and dirt is dissimilar, since we have no reason to believe—at least the rights view itself does not aspire to offer any reason to believe—that these objects have any moral rights that may or may not be violated.

Summary and Conclusion

The principle basic moral right possessed by all moral agents and patients is the right to respectful treatment. . . . [A]ll moral agents and patients are intelligibly and nonarbitrarily viewed as having a distinctive kind of value (inherent value) and as having this value equally. All moral agents and patients must always be treated in ways that are consistent with the recognition of their equal possession of value of this kind. These individuals have a basic moral right to respectful treatment because the claim made to it is (a) a valid claim-against assignable individuals (namely, all moral agents) and (b) a valid claim-to, the validity of the claim-to resting on appeal to the respect principle. . . . It was also argued that all moral agents and patients have a prima facie basic moral right not to be harmed.

To say that this latter right is a prima facie right means that (1) there are circumstances in which it is permissible to override it but (2) anyone who would override it must justify doing so by appeal to valid moral principles that can be shown to override this right in a given case. . . .

Thus has the case for animal rights been offered. If it is sound, then, like us, animals have certain basic moral rights, including in particular the fundamental right to be treated with respect that, as possessors of inherent value, they are due as a matter of strict justice. Like us, therefore—assuming the soundness of the arguments that have gone before—they must never be treated as mere receptacles of intrinsic values (e.g., pleasure, or preference satisfaction) and any harm that is done to them must be consistent with the recognition of their equal inherent value and their equal prima facie right not to be harmed. ◣

One common response to the claim that animals have rights is simply to dismiss it as crazy. This was certainly the view of Thomas Taylor, noted above. However, this response is neither thoughtful nor historically supported. There was a time when many people thought it was crazy to suggest that women or humans considered "savages" (i.e., non-Europeans or non-whites) have rights. Simply labeling a view as crazy obviously does not provide reasons, much less an argument, against it. Nonetheless, many people have offered many arguments against the view that animals are rights holders. Before we turn to such arguments, an important point must be made: Denying rights to animals is not at all the same thing as denying duties regarding them or concern about their well-being. In the reading below, for instance, Carl Cohen resoundingly rejects the notion of animal rights, but he accepts the notion that we have duties not to mistreat animals. Many people who defend the well-being and humane treatment of animals, including

many vegetarians and vegans, accept those duties without endorsing the concept of animal rights. So, rejecting animal rights, or animals as rights holders,
is not the same thing as rejecting the duty of humans to treat animals in humane ways. For these people, there are other moral constraints on our behavior toward animals than the constraint of not violating their rights.

Having said that, what are the primary arguments against animal rights?
One—and this was mentioned above—holds that animals are simply not
moral agents. The concept of moral behavior and action is totally irrelevant
to animals. They cannot behave rightly or wrongly. Animals are totally outside the realm of moral behavior. Rights, however, are a moral concept and,
as a result, do not have any relevance to animals. While Regan and animal
rights advocates state that animals are moral patients (not moral agents), this
is also irrelevant, say animal rights opponents. Cohen notes that rights are
valid claims and make sense only within the realm of moral behavior. Rights
have a possessor, a target, and content. But animals cannot be the target of
rights; no agent can have a right against some animal. It simply makes no
sense, animal rights opponents say. In addition, a right puts others in some
dutiful relation (as the last chapter shows, one agent's rights puts a duty on
others either not to interfere or to provide something). But it is also nonsense to suggest that animals could ever be put in a dutiful relation to anything. Animals have no duties. Again, they are simply outside the realm of
morality, and for animal rights opponents, labeling them as moral patients
does not place them within the bounds of possessors or targets of rights.

In Chapter 1 I mention that Heather Gert has asked whether our rights
can be violated if we are attacked by Bertha, and Bertha turns out to be a wild
bear. Her answer, and probably just about everyone else's, is, No, bears cannot
violate our rights even if they behave in ways that would violate our rights if a
person performed the same act. Likewise (this is not Gert's example), if Bertha
turned out to be a hurricane, it, too, could not violate our rights by destroying
our homes or killing us. For Cohen, that is exactly right! Animals (and nature)
cannot violate our rights or have any other kind of relation to us with respect
to rights; they are totally outside the realm of rights. Once again, animals are
neither the target nor the possessor of rights.

A second argument sometimes given against animal rights maintains that
advocates for animal rights confuse interests and rights. Of course, animals
have interests, but interests are no more the basis or justification of rights than
wishes or desires are. Rights are moral, social regulations of behavior. Interests

might be relevant to why we regulate behavior and in what ways, but they are not rights and are not sufficient to account for rights.

There is, of course, a utilitarian argument against the concept of animal rights—namely, that applying rights to animals would reduce the general level of happiness. Specifically, this would result from the wide-ranging implications noted earlier if animals really did have rights: Medical experimentation would be extremely restricted, farming and food-production practices would be dramatically altered, and so forth.

Finally, animal rights opponents do not accept Regan's argument about animal rights being implied by the principle of inherent value. Two sorts of responses are given: (1) denial that all living beings have inherent value, and (2) denial that inherent value implies equal rights (or the right to equal consideration). Below, Cohen speaks to both of these concerns by claiming that Regan's view of inherent value plays on an ambiguity. For Cohen, the notion of inherent value can mean either that every living thing is unique and individualized or that all things are equal to all other things. The first, he says, is true, but the second is not. The assertion that (equal) rights follow from inherent value, then, Cohen says, is not correct.

One final remark before we see what Cohen has to say: In the reading below, he begins with the comment that criticisms of animal experimentation come from animal rights advocates. As already mentioned, animal rights advocates claim that if they are correct that animals do have (certain) rights, then this might well mean altering our use of animals, including in medical experimentation. Some, but not all, animal rights advocates have lobbied for the end of all experimentation on animals. Others have lobbied for cessation of all such experimentation that does not benefit those animals. Yet others have lobbied for continued experimentation only as long as the conditions are genuinely humane and not harmful to the animals. Spanning this spectrum of views among animal rights advocates is the recognition that a great deal of experimentation involving animals has not been humane (see Peter Singer's *Animal Liberation* for just one exposé). Also, in almost all cases, regardless of whether the conditions are humane, animal experimentation is conducted for the benefit of humans, not the animals involved. Since many of the results of such experimentation must be "translated" into applications for humans (after all, humans are different organisms and species than these other animals), the value of such experimentation is outweighed by the (moral) harm done to the animals. As you might expect, animal rights opponents have responses to these claims. The point here is not to engage in this particular debate but to note that the reading below begins after Cohen has raised the issue of criticisms of animal experimentation. So, here is Cohen:

CARL COHEN, "IN DEFENSE OF THE USE OF ANIMALS"*

Rights and Interests

The central attack on animal experimentation comes from those who contend that animals have rights. Whether animals do have rights is a question of very great importance, because if they do, as these critics claim, those rights must be respected—and they must be respected . . . even if doing so imposes great costs or burdens on human beings. Rights count; they are dispositive; they cannot be ignored. The meaning of *right* is therefore absolutely critical in this debate; it deserves the most careful reflection at the outset.

A *right* is a valid claim, or potential claim, that may be made by a moral agent, under principles that govern both the claimant and the target of the claim. Every genuine right has some *possessor* and must have some *target* and some *content*.

You, the reader, possess many rights, of course. The *content* of your rights may vary greatly: You may have a right to the repayment of a loan or deposit, a right to nondiscrimination by an employer on account of race, a right to noninterference by the state in some protected activity like political speech, and so on. The *target* against whom some rights claim of yours may be registered may also vary greatly. It can be a single person (say, your landlord), or a group (say, some profit-making corporation), or a community (say, the city in which you live). You may, conceivably, have a right against all humankind. To comprehend any genuine right fully, therefore, we must know *who* holds the right, *to what* it is a right, and *against whom* it is held.

Rights are very different from *interests*, and this distinction is of profound importance in moral reasoning. It may be much in my interest for

---

*In *The Animal Rights Debate*, ed. Carl Cohen and Tom Regan (Lanham, MD: Rowman & Littlefield, 2001), 17–19, 30–36, 52–54.

you to employ me or promote me—and yet I may have a right to neither. I may have a very strong interest in the passage of some legislation or in having a particular decision reached by a judge or jury—and yet have no right to those outcomes. . . .

If you have a right that conflicts with my interests, there can be no serious doubt how that conflict is to be resolved. Interests are for the most part transient and subjective. Rights are objective and commonly endure; they are legitimate demands made within a moral system. *Rights trump interests*. This is a point of the most fundamental importance. The animal rights movement takes rights very seriously, and so should we all. . . .

In all morality the key concept is that of *rights*. In the life of the community what is most precious to its members are its rights. We have a weighty interest in protecting our rights, of course—but we certainly do not have a right to have all our interests satisfied. An interest, even if it is weighty, does not for that reason become a right. Rights have a commanding place in moral relations that interests cannot usurp. Rights, but not interests, are valid moral claims that other moral agents have the obligation to recognize and to respect. . . .

Why Animals Do Not Have Rights

Animals cannot be the bearers of rights because the concept of right is *essentially human*; it is rooted in the human moral world and has force and applicability only within that world. Humans must deal with rats—all too frequently in some parts of the world—and must refrain from cruelty in dealing with them. But a rat can no more be said to have rights than a table can be said to have ambition or a rock to exhibit remorse. To say of a pig or a rabbit that it has a right is to confuse categories, to apply to its world a moral category that can have content only in the human moral world. . . .

Humans, on the other hand, certainly do have rights. And at this point we are likely to ask how this difference is to be accounted for. Rabbits are mammals and we are mammals, both inhabiting a natural world. The reality of the moral rights that we possess and that they do not possess we do not deny, and the importance of this great difference between us and them we do not doubt. But we are unsure of the ground of these rights of ours, their warrant, their source. Where do our rights come from? We are animals, too; we are a natural species too, a product of evolution as all animals are. How, then, can we be so very different from the zebras and the rats? Why are we not crudely primitive creatures as they are, creatures for whom the concept of moral right is a fiction? . . .

To be a moral agent is to be able to grasp the generality of moral restrictions on our will. Humans understand that some acts may be in our interest and yet must not be willed because they are simply wrong. This capacity for moral judgment does not arise in the animal world; rats can neither exercise nor respond to moral claims. My dog knows that there are certain things he must not do, but he knows this only as the outcome of his learning about his interests, the pains he may suffer if he does what has been taught is forbidden. He does not know, he cannot know (as Regan agrees), that any conduct is *wrong*. The proposition "It would be highly advantageous to act in such-and-such a way, but I may not do so because it would be morally wrong" is one that no dog or rabbit, however sweet and endearing, however loyal or loving or intelligent, can ever entertain, or intend, or begin to grasp. *Right is not in their world*. But right and wrong are the very stuff of human moral life, the ever-present awareness of human beings who *can* do wrong and who by seeking (often but not always) to avoid wrong conduct prove themselves members of a moral community in which rights may be exercised and must be respected.

Every day humans confront actual or potential conflicts between what is in their own interest and what is just. We restrain ourselves (or at least we can do so) on purely moral grounds. In such a community the concept of a right makes very good sense, of course. Some riches that do not belong to us would please us, no doubt, but we *may* not take them; we refrain from stealing not only because we fear punishment if caught. Suppose we knew that the detection of our wrongdoing were impossible and punishment out of the question. Even so, to deprive others of what is theirs by right is conduct forbidden *by our own moral rules*. We return lost property belonging to others even when keeping it might be much to our advantage; we do so because that return is the act that our moral principles call for. Only in a community of that kind, a community constituted by beings capable of self-restricting moral judgments, can the concept of a *right* be intelligibly invoked.

Humans have such moral capacities. They are in this sense self-legislative, members of moral communities governed by moral rules; humans possess rights and recognize the rights of others. Animals do not have such capacities. They cannot exhibit moral autonomy in this sense, cannot possibly be members of a truly moral community. They may be the objects of our moral concern, of course, but they cannot possibly possess rights. Medical investigators who conduct research on animal subjects, therefore, do not violate the rights of those animals because, to be plain, they have none to violate.

One *caveat* of the utmost importance I repeat. . . . It does not follow from the fact that animals have no rights that we are free to do anything we please to them. Most assuredly not. We do have obligations to animals, weighty obligations—but those obligations do not, because they cannot, arise out of animal rights. . . .

Regan's case [for animal rights] is built entirely on one principle, a principle that allegedly carries over almost everything earlier claimed about humans and their rights to mice and rats and almost all other animals. What principle is that? It is the principle, put in italics but given no name, by which "moral agents" (humans) and "moral patients" (animals) are held unconditionally equal. Regan writes (the italics are his): *"The validity of the claim to respectful treatment, and thus the case for the recognition of the rights to such treatment, cannot be any stronger or weaker in the case of moral patients than it is in the case of moral agents."*

If this assertion were true, Regan would be home free, of course. What it says, in erudite and appropriately "philosophical" language, is that humans and animals are in fundamental respects equals, that they have rights equally, and that the rights they have are equally entitled to moral respect. But why in the world would anyone think this principle to be true? Why should one think the moral patient, the animal, is in precisely the same moral situation as the moral agent, the human? . . .

[Regan says] he is chiefly concerned for those moral patients, those animals, which are like humans in having "inherent value." This is the key to Regan's argument for animal rights: *the possession of inherent value*. This concept and its uses are absolutely critical to the success of his defense of animal rights.

The argument fails completely. It fails because, as close scrutiny reveals, "inherent value" is an expression used by Regan with two very different senses—and in one of these senses it may be reasonable to conclude that those who have inherent value have rights, while in the other sense of the term that inference is wholly unwarranted. . . .

The equivocation works like this: The concept of "inherent value" first enters Regan's account . . . at the point at which his principle object is to fault and defeat utilitarian moral arguments. Utilitarians, with lesser or greater sophistication, depend ultimately on some calculation of the pleasures and pains that moral agents experience. But, Regan argues there, the real value of human beings must rest not in their experiences but in them*selves*. It is not the pleasures or pains that go "into the cup" of humanity that give value, but the "cups" themselves; all humans are in a deep sense equal in value because of what they are: moral agents having *inherent value*. That is what underlies the principle of human equality. We are, all of us, equal in being *persons* who have this inherent value. . . . And all moral agents (he contends) are "equal in inherent value." . . . This is *inherent value* in sense 1.

The expression "inherent value" has another sense, however, a very different sense that is also quite intelligible and also commonly invoked. In this second sense my dog has inherent value too, and so does every wild animal, every lion and zebra, every fish and helpless stranded whale—because each living creature we know to be unique, in itself not replaceable by another creature or by any rocks or clay. The recognition of inherent value in this second sense helps to explain our repugnance for the hunting of animals for mere amusement, and for the wanton slaughter of elephants and sea turtles, tigers and eagles, and all endangered species, including even kinds of fish or lizards we ourselves have never seen. Animals, like humans, are not just inert matter; they *live*. . . . This is inherent value in sense 2.

But used in this second sense the phrase "inherent value" means something entirely different from what is meant by those who use it in the first . . . sense earlier described. Inherent value in sense 1, characterizing humans and warranting the claim of rights by humans, is very much more than inherent value in sense 2, which (possessed by every living creature) warrants no such claim. The uniqueness of animals, their intrinsic worthiness of consideration as individual living beings, is properly noted, but it does not ground the possession of rights, has nothing whatever to do with the moral condition in which rights arise. Tom Regan's argument reaches its critical objective with almost magical speed because, having argued (sensibly) that beings with inherent value (sense 1) have rights that must be respected, he quietly glides to the assertion (putting it in italics lest the reader be inclined to express some doubt) that rats and rabbits also have rights, since they, too, have inherent value (in sense 2). Rats and rabbits do have inherent value, but their inherent value cannot yield rights.

The argument for animal rights that is grounded on their "inherent value" is utterly fallacious, an egregious example of the fallacy of equivocation—that informal fallacy in which two or more meanings of the same word or phrase are confused in the several propositions of an argument. . . . The fallacy that underlies such equivocal arguments is often inadvertent; in some instances it is a deliberately deceptive maneuver. But whether it be deliberate or accidental, an argument that employs when convenient (as Regan's does) alternative meanings of a key term is dreadfully unsound. Recognizing that there has been an unmarked shift from one meaning of "inherent value" to another, we see immediately that the argument built on that shift is worthless. The "case" for animal rights evaporates. ◢

Questions for Discussion

1. It is obvious that some people are discriminated against on the basis of being a member of some group, so group identity functions as a relevant category in people's behavior not only among individuals but also at the level of laws that apply specifically to some groups. Is this behavior sufficient evidence that groups do have an ontological status above and beyond individual members, as Gould claims? Why or why not? Do her notions of "constituted entities" and "individuals-in-relations" apply to interest-based groups (e.g., political parties), since the members of such groups might see their individual identities as very closely interwoven with others of like interest? If so, would there then be, say, Democrat rights or Republican rights?

2. Wall says that Gould's argument for group rights fails in large part because only individuals can be agents. Is it true that groups cannot be agents? What about a team (not the individual players) winning a game? Is that not a case of group agency? Why or why not? In addition, could groups be moral patients? If not, why not? If so, as Regan argues for animal rights, could groups, as moral patients, have rights?

3. For Regan, all animals deserve to be treated with respect. What exactly does that mean? Does it follow that one should not kill mosquitoes? Does it follow that one should not make any changes to the natural environment, since that is the habitat of animals? Also, does the concept of animals as moral patients yield the conclusion that they therefore have rights? Why does the status of moral patients not "merely" lead to the conclusion that moral agents must consider animal well-being, without framing it as a matter of rights?

4. Cohen claims that although animals do not have rights, it does not follow that we can mistreat them. Why not? If animals are not moral agents, and the concept of their being moral patients does not provide them with the protective bubble of rights, then why would the same argument not apply to speaking of animal well-being (rather than animal rights)? In addition, does Cohen's claim of two senses of inherent value really rebut Regan's claim that all beings deserve equal respect? Why or why not?

5. How do the various views and arguments concerning group and animal rights contained in this chapter relate to the various conceptions of the nature of rights outlined in Chapter 1?

6. How do the various views and arguments concerning group and animal rights contained in this chapter relate to the various justifications of rights outlined in Chapter 2?

7. How do the various views and arguments concerning group and animal rights contained in this chapter relate to positive versus negative rights and the question of moral (versus legal) rights outlined in Chapter 3?

Further Reading

Cohen, Carl. *The Animal Rights Debate*. Lanham, MD: Rowman & Littlefield, 2001. A fine collection of essays from different perspectives on various issues connected to animal rights.

Crawford, James, ed. *The Rights of Peoples*. Oxford: Clarendon Press, 1988. A thorough collection of essays debating the notion of human groups as legitimate rights holders.

Dolins, Francine L., ed. *Attitudes to Animals: Views in Animal Welfare*. Cambridge: Cambridge University Press, 1999. A collection of essays focusing on human interactions with animals, including discussions of animal rights.

Frey, R. G. *Interests and Rights: The Case Against Animals*. Oxford: Clarendon Press, 1980. A classic statement against nonhuman animals as rights holders.

Ingram, David. *Group Rights: Reconciling Equality and Difference*. Lawrence: University of Kansas Press, 2000. An analysis of the nature of human groups, focusing on group identities and their relation to rights.

May, Larry. *The Morality of Groups: Collective Responsibility, Group-Based Harm and Corporate Rights*. Notre Dame, IN: University of Notre Dame Press, 1987. An analysis of the nature of human groups, including a discussion of group rights.

Regan, Tom. *The Case for Animal Rights*. Berkeley: University of California Press, 2004. The classic statement in favor of nonhuman animals as being rights holders.

Sistare, Christine, Larry May, and Leslie Francis, eds. *Groups and Group Rights*. Lawrence: University of Kansas Press, 2001. A fine collection of essays on various aspects of group rights.

Stapleton, Julia, ed. *Group Rights: Perspectives Since 1900*. Bristol, UK: Thoemmes Press, 1995. Reprints of historical essays detailing and debating the notion of groups as rights holders.

Sunstein, Cass R., and Martha C. Nussbaum, eds. *Animal Rights: Current Debates and New Directions*. Oxford: Oxford University Press, 2005. A comprehensive collection of essays representing a "second wave" of concerns and issues related to animal rights.

CHAPTER 5

CRITICISMS OF RIGHTS

In Chapter 3 we saw several criticisms of rights, at least of certain kinds of rights. We saw that some people see positive rights—rights that place others under a duty to provide the rights holder with some good or service—as necessarily infringing on others' negative rights—rights that place others under a duty of noninterference. So, if you have a right to education, then the duty on others is not simply to leave you alone. Indeed, simply leaving you alone will not get you an education. Rather, the duty on others is to provide you with whatever is necessary for you to truly exercise your right to education (presumably, books, teachers, and so forth). Of course, many people embrace positive rights and see them either as not an infringement on the negative rights of others or as a legitimate and justifiable infringement on them. This points to the issue of a hierarchy of rights, which we consider below.

First, however, it is worth noting that we have also already seen criticisms of a broader notion of rights, the notion of moral rights. Again, Chapter 3 shows that some people see the notion of moral rights—rights grounded in or justified on the basis of some moral principle(s)—as empty or meaningless. Legal rights—rights grounded in or justified on the basis of some legal rule—are legitimate, say these critics, because rights, as a means of regulating the behavior of agents, make sense only in the context of some set of agreed-upon rules of conduct (i.e., a legal system). We do not need to rehash that discussion here, and, of course, we have seen that not everyone agrees with those criticisms. The point here is merely that we have already encountered criticisms of at least some kinds of rights, although those kinds are quite broad and sweeping.

We also all know, though we have not covered this specifically so far, that there are criticisms of specific (purported) rights. For example, many people criticize the (purported) right to same-sex marriage or to assisted suicide or to particular interpretations of, say, the right to bear arms, the right to due process, or the right to be free of unwarranted search and seizure of property. Upcoming chapters consider various specific rights and criticisms of them, such as the right to privacy or victims' rights. But, again, the present point is merely that many people have concerns about and criticisms of rights, both broad kinds of rights and specific rights.

HIERARCHY AND FEATURES OF RIGHTS

I noted above that some defenders of positive rights acknowledge that one agent's positive right (say, a right to health care) may infringe on another agent's negative right to liberty because true exercise of that right requires others to provide some good or service, whether or not they want to. A right, remember, as opposed to a privilege or liberty, places others under a duty, and a positive right places them under a duty to do something for the right holder, even if they do not want to. (As an aside, many people claim that negative rights also place others under a duty to do something even if they do not want to—you must refrain from interfering with me even if you do not want to— and as a result the difference between negative and positive rights is not very sharp. Not everyone agrees with that argument though, so we will leave it aside. It is a good topic for your consideration however.)

Now, the present point connected to positive and negative rights is the issue of a hierarchy of rights. That is to say, there are times when one person's rights conflict, or at least seem to conflict, with someone else's rights. How should such a conflict (real or apparent) be resolved? Which right trumps the other? For example, we all know that the abortion issue is often portrayed as a conflict of rights: a woman's right to self-determination versus a fetus's right to life. If this portrayal is reasonable, then a resolution of the conflict will certainly rely on one of these rights trumping the other, which is to say that in a hierarchy of rights, one is more important. Or, to give another example, in some towns on the Oregon coast, there are many vacation rental homes (i.e., dwellings specifically intended to be rented out to vacationers), and the owners of these rental homes claim them as their property, which they have a right to rent out if they so choose. Many other residents in these towns argue that the owners of these rental homes fail to maintain proper upkeep of them, thereby lowering of the value of their own homes (because they are situated next to run-down rentals often tenanted by loud and obnoxious vacationers). Consequently, this conflict has been portrayed, at least by some, as the property rights of one agent or group (rental home owners) versus the property rights of another agent or group (resident home owners). The former claim they can do as they wish with their property (as long as no laws are violated); the latter claim that they are being indirectly harmed and want laws passed to insure greater control over the former. The point here is that each frames this debate as a conflict of rights.

So, the general issue is this: Is there a legitimate hierarchy of rights, and if so, how can it be determined? In addition, for the purposes of this chapter, the real issue here is that there is no uncontroversial answer to this question, which is one of the criticisms of rights. There have, of course, been many attempts to identify some basic rights—that is, the most fundamental and important rights. As shown in Chapter 3, Henry Shue claims that the right to physical security and subsistence are two such basic rights, whereas Tibor Machan and other libertarians claim that life, liberty, and property are the basic rights (while also rejecting positive rights). Although some rights are obviously derived from others—for example, one's right to vote is said to be derived from one's right to self-determination, which itself is derived from a right to liberty—it is still not clear how, say, two cases of the right to self-determination relate to each other, should they conflict. For instance, should one agent's right to privacy be trumped by another agent's right to (access to) information (think of paparazzi hounding celebrities)?

Medieval philosopher and theologian Saint Augustine famously said that before he was asked what time was, he knew, but after he was asked (so that he really thought about it), he did not know. A related question and concern about rights is that, for many people, they are vague. In one sense they are vague because their content is ill-defined. For example, when we speak of a "right to life," the phrase actually has multiple meanings. If someone says that a fetus has a right to life, this actually means that a fetus has a right to be born or brought to term. Once an agent is born, however, a right to life means that other agents do not have the right to kill that particular agent. For some people, however, the distinction between killing and letting die is not at all clear or obvious, so there is disagreement as to whether a right to life, meaning a right not to be killed, is a negative right (other agents have the duty to leave you alone) or a positive right (your right not to be killed includes, at least in some circumstances, having your life saved). Consider, for instance, if I, as an expert swimmer or perhaps a former lifeguard, watch you drowning and crying out for help. Assuming that I could very easily save you but choose not to, have I violated your right to life? In this situation I have not actively killed you, but I have let you die. Is that a morally relevant distinction in this case? (Make this case as complex as you want: Have the person who is drowning be a young infant who has accidentally fallen out of a boat.) If not, then one issue is whether or not a right to life includes a right not to be allowed to die as well as not to be killed.

This general concern that rights are vague—and, so, difficult to use meaningfully as a means of appropriately regulating behavior—extends to other basic features of rights. Among those features are the notion that rights are inalienable (they cannot be taken away) or universal (if one person has a right to worship as she wishes, then that same right belongs to any other person) or self-evident (what evidence or argument would be needed to demonstrate that torturing innocent babies is wrong and a violation of some basic right?). As with the content of rights, when the various purported features of rights are analyzed, they turn out to be much less clear than one might think. It is just this lack of clarity that leads to so many disputes about specific rights as well as to pleas for legal interpretations of rights claims. Is the right to private property really inalienable? Well, not in any legal system (including in the United States) if the right to private property means that the state cannot tell you what to do with it or even take it from you! One very broad kind of criticism of rights, then, is that they are unhelpfully vague.

GENERAL CRITICISMS OF (HUMAN) RIGHTS

Rights seem fundamental and important in our lives as a means of recognizing and protecting the well-being of agents and allowing them to flourish. So, why would someone criticize them? As we just saw, there is genuine concern about their vagueness. In addition, as each of the earlier chapters have shown, there are strong and definite disagreements about the nature of rights (what exactly are rights?), about the justification of rights (what exactly legitimizes claims to rights?), about the content of rights (what exactly do agents have rights to?), and even about the holders of rights (who or what exactly has rights?).

Putting all of these matters aside, other concerns have been raised about rights. These concerns are reflected in the four readings below. The first two readings, by Alasdair MacIntyre and Douglas Husak, both deny that there exist human rights, but for different reasons. The final two readings, by Elizabeth Wolgast and Radha D'Souza, offer critiques of rights generally, at least of their role and value in addressing social matters and injustices. So, first, we turn to MacIntyre's criticism of human rights.

Philosophers from across the political spectrum have raised criticisms of human rights for centuries. Writing from what today many would consider the political right wing (although in his time he was definitely seen as a reformer), Jeremy Bentham, at the end of the 1700s, called natural rights, or the "rights of man" (what we would today refer to as human rights), "nonsense . . . rhetorical nonsense,—nonsense upon stilts." Assertions proclaiming human rights are nonsensical, for Bentham, because rights only come about and make sense in the context of legal systems. Beyond being nonsensical, however, assertions of human rights are "mischievous" (i.e., dangerous) because, for Bentham, they provoke people into thinking that they can justifiably challenge the legitimate authority of the government. Bentham fully supported the notion of legal, civil rights and, for that matter, limiting the role and power of government, but not by the illegitimate means of insurrection, which he associated with the mischief caused by a belief in human rights. Decades later, coming from the political left wing, Karl Marx also wrote critically about natural (human) rights, declaring that they presuppose a meaningful distinction between individuals as persons and individuals as citizens, or, in his language, between "the rights of man and the rights of the citizen." But, Marx asked, "Who is man distinct from the citizen?" For him, no one is merely a human, totally independent of being a member of civil society; no one is purely isolated, "withdrawn into himself." So, assertions of human rights, particularly human rights as opposed to legal, civil rights, are based on mistaken assumptions about what kind of beings we are. We see this concern fleshed out much more fully in Chapter 6. For now, the point is that claims about human rights have been challenged for a long time by people with very different political, social, and philosophical views.

In the first reading below, Alasdair MacIntyre claims boldly that human rights are "fictions" on a par with unicorns and witches. People might believe in them, but that does not make them real. The reason he confidently claims that they are fictions is that no one has been able to give a convincing argument that they are real, even after centuries of wrestling with them.

But MacIntyre does not merely assert that human rights are fictions. The broader context for his claim is that the notion of human rights (or natural rights) emerged historically after the decline of traditional ethical theories based on classical Greek and biblical views. In Europe, during the sixteenth and seventeenth centuries, tremendous social changes occurred, including a pronounced movement toward secular conceptions of the natural and social worlds. As classical and religious institutions lost much of their social authority, questions arose concerning the legitimacy of governments and states as well as about the relationship between individuals and social collectives. As part of the Enlightenment (especially during the eighteenth and into the nineteenth centuries), MacIntyre claims, social, political, and moral philosophers wrestled with providing new perspectives and justifications for regulating people's behavior. Two broad views emerged: utilitarianism and natural rights. Only by understanding how and why the concept of human (as opposed to legal) rights emerged, says MacIntyre, can we really understand why they are fictions. Ultimately, it is their role in moral and social theory—for MacIntyre, their flawed role because they are housed in flawed theories—that is mistaken. Where traditional morality focused on virtues and what was good, Enlightenment morality focused instead on principles of action and what was right. The result was an emphasis on individuals as social atoms and the need for a justification of why and how they were part of a "social compact," that is, part of communities. Inevitably, for MacIntyre, tensions and difficulties arose around providing a legitimate account of why and how individuals' liberty could and should be regulated, with both utility and rights being offered as answers. So, for MacIntyre the larger concern is the social, conceptual housing of which human rights are a part. In Chapter 7, we see this social, conceptual housing being questioned again within the discussion of global and international discourse about rights. For now, though, here is MacIntyre:

ALASDAIR MACINTYRE, *AFTER VIRTUE: A STUDY IN MORAL THEORY**

The problems of modern moral theory emerge clearly as the product of the failure of the Enlightenment project. On the one hand the individual moral agent, freed from hierarchy and teleology, conceives of himself and is conceived of by moral philosophers as sovereign in his moral authority. On the other hand the inherited, if partially transformed rules of

---

*(Notre Dame, IN: University of Notre Dame Press, 1981), 60–68.

morality have to be found some new status, deprived as they have been of their older teleological character and their even more ancient categorical character as expressions of an ultimately divine law. If such rules cannot be found a new status which will make appeal to them rational, appeal to them will indeed appear as a mere instrument of individual desire and will. Hence there is a pressure to vindicate them either by devising some new teleology or by finding some new categorical status for them. The first project is what lends its importance to utilitarianism; the second to all those attempts to follow Kant in presenting the authority of the appeal to moral rules as grounded in the nature of practical reason. . . .

[Following Kant, the modern rights theorist Alan Gewirth] argues that anyone who holds that the prerequisites for his exercise of rational agency are necessary goods is logically committed to holding also that he has a right to these goods. But quite clearly the introduction of the concept of a right needs justification. . . .

It is first of all clear that the claim that I have a right to do or have something is a quite different type of claim from the claim that I need or even want or will be benefited by something. From the first—if it is the only relevant consideration—it follows that others ought not to interfere with my attempts to do or have whatever it is, whether it is for my own good or not. From the second it does not. And it makes no difference what kind of good or benefit is at issue.

[A] way of understanding what has gone wrong with Gewirth's argument is to understand why this step is so essential to his argument. It is of course true that if I claim a right in virtue of my possession of certain characteristics, then I am logically committed to holding that anyone else with the same characteristics also possesses this right. But it is just this property of necessary universalizability that does not belong to claims about either the possession of or the need or desire for a good, even a universally necessary good.

One reason why claims about goods necessary for rational agency are so different from claims to the possession of rights is that the latter in fact presuppose, as the former do not, the existence of a socially established set of rules. Such sets of rules only come into existence at particular historical periods under particular historical circumstances. They are in no way universal features of the human condition. . . . [B]oth the utilitarianism of the middle and late nineteenth century and the analytic

moral philosophy of the middle and late twentieth century are alike un-
successful attempts to rescue the autonomous moral agent from the
predicament in which the failure of the Enlightenment project of providing him with a secular, rational justification for his moral allegiances
had left him. . . .

Contemporary moral experience . . . has a paradoxical character. For
each of us is taught to see himself or herself as an autonomous moral
agent; but each of us also becomes engaged by modes of practice, aesthetic or bureaucratic, which involve us in manipulative relationships
with others. Seeking to protect the autonomy that we have learned to
prize, we aspire ourselves *not* to be manipulated by others; seeking
to incarnate our own principles and stand-point in the world of practice, we find no way open to us to do so except by directing towards
others those very manipulative modes of relationship which each of us
aspires to resist in our own case. The incoherence of our attitudes and
our experience arises from the incoherent conceptual scheme which
we have inherited.

Once we have understood this it is possible to understand also the
key place that three other concepts have in the distinctively modern
moral scheme, that of *rights*, that of *protest*, and that of *unmasking*. By
"rights" I do not mean those rights conferred by positive law or custom
on specified classes of person; I mean those rights which are alleged to
belong to human beings as such and which are cited as a reason for
holding that people ought not to be interfered with in their pursuit of
life, liberty, and happiness. They are the rights which were spoken of in
the eighteenth century as natural rights or as the rights of man. Characteristically in that century they were defined negatively, precisely as
rights *not* to be interfered with. But sometimes in that century and much
more often in our own positive rights—rights to due process, to education or to employment are examples—are added to the list. The expression "human rights" is now commoner than either of the eighteenth
century expressions. But whether negative or positive and however
named they are supposed to attach equally to all individuals, whatever
their sex, race, religion, talents or deserts, and to provide a ground for a
variety of particular moral stances.

It would of course be a little odd that there should be such rights at-
taching to human beings simply *qua* human beings in light of the

fact . . . that there is no expression in any ancient or medieval language correctly translated by our expression "a right" until near the close of the middle ages: the concept lacks any means of expression in Hebrew, Greek, Latin or Arabic, classical or medieval, before about 1400, let alone in Old English, or in Japanese even as late as the mid-nineteenth century. From this it does not of course follow that there are no natural or human rights; it only follows that no one could have known that there were. And this at least raises certain questions. But we do not need to be distracted into answering them, for the truth is plain: there are no such rights, and belief in them is one with belief in witches and in unicorns.

The best reason for asserting so bluntly that there are no such rights is indeed of precisely the same type as the best reason which we possess for asserting that there are no witches and the best reason which we possess for asserting that there are no unicorns: every attempt to give good reasons for believing that there *are* such rights has failed. The eighteenth-century philosophical defenders of natural rights sometimes suggest that the assertions which state that men possess them are self-evident truths; but we know that there are no self-evident truths. Twentieth-century moral philosophers have sometimes appealed to their and our intuitions; but one of the things that we ought to have learned from the history of moral philosophy is that the introduction of the word "intuition" by a moral philosopher is always a signal that something has gone badly wrong with an argument. In the United Nations declaration on human rights of 1949 what has since become the normal UN practice of not giving good reasons for *any* assertions whatsoever is followed with great rigor. And the latest defender of such rights, Ronald Dworkin (*Taking Rights Seriously*, 1976) concedes that the existence of such rights cannot be demonstrated, but remarks on this point simply that it does not follow from the fact that a statement cannot be demonstrated that it is not true (p. 81). Which is true, but could equally be used to defend claims about unicorns and witches.

Natural or human rights then are fictions—just as is utility—but fictions with highly specific properties. In order to identify them it is worth noticing briefly . . . the other moral fiction which emerges from the eighteenth century's attempt to reconstruct morality, the concept of util-ity. When Bentham first turned "utility" into a quasi-technical term, he did so . . . in a way that was designed to make plausible the notion of summing individual prospects of pleasure and pain. But, as John Stuart Mill and other utilitarians expanded their notion of the variety of aims which human beings pursue and value, the notion of its being possible to sum all those experiences and activities which give rise to satisfaction became increasingly implausible. . . . The objects of natural and educated human desire are irreducibly heterogeneous and the notion of summing them either for individuals or for some population has no clear sense. But if utility is thus not a clear concept, then to use it as if it is, to employ it as if it could provide a rational criterion, is indeed to resort to a fiction.

A central characteristic of moral fictions which comes clearly into view when we juxtapose the concept of utility to that of rights is not identifiable: they purport to provide us with an objective and impersonal criterion, but they do not. And for this reason alone there would have to be a gap between their purported meaning and the uses to which they are actually put. Moreover, we can now understand a little better how the phenomenon of incommensurable premises in modern moral debate arises. The concept of rights was generated to serve one set of purposes as part of the social invention of the autonomous moral agent; the concept of utility was devised for quite another set of purposes. And both were elaborated in a situation in which substitute artifacts for the concepts of an older and more traditional morality were required, substitutes that had to have a radically innovative character if they were to give even an appearance of performing their new social functions. Hence when claims invoking rights are matched against claims appealing to utility or when either or both are matched against claims based on some traditional concept of justice, it is not surprising that there is no rational way of deciding which type of claim is to be given priority or how one is to be weighed against the other. Moral incommensurability is itself the product of a particular historical conjunction.

This provides us with an insight important for understanding the politics of modern societies. For what I have described . . . as the culture of bureaucratic individualism results in their characteristic overt political debates being between individualism which makes its claims in terms of rights and forms of bureaucratic organization which make their claims in terms of utility. But if the concept of rights and that of utility are a matching pair of incommensurable fictions, it will be the case that

the moral idiom employed can at best provide a semblance of rationality for the modern political process, but not its reality. The mock rationality of the debate conceals the arbitrariness of the will and power at
work in its resolution. ▶

Not everyone who has concerns about human rights bases those concerns
on issues about the historical moral theories in which rights emerged. Another critic of human rights, Douglas Husak, has more straightforwardly conceptual concerns. He claims that there are no human rights because, quite
simply, nothing morally relevant is shared by all humans that could account
for such rights. As we have noted repeatedly, rights are a relation between
agents that regulates behavior. It is fairly clear what constitutes and justifies
legal rights, namely, appropriate processes within recognized and legitimate
legal systems (e.g., we vote on whether there will be the right to abortion on
demand). To have rights as an Oregonian, one needs to be a citizen of Oregon, and to have American rights, one must be an American citizen. To call
something an "Oregonian right" would mean that it applied to all and only
Oregonians, or perhaps to all and only actions in Oregon. So, Oregonians
have the right to vote for the governor of Oregon but not for the governor of
California (and Californians do not have the right to vote for the governor of
Oregon). Likewise, Americans have the right to vote for the president of the
United States but not for the president of Rwanda.

For Husak, however, it is not so clear what it would mean to have human
rights. It is not enough simply to say that one needs to be a human. What
about being human justifies all humans' having rights? Chapter 4 discusses
some serious questions about what counts as a rights holder. Husak claims
that no features apply to all (and only) humans that are at all morally relevant to having rights. As he says, the sorts of features usually suggested—
such as having some level of rationality or ability to use language or sense
of self or self-motivated activity—fail either to be true of all humans (and
might not be unique to humans) or to be morally relevant. Of course, we
might be able to come up with some feature that all humans share, such as
having some basic genetic code that separates us from other species, but simply having a particular genetic structure seems irrelevant morally. The result
of this sort of claim is that we have human rights because we are human, but
that merely argues in a circle.

Besides claiming that there are no human rights, Husak stresses that he is really concerned with why people are so reluctant to acknowledge that there are none. His answer is that we think that denying human rights must put us in company with bad people, people who perpetrate injustices, and we do not want to be in their company. In addition, he says, denying human rights seems to land us in a position of moral relativism, in which we have no good basis for critiquing injustices, a position that, again, we do not want to be in. But, he says, we can acknowledge that there are no human rights without being forced into either of those unsavory positions.

DOUGLAS HUSAK, "WHY THERE ARE NO HUMAN RIGHTS"*

There are no *human* rights. The chief difficulty in defending this thesis is not in providing a sound argument in its favor. Such an argument (discussed below) has in fact been familiar to philosophers for some time. Instead, the difficulty is in offering an explanation of why so few theorists have been persuaded by this argument. An attack on human rights is bound to give rise to misunderstandings I am anxious to dispel. My purpose is not to discredit the noble purposes to which human rights have been put, but to suggest that these purposes are better served without the highly problematic contention that all human beings share rights. Thus my central project is to undermine the philosophical motivation for believing that human rights must exist. Once the obstacles to rejecting human rights have been identified and removed, my thesis will be found much more palatable.

A preliminary difficulty is to characterize what human rights *are*. Otherwise it is unclear whether philosophers who debate about the existence of human rights are in genuine agreement or disagreement. Unfortunately, there is no consensus about the definition of human rights. I will borrow from philosophers sympathetic to human rights, first an account of what makes a right a *human* right, and second, a theory of *rights*.

All philosophers agree that a right cannot be a human right unless it is possessed (a) *by all human beings*. But apart from this first condition,

---

Social Theory and Practice 11 (1984): 125–141.

there are two others that may or may not be necessary for a right to qualify as a human right. Some philosophers insist that the right must be possessed (b) *only by human beings*; and/or (c) *by all human beings equally*. The doctrine of human rights I will attack includes the first condition but rejects the second; thus, if a given right is shared by nonhumans, it is not thereby disqualified as a human right. The third condition, however, is more problematic, largely because it is unclear what is meant by the claim that a given right is possessed equally or unequally. It is not easy to appreciate how the possession of a given right could admit of degrees. If my right is said to be greater or lesser than your right, why suppose we possess the *same* right to different degrees? There simply is no agreement among philosophers about how rights are to be individuated. Thus it seems sensible to adopt a definition of human rights that is noncommittal about this third condition. Hence my attack upon human rights construes them weakly, including only the first condition. If I can show that there are no rights possessed by all human beings, any stronger doctrine of human rights will have been refuted as well.

Differences among philosophers about what makes a right a *human* right account for only a small part of the controversy about the existence, basis, and content of human rights. Of far greater significance is the fact that philosophers are unclear about what *rights* are. Human rights are, presumably, a kind of right, and any confusion about rights is bound to create uncertainty about human rights. Once again, it is fair to conclude that there is no consensus among philosophers about the role played by rights in moral theory. How, if at all, would a moral theory without a concept of rights differ from one in which rights are included? Though there is much room for controversy here, I will assume the truth of a theory about rights that has gained a substantial following among several of the most distinguished moral and political philosophers to have addressed these questions.

According to this theory, rights function to protect their possessors from being subjected to treatment solely in accordance with the outcomes of utilitarian calculations. In many circumstances, acts are justified—even when coercive and contrary to some person's interests—when they produce a net balance of benefits over harms. But when a *right* of such a person is violated, this utilitarian rationale is insufficient to justify the act in question. Thus it is sometimes said that rights "trump" countervailing utilitarian considerations. Many philosophers contend that the chief difficulty with utilitarianism is that it provides a defective account of rights. Hence a moral theory that did not include rights would be vulnerable to many of the difficulties urged against utilitarianism—it would allow the unjust sacrifice of one person's welfare for the greater good, and thus would exhibit disrespect for persons. Despite widespread differences in their moral and political theories, [John] Rawls, [Ronald] Dworkin, and [Robert] Nozick each share this basic conception of the nature and value of moral rights.

If the above theory of rights is juxtaposed with the earlier description of what makes a right a human right, the following account results. Human rights are those considerations that protect each and every human being from being subjected to treatment solely in accordance with the outcomes of utilitarian calculations. If they did not protect *every* human being, they would not be *human* rights; if they did not afford protection from being subjected to the outcomes of utilitarian calculations, they would not be *rights*. . . .

The argument against human rights is familiar, but only because champions of human rights regard its appeal as a challenge to be overcome rather than as an insight to be accommodated. The key premise in the argument is that no morally relevant characteristic(s) that could provide the basis or ground of such rights is possessed by all human beings. Whatever property (or properties) is adduced as a possible foundation for such rights is defective in one or both of two respects. Either it is not shared by each and every human being, or it provides no reason for believing that its possessor enjoys rights. In other words, each proposed foundation of human rights fails what might be called the *universality* or *relevancy* tests. I would not make an original contribution to the voluminous literature on human rights by showing in detail how each of the several candidates put forth as a basis or ground of human rights—e.g., rationality, the ability to use language, reciprocity, the capacity to conform to moral requirement, self-motivated activity, self-consciousness, etc.—fails either or both of these tests. My central project is not to defend this argument so much as to explain why so many sensible moral and political philosophers have gone to such extraordinary and desperate lengths to resist it. . . .

Finally, we come to the crux of the matter. If there is no sound argument establishing the existence of human rights and numerous difficulties in any attempt to defend them, why have moral philosophers not abandoned them? A mere lapse of critical faculties does not explain why good philosophers are persuaded by bad arguments. More typically they are convinced of a conclusion not because of the arguments they marshall in its support, but for independent reasons not explicitly identified. I conjecture that they countenance human rights because of the allegedly devastating implications of the contrary supposition, and therefore reason that if a belief in human rights must be correct, then there must be some good arguments in favor of so believing. Thus they are less likely to be critical of unsound arguments, convinced as they are that *some* good arguments must be available.

This conjecture explains why virtually all defenses of human rights share a similar tone. Typically philosophers begin with the conviction that there are human rights and define their project as "providing an account" of them. Few philosophers seem to approach this area without prejudice, allowing themselves to be carried wherever their arguments might take them. The ground of their antecedent conviction is rarely identified for critical scrutiny. It is this lacuna I now attempt to fill by speculating about (and then undermining) a number of reasons why so few philosophers exhibit skepticism about the existence of human rights.

What are the allegedly devastating consequences that follow from a repudiation of human rights? In what follows I identify three such fears, and argue either that the consequences, though unacceptable, are not genuine implications of my thesis, or that the consequences, though genuine implications of my thesis, are not unacceptable.

1. A philosopher who abandons human rights places himself squarely within a tradition with highly dubious historical credentials. He is understandably uncomfortable to join company with Nazis, racists, and sexists. This is not simply a "guilt by association" objection. The undeniable fact is that repudiations of human rights have frequently been employed by warped theorists to promote pernicious ideologies. Too much bad political theory has traded upon an "us persons versus those nonpersons" mentality. Much of the resistance to skepticism about human rights is an overreaction to such misguided political theories. The claim that some human beings are nonpersons is certain to earn the scorn of well-intentioned philosophers who will remind me of this disastrous legacy. . . .

2. A study of the primary use to which human rights have been put suggests a second reason why philosophers have been largely uncritical

of them. Human rights have been a cornerstone of American foreign policy, and function as an effective tool for denouncing political regimes which show a callous disregard for them. Torture, denials of religious freedoms, and racial discrimination are only a small sample of the widespread atrocities that evoke criticism in the name of human rights. If human rights do not exist, this humanitarian movement might have to be reinterpreted as shallow propaganda. The alternative to human rights might be thought to be a kind of relativism, where the only moral rights possessed by persons are products of their particular social, political, and legal systems. Thus a useful device for comparing and contrasting such systems would be lost.

Such fears, however, are grossly exaggerated. Nearly all of the criticisms made about human rights violations throughout the world involve the maltreatment of persons. The victims of torture and religious oppression quite obviously satisfy the criteria of personhood, whatever they might be. . . . We can and should continue to protest the unjust treatment of persons, and to evaluate various social, political and legal systems to the extent that they exhibit respect for persons. But the existence of *human* rights is not required for this noble purpose. The crucial point is that the vast majority of sensible criticisms of unjust political systems can be preserved as intelligible even if it is conceded that no human rights exist.

3. Perhaps the most compelling reason for countenancing human rights is the fear of how it would be permissible to treat human nonpersons in the event that they are held to be without rights. Though it may be controversial whether human nonpersons are entitled to the same concern and respect as persons, the alternative that would treat them as mere things, to be used for our convenience and amusement, seems even more repellent. Does anyone seriously suggest that it would be permissible to breed and eat human nonpersons, provided that the public should develop a taste for their flesh? If not, how can such creatures be without rights?

There is admittedly something appealing in the conception of the moral universe as neatly divided into persons, who have rights and a high moral status, and nonpersons, who have neither. But this picture is an extreme oversimplification. There are any number of living (or extinct) creatures whose moral status is somewhere between persons and inanimate objects with no moral status whatever. . . .

Philosophers have dreamed of specifying rights which human beings share regardless of their race, religion, sex or nationality. This dream is noble: most discriminations between human beings based on the above differences are unquestionably unjust. But when such philosophers attempted to answer the question of why all human beings possessed rights by specifying their ground or basis, they identified a characteristic(s) that is not shared by all human beings. Thus their projects are better understood as defenses of the rights of *persons* rather than of *human beings*. As so construed, their projects remain interesting and important. I have tried to show why philosophers should not lament the passing of *human* rights. ◣

Whereas MacIntyre and Husak both offer critiques of human rights, Elizabeth Wolgast claims that the broader concept of rights per se—or at least the appeal to rights as a means of regulating behavior and addressing injustices—needs to be questioned. Echoing concerns that have already been raised, Wolgast states that rights derive from a particular notion of what it is to be a person, and that notion is atomistic. In other words, rights—as a relational means of regulating behavior—effectively provide each individual with a protective "social bubble," as it were, that isolates each one from the impact of all the others. So, my rights protect me from you (you do not get to do certain things to me) and allow me to do certain things even if you do not like it (unless I infringe on your protective bubble). The point is that rights function by treating each agent as a social atom, isolated and insulated. In addition, rights function, perhaps necessarily, in assertive, even combative, ways. That is to say, when we bring our rights to bear, we do so to make someone do something or other (either leave me alone or provide me with something). Rights are not bridges but shields and swords. As a result, for Wolgast, rights—or, again, appeals to rights—reflect an atomistic, combative view of agents. Also, they do not simply reflect but perpetuate such a view. In this way, she says, rights can be harmful; they can run counter to establishing and maintaining useful, valuable interrelationships between agents.

Another concern about rights, for Wolgast, is that they are sometimes beside the point and irrelevant to addressing moral concerns. Imagine a married couple (this is not her example). The husband, say, very much wants to have children, while the wife does not. Assuming that they wanted to stay married, it would be truly beside the point and genuinely unhelpful in addressing this conflict for the husband to assert his right to have children and the wife to assert her right not to have children. Assertions of rights in this case (equivalent to stamping one's foot) simply do not resolve the conflict. So, for Wolgast, in many situations, including ones of conflict, assertions of rights (especially with the assumption that rights will function as trumps) are simply misguided and unhelpful. As an example, in the reading below Wolgast discusses the notion of the doctor-patient relation and, for her, the questionable value of bringing in patients' rights when there has been a problem with this relation. (In her full article, she covers other examples, such as children's rights.)

A final word here: As Wolgast states at the end of this reading, she is not claiming that all rights—rights per se—are illegitimate, wrongheaded, destructive of relationships, or unhelpful in addressing injustices. Rather, she is saying that sometimes they are and that appealing to rights as the first or only means of addressing such concerns and conflicts is problematic. So, here is what she says:

ELIZABETH WOLGAST, "WRONG RIGHTS"*

The concept of individual rights which derives from an atomistic view of society gives us a way of looking at wrongs. It is a conceptual grid, a schema, a language which both gives us a sense of *how* a wrong is wrong and points the way to address it. Though powerful and useful, the terminology is unfitted to some of the uses we make of it. It is capable of binding us, stereotyping our reasoning and leading to remedies that are grotesque. Our commitment to this language is deep all the same. I examine both its anomalies and the source of its fascination.

Rights are often spoken of in the language in which we speak of possessions. . . . Conceiving of rights as moral property and as belonging to individuals the way property does is important among the implications of speaking of rights. It focuses attention upon the person to whom something is due, rather than on the misdeeds of the one who offends. It says something positive, that a *right* exists, and doesn't merely con-

---

Hypatia 2 (1987): 25–43.

demn an action or the person doing it. It is as if we had here a moral metaphysics. What is it that exists? Can one prove that it does? I think we are complacent in thinking that all the rights we invoke can't be denied any more than the law of gravitation.

The point of having a right is that having it guarantees a benefit to the possessor. . . . [Philosopher David Lyons] provides an important feature of the language of rights, namely, the power it puts in the hands of the owner to press his right against someone or some agency. Rights are there to be *claimed*—asserted, demanded, pressed—or, on the other hand, waived.

A right puts its possessor in an assertive position, one in which he may claim something, and that means claim it against another. So a right to a free education may be claimed by any child *against* the state, the right to vote may be asserted by any citizen *against* whoever would interfere, the right of habeas corpus may be demanded *against* the court by anyone charged with a crime, and so on. But these are quite a bit different from benefits, since a gift doesn't need to be claimed, and the giver doesn't *owe* it if it is.

The language of rights has advantages over the language of benefits. Rights put the right-holder in the driver's seat; the right-holder may be seen as active while the recipient of a benefit is passive. A world with rights is a better one than a world without them, [Joel] Feinberg argues. . . . Men need to think of themselves as equal to others and claim their rights against others: that is a large part of what it is to be in the fullest sense a person. In that case nothing is more appropriate to a person than the possession of individual rights, rights which by their nature should be equal; and in Feinberg's view the claiming of these possessions has a moral value of its own. . . .

The language in which Feinberg praises rights is recognizably atomistic. He is thinking of individuals as independent entities, whose self-respect is important to them as separate entities. And their capacity to claim rights is part of their active pursuit of their interests. Such talk of rights confirms the main features of the atomistic model and relies on its implicit values.

My argument is that such a conception of individuals and their rights is sometimes a misguided way of addressing injustices.

Consider the issue of the maltreatment of patients by doctors and medical staff in hospitals. In a hospital a patient is entirely at the mercy of medical people whose expertise and positions give them great power. This means that their patients are vulnerable to abuses of power. The patient who is weak and frightened is by definition dependent upon the staff; and they, in virtue of their practical knowledge and ability, are in the position of his rescuers—can instruct him and help him to survive. Abuse of this power and authority is in view of the patient's helplessness a frightening kind of abuse.

Historically, Michel Foucault argues, with the development of clinics and the opportunities they offer to study disease, a new doctor-patient relationship develops. "If one wishes to know the illness from which he is suffering, one must abstract the individual, with his particular qualities" (*The Birth of the Clinic*, New York: Random House, 1975; page 14). The doctor has to look through the patient at the disease.

On the one side of the patient is the family whose "gentle, spontaneous care, expressive of love and a common desire for a cure, assists nature in its struggle against the illness"; on the other side the hospital doctor who "sees only distorted, altered diseases, a whole teratology of the pathological." In contrast, the family doctor cannot have the clinical detachment of the hospital doctor, but such medicine "must necessarily be respectful" of the patient (Foucault, *ibid.*, page 17). Thus Foucault's account provides a plausible explanation as to how the problem of disrespectful treatment of patients in a modern hospital comes about. Moreover the search for knowledge and the holding of power go hand in hand, and as the doctor seeks knowledge of a scientific kind, his patient becomes increasingly an object under his control and less and less someone to be dealt with in personal terms.

Here's the problem then. The patient is weak, frightened, helpless, but needs to be treated in many ways the way a normal person is— needs to be respected, even in his wishes regarding treatment, and ultimately perhaps his wish to die or be sent home uncured. The issue can be framed in different ways, but the most common way of dealing with it is to say that the patient has a *right* to respectful and considerate treatment, a right to have his wishes respected with regard to that type of treatment, a right to be informed about the character of his treatment, etc. To force decisions upon him which he might make differently if he weren't ill and dependent seems a kind of subjection. . . .

The hospital is an awesome environment for a patient and a morally sensitive one for medical staff. In the wake of protests over mistreatment of patients, the American Hospital Association instituted a code of patient's rights which has been widely adopted in this country. The first of these rights is "the right to considerate and respectful care," the fourth is the "right to refuse treatment to the extent permitted by law and to be informed of the medical consequences of his action," the eighth refers to his "right to obtain information as to the existence of any professional relationships among individuals . . . who are treating him." . . . These rights are posted prominently in the hospital so that both patient and staff will be reminded of them as they go about their routines.

Now what can be wrong with this way of dealing with patient care? First, the rights give us a picture of abuses by implication, similar to the "right not to be beaten by your spouse." They incriminate doctors as commonly guilty of unethical or insensitive conduct; otherwise there would be no need to "protect" patients from them. Secondly, it focuses upon a patient as a complainant. In the language of rights the person holding a right holds a license to protest against others when his right isn't respected. That is part of the language and one reason why it's connected with self-respect. Now what is wrong with instituting rights which a patient can claim against the hospital and doctors and nursing staff is that the patient is in no position to *exercise* such rights. He may be in pain or drugged through medication, frightened about his future and dependent upon others. Who is he to complain? To give him rights puts him in the role of an assertive and able individual, but this is inconsistent with his being ill.

Someone who presses a claim and demands respect for his rights does so from the stance of a peer *vis-à-vis* the one complained against, as Feinberg says. But the doctor-patient relationship is not one of peers. As one writer observes, "Strong statements of patient rights imply a parity between physician and patient not usually possible in the situations under which . . . physician-patient relationships are developed" (H. Tristram Englehart, "Rights and Responsibilities of Patients and Physicians," in *Contemporary Issues in Bioethics*, eds. T. Englehart and L. Walters, Beaumont: Wadsworth, 1978; page 136). The patient *needs* the doctor who doesn't in the same way need him. Moreover the patient "often enters into the arms of medicine as one might enter passionately into the arms of a lover—with great haste and need, but little forethought" (*ibid.*); in such circumstances a cool consideration of one's situation is impossible. Once recovered and out of the hospital the patient can *then* exercise his rights—take the doctor to court and sue the hospital for damages. But this remedy is no remedy at all. What a sick and dependent person needs is responsible treatment *while unable to press any claim against anyone.*

How then ought the problem be addressed? The moral difficulty comes to roost in the doctor-patient or staff-patient relationship; something isn't right there. As the Patient's Bill of Rights asserts, a doctor *ought to* treat his patients with respect and concern, for that is his responsibility and part of his professional role. If he doesn't do so he fails to be a good doctor no matter now knowledgeable he is. Then why is a set of rights given to the patient?—it's the doctor who needs to be reminded of his charge. Here is where the focus ought to be, logically— on the doctor's fulfilling his responsibility. . . .

In the atomistic model [of persons and society] connections of responsibility or dependence don't appear; there aren't any. In the same way molecular theory cannot allow that some molecules take care of others or defer to them. The language of rights reflects the atomistic fact that relations of individuals to one another are relations between autonomous entities who are peers. And these peer-relations give rise to contracts in which both parties pursue their self-interests. Looking at the doctor-patient relation in this light, there is no room for—no representation of—the doctor's *responsibility for the patient.* There is similarly no room for anyone's responsibility for another; everyone is responsible for himself and that's all.

Thus, we are blocked from dealing with the problem in terms of the medical profession's responsibility for the patient. Atomism prefers to give the patient rights.

But it doesn't make any sense to do what we do in this case, *viz.,* to put the burden of straightening out the problem of medical negligence and disrespect on the shoulders of those already unable to handle the practical details of life—to say to such people, "Here are your rights; now you may press a claim against the doctor in whose care you placed yourself or waive your right, just as you please." The relationship between doctor and patient is appropriately one of trust, while this remedy implies an absence of trust.

It also makes no sense to assume that a patient has a healthy person to speak for him and press his rights. For even though such a person exists, the patient's dependency may still prevent his taking action against those who are supposed to *care* for him. When he is well (if he recovers), he—and his representative—can then go about bringing a suit against the doctor or whomever. But this simply shows that the right he possesses is a right appropriate to a *well* person, not a sick one. This conception of patients' rights is irrational and impractical. . . .

Without doubt rights have an important place in our legal and political systems and they often *do* give reasons for condemning actions which would be permissible without them. But seeing them as justifications in some instances—as e.g., the right to vote justifies calling a poll tax wrong or unjust—we are led to think that they are always valuable, that without them our censure of wrongs is weakened, and this conclusion is mistaken. Rights sometimes supply only the appearance or form of a justification and in reality may be superfluous.

The corrective to this tendency to supply rights as justifications, as if they added substance to our condemnation of wrongs, is realizing that we know some things to be wrong more securely and fundamentally than we know what rights people have or ought to. ◣

In the final reading in this chapter, law professor Radha D'Souza argues that many people's conception of rights does not match up well with today's economic and technological reality. Like MacIntyre, D'Souza insists that we need to understand our common notions of rights in light of their historical framework. But, she says, social conditions have changed dramatically since rights emerged in eighteenth-century Europe. Given today's economic and technological structures, with enormously powerful corporations functioning as social agents and rights holders, the traditional notions of rights no longer function as they did when rights were conceived as protections for individual persons against powerful governments. As she says, talk of rights must be backed up with conditions for exercising those rights. Those conditions are quite different in the twenty-first century than they were in the eighteenth. As she puts it, "[W]hile the political idea of 'rights' promotes the idea of equal opportunities for all, the juridical idea rests on the foundational myth that the 'corporate person' stands on the same footing as the 'natural person.' The size and reach of corporations today are vastly different from what they were in the eighteenth or nineteenth centuries, and make the legal myth of the corporate person an absurdity." Particularly in the Third World, where nondomestic corporations are often influential legal agents, the property rights, say, of powerful corporations simply overwhelm the property (or other) rights of individuals. D'Souza concludes not, of course, that rights are irrelevant or even harmful but that a particular notion of rights, associated with particular historical, now outdated conditions, can be irrelevant or even harmful.

RADHA D'SOUZA, "WHAT'S WRONG WITH RIGHTS?"*

Before we look at the problems associated with "rights" it is important to understand what the word means, not least because it means different things to different people at different times. "Rights" are commonly understood to mean entitlements to do or not do something, and for others to respect that entitlement. Social justice activists often believe that the corollary of "rights" is obligations and responsibilities, and that social injustices exist not because of problems with the concept of "rights" as such but because the concomitant of "rights"—"obligations" and "responsibilities"—have been erased from our thinking and from debates about "rights." These beliefs are based on misunderstandings of the real nature of "rights." The misunderstandings arise partly because "rights" are a philosophical, political and juridical idea, and the concept and its meanings in philosophy, political theory and law are not the same. Confusions arise because the three overlapping fields are used interchangeably in different contexts.

In part, misunderstandings about "rights" persist within social justice movements because they have forgotten the history of "rights" and the critique of "rights" by revolutionary thinkers of the late nineteenth and early twentieth centuries, and the political programs of the successful movements for socialism and national liberation struggles to alter the nature of "rights." As a result, social movements, instead of learning from and developing those revolutionary experiences, have discarded the history of struggles against "rights" and feel frustrated that "rights" do not work, but have nothing to offer beyond "rights." If we wish to move forward, it is important therefore to grasp the concept of "rights," its history and the critique of "rights" by radical movements of working people in the past.

Seedling, October 2007, www.grain.org/seedling/?id=505#.

It may be noted that the concept of "rights" is peculiar to Greco-Roman civilizations, but its history need not concern us here except to note that the philosophical concept was an objective concept associated with ethical and moral ideas of what is right or wrong. As all human beings are required to do "right" and abstain from doing "wrong," the philosophical concept was supposed to guide people in "right" actions.

Philosophers of Capitalism

The philosophers of capitalism in the eighteenth and nineteenth centuries radically transformed the classical idea of "rights" into a subjective political idea attached to individuals who became "right bearers" vis-à-vis the state and society. The idea of "rights" was transformed into "freedom from state" and social constraints. As such, the corollary of "rights" is "freedom," "choice" and absence of restraint. Today, the philosophical idea of "rights" exists at best as a moral ideal because the political philosophers of capitalism have put rights on a different institutional and juridical foundation. When social justice activists speak of "rights" they have in mind this classical ideal, but often it is forgotten that the institutional and legal basis for objective "rights" do not exist any more. Capitalism developed the idea of "rights" to new levels by introducing two components that radically altered the nature of "rights." First, philosophers of capitalism introduced the novel idea that property was a natural and inalienable right attached to every person in the same way as life, and the conditions that sustain life: air, water and food. Second, "rights" were articulated as negative juridical concepts, in that "rights" only guarantee the possibility of something, not the actual thing.

Thus the right to collective bargaining creates the possibility of a living wage but does not guarantee a living wage; the right to property makes it possible to own a home but does not promise everyone a house to live in. It is therefore wrong to think that through default, somehow, "rights" have come to be equated with property rights. "Rights" in its modern form and as a political idea owes its very existence to property rights, and is inseparable from it; and the concomitant idea of freedom is about freedom to own and accumulate property without interference from the state. Circumscribing property rights for social purposes does not take away its primacy in the political and legal order. Capitalism will be impossible if property rights are taken out of the scope of "rights."

The Revolutionary Critique

Revolutionary social movements of the early twentieth century advanced three main philosophical criticisms against "rights," which are still valid. First, the "empty shell" argument: liberal rights are negative endowments that promise the possibility of, but do not create the conditions for, their fulfillment. Second, that any talk of "rights" in politics must be backed by an economic system that facilitates it, and capitalist individualism, commodity production and market economy do not create the conditions for freedom from want and other freedoms; to the contrary they create bondage and oppression. Third, the "means to an end" argument: "rights" free laboring people from feudal obligations and old forms of oppression (caste, gender, and so on) and allow limited political space for organized dissent, which is useful not for its own sake but only if people actually organize themselves to create the conditions for real freedoms.

Socialist revolutions of the early twentieth century extended the philosophical critique to the political arena and removed property from the idea of "rights" and tried to infuse the idea of "rights" with positive substance, so that the right to a job meant that everyone should have a job, not just the possibility of finding a job; the right to education meant that schools should be free so that every child could go to one, and not just the possibility of education for those who could afford it, or those supported by charities. Given this backdrop, is fighting for "rights" the road to follow? To say yes is effectively to go backwards in history or to argue, as some modern day philosophers of capitalism such as Francis Fukuyama argue, that there is no alternative to liberalism in philosophy, politics and law, the foundations of which stand on the idea of "rights." For emancipatory social movements, a more useful way of understanding the question of "rights" would be to interrogate critically the *return* of the "rights" discourse in the contemporary context of neo-liberalism. The socialist and national liberation struggles articulated and attempted to achieve "human emancipation" and "liberation" from oppression, not "rights." Neo-liberalism claims legitimacy on the grounds that this aspiration can no longer be fulfilled because socialism has been defeated. The real question then is: are we willing to concede the hope of human emancipation to "empty shell" possibilities of "rights" based on the primacy of property, which very few possess? Are we ready to concede that liberation from oppression is not possible because the economic system cannot be changed?

Limits of Statute Law

Turning to law, legal theorists, following in the footsteps of political theorists of capitalism, developed legal principles and innovated institutional mechanisms that sustain capitalism. The most significant legal development was the idea of statute law, by which we mean different Acts of legislature on different social issues enforced by a court system backed by police powers. This form of law, which most people today think is "natural," as if that is how law has always been, came into existence only with capitalism, and is far from being "the way law has always been." Under statute law, each aspect of social life is cast into a distinct legislation or statute which makes it difficult to envisage the social whole. What one statute gives another can take away. For example, a statute may provide for a minimum wage, but if prices go up as a result and cancel out the wage gains, that is not an issue that can be addressed within the scope of the minimum-wage legislation. A statute may grant the "right" to education, but treasury and fiscal management rules may simultaneously require cuts in spending. "Choice" then is limited to whether we allow budget cuts to affect the "right" to education or some other "right," like health for example. Socialist movements, while strong on philosophical critique and political action, were weakest in legal development and institutional innovation. If we wish to advance, and not go backwards, we need to rethink how we can recover the gains made by liberation struggles, what the weaknesses of those struggles were, why working people everywhere lost, and how we can regain the ground and consolidate the gains when they are recovered. Those who say there is no alternative to "rights" do so by forgetting the history of struggles against "rights," and implicitly deny the possibility of emancipation and liberation.

Five Themes

Social justice movements need to reflect on five broad themes in relation to "rights." The first and most important is what may be called the "colonial question." Neither liberal theory, nor politics, nor law extended "rights" to colonial subjects in the colonial era. Although based on liberal ideas and "rights" talk, the power structures of the post World Wars world privileged the victors, primarily the Allies, whether it be through the United Nations Security Council veto, or the weighted voting rights in the World Bank and the International Monetary Fund, or the dispute resolution mechanisms in organizations like the World Trade Organization. The UN Charter by institutionalizing and privileging the "rights" of the Allies and the victors in the Second World War has perpetuated neocolonialism, poverty and wars. Without challenging the constitution of the UN, any "rights" talk at nation-state level today is a non-starter. The "colonial question" in the neo-liberal era is a philosophical and political question, and it is not possible to find a juridical solution to a more fundamental problem of our times, as many social justice movements try to do when they advocate "rights" as the solution. Besides, the legal systems in "Third World" countries by and large were created by colonial powers and remain neocolonial institutions. To speak of juridical ideas of "public goods" and "commons" and "community" without evaluating how their social substance has been warped by imperialism past and present is to insist on confusing appearance with reality. Second, the impulse for "rights" talk today is largely driven by environmental questions, and is primarily about extending private property regimes to aspects of nature and natural resources, something that was impossible before but made possible today by technology. For example, water was attached to land rights until technology made it possible to separate water from land and deliver it across continents, a development that required legal and institutional innovation. Third, while the political idea of "rights" promotes the idea of equal opportunities for all, the juridical idea rests on the foundational myth that the "corporate person" stands on the same footing as the "natural person." The size and reach of corporations today are vastly different from what they were in the eighteenth or nineteenth centuries, and make the legal myth of the corporate person an absurdity. The real issue is whether "rights" claimed for the natural person can be extended to corporations. Cracking the juridical myth on which modern society is founded is a task that needs to be taken more seriously and fleshed out programmatically in politics. Fourth, capitalism has transformed the structure of communities. Communities too are formed on market principles based on common "interests" in the marketplace, and not allegiance to "people in places." For example, a person joins a trade union because of common interest with others in the labor market, and joins a consumer organization because of common interest in commodity prices, and joins a "water rights" movement because of interest in water, and so on. Interest-based communities alter the character of "rights" in fundamental ways. As each interest is governed by a different statute law enforced by a different set of institutions, it is no longer possible to find institutional and legal recognition of "people-in places," whose well-being requires the convergence of several interests. It is sometimes argued that, notwithstanding all of the above, it is possible to create parallel enclaves where indigenous communities and knowledge flourish. This may be possible in the short term, but not in the long term, because imperialism is capitalism plus militarism, and both are by their very nature expansionist. Customs and traditions grow from economic and production relations. Colonialism arrogated to itself power over economic relationships and allowed "freedom" for cultural practices whether in the economy or society, as if tradition could exist without economic foundations. By doing that, imperialism appropriated the productivity and social stability following from the space provided for customary knowledge and practices. To insist on "customary rights" without considering the imperialist context and colonial history within which it survives is only to insist on being blind. Fifth, there are three interrelated battlegrounds on which movements desirous of human emancipation must fight: the philosophical, the political and the economic. Each of these involves very different types of struggle, and yet emancipation is impossible without fighting on all three fronts. Of the three, economic struggles were prominent in the Cold War era; the end of the Cold War has seen the return of political struggles, and on both fronts emancipatory movements have gained considerable experiences and successes everywhere. On the philosophical front, emancipatory movements have more or less abandoned the field; and the conundrum of "rights" exemplifies this failure. Dismissed by social justice movements as "too academic" or irrelevant or simply talk-shops, and sometimes, sadly, with contempt for people's intellectual capabilities—evidenced by arguments like "ordinary people will not understand philosophical issues"—abandoning this field of struggle is an important reason why emancipatory movements have become stuck in conceptual grooves. This is a problem in its own right for those who wish to get to the bottom of the "rights" conundrum. ▶

Questions for Discussion

1. MacIntyre claims that the best reason for asserting that there are no human rights is that no one has been able to give a good enough justification for them. Is that a good enough reason for denying that there are any human rights? Behind his claim also lies the belief that, as a moral concept, rights are part of larger moral theories and views and that the prevailing modern moral theories and views (namely, utilitarianism and some form of Kantian emphasis on the autonomous individual) not only conflict but fail to provide a coherent moral framework to guide and justify moral interaction. Is MacIntyre correct? Finally, MacIntyre claims that rights, but not goods or benefits, presuppose socially established sets of rules (which, he also says, are not universal). Is this correct?

2. Husak argues that there are no human rights because there are no features morally relevant to rights that all humans share. Is he correct (1) that human rights must pertain to all humans, and (2) that there are no morally relevant features held by all humans? In addition, Husak claims that people are reluctant to criticize or deny human rights because (1) those critics would be associated with "bad" people, (2) human rights, or at least the rhetoric of human rights, is a useful tool for regulating bad behavior, and (3) without human rights there would be no definitive argument against mistreating humans in the ways we (sometimes) justify our treatment of nonhumans (e.g., we keep them as pets and even eat them). Do those reasons in fact deter people from criticizing or denying human rights? Are Husak's responses to those concerns correct?

3. Wolgast enunciates several concerns about rights broadly speaking (not just human rights). One is that rights derive from an atomistic view of moral agents, that is, that each agent is a separate social entity unto itself. This presupposition, says Wolgast, misses the importance and relevance of interrelationships in terms of interactions and regulating behavior. Another concern is that rights put agents in aggressive, even combative, positions because rights are asserted as trumps, as means of forcing others to behave in ways consistent with the interests of the rights holder. As a result, for Wolgast, sometimes the appeal to and insistence on rights can be a misguided way of addressing injustices. Is she correct that rights presuppose (and reinforce) an atomistic view of agents? If not, why? If so, why is that bad? Also, is she correct that appeals to (and insistence on) rights are necessarily aggressive or combative? If not, why? If so, why is that bad?

4. D'Souza argues that rights need to be understood historically and that conditions today are quite different from when rights theory was formulated and constructed (i.e., in eighteenth-century Europe). Relations between rights and concerns about social justice have changed dramatically, she says. The contemporary world of economic and technological structures render "standard" conceptions of rights and rights holders awkward at best and perhaps inappropriate. Is D'Souza correct that the nature, justification, and content of rights are so historically bound that they are misapplied in the economic and technological realities of today?

5. Do any proposed justifications for rights (from Chapter 2) adequately or successfully reply to, or even rebut, the various criticisms of rights presented in this chapter?

Further Reading

Bentham, Jeremy. "Anarchical Fallacies." In *The Works of Jeremy Bentham*, edited by John Bowring, 2:489–534. New York: Russell & Russell, 1962. The classic utilitarian essay against the concept of natural rights.

Boersema, David. "What's Wrong with Rights?" In *Law, Justice and the State*, edited by Aleksander Peczenik and Mikael M. Karlsson, 149–155. Stuttgart: Franz Steiner Verlag, 1995. A brief survey of concerns about rights from a pragmatist perspective.

Charvet, John. "A Critique of Human Rights." In *Human Rights*, edited by J. Roland Pennock and John W. Chapman, 31–51. New York: New York University Press, 1981. A criticism of the concept of nonlegal (or extralegal) rights.

Cranston, Maurice. "Human Rights, Real and Supposed." In *Political Theory and the Rights of Man*, edited by D. D. Raphael, 43–53. Bloomington: Indiana University Press, 1967. A modern-classic critique of positive human rights.

D'Souza, Radha. "What's Wrong with Rights?" *Seedling*, October 2007, www .grain.org/seedling/?id=505#. A critique of how rights are carried out in practice by neoliberalism and multinational corporations.

Flynn, David. "What's Wrong with Rights?" *Australian Social Work* 58 (2005): 244–256. A critique of rights, without corresponding responsibilities, as a framework for social work theory or practice.

Greer, Steven. "What's Wrong with the European Convention on Human Rights?" *Human Rights Quarterly* 30 (2008): 680–702. A critique of the practices of the

European Convention on Human Rights, with an argument for member states to "constitutionalize" rights.

Kingdom, Elizabeth. *What's Wrong with Rights: Problems for Feminist Politics and Law*. Edinburgh: Edinburgh University Press, 1992. A feminist critique of philosophical and political presumptions underlying rights as the means of addressing social ills.

Rorty, Richard. "What's Wrong with Rights?" *Harper's Magazine*, June 1996, 15–18. A critique of rights as having failed to improve the condition of the poor in America.

Sajó, András. *Human Rights with Modesty: The Problem of Universalism*. Boston: Brill Academic Publishers, 2004. A collection of essays on concerns about the universalization of human rights, particularly as they are implemented in different national legal systems.

PART II

PRACTICE AND
APPLICATIONS

The chapters in this part concern matters related to how we understand and "use" rights in our social and political contexts. Also, specific rights, such as the right to free expression and children's rights, are examined. Having looked at some fundamental issues about the very nature of rights in Part I, we turn here to questions about how rights actually play out in domestic and global interactions. Whatever the theoretical issues and arguments about rights, they in fact play a significant role in our social and political behavior. How do we consider rights in our everyday lives? Chapter 6 considers the issue of what has come to be called "rights talk." This is the notion that, at least in the United States, the language of rights frames more and more social conflict and interaction. It is said that we address social conflicts and interactions as matters in which people's rights, as opposed to some other basis, determine what others must or may not do. Chapter 7 extends this matter of rights talk to the international and global levels. Are rights (merely) a reflection of Western cultural values? How do, and how should, we understand rights across different cultures?

Chapters 8 through 13 look at specific rights (or applications of the issues from earlier chapters to specific rights). These include the right to free expression, employment rights, the right to privacy, intellectual property rights, victims' rights, and children's rights. These are a few of the many particular rights claimed or acknowledged by people and by legal systems. These chapters have two primary concerns. One is to look at claims for and against each of these rights. That is, what arguments have been raised for and against, say, regulating hate speech or for and against children having rights as children (rather than as humans or as citizens)? To the extent that rights are intended to regulate our collective behavior and enhance our well-being, what matters is how they do so in practice and application, not only in theory. So, by looking at specific rights, we can better assess the underlying theory and conceptual concerns raised in Part I. For example, can certain conceptions of the nature of rights make sense of how we actually treat children's rights or a right to privacy? By looking at specific rights, we can test the theory, so to speak, by applying it to these specific cases.

The second primary concern here is to use the conceptual and theoretical insights from Part I to help assess the claims that people make about specific rights. In other words, we can use these conceptual and theoretical insights to analyze and evaluate specific cases. For instance, can the notion of intellectual property rights stand up to the scrutiny of fundamental conceptions of the nature or justification of rights? There is a valuable give-and-take, a valuable cross-pollination, between theory and practice. The chapters in this part are to be tests of the theoretical claims in Part I and at the same time to be assessed by those conceptual and theoretical claims.

CHAPTER 6

RIGHTS AND POLITICAL DISCOURSE

Having looked at various issues related to the fundamental theory of rights—what they are, who or what can have them and why, and so forth—this chapter and the next focus on how rights play out in society. This chapter zeros in on how rights factor into domestic American social and political discourse. The discussion does not take place at the level of specific rights, such as the right to have an abortion or to bear arms, or how different political parties line up with respect to advocacy for or opposition to some right or other. Instead, the emphasis is on a broader, sociological perspective: how, especially in the past half-century, rights have been an important factor in our collective social and political engagement with each other. We look at different perspectives and evaluations of what has come to be seen as "rights talk." Chapter 7 looks at these same sorts of issues with respect to international and global perspectives.

THE GROWTH OF RIGHTS AND RIGHTS TALK

In *Rights from Wrongs*, Harvard law professor Alan Dershowitz compiles a list of many rights that recently have actually been claimed along with claimed counterrights. This list is drawn from actual court cases and, of course, represents only a small number of the kinds of rights that people have claimed. Quite a few of the examples could be grouped together into broader and more

Right	Counter-right
Right to life of fetus	Right to choose abortion
Right to life of dying person	Right to assisted suicide
Right not to be executed	Right to have loved one avenged
Right to be well fed	Right of animals not to be eaten
Right to keep and bear arms	Right to safe streets
Right of criminal defendants	Right of victims
Right to free speech	Right not to be offended
Right to keep one's money	Right to equitable distribution of wealth
Right-to-work law	Right to collectively bargain
Right to sexual privacy	Right to a moral society
Right to influence election by voters	Right to equality of contributions
Right to be a free agent in sports	Right of team to continuity
Right of employee to a four-day work week	Right of employer to labor of work-week employee
Right to privacy and anonymity	Right to know who is criticizing you on the Internet
Right to confidentiality (lawyer, minister, doctor, rape counselor, etc.)	Right to subpoena relevant information
Right of parents to control access to children	Right of grandparents to visit grandchildren
Right of parent to remove child from school for religious reasons	Right of child to education and to choose different life
Right of parent to refuse medical treatment for child on religious grounds	Right of child to live and choose different religion
Right of parent to discipline harshly	Right of child to be free from abuse
Right of husband to connubial relations	Right of wife to refuse connubial relations
Right to smoke	Right not to be subjected to secondhand smoke
Right to clean environment	Right to a job that would be eliminated by environmental concerns
Right to a bilingual education	Right to linguistic uniformity
Right to an organ from dead persons	Right of person to be buried with organs
Right of parents to know of underage daughter's abortion	Right of daughter to choose abortion without parents knowing
Right to choice of doctors	Right to equal medical care
Right not to be tested for DNA	Right to evidence of innocence
Right to build a church, synagogue, or mosque in neighborhood	Right to residential control

Right	Counter-right
Right to fair housing practices	Right to live in homogeneous neighborhood
Right to proselytize	Right to be free from proselytization
Right to treatment	Right to refuse treatment
Right to confidentiality of tax information	Right to relevant information
Right of animals	Right of humans to use animals for medical experimentation
Right to genetic privacy	Right of insurer or employer to assess risks
Right of defendant to have victim's body disinterred for DNA testing	Right of victim's family to peace for victim's body
Right of rape victim to have defendant tested for sexually transmitted disease	Right of defendant to presumption of innocence and privacy
Right of rape victim to have her identity undisclosed	Right of defendant to disclose name of alleged victim in order to elicit challenge to her credibility
Right of gay couple to adopt	Right of child to be adopted by heterosexual family
Right to quote from and parody any written work	Right to author of copyright
Right of owner to alter art	Right of artist to integrity of his art
Right to know of sex offenders in neighborhood (Megan's Law)	Right of privacy after serving sentence
Right to your name and identity	Right of property in domain names fairly purchased
Right to prevent stranger from changing his name to yours	Right to choose an identity
Right to express sexist, racist, homophobic and other bigoted views	Right to be free from hostile environment
Right to jury nullification	Right to equal protection of law
Right to procreate without limits	Right to live in an uncrowded world
Right to borrow money without excessive interest	Right to make profit on risk
Right to refuse to testify against your child, parent, spouse, friend, etc.	Right to everyone's testimony
Right to hand recount of machine votes	Right to a final machine vote without "subjective" recount
Right to be free from racial or ethnic profiling	Right to be safe from hijackers and other criminals
Right to anonymity	Right to be protected from identity theft by foolproof national identity card

basic kinds of rights—for example, the right to free expression or to privacy or children's rights. Nevertheless, the list is quite revealing and, for many people, quite sobering. It is revealing in the sense that it demonstrates the proliferation of rights claims—if not of rights themselves—in our courts and society generally. It is exactly this proliferation that some people find sobering because it speaks to how we understand ourselves in the context of engaging with others and how we address social and interpersonal conflict.

Many rights theorists, political philosophers, and social commentators often refer to this expansive (and insistent) use of rights as "rights talk." Rights talk is the tendency toward and practice of understanding and addressing social and interpersonal discord primarily, perhaps exclusively, in terms of rights, often (as the list above illustrates) competing or conflicting rights. As the readings in this chapter show, some theorists bemoan what they see as the expansion and shrillness of contemporary rights talk, while others do not. We will also see that perspectives about contemporary rights talk connect up with basic views about political philosophy. In particular, we will note two broad perspectives, usually referred to as liberalism and communitarianism.

LIBERALISM

Most of us know, at least vaguely, the following words contained in the U.S. Declaration of Independence from 1776:

> We hold these truths to be self-evident, that all men are created equal, that they are endowed by their Creator with certain unalienable Rights, that among these are Life, Liberty and the pursuit of Happiness.—That to secure these rights, Governments are instituted among Men, deriving their just powers from the consent of the governed,—That whenever any Form of Government becomes destructive of these ends, it is the Right of the People to alter or to abolish it, and to institute new Government, laying its foundation on such principles and organizing its powers in such form, as to them shall seem most likely to effect their Safety and Happiness.

These famous words speak to the heart of the political philosophy known as liberalism. Like any "ism," liberalism encompasses many varied principles and tenets, and not all people who call themselves liberals agree on all of them. Many political philosophers speak of classical liberalism (such as the views expressed in the Declaration of Independence) versus modern liberalism, which embraces more positive rights. For example, President Franklin Delano Roosevelt's famous 1944 speech on economic rights—in which he spoke of freedom from want and a right to employment, a decent home, adequate medical care, a good education, and so forth—is supported by many modern liberals, but not necessarily by classical liberals.

It is important to note and to remember that "liberalism" does not mean the same thing as "liberal"—at least what most people mean by "liberal" in today's political climate. The root, of course, is *liber*, which is Latin for "free." Classical liberals understood this sense of freedom or liberty primarily as *freedom from* restraint or constraint, that is, freedom from the clashing interests of others (and, so, protection against them from the government) or even freedom from an oppressive government. Many modern liberals, however, understand freedom also, perhaps even primarily, as *freedom to* have not only security against a repressive or oppressive government but conditions—often provided by the government—such as health care and education, that protect and enhance an individual's well-being. Again, politically, today's liberals are more aligned with modern liberalism, while many of today's political conservatives are fully aligned with classical liberalism. But the liberalism/conservativism distinction rampant in today's political rhetoric is not the same as the liberalism/communitarianism distinction that this chapter discusses.

So, although there is variation among liberals regarding what rights and freedoms an individual has, they nonetheless share some basic principles or commitments: an emphasis and focus on the individual as the primary social entity rather than the state, community, religious group, or any other collective; individuals as the primary rights holders, with any other entity (such as a corporation or the government) holding rights only in a derivative way; the role and function of the state as protecting the rights of individuals/citizens; the fundamental importance of freedom understood as personal choice, as long as one's choices do not infringe on the rights of others.

A corollary of these basic principles is a doctrine that has come to be called "neutralism," or the notion that the state must be neutral with respect to what individuals choose in terms of their conceptions of a good life. In other words, the government has no appropriate or legitimate role in promoting or enforcing any particular moral agenda; it is up to individuals to decide their own interests, goals, and life plans. This is sometimes phrased as individuals having the right to do wrong, where that means they have the right to choose things that—objectively or subjectively—are considered wrong or bad. For example, if someone wants to be a smoker, it is that person's right to smoke (and harm her own body; i.e., do what's wrong). Or if someone wants to be a couch potato, watch inane television shows, or look at YouTube for hours on end, it is not the appropriate role or function of the government to restrict that person. Of course, if one's choices infringe on the rights of others, then that is not acceptable to liberals. So, for example, while many liberals do not endorse pornography, they allow it as a form of free expression; however, they would not allow rape as a form of free expression. Or, as the reading by Gilbert Harman in Chapter 2 shows, most liberals would agree that although there is a right not to be harmed by others, there is no right to be helped by others (because your right to be helped by me is an infringement on my prior right to liberty).

COMMUNITARIANISM

As you can imagine, there is substantial support for liberalist principles, certainly in the United States and Western culture (but not only there). Although Chapter 5 surveys various criticisms of rights, many people see liberalism not only as appropriate and legitimate but as the best form of political philosophy exactly because it promotes the rights of individuals and insists that collectives, whether in the form of governments or other groups, not repress or oppress individuals. No social or political system is ideal in the sense of fully realizing the well-being of all citizens and individuals, but liberalism forthrightly promotes the rights of individuals to seek and attempt to fulfill their interests and goals.

Nonetheless, there have been, and continue to be, many critics of liberalism. One prominent alternative political philosophy some of them endorse is often called "communitarianism." Like liberals, communitarians fall along a spectrum and do not agree on all points or issues. They do, however, broadly agree on several criticisms of liberalism and on the significance of community. One criticism holds that liberalism rests on a mistaken conception of the individual, in one common phrase, as an "unencumbered self." By this communitarians mean that liberals see individuals as separate, unique, and fundamentally isolated entities that happen to be part of communities or society and communities and society as essentially aggregates or collections of individuals. But, say communitarians, we are not unencumbered selves. Individuals are inherently and always members of communities. Of course, some associations we can and do choose, such as membership in a political party, but on a deep and basic level, we are connected to others in vast networks of relations. Communities and society as a whole are not simply add-ons to who and what we are. In short, we are at our core communal beings.

A consequence of this rejection of the unencumbered self is the recognition, for communitarians, of a balance between rights and responsibilities. Liberalism's view of persons as unencumbered selves places a primary emphasis on individual rights with little or no concern for responsibilities to others (beyond not infringing on others' rights). This overemphasis on rights, based on the view of the unencumbered self, leads to the neglect of care for others and for the common good. Minimally, say communitarians, we need to balance the rights of individuals with those of communities. While most liberals speak of individual rights held *against* communities (i.e., protecting individuals against the constraints and restraints of communities), communitarians often speak of rights *in* communities and rights *of* communities. The notion of rights in communities recognizes rights as social relations that arise because we are social, communal beings. For communitarians, the very concept of rights would make no sense outside of communities and interactions with other moral agents. In addition, there are rights of communities, meaning that some collectives, at least, have legitimate moral status, and their interests and well-being are one component—along with the rights of individuals—of the appropriate regulation of behaviors.

But beyond minimally including communities as rights holders, communitarians insist that more than simply expanding rights to communities, it is equally important to recognize and ensure responsibilities to other individuals and communities. Rights are one important feature of moral interactions, but so are justice and equality (at least some forms of equality). Rights are not an end in themselves; they are a means for promoting and protecting the well-being of moral agents. Liberty is important, say communitarians, because it enhances the flourishing of moral agents. A corollary of this, they hold, is the need to balance "right and good." That is, communitarians object to what they see as the neutralism of liberalism with respect to the good life. If what really matters is the flourishing and well-being of moral agents, then we cannot, or at least should not, have a social structure that promotes neutrality about values. What is needed certainly is not anyone or any collective dictating "the good life" to individuals, but, again, a balance of individual rights and the common good. Here, then, is a statement of communitarians, a document entitled, "The Responsive Communitarian Platform: Rights and Responsibilities":

"THE RESPONSIVE COMMUNITARIAN PLATFORM: RIGHTS AND RESPONSIBILITIES"*

Preamble

American men, women, and children are members of many communities—families; neighborhoods; innumerable social, religious, ethnic, work place, and professional associations; and the body politic itself. Neither human existence nor individual liberty can be sustained for long outside the interdependent and overlapping communities to which all of us belong. Nor can any community survive unless its members dedicate some of their attention, energy, and resources to shared projects. The elusive pursuit of private interests erodes the network of social environments on which we all depend, and is destructive to our shared experiment in democratic self-government. For these reasons, we hold that the rights of individuals cannot long be preserved without a communitarian perspective.

A communitarian perspective recognizes both individual human dignity and the social dimension of human existence.

A communitarian perspective recognizes that the preservation of individual liberty depends on the active maintenance of the institutions of civil society where citizens learn respect for others as well as self-respect; where we acquire a lively sense of our personal and civic responsibilities, along with an appreciation of our own rights and the rights of others; where we develop the skills of self-government as well as the habit of governing ourselves, and learn to see others—not just self.

A communitarian perspective recognizes that communities and polities, too, have obligations—including the duty to be responsive to their members and to foster participation and deliberation in social and political life.

A communitarian perspective does not dictate particular policies; rather it mandates attention to what is often ignored in contemporary policy debates: the social side of human nature; the responsibilities that must be borne by citizens, individually and collectively, in a regime of rights; the fragile ecology of families and their supporting communities; the ripple effects and long-term consequences of present decisions. . . .

---

*Amitai Etzioni, ed. *The Essential Communitarian Reader* (Lanham, MD: Rowman & Littlefield, 1998), xxv–xxxix.

Within History

The basic communitarian quest for balances between individuals and groups, rights and responsibilities, and among the institutions of state, market, and civil society is a constant, ongoing enterprise. Because this quest takes place within history and within varying social contexts, however, the evaluation of what is a proper moral stance will vary according to circumstances of time and place. If we were in China today, we would argue vigorously for more individual rights; in contemporary America, we emphasize individual and social responsibilities. . . .

Not Majoritarian but Strongly Democratic

. . . Communitarians do not exalt the group as such, nor do they hold that any set of group values is ipso facto good merely because such values originate in a community. Indeed, some communities (say, neo-Nazis) may foster reprehensible values. Moreover, communities that glorify their own members by vilifying those who do not belong are at best imperfect. Communitarians recognize—indeed, insist—that communal values must be judged by external and overriding criteria, based on shared human experience. . . .

Rights Versus Rightness

The language of rights is morally incomplete. To say that "I have a right to do *X*" is not to conclude that "*X* is the right thing for me to do." . . . Rights give reasons to others not to coercively interfere with the speaker in the performance of protected acts; however, they do not in themselves give a person a sufficient reason to perform these acts. There is a gap between rights and rightness that cannot be closed without a richer moral vocabulary—one that invokes principles of decency, duty, responsibility, and the common good, among others.

Social Justice

At the heart of the communitarian understanding of social justice is the idea of reciprocity: each member of a community owes something to all the rest, and the community owes something to each of its members. Justice requires responsible individuals in a responsive community.

Members of the community have a responsibility, to the greatest extent possible, to provide for themselves and their families: honorable work contributes to the commonwealth and to the community's ability to fulfill its essential tasks. Beyond self-support, individuals have a responsibility for the material and moral well-being of others. This does not mean heroic self-sacrifice; it means the constant self-awareness that no one of us is an island unaffected by the fate of others.

For its part, the community is responsible for protecting each of us against catastrophe, natural or man-made; for ensuring the basic needs of all who genuinely cannot provide for themselves; for appropriately recognizing the distinctive contributions of individuals to the community; and for safeguarding a zone within which individuals may define their own lives through free exchange and choice.

Communitarian social justice is alive both to the equal moral dignity of all individuals and to the ways in which they differentiate themselves from one another through their personal decisions. . . . ▰

COMMUNITARIAN CRITIQUE
OF CURRENT RIGHTS TALK

As just noted above, communitarians embrace moral and legal rights as a crucial component of social interaction. They criticize, however, what they see as the current practice of rights talk in America: relying on rights as winner-take-all trumps in settling interpersonal disputes; addressing social problems and conflicts via the courts, which frame the issues at hand as issues of rights, again with (some) rights functioning as trumps over the concerns of others; placing a hyperemphasis on an understanding of rights as individualistic; and so forth. For communitarians, it is not rights per se that are troubling or troublesome; it is our current practice of using rights as trumps with little, if any, acknowledgement of or regard for duties and responsibilities to others or to communities.

Among communitarians, Mary Ann Glendon is particularly well known for her critique of rights talk. In *Rights Talk: The Impoverishment of Political Discourse*, she offers a clear and sustained critique of current American practice and appeals to rights. While the reading below speaks primarily to broad conceptions of and arguments about American rights talk, her book contains many specific examples of what she calls "the missing language of responsibility" and "the missing dimension of sociality," as well as striking cases of both mistaken historical understanding of the "absoluteness" of rights and undesirable isolation and insulation generated by an overemphasis on individual rights. In the reading below, Glendon identifies what she sees as mistaken assumptions about the content and significance of rights as well as unwelcome consequences of our overreliance on rights:

MARY ANN GLENDON, *RIGHTS TALK: THE IMPOVERISHMENT OF POLITICAL DISCOURSE**

. . . Two months before the 1988 presidential election, polls revealed that half the voting-age public did not know the identity of the Democratic vice-presidential candidate and could not say which party had a majority in Congress. In that election, only half the eligible voters cast ballots, thirteen percent less than in 1960. . . .

Poor voter turnouts in the United States are, of course, mere symptoms of deeper problems, not least of which are the decline of broadly representative political parties, and the effect of the "sound-bite" on serious and sustained political discussion. On this deeper level lies . . . the impoverishment of our political discourse. Across the political spectrum there is a growing realization that it has become increasingly difficult even to define critical questions, let alone debate and resolve them.

Though sound-bites do not permit much airing of issues, they seem tailor-made for our strident language of rights. Rights talk itself is relatively impervious to the other more complex languages we still speak in less pubic contexts, but it seeps into them, carrying the rights mentality into spheres of American society where a sense of personal responsibility and of civic obligation traditionally have been nourished. An intemperate rhetoric of personal liberty in this way corrodes the social foundations on which individual freedom and security ultimately rest. . . . In the home of free speech, genuine exchange of ideas about matters of high pubic importance has come to a virtual standstill. . . .

---

*(New York: Free Press, 1991), ix–xi, 4–8, 15–16, 175.

[T]he prominence of a certain kind of rights talk in our political discussions is both a symptom of, and a contributing factor to, this disorder in the body politic. Discourse about rights has become the principle language that we use in public settings to discuss weighty questions of right and wrong, but time and again it proves inadequate, or leads to a standoff of one right against another. The problem is not, however, as some contend, with the very notion of rights, or with our strong rights tradition. It is with a new version of rights discourse that has achieved dominance over the past thirty years.

Our current American rights talk is but one dialect in a universal language that has developed during the extraordinary era of attention to civil and human rights in the wake of World War II. It is set apart from rights discourse in other liberal democracies by its starkness and simplicity, its prodigality in bestowing the rights label, its legalistic character, its exaggerated absoluteness, its hyperindividualism, its insularity, and its silence with respect to personal, civic, and collective responsibilities.

This unique brand of rights talk often operates at cross-purposes with our venerable rights tradition. It fits perfectly within the ten-second formats currently preferred by the news media, but severely constricts opportunities for the sort of ongoing dialogue upon which a regime of ordered liberty ultimately depends. A rapidly expanding catalog of rights—extending to trees, animals, smokers, nonsmokers, consumers, and so on—not only multiplies the occasions for collisions, but it risks trivializing core democratic values. A tendency to frame nearly every social controversy in terms of a clash of rights (a woman's right to her own body vs. a fetus's right to life) impedes compromise, mutual understanding, and the discovery of common ground. A penchant for absolute formulations ("I have the right to do whatever I want with my property") promotes unrealistic expectations and ignores both social costs and the rights of others. A near-aphasia concerning responsibilities makes it seem legitimate to accept the benefits of living in a democratic social welfare republic without assuming the corresponding personal and civic obligations.

As various new rights are proclaimed or proposed, the catalog of individual liberties expands without much consideration of the ends to which they are oriented, their relationship to one another, to corresponding responsibilities, or to the general welfare. Converging with the language of psychotherapy, rights talk encourages our all-too-human tendency to place the self at the center of our moral universe. In tandem with consumerism and a normal dislike of inconvenience, it regularly promotes the short-run over the long-term, crisis intervention over preventive measures, and particular interests over the common good. Saturated with rights, political language can no longer perform the important function of facilitating public discussion of the right ordering of our lives together. Just as rights exist for us only through being articulated, other goods are not even available to be considered if they can be brought to expression only with great difficulty, or not at all. . . .

The marked increase in the assertion of rights-based claims, beginning with the civil rights movement of the 1950s and 1960s, and the parallel increase in recognition of those claims in the courts, are sometimes described as a rights revolution. If there is any justification for using the overworked word "revolution" in connection with these developments, it is not that they have eliminated the ills at which they were aimed. Indeed, the progress that has been made, substantial as it is, serves also to heighten our awareness of how deep, stubborn, and complex are the nation's problems of social justice. What do seem revolutionary about the rights-related developments of the past three decades are the transformations they have produced in the roles of courts and judges, and in the way we now think and speak about major public issues.

At least until the 1950s, the principle focus of constitutional law was not on personal liberty as such, but on the division of authority between the states and the federal government, and the allocation of powers among the branches of the central government. . . . Today the bulk of the Court's constitutional work involves claims that individual rights have been violated. In the 1980s, even though a majority of justices on the United States Supreme Court began to adopt a slightly more deferential attitude toward the elected branches of government, the rights revolution continued, as many state supreme courts began interpreting state constitutions to confer more rights on individuals. . . . The rights revolution has contributed in its own way to the atrophy of vital local governments and political parties, and to the disdain for politics that is now so prevalent in the American scene. . . .

Gradually [following the Civil Rights Act of 1964], the courts removed a variety of issues from legislative and local control and accorded broad new scope to many constitutional rights related to personal liberty. Most dramatic of all, perhaps, from the average citizen's point of view, was the active role the lower federal court judges assumed in many parts of the country, using their remedial powers to oversee the everyday operations of prisons, hospitals, and school systems. Court majorities with an expansive view of the judicial role, and their academic admirers, propelled each other, like railwaymen on a handcar, along the line that led to the land of rights. The example of the civil rights movement inspired many other victims of injustice to get on board. In the 1970s, the concerns of women crystallized around the idea of equal rights. Soon, persons and organizations devoted to social and related causes—such as preventing the abuse and neglect of children, improving the treatment of the mentally and physically disabled, eliminating discrimination based on lifestyle, protecting consumers from sharp practices, preventing cruelty to animals, and safeguarding the environment—began to articulate their concerns in terms of rights. . . .

We do not, of course, normally think of our own way of speaking as a dialect. But American rights talk does possess certain distinctive characteristics that appear both in our official declarations and in our ordinary speech. As an initial example of the latter, consider the lively discussions that took place in the wake of the Supreme Court's first controversial flag-burning decision in June 1989. On the day after the Court ruled that burning the American flag was a form of expression protected by the First Amendment to the Constitution, the *Today* show invited a spokesman for the American Legion to explain his organization's discontent with that decision. Jane Pauley asked her guest what the flag meant to the nation's veterans. He gave a standard reply: "The flag is the symbol of our country, the land of the free and the home of the brave." Jane was not satisfied. "What exactly does it symbolize?" she wanted to know. The legionnaire seemed exasperated in the way people sometimes get when they feel there are certain things that should not have to be explained. The answer he came up with was, "It stands for the fact that this is a country where we have the right to do what we want." Of course he could not really have meant to espouse a principle that would have sanctioned the very act he despised. Given time for thought, he almost certainly would not have expressed himself in that way. His spontaneous response, however, illustrates our tendency, when we grope in public settings for the words to express strong feelings about political issues, to resort to the language of rights.

Later that same day, a man interviewed on National Public Radio offered a defense of flag-burning. He said, "The way I see it, I buy a flag. It's my property. So I have a right to do anything I want with it." Let us put aside the fact that the flag involved in the case happened to be a stolen one. What is striking about this man's rights talk is that, like the outburst of the legionnaire, it was couched in absolute terms. In neither case was the choice of the words idiosyncratic. How often, in daily speech, do all of us make and hear claims that whatever right is under discussion at the moment trumps every other consideration? . . .

The critique of the American rights dialect presented here rejects the radical attack on the very notion of rights that is sometimes heard on both ends of the political spectrum. It is not an assault on specific rights or on the idea of rights in general, but a plea for reevaluation of certain thoughtless, habitual ways of thinking and speaking about rights. Let us freely grant that legally enforceable rights can assist citizens in a large heterogeneous country to live together in a reasonably peaceful way. They have given minorities a way to articulate claims that majorities often respect, and have assisted the weakest members of society in making their voices heard. The paradigms of civil rights at home and universal human rights around the world undoubtedly have helped to bring to light, and to marshal opinion against, oppression and atrocities. We Americans justifiably take a great sense of pride in our particular tradition of political liberty. Many of us harbor, too, a patriotic conviction that, where freedom is concerned, the United States was there first with the best and the most. From there, however, it is but a step to the more dubious proposition that our current strong, simple version of rights is the fulfillment of our destiny toward freedom, or to the still more questionable notions that, if rights are good, more rights must be even better, and the more emphatically they are stated, the less likely it is that they will be watered down or taken away. . . .

It is ironic that Americans have saturated their political language with what is only a secondary language of the law. The predilection for exaggeration and absoluteness that all of us indulge when speaking of rights seems recognizably related to the strategic use of language by courtroom performers, hardball negotiators, takeover artists, and other zealous advocates ready to go to almost any lengths on behalf of a client or a cause. The majority of lawyers in the United States, however, spend most of their working hours engaged in the legal equivalent of preventive medicine.

The rank and file of the legal profession help their clients to plan and maintain relationships that depend on regular and reliable fulfillment of responsibilities. They know that the assertion of rights is usually a sign of breakdown in a relationship. They endeavor to prepare arguments, leases, estate plans, charters, and bylaws, so as to minimize occasions for friction. They are careful—often to a fault—in their use of language. When discord arises, they assist in negotiation and adjustment. Only when something goes drastically wrong is the matter turned over to a litigator, and even then, her initial efforts normally will be directed toward settlement. Most lawyers (like most other people) understand that, over time, selective exaggeration and omission undermine relationships as well as credibility. They, too, tell their children the cautionary tales of Chicken Little and the little boy who cried "Wolf." Abraham Lincoln's exhortation to lawyers to be "peacemakers" still reflects the commonsense ideals, and the way of life, of lawyers engaged in what is still the main business of the profession—helping citizens live decently together. ▴

LIBERAL RESPONSE

While communitarians insist that their agenda is not one of repudiating the importance of rights for either individuals or communities, many other philosophers, political scientists, and social commentators see in communitarianism a wolf in sheep's clothing. These critics claim that, although communitarianism might appear to be a reasonable balance of the well-being of individuals and their communities, in fact it is—intentionally or not—a conservative political program based on mistaken assumptions and carries with it undesirable goals and results. These critics, often associated with liberalism as a political philosophy, argue that communitarianism is faulty in a number of respects: It relies on vague platitudes about "community"; it is based on questionable, false, or even regrettable historical claims; it results in, and even strives for, undesirable policies and practices (e.g., regarding abortion and free expression).

The argument that communitarians rely on vague platitudes about "community" rests on the vagueness of the concept of "community" as well as on communities' unclear social and political status. As even communitarians themselves acknowledge, the term *community* is not precise or obvious. There are "natural" communities, such as biological families of persons. But even the notion of family is not a simple given, since we recognize extended families and adopted family members, and so forth. There are geographical communities, such as states, towns, and neighborhoods, but in a mobile society, such communities are not necessarily obvious or even meaningful to the individuals who live in them. There are religious communities (such as the Church of Latter Day Saints), political communities (such as the Libertarian Party), ethnic communities (such as Lebanese Americans), work-related communities (such as labor unions), perhaps even historical communities (such as World War II veterans), and so forth. There are communities to which the members choose to belong (such as the Libertarian Party) and into which they are born (such as Lebanese Americans). In addition, membership in many communities can vary; I can choose to be a member of a political community at one time and then opt out of that community at a later time. But I never can opt out of being an individual. The point, of course, is that, for these critics, the notion of "community" does not serve very well as a basic political concept, at least not with respect to balancing it with individual rights (or freedoms or privileges).

A second criticism that has been raised, as seen in the case of Reitz van Winkle in the reading below, is that, intentionally or not, communities can be repressive, and even oppressive, of their members. We have already seen aspects of this concern in Chapter 4's discussion of group rights. Nor is this a hypothetical, theoretical claim. In the reading below, Samuel Walker argues that history, even recent American history, reveals constraints and restraints on individual freedoms—constraints and restraints necessarily overcome by the recognition and enforcement of the rights of individuals.

Along with this historical argument, critics of communitarianism claim that when it comes down to actual specific positions and policies, communitarians actually advocate conservative agendas. For example, under the umbrella of balancing the interests and well-being of both individuals and communities, many communitarians advocate restrictions on individual liberties—for example, by opposing same-sex marriage and abortion on demand, lobbying for stricter controls on free expression such as pornography, and so forth. (On the other hand, many communitarians also advocate policies rejected by most political conservatives. For example, the Responsive Communitarian Platform quoted earlier in this chapter includes a call for fairly strict gun-control laws.)

In the reading below from *The Rights Revolution: Rights and Community in Modern America*, Samuel Walker responds directly to what he sees as a communitarian challenge to the primacy of individual rights. Walker argues that the emphasis on and expansion of the rights of individuals (as well as the growth of types of rights holders) have, in fact, been good, not bad. Such focus on rights over the past half century, for Walker, has not impoverished American society but rather made it more inclusive.

▍SAMUEL WALKER, *THE RIGHTS REVOLUTION**

How quickly we forget. Patterns of daily life that were once familiar are swept aside, and old ways of life are forgotten. And for each new generation, past ways of life are "history," something remote and not personally experienced. Americans in particular are people without a sense of history, forever inventing a new society and casting off the past. We take the present for granted and implicitly assume that life was always this way. But of course it wasn't. Change continues to alter the way we live and how we think about the way we live.

This book is about one of the great transformations of American society. I believe it involves the most important change of the past half century, which I call the *rights revolution*, the growth of a comprehensive set of individual rights. This revolution includes a broad array of formal rights codified in laws and court decisions; but even more important, it involves a new rights consciousness, a way of thinking about ourselves and our society. As some observers point out, this new "rights culture" is marked by an almost reflexive habit of defining all problems in terms of rights. The words, expressed as demands, fall quickly from our lips: "I have a right to . . . " These rights include an expectation of personal liberty, freedom from unwarranted government regulation of both public and private matters, a right to speak freely on public affairs, and a freedom to conduct our private—including especially our sexual—lives as we choose.

It was not always so. In fact, we need go back scarcely forty years, and in some cases less, to a time when these notions of rights did not even exist as concepts, much less as formal legal rights. The now highly prized right to privacy, for example, is a little more than thirty years old. The challenge for the historian, writing for an audience that is so ahistorical, is to make the dimensions of this transformation of American

---

*(Oxford: Oxford University Press, 1998), vii–xviii, 25–28, 180–183.

society come alive. So, as an imaginative exercise, I offer the following fable, adapted from a well-known part of our literary heritage.

The Adventures of Reitz van Winkle

The story is told about Reitz van Winkle, the ne'er-do-well son of an old Atlanta family. With a family inheritance, Reitz could afford to indulge his preference for drink and spend his days wandering around the city, conversing with whomever he met.

One day in the summer of 1956, Reitz drank a bit more than even he was accustomed to, and in a drunken stupor he slid down a ravine on the outskirts of town and fell into a deep sleep. He slept so well, in fact, that he did not awaken for forty years. Then, on a morning in the spring of 1996, he awoke, an old man with a long gray beard and tattered clothes.

After reviving, Reitz looked around to find himself at the bottom of a ravine that was now crossed by a series of massive highways. Later, he would learn that they were called "interstates," but he had not yet heard of such a thing, much less seen one. The steady stream of rush hour traffic over all four lanes immediately suggested that the pace of life in his hometown had quickened substantially. Slowly, and with much effort, he climbed up through the underbrush and out of the ravine. He marveled at the many skyscrapers that marked the center of the city. These, too, were new. After catching his breath, he set off in the direction of downtown.

As he wandered into the city, one of the first things to catch his eye was an adult movie theater advertising "Hard-Core Double Penetration." Nearby bars advertised "Live! Nude! Women!" These sights were truly shocking to poor Reitz. Such blatant displays of explicit sex were just not allowed—or at least they weren't when he fell asleep in 1956. Why, he wondered, weren't these establishments closed immediately, and their proprietors arrested?

Continuing on to Peachtree Street, Reitz looked up at the gleaming office buildings that were the symbols of Atlanta's booming economy and the city's role as the economic hub of the New South. The pace of life on the streets was much faster than he remembered, with everyone in a hurry. He also noticed that many of the people streaming in and out of these buildings were "Nigras." Only later would someone explain to him that this word was not used in polite company. Over the years it had been replaced first by "Negro," then by "black," and more recently by

"African American." Just watching the fast parade of multiracial, professional Atlantans made Reitz's head spin.

Whatever the correct name, Reitz noticed that these African American people were well dressed. He didn't remember ever seeing so many who were evidently in business or some profession. Equally startling, they were often in the company of equally well-dressed white men and women. A few of these interracial couples exchanged kisses. Noticing their wedding rings, Reitz concluded that they were actually married. His head spun even faster. He had never seen such casual intermingling of the races, and certainly not between black men and white women. Any fool knew that interracial marriage was illegal, he said to himself. In 1956 such behavior would have resulted in arrest, at the very least. The reprisals by vigilantes—a very real possibility—would be much worse.

The bewildered Reitz wandered down a side street, where he saw something even more bizarre. There, in broad daylight, were two men holding hands and engaged in what was obviously a very intimate conversation. He had always heard about such things, of course, but had never actually seen two people of the same sex acting like this, and certainly not in public. Behavior like this was not tolerated in public. In the world of 1956 Atlanta that he knew, such behavior quickly drew the attention of the police. Why were these men not promptly arrested and jailed for their gross and immoral conduct? . . .

Somewhere along the way, Reitz passed an abortion clinic. This, too, amazed him. Like homosexuality, abortion was something that existed only in the shadows. It was whispered about, but never discussed openly in polite society. Moreover, it was illegal. Rumor had it that you could get one, if you had the right connections, but it was risky in terms of both the law and the woman's health. . . .

Eventually, Reitz located some members of his family. The van Winkles had not done well over the past forty years, but they were hardly destitute. A younger cousin, who was now in his sixties, lived in the old family mansion, which had fallen into a state of disrepair. The cousin took Reitz in and, with much excitement, introduced him to other family members. . . .

Reitz was naturally fascinated by all of the new technology: the computers, CDs, and VCRs. But he also seemed utterly unaware of the new rules of life, particularly about sex, race, and gender. . . . As he badgered his family with questions over the next few weeks, he gradually pieced together the story. A social revolution had occurred in America while he slept. All sorts of new things, previously forbidden, were now possible. The common denominator, Reitz concluded, was a revolution in rights. Everything seemed to revolve around the right to do this or the right to do that. You could see dirty movies anytime you wanted, or even kiss someone of the same sex in public. And African Americans (Reitz was still slow in learning the new terminology) could do almost anything they wanted as well.

Our fable about Reitz van Winkle dramatizes the fact that something dramatic happened in American society over the past forty years. Our daily lives are very different as a result of the explosive growth of a set of individual rights. At a formal level, these rights are defined in a vast body of court decisions and federal, state, and local laws. The real revolution in American life, however, goes much deeper and involves a profound change in what we expect out of life, how we define ourselves, how we treat others and expect them to treat us, and what we demand of government.

Many of our most cherished assumptions about personal liberty are a product of the rights revolution. And yet these assumptions, indeed the rights revolution itself, are under attack. A number of critics argue that the rights revolution has destroyed community in America, cultivating an unhealthy set of values and undermining the fabric of daily life.

My reply . . . is that the growth of rights has enlarged and enriched the dimensions of community in America, fulfilling the core values of American democracy. . . .

The Communitarian Vision

Rising liberal and moderate concerns about the role of rights in American society eventually coalesced into a movement known as *communitarianism*. In brief, communitarianism holds that in matters of law and policy we have given far too much attention to individual rights and have neglected both the needs of the larger community and the importance of individual responsibility. . . .

The most intellectually gifted communitarian spokesperson is Harvard law professor Mary Ann Glendon. Her book *Rights Talk* is the most articulate discussion of the extent to which the growth of rights has produced a new culture of rights. Better than any other critic, she grasps the nature of the fundamental changes in our society. She argues that we think reflexively in terms of rights, defining virtually every issue that arises in those terms. Problems related to children, for example, are immediately defined in terms of "children's rights," the problems of the poor are immediately defined in terms of the "rights of the poor," and so on.

Glendon is especially perceptive in seeing how deeply the language of rights has penetrated the lives of ordinary people. Concepts and terminology that were once the exclusive province of lawyers now fall easily from the lips of nearly everyone. She believes we have almost lost the capacity to express thoughts about personal responsibility and the common good. We are quick to talk about our rights, but we maintain a near-complete "silence with respect to personal, civic, and collective responsibilities." . . .

[However, I] argue that these critics lack a proper historical perspective. They assume, implicitly but without justification, that all was well with American society forty years ago. They fail to see what was wrong, particularly the narrow and exclusionary definition of community that prevailed. And thus they have no appreciation of the positive contributions of the rights revolution in that regard.

New Rules for American Society

. . . Can it be that the pursuit of individual liberty—the highest ideal of American constitutional democracy—is indeed responsible for the many social ills attributed to it? Has it really led us into a moral abyss? Has it unleashed a poisonous balkanization that divides rather than unites us? Has it undermined the foundations of community in America? . . .

[D]espite the many problems created by our new rights culture, the gains far outweigh the costs. The critics fail to appreciate what has happened in American society for several reasons, which can be summarized as follows.

First, and most important, the critics lack a proper historical perspective. Their "decline and fall" view of recent American history rests on an invented view of our society in the 1950s. They imagine it to have been a time of peace and harmony . . . [but] the critics simply ignore the many forms of discrimination and exclusion that were taken for granted at that time: from the blatant race discrimination of de jure segregation to the more hidden exclusion of helpless mentally retarded children.

Second, the critics fail to appreciate the extent to which the rights revolution has produced a more inclusive and tolerant community. They focus on the liberating side of the rights revolution—the expressive individualism—and do not see that every new right embodies a consequent set of constraints. For the most part, those constraints prohibit those in power from limiting the full participation of other groups in American society.

Third, many critics fail to appreciate the dilemmas of difference in a society with a powerful legacy of discrimination and equality. They attach "identity politics" but fail to offer any reasonable solution to the question of how those who are excluded because they are "different" can overcome that exclusion without heightening awareness of that difference in the process. There is no easy resolution to this dilemma, but it does not help us to move in the direction of full equality by asking the historic victims of discrimination to pretend that they have not been treated differently.

Fourth, some of the most prominent critics believe that European countries, and the standards of the international human rights movement in particular, offer a better balance of rights and responsibilities than we currently have in the United States. Yet, on closer inspection, it turns out that the balancing principles used elsewhere are couched in vague terms ("national security," "public health and morals") that we have wrestled with in our struggles over constitutional law and have rejected.

Fifth, many of the critics of rights improperly assess the blame for the problems that do afflict American society. If there is an inadequate network of social services—leaving the single pregnant woman and the homeless man without needed support—that is hardly the fault of our rights advocates. The critics of our rights culture consistently refuse to blame the conservative opponents of a wider and stronger social safety net. On the issue of the responsibility of corporations to the communities where they operate, the critics refuse to even suggest any laws or policies that might arouse the wrath of the truly powerful.

Sixth, the most comprehensive alternative to a rights-oriented society is the philosophy of communitarianism. Yet those who posit a conflict between "rights" and "community" rarely, if ever, define what they mean by community . . . [and] there are many different forms of community in America. Moreover, there are often fundamental conflicts between these notions of community: between neighborhood residents and the groups they do not like; between the national government and religious community traditions; between the majority (be it national, regional, or local) and minority groups. Simply invoking the word "community" as some kind of mantra does not help us address the very real conflicts we face.

Seventh, the critics attack the new rights culture as lacking a moral voice and encouraging an excessive and amoral individualism. They fail to see the values inherent in a society organized around a system of rights: the values of tolerance, equality, fair play, and privacy. These values constrain as much as they liberate, and they constitute the new rules for American society.

The American experiment in constitutional democracy is now in its third century. The United States is the oldest such constitutional democracy in the world. The experiment continues. The last forty years have witnessed a crucial new era in that experiment. We are still coming to terms with the full ramifications of some of the new ideas that have arisen, just as we are still attempting to come to terms with the implications of the promise of freedom set forth in the Declaration of Independence, the Constitution, and the Bill of Rights. ◣

REALITY OF RIGHTS TALK?

Given the two readings above, clearly there are, at least some, very fundamental disagreements between Glendon (as a spokesperson for communitarianism) and Walker (as a spokesperson for liberalism). One point on which they seem to agree, however, is that there has indeed been a growth of appeals to rights over the past half-century. In the next reading, however, legal theorist Amy Bunger argues that American society is not more "rights conscious" than in the past. Having surveyed multiple areas of law reviews spanning multiple decades, Bunger claims that there has indeed been a shift, though not necessarily an expansion, in the types of topics that Americans have associated with rights. In particular, Bunger notes a shift toward framing issues as positive rather than negative rights and even toward identifying appropriate rights of the government to enact and to set and follow certain minimum standards that then promote and recognize entitlements for rights holders. So, while agreeing that how Americans conceive and speak of addressing many social concerns has changed over the years, Bunger does not see this as a dramatic growth in rights talk.

AMY BUNGER, "RIGHTS TALK AS A FORM OF POLITICAL COMMUNICATION"*

In *Rights Talk: The Impoverishment of Political Discourse* (1991), law professor Mary Ann Glendon asserts that rights occupy a large part of the public conversation, often at the expense of other topics (such as responsibilities). It is hard to measure conversations about rights, for that quickly becomes a highly subjective procedure, and some might argue that almost all human conversations, to some degree or another, are about rights. Glendon argues that we phrase much of our societal conflict in the language of rights, and scores of scholars now debate the degree to which an overabundance of rights talk has resulted in excess litigiousness. . . .

This work argues that rights talk isn't new to Americans. Quite the contrary, it is part of our national identity. What have changed are the types of topics sharing sentences with the words "right to." Why have our conversations about rights changed from a focus on negative rights (freedom from) to positive rights (entitlement to). Why were discussions of rights in the early part of the twentieth century predominantly about economics and property while they are now focused on social policy and privacy? By choosing not to focus on case law, the de facto frame used by political scientists to analyze changes in rights, we can "hear" more of what Americans are really saying when they speak the language of rights. . . .

My research traces how the discourse of rights has come to encompass many different variations. Three major thematic categories emerge from my research: first, "rights" is used interchangeably with the terms "privilege" and "liberty." Second, positive rights (entitlements) are now being more frequently discussed. This represents a change from what is

---

*In *Politics, Discourse, and American Society: New Agendas,* ed. Roderick P. Hart and Bartholomew H. Sparrow (Lanham, MD: Rowman & Littlefield, 2001), 71–90.

generally agreed to be the basis of the U.S. Bill of Rights, at minimum a document of negative liberties that frames restrictions on what the government cannot do and how citizens can maintain freedom from government intrusion. Third, the data show the roots of this growth in the debate over positive rights, including the actual "right of the government to act" and the "obligation to set standards, and promulgate regulation."

Methodology

. . . While case law is used by political science scholars to study and analyze changes in rights, it only tells us what cases and issues are successful in getting before the court—generally less than a couple of hundred cases per year. Case law tells us the *outcome* of a given rights orientation, but it doesn't explain what combination of factors came together for an assertion of rights to begin with, and it doesn't tell us why particular cases were put forth at a given time. . . .

Law review articles are therefore an interesting forum for tapping public discourse. Law reviews provide a forum where people debate ideas about rights and how those rights should be secured. Law reviews are also more representative of the wider range of societal conflict in a given period than are actual court cases, which often have more to do with legal issues (that is, standing and justiciability) than with the range of ideas about which people are debating. Rights talk, in short, is "old"—the United States is known for it. What is new is what Americans are now talking about and how these topics are being incorporated into lawsuits and thereby becoming a de facto mechanism of governance.

While the topics analyzed here varied widely, they can be thematically organized into the overarching category of negative and positive rights. The data demonstrate the growing prevalence of discussions of positive rights. In the discussion of "the rights of government," one finds a change in the type of issue or entity said to possess a positive right. Regarding positive rights, one also finds significant discursive changes across time. The data illustrate a conscious attempt to reframe positive rights into negative ones, a frame that is much more familiar to American political philosophy. The creation of minimum standards is a good example of this discussion, because the failure to adhere to a newly created minimum standard is often talked about as a deprivation. The data also show that many key phrases became associated with securing positive rights, in particular, actions pursued "in the public interest."

Negative and Positive Rights

Commentary on the Bill of Rights in the late 1940s was solidly rooted in the negative rights interpretation: "These amendments [the first ten known as the Bill of Rights] *were based on a fear of tyranny*" (Tom Clark, "A Federal Prosecutor Looks at the Civil Rights Statutes," in *Columbia Law Review*, 1947; emphasis added). In this post–New Deal period, author Tom Clark explained the organizing notions of the Founders as "distrusting all government, they set forth what their newly created government must not do to them and included amongst these the freedom of religion, freedom from unreasonable search and seizure and *due process of law*." Unlike many of his contemporaries in more progressive mid-century thought, Clark attempted to pair due process, often used as justification for the recognition of positive rights, with negative liberty. Clark added that our forefathers "aimed the Bill of Rights against the federal government only, by giving it no power to protect *fundamental personal rights* against infringement by either the states or individuals."

Negative rights highlight protection from an intrusive government and enshrine the idea of a private, protected sphere. "The protection of private rights from governments' wrongs and the maintenance of a federal system and a strong federal government have been important objectives of the Court at every period in its history," said Malcolm Sharp [in a 1933 issue of the *Harvard Law Review*]. Sharp's interpretation was quite typical. Throughout the twentieth century, discussions of negative rights never lessened. To the contrary, positive rights were frequently disguised as negative ones (an interesting development to be explored later). . . .

The Emergence of Positive Rights

Between 1930 and 1960, many articles referred to positive rights in passing [although there were some] who explicitly advocated the recognition of positive rights. For the most part, positive rights were largely distinguished from negative rights. C. B. Elder [in a 1934 issue of the *Illinois Law Review*], for example, discusses a positive right to employment versus the negative right of protection of private property. He asked, "If price fixing for homes and places of business after the war was justified because of the social emergency," then why can't policy support fixing prices for labor if there is a shortage of work? He justified his view by arguing that if a society can provide welfare for those out of work, why wouldn't furnishing employment be appropriate?

The Rights of Government: In the Public Interest

Discussions of positive rights took some important discursive turns over the years. Actions said to be "in the public interest" began to appear in combination with discussions of public welfare and the right of the government to act. Phraseology was crucial here because there is a difference between the *duty of the government to provide something* and *the right of the government to engage in an activity*. Throughout the years studied, rhetoric about *rights possessed by the government* clearly increased. The main turning point of the argument was whether the government had pursued a course of action or inaction. The main portion of the Constitution (as opposed to the Bill of Rights) delineates the power structure built into the American form of government, and yet one finds numerous examples of scholars discussing the "rights of" a government entity to pursue a given course of conduct. It is possible that these scholars were offering a defense of *delegated* power associated with the rise of the administrative state. What is significant, however, is that the authors frame such powers in terms of rights. . . .

In 1910, the noted progressive Louis Greeley was complimentary of the Supreme Court for actively endorsing regulation in the name of the public good, while de-emphasizing the importance of contractual or property rights. Data from this time period shows the emergence of a spirited defense of the "right" of the public good and of the notion that it be placed on equal footing with individual rights. Greeley quoted from *People v. Strollo* that "under a judicial system which has for centuries magnified the sacredness of individual rights, there is much less danger of doing injustice to the individual than there is in overlooking the obligations of those in authority to organized society."

The defense of governmental action demonstrated how a mixture of due process became integral in the developing rights rhetoric. According to that rhetoric, the right to regulate hinged on the interpretation of due process. "The cornerstone of regulation is the 'governmental interest' concept of due process," said Richard Speidel. Louis Henkin, a prominent liberal legal philosopher, advocated the link between positive rights and government interest when writing about past offenses to American Indians. Henkin argued that reparations to victims may be part of a "seamless general welfare," which may stem from "a sense that such particular welfare is the moral responsibility of all." Henkin's rhetoric underscores the movement away from a purely individualistic notion of the law to a system concerned with communitarian goals or public values. The rise in such discussions of public interest graphically illustrates the expansion of rights rhetoric over the years.

Minimum Standards and Positive Rights

The discourse of positive rights developed into the idea of a guarantee of "minimum standards" with a consideration of how much of something—protection or services—the government must provide. Actions of the legislature, and regulations in the name of the public interest, went a long way toward arguing for the development of minimum standards. Once minimum standards are made law, of course, they can become positive rights and part of the discussion of due process. Due process, after all, is a citizen's guarantee against deprivations on the part of the state. If minimum standards are developed, then the absence of minimum standards can be claimed to be a deprivation. . . .

[For example, a] 1969 article [by J. Etelson and F. Smith in the *Harvard Law Review*] recommended a "uniform requirement of full written notice" for union disciplinary proceedings. Like right-to-counsel cases earlier in the decade, the authors asserted that "the guarantee of lay representation is an important *minimum* safeguard to the right of a fair hearing" [emphasis added]. Again, the notion of a minimum underscored a kind of public responsibility or obligation, the absence of which would result in a deprivation.

Discussions of minima were also present in the area of social policy, such as abortion. Laurence Tribe, for example, wrote [in a 1973 issue of the *Harvard Law Review*], "If the developing concept of *minimum protection were thus shaped so as to reflect an underlying governmental* duty," and if there were a failure to meet such a need, "it would appear to follow that no woman could be denied public assistance for a lawful abortion which she says she cannot otherwise obtain."

Cass Sunstein, in 1987 [in the *Columbia Law Review*]—fourteen years after Tribe—illustrated how equating rights with "minima" had gained ground throughout the course of the century. "Claims for 'positive rights' cannot be dismissed," he said, "by reference to the 'negative' character of constitutional guarantees of the word 'deprive' in the Fourteenth Amendment." Sunstein notes that were there to be a preexisting right to welfare, the failure to deliver it would be a deprivation and thus it could be claimed *"that in the modern era the right to a minimal level of material goods,* like the right to protection against trespass, has constitutional status" [emphasis added].

Conclusion

The data gathered here suggest an ongoing struggle to categorize and define rights, as well as confusion when the term *rights* is used to reflect both "privilege" and "liberty." Confusion has occurred because the Court has held many aspects of procedure to be rights instead of privileges. Definitions of rights have gone from being based in a purely legalistic realm to one featuring strong sociological, political, and philosophical undercurrents. Rights, as we have seen, have been discussed in debates sprinkled with the terms "justice," "equality," "duty," and "morality."

Confusion has also permeated debates about positive and negative rights. For traditionalists, the Bill of Rights was thought to be, at minimum, a charter of negative liberties. Increasingly, though, there has been significant disagreement about the degree to which it also contains or secures positive rights. The distinction between positive and negative rights has been blurred over the course of the century, particularly in the discourses of "minima" and deprivation, where scholars have argued for declarations of minimum standards so that the failure to meet such standards could be declared a deprivation under the Fourteenth Amendment's due process clause. The discourse of positive rights reflects tenets embodied in other twentieth century constitutions in other Western countries. In the United States, however, the Constitution is largely silent about such matters, thereby giving rise to the public arguments about affirmative welfare or group rights profiled here.

There has also been a continuing tendency to confuse other terms with rights. More commonly, and indeed more importantly, there was a related tendency to label political desires and ideals as "rights." Specifically, references to the "public interest" included the assertion of the right of the government to act. This tendency became more pronounced with the rise of the regulatory state where the conflict between the rights of the individual and the rights of the state has increased. Here the state asserts a right to a particular action (often regulatory) that a citizen then claims to be an infringement of individual rights. There is considerable evidence of a tendency to discuss the powers granted in the first two portions of the Constitution as issues of rights contained in its latter portion, the Bill of Rights. The amalgamation of rights with an idea closer to liberty happened concurrently with the changes in the structural aspects of the Constitution. The twentieth century's centralization and proliferation of the administrative state also has increasingly conflated individual and group desires with the notion of rights, in part because rights are the language of the courts—the ultimate path to power in a democratic society. To be sure, the categorizations and definitions of rights presented here represent only a portion of the discourse studied. The sources of rights, be they common law, constitutional law, statutory law, or natural law, have become a significant portion of this nation's most diverse discourse and it is not likely that such debates will be resolved soon.

This [essay] argues that Americans are not more rights conscious per se than in previous times—although rights are surely still normal parts of public conversation in the United States. What is different, and what has changed, are (1) the types of issues now being discussed as rights, (2) what we mean when we speak in the language of rights, and (3) what all of this says about the relationship between citizen and state. ▲

Questions for Discussion

1. Are the various social ills that Glendon identifies, such as poor voter turnout or "sound-bite" political discussion, the effect primarily, or even in large part, of the proliferation of rights talk or of some other cause(s)?

2. Is American rights dialect more strident than in the past? Is it more strident than other rights dialects (i.e., in other cultures)? If not, why? If so, is this the cause or effect of other social changes?

3. Is it a problem for communitarianism that the notion of community is very open-ended?

4. Does Reitz van Winkle show what Walker intends, namely, that contemporary American rights talk has benefited individuals and made American culture more inclusive?

5. Is it the liberalist perspective that the well-being of individuals (always) trumps the well-being of communities? If not, why? If so, is that acceptable? For example, are communities harmed (acceptably) by being prevented or restricted from censoring pornography?

6. Given the list of rights claims and counterclaims noted by Dershowitz, is Bunger correct that there has been a change but not an expansion in rights talk?

7. Bunger claims that data show a growth in the notion of positive rights and of the rights and responsibilities of government to recognize and enforce rights. Is this more compatible with liberalism or communitarianism (and in what ways)?

8. Which models of the nature of rights from Chapter 1 are more or less compatible with how liberalism and communitarianism seem to understand rights?

Further Reading

Avineri, Shlomo, and Avner de-Shalit, eds. *Communitarianism and Individualism.* Oxford: Oxford University Press, 1992. A fine collection of essays for and against communitarianism.

Daly, Markate, ed. *Communitarianism: A New Public Ethics.* Belmont, CA: Wadsworth, 1994. A collection of classic and contemporary essays on the liberalist-communitarian debate, somewhat sympathetic to the communitarian view.

Etzioni, Amitai, ed. *The Essential Communitarian Reader.* Lanham, MD: Rowman & Littlefield, 1998. A collection of essays detailing a communitarian philosophical and political perspective.

Flathman, Richard E. *Toward a Liberalism.* Ithaca, NY: Cornell University Press, 1989. A detailed philosophical statement in favor of liberalism, with a sustained argument for individual rights.

Forst, Rainer. *Contexts of Justice: Political Theory Beyond Liberalism and Communitarianism.* Berkeley: University of California Press, 2002. A critique of various aspects and claims of both liberalism and communitarianism.

Gray, John. *Liberalism*. Minneapolis: University of Minnesota Press, 1986 (2nd ed., 1995). A fine statement of the history and basic political philosophy of liberalism.

Jumonville, Neil, and Kevin Mattson, eds. *Liberalism for a New Century*. Berkeley: University of California Press, 2007. A collection of essays addressing social and political issues from a liberal perspective.

May, Larry. *The Socially Responsive Self*. Chicago: University of Chicago Press, 1996. A communitarian statement of social and moral theory and practice.

Smith, Patricia. *Liberalism and Affirmative Obligation*. Oxford: Oxford University Press, 1998. An analysis of social and political duties, including their relations to rights.

Wellman, Carl. *The Proliferation of Rights: Moral Progress or Empty Rhetoric?* Boulder, CO: Westview, 1999. A historically based analysis and critique of specific rights.

CHAPTER 7

GLOBAL RIGHTS DISCOURSE

Following the end of World War II, in acknowledgment of the widespread horrors and abuses of peoples around the globe, the International Court of Justice (also called the World Court) was established in 1946. Recognizing and labeling some actions as "crimes against humanity," in December 1948 the UN General Assembly adopted the Universal Declaration of Human Rights (UDHR) (see Part III). Forty-eight of the then fifty-eight member states of the United Nations voted in favor of the UDHR, with the nations abstaining being from the then Soviet Bloc countries, as well as South Africa and Saudi Arabia. (In 1990, Saudi Arabia, along with other member states of the Organization of the Islamic Conference, signed on to the Cairo Declaration of Human Rights in Islam. See Part III.) Since its adoption, states that have joined the United Nations have also signed on to the UDHR. By the end of the twentieth century, support for the UDHR was truly international, though not universal, and many of the articles it contained served as the basis for new national constitutions around the globe. Indeed, at a time when genuine concern has been raised about rights, as discussed in Chapters 5 and 6, there has been an ever-increasing appeal to the UDHR and to an attention on human rights in terms of international diplomacy and policy. For example, following the adoption of the UDHR, numerous rights agreements have been ratified by nations across the world, such as the International Covenant on Civil and Political Rights (1966), the International Covenant on Economic, Social, and Cultural Rights (1966), the Helsinki Agreement (1975), the Convention on the Elimination of All Forms of Discrimination Against Women (1979), the African

Charter on Human and Peoples' Rights (1986), the Convention Against Torture and Other Cruel, Inhuman, and Degrading Treatment and Punishment (1987), the Cairo Declaration of Human Rights in Islam (1990), the Universal Declaration on the Human Genome and Human Rights (1999), the Declaration on the Rights of Indigenous Peoples (2007), and many others.

In addition to signing on to international agreements and accords such as those just mentioned, nearly every nation with a constitution has now incorporated the language of human rights into it. For example, the constitution of Brazil lists many "fundamental rights and guarantees," including all persons as "equal before the law, without any distinction whatsoever, and Brazilians and foreigners resident in Brazil are assured of inviolability of the right of life, liberty, equality, security, and property." In addition, "education, health, work, leisure, security, social security, protection of motherhood and childhood, and assistance to the destitute, are social rights under this Constitution." The constitution of Zimbabwe guarantees the protection of fundamental rights and the freedom of the individual, covering freedoms of conscience, expression, movement, assembly, and association, as well as protection against inhuman treatment, deprivation of property, discrimination, and so forth. The Canadian constitution notes various kinds of rights, such as democratic rights (e.g., the right to vote), mobility rights (e.g., the right to move and gain livelihood), legal rights (e.g., the right to due process under the law), and equality rights (e.g., the right to freedom from discrimination). The constitution of Iran speaks explicitly of "the rights of the people," including all citizens to "equally enjoy the protection of law and enjoy all human, political, economic, social, and cultural rights in conformity with Islamic criteria," covering both negative rights, such as freedom of belief and association, and positive rights, such as social security and education. Likewise, the constitution of the People's Republic of China addresses "fundamental rights and duties of citizens." These rights include the right to vote and stand for election; freedom of speech, press, assembly, procession, demonstration, and religion; freedom from unlawful search or intrusion into one's home; and the right to social security, education, and gender equality. The point here is that across the world, even in nations that have been criticized with respect to their protection of human rights, such rights have been codified into their respective legal structures, which speaks to the internationalization of human rights (however well or poorly those rights have been interpreted and implemented in practice).

Nonetheless, since the initial adoption of the UDHR, many people have raised concerns about and objections to it, relating sometimes to specific parts and other times to broad assumptions of commitments attached to it. Among the objections to specific parts have been criticisms that it includes a "wish list" of illegitimate rights. For example, Article 24 states that everyone has a right to rest and leisure, including reasonable limitation of working hours and periodic holidays with pay. Or Article 27 states that everyone has the right to participate freely in the cultural life of the community, to enjoy the arts and to share in scientific advancement and its benefits. Critics have claimed that besides being illegitimate (as they carry correlative duties on others), these rights are not feasibly enforceable, especially in developing nations with limited resources.

Another, broader type of concern raised has involved the appropriateness of the universal language of the UDHR. Many people insist that the focus of human rights must not be unbalanced in such a way as to emphasize individuals at the expense of groups (or, at least, the focus on individuals must not outweigh the focus also on groups). Many argue that individuals are inherently and inextricably related to the cultures in which they are raised, so the applicability of the UDHR is lessened to the extent that such relations are not respected and taken into account. One example of this view appears in what is called the Bangkok Declaration. In preparation for the World Conference on Human Rights in 1993, ministers and representatives from many Asian countries met and formulated the Bangkok Declaration, in which they affirmed a commitment to the Charter of the United Nations and the principles of the UDHR, but also emphasized a recognition that "while human rights are universal in nature, they must be considered in the context of a dynamic and evolving process of international norm-setting, bearing in mind the significance of national and regional particularities and various historical, cultural and religious backgrounds." Such recognition, they said, entailed "respect for national sovereignty, territorial integrity and non-interference in the internal affairs of States," and "the promotion of human rights should be encouraged by cooperation and consensus, and not through confrontation and the imposition of incompatible values." From its very inception, then, the UDHR has faced the "challenge" of cultural relativism.

CULTURAL RELATIVISM AND HUMAN RIGHTS

One broad concern raised about human rights has been that, as a means of regulating behavior, they reflect particular assumptions, traditions, and moral perspectives—specifically, Western ones. As noted above, one of the states that

abstained from approving the UDHR in 1948 was Saudi Arabia. It did so because some of the language contained in the UDHR did not resonate well with
Shari'ah (i.e., the legal system derived from Islamic religious scripture and doctrine). This broad concern that the UDHR and the doctrine of human rights
in general are Western based is expressed in various ways. At the mildest level,
the concern is that they are too narrow and do not reflect different cultural understandings and practices; in a word, they are not sensitive enough to cultural
differences. At a stronger level, the concern is that they are culturally imperialistic; in a word, they are attempts (whether explicit or implicit) to impose
Western values on all cultures and societies. In the readings below, we see both
of these sentiments expressed as well as a non-Western—at least, South American, thus Third World—endorsement of the UDHR and human rights.

These concerns are usually framed within the context of cultural relativism. The notion of cultural relativism, in the broadest sense, claims that
standards of right and wrong behavior are relative to cultures; there are no
universal standards. There is disagreement, however, as to exactly what this
claim means. One interpretation of cultural relativism is descriptive: It is a descriptive fact about the world that different cultures and societies have different perceptions of (standards of) right and wrong. We all know that different
cultures and societies have different views on what is acceptable as far as decent and modest dress in public. We all know that different cultures and societies have different levels of tolerance for abortion on demand. So, this
descriptive interpretation seems quite straightforward and uncontroversial.
However, it turns out not to be as obviously true as it at first seems because
the cultural variation that exists concerning acceptable behavior might be
more at the surface than at a deeper level. For example, one culture might find
it permissible for a person to have multiple spouses at the same time, while
another culture might not. This is certainly a difference, but the underlying
institution of marriage, including what is believed to be its important func-
tion(s) and purpose(s) for individuals and communities, might very well be an
underlying value shared by all cultures. The specific features and practices
(such as who can be married to whom or who has authority to sanction marriages) might vary across different cultures, but the deeper meaning and value
of marriage might not. Just as wings for birds and fins for fish and legs for
mammals all clearly differ from each other, all are used for propulsion within
the relevant environments of these different animals. So, the argument goes,
the differences and variations are real, but all three features share a deep, underlying adaptive value: They allow the relevant organism to survive. Indeed,

in a classic compendium of "human universals," American anthropologist George P. Murdock compiled a list of sixty-seven features that he found in all cultures across the globe, including age grading, bodily adornment, eschatology, food taboos, gift giving, kinship nomenclature, penal sanctions, and residence rules, to name a few. He claimed that every culture exhibits these features. The particulars vary (e.g., different cultures identify different things as appropriate or inappropriate as food), but the underlying feature is universal. The basic point, then, is that even the seemingly obvious descriptive interpretation of cultural relativism—that, in fact, different cultures and societies have different values—might be less significant than it seems at first glance.

A second interpretation of cultural relativism is normative: It is not simply the case that people *do* have different values associated with different cultures, but they *ought* to have different values based on different cultures. Under this interpretation of cultural relativism, culture is not only the source but the justification of one's values. A corollary of this claim is that there are no absolute or universal standards of values that transcend or trump cultural standards. If there are any normative universals—that is, moral principles that all cultures accept, such as some form of the Golden Rule—that is perhaps a happy outcome, but it is just general agreement, not evidence of a universal standard of right or wrong (except in a descriptive sense). Furthermore, if culture is the predominant determinant of values, then, at least for many people, criticism of values internal to a culture by others outside of that culture is cultural imperialism. It is one thing to say that some standard or principle is accepted across different cultures, but it is another to say that some standard or principle applies—that is, should be accepted—across different cultures. This latter claim is said to be imperialistic and is rejected by normative cultural relativism.

With respect to the issue of human rights, it is the normative, not the descriptive, view of cultural relativism that matters. Those who advocate human rights as applying to all humans, regardless of when or where they live (i.e., regardless of their cultural context), claim that these rights are not relative and trump any cultural values that violate them. So, these people say, if there is a human right to self-determination, then that right pertains to all humans, not just Americans or Westerners. The rights outlined and specified in the UDHR, these people argue, are indeed *human* rights, held by all humans, even if their respective cultures do not recognize or protect them.

Needless to say, not everyone agrees with this view. In the first reading below, Korean scholar Manwoo Lee argues in favor of the cultural relativist view. Lee posits that the very concept of individual human rights, rights held by individuals against their communities and governments, is one that not only arises from Western history, traditions, and values but perpetuates and imposes such values on others who do not share that history or traditions (in this case, North Koreans). The individualism that underlies the basic concept of human rights is foreign, he says, to Korean culture. To criticize Korean, especially North Korean, traditions and practices—including the obligations and expectations of North Koreans vis-à-vis their government—is simply Western cultural imperialism. For Lee, there is no single, absolute, universally correct understanding of what rights are; instead, rights, like all other moral concepts, must be understood always and only within the context of a culture and its traditions. Human rights violations, then—including determinations of what sorts of things even count as violations—also must be understood always and only within such contexts.

MANWOO LEE, "NORTH KOREA AND THE WESTERN NOTION OF HUMAN RIGHTS"*

The concept of human rights and the demand for a constitutional government do not arise from human nature. These ideas are not innate in the human mind, but are products of reflection by philosophers like John Locke and John Stuart Mill who lived in a particular society with a particular culture. It would be fascinating to probe the question of why in the West the idea of equality, the dignity of law, the evil of tyranny, and the demand for self-government came to be the lanterns of political civilization, while in Eastern societies such as China and Korea these ideas did not grow indigenously. For simplicity of argument, it is stated here that for a variety of cultural reasons the concept of human rights as understood in the context of Western cultures did not emerge in East Asia. While Western societies developed their sensitivities to the idea of human rights, East Asian societies as a whole preoccupied themselves not with the rights of individuals but with their duties. Here lies one of the major differences between the two civilizations. Naturally there are

---

*In *Human Rights in East Asia: A Cultural Perspective*, ed. James C. Hsiung (New York: Paragon House, 1985), 129–151.

tremendous differences in the life style and the political and ethical outlook between duty-bound individuals of the East and "rights-seeking"
individuals of the West. It is no accident that where the adversarial notion of democracy became rooted, as in the West, the concept of human rights and individualism has also developed.

Barrington Moore has written that the development of Western liberal
democratic politics and rights involved "a long and incomplete struggle
to do three related things: (1) to check arbitrary rules; (2) to replace arbitrary rules with just and rational ones; and (3) to obtain a share for the
underlying population in the making of rules." If what Moore said captures the essence of the historical struggles for Western democracy and
rights, none of what he said is even remotely related to the historical
development of North Korean politics. Only in South Korea in recent decades has there been a series of frustrated efforts to achieve a democratic
political system. Korea's 5000-year history is replete with stories of struggles for position, honor, power, property and perhaps sometimes justice,
but not about the individual consciously fighting for his autonomy and
rights, or about the people trying to limit the arbitrary power of state. Korea produced no thinkers comparable to Aristotle, Aquinas, Rousseau,
Locke or (John Stuart) Mill.

The absence of these types of thinkers associated with the idea of a
government of law, human dignity, constitutionalism and liberty does not
imply, however, that the Korean people have lived like barbarians. Korea
had (and still has) its own Shamanistic world view, perhaps unintelligible
and even exotic to the Western mind. The Shamanistic world view refused to share many of the fundamental assumptions of Western civilization. . . . The Shamanistic man was truly free of . . . preoccupations that
characterized the development of Western civilization, which ultimately
gave birth to the concept of natural rights of man, human rights, democracy, or individualism. Instead, he was preoccupied with what Hahm
Pyongchoon calls attaining "a fully human condition," which meant that
he was deeply interested in procreation, kinship and blood ties. . . .

This meant that a doctrine or practice based on the assumption that
the individual and not kinship or society is the paramount consideration or end could not develop in Korea. In a society where a clear-cut
ego boundary is de-emphasized, as in Korea, the pursuit of individual
rights becomes secondary. . . .

Thus, a theory maintaining that individual initiative, action and interests should be independent of the family, group, or state is an absurd concept to the Shamanistic man.

Clearly, what a Korean Shamanistic man feared most was exclusion from the familial or communal life of human interaction in which separate egos overlapped. The Shamanistic man was lost if he was not able to develop and maintain a personal relationship with deep human emotional involvement. He was not interested in being different from others. He always sought uniformity and harmony with others. Ostracism and communal condemnation were greatly feared (and still are). Given this kind of psycho-cultural background, Korea was not a place where individualism or autonomous identity with its accompanying rights could flourish. . . .

There are other interesting Korean psycho-cultural elements that discouraged the development of democratic rights. A strong tradition of family system in Korea meant that a family was the center of the universe. State, nation, and community had to be understood in the context of a family analogy. The traditional Korean man never understood state or nation as an abstract entity. He always regarded it as a large extended family with the ruler as its head. He could transfer his loyalty and affection only to the father of the nation, not to such abstractions as nation or state. This is why, even to this day, most Koreans, whether they live in the South or the North, find it difficult to distinguish between a ruler and the state he heads. Also, private and public spheres have never been clearly and strictly defined. In the West, the distinction between a temporary ruler and the state itself was made long ago, and that issue has been settled. The two Koreas have not made a functional differentiation of the two. . . .

With the importance of loyalty, hierarchy, family, unity and uniformity emphasized by both Confucianism and Shamanism, the potential for arbitrariness and authoritarianism is firmly imbedded in the culture. The concept of the limitation of governmental power—the most important ingredient of democracy—could not emerge in Korea. . . .

To sum up, the collective consciousness of the Korean people still retains many traditional cultural traits. Aversion to individualism, diversity, abstract conceptualization and rationalism is still deeply ingrained. While Western societies have deliberately fostered and promoted individualism, rationality, and diversity, producing autonomous and heterogeneous individuals, Korean societies have stressed the development of a people homogeneous in thought and behavior. Koreans still feel an antipathy toward heterogeneous elements in society. They believe people must share homogeneous substance and quality—*dongjil*—in personality, ideas, and way of life. A strange and different behavior is not easily tolerated. North Korea's strong desire to homogenize the entire population stems in part from the cultural tradition of Korea that stressed the importance of *dongjil*, though its actual practice, tinged by Marxism-Leninism, is excessive by any standard. The importance attached to the notion of *dongjil* also explains the extent of hatred between the two Koreas. Under these circumstances, human rights have never succeeded in asserting themselves in Korea, especially in North Korea. . . .

> The sources of human misery vary from one culture to another; each society inflicts its own version of injustice, develops its own way of not seeing the suffering of its victims, builds up its own myths to maintain the claim of the winners.
>
> —FOUAD AJAMI

Perhaps the above statement may apply to all societies, including those that show outrage and concern with their endless tales of repression and brutality in places other than their own. It is much harder to look into violations in one's own country. A listing of any nation's sins can be abundantly documented. No one can deny that the North Korean system has inflicted immense suffering on its own people in the name of revolution and progress, and that the people of North Korea have not been given a chance to reflect on their own society, to examine the myths and claims, and to confront the human and social costs of their own arrangements. Even if they had the chance, they might not have the conceptual framework. The blending of the traditional Korean world view with Marxism-Leninism in North Korea effectively impeded the development of any human rights theory as understood in Western societies. The current regime, by attempting to enforce its vision of conformity, further discourages such a development. At the same time, there is no compelling reason for North Korea to emulate the Western values of human rights. These have no universal applicability to other peoples, times, or places. As [the Mexican diplomat and intellectual

Carlos] Fuentes eloquently suggested, the clocks of all societies are not set at the same hour.

The North Korean system under [former leader Kim Il-sung] was purposefully designed to use unlimited power to institutionalize the "politics of redemption." Its vision of human brotherhood, arising from the conquest of poverty, oppression, and injustice, has been the hallmark of the "politics of redemption." Kim . . . called for the creation of a paradise in which there is no room for the "viles" of individualism. Into how much terror and disappointment has he led his people? Would he have been nobler if he had no such thought? Perhaps. In any case it makes no sense to view such a system through a narrow, Western, human rights lens. Furthermore, given North Korea's indigenous psycho-cultural idiosyncrasies combined with Marxism-Leninism, the North Korean people . . . do not even seem to be conscious of the human rights debates going on outside their own country. In this sense, North Korea is truly an isolated nation. Kim's revolutionary ethos and the passion of North Korean communal solidarity demand a different conception of human well-being. The individual is forced to integrate into a larger socio-political entity. Only a person fully integrated into the system can function and remain "free."

This un-Lockean tradition is not only deeply rooted in Korean culture, but further reinforced by the application of Marxism-Leninism. Hence, a different conception of freedom and human rights emerges. The system can guarantee freedom from starvation, unemployment, and individual loneliness. It can provide education and health facilities. But the freedoms of speech, assemblage, movement and religions are, by nature, incompatible with the functioning of the North Korean system. In North Korea an individual wholly preoccupied with his private interest and acting in accordance with his private caprice is a criminal deserving banishment from the community. This system indeed evokes a crude version of Rousseau's paradoxical assertion that a human being can be forced to be free. Western societies that practice the "politics of convenience" in the liberal tradition of Locke will always find the North Korean version of the politics of redemption repulsive because, in the Lockean tradition, the greatest security is still the private realm, with the state being seen primarily as a threat to human well-being. Nevertheless, it must be acknowledged that a totally different definition of human purpose exists in North Korea. ◣

Chapter 4 presents differing views about whether groups *as groups* are legitimate rights holders. One concern raised in that context is, even if groups are rights holders, do their rights trump the rights of their individual members, or vice versa? This issue returns here in the context of different cultures and how we should understand rights in a global context. As we have just seen, Lee argues that we should understand rights only locally, that is to say, only *within* particular cultural traditions. For Lee, if Korean culture understands the role and content of individual rights in certain ways, then those ways are legitimate and appropriate for Koreans, regardless of whether they are legitimate and appropriate for Americans. To insist that there is one single correct conception of human rights is, says Lee, cultural imperialism.

While others agree with Lee, yet many others see his claims regarding cultural imperialism as minimally mistaken and, worse, as illegitimate efforts to deflect scrutiny and criticism. Chinese scholar Xiaorong Li, for example, claims that bad regimes can and do use the notion of cultural relativism to justify repression of their citizens. By saying that rights are culturally specific (or that they are a matter of national sovereignty or must be balanced against the priority of the community), bad regimes violate individuals' human rights with impunity. This criticism is shared in the reading below by Argentinean legal scholar Fernando Tesón.

Tesón's primary concern is that a cultural relativist view of rights is mistaken (and, on the heels of this problem, that such a view is used to justify violations of human rights, though that issue is not included in the reading below). For Tesón, cultural relativism with respect to rights is mistaken for several reasons. One is that, intentionally or not, the cultural relativist view conflates descriptive and prescriptive (or normative) relativism. The fact that different people or cultures have different values or practices does not necessarily justify any specific values or practices. Just because Nazi Germany "restrained" Jews and others, such practices were not thereby justified. As noted in Chapter 4's discussion of group rights, in the words of Will Kymlicka, "tradition is not self-validating."

A second reason Tesón thinks that cultural relativism is mistaken has to do with the vagueness of the very notion of culture and of whose values constitute a culture's values. Cultures and societies include many different communities often at odds with one another (just think of Republicans and Democrats in the United States!). A worrisome aspect of this vagueness arises when the values and traditions of the more powerful elements within a culture or society become equated with the values and traditions of the culture itself. In particular, a culture is not necessarily the same thing as the government or the state. Even more, a culture is not the same thing as the specific regime in power at any given time. Yet, such a conflation of culture = government = this regime can and does get used to insulate a given regime from outside criticism. In Tesón's view, normative cultural relativism is actually a very conservative political philosophy because it claims there is no basis for critiquing the status quo.

Tesón also thinks that a cultural relativist view of rights is mistaken because humans are not just citizens; they have value as persons as well. Humans have universal needs that transcend, for Tesón, their citizenship. All humans— regardless of when or where they live—require a basic level of food and shelter, for example. Such needs have nothing to do with whether someone is American or Kenyan or Indian. There exist moral concerns, no less than biological concerns, that are universal and, indeed, universalizable, says Tesón.

A final reason Tesón gives for rejecting a cultural relativist view of rights is that such a perspective generates two disturbing by-products: elitism and conspiracy fears. By the claim of elitism, he means that as a consequence of a normative cultural relativist view, some, perhaps many, rights enjoyed in Western nations are not enjoyed in others, with the underlying view being that while repressive regimes are not acceptable in modern, sophisticated cultures, they are fine for others (almost always meaning for Third World cultures). By the claim of conspiracy fears, Tesón refers to the view that advocacy of human rights as transcending national and cultural boundaries clearly reflects the effort of Western cultures (and regimes) to impose their values on others, with their own selfish interests at heart (not the well-being of those other nations or cultures). An example of this attitude is a remark by an Iranian official during the 1979 Islamic Revolution: "The Beatles are more dangerous than bombs." While bombs represent overt military action that can be openly addressed, The Beatles represent cultural values that can undermine another culture from within. In response to such fears, Tesón claims that there is simply no evidence of such a conspiracy (and certainly not from international agreements such as the UDHR). In addition, even if the predominant human rights views have come from Western culture, that in itself does not mean that they are wrong or inapplicable to other cultures. Such views are not false or illegitimate simply because they originate in one place rather than another. Here, then, is Tesón:

FERNANDO R. TESÓN, "INTERNATIONAL HUMAN RIGHTS AND CULTURAL RELATIVISM"*

In the context of the debate about the viability of international human rights, cultural relativism may be defined as the position according to which local cultural traditions (including religious, political, and legal practices) properly determine the existence and scope of civil and political rights enjoyed by individuals in a given society. A central tenet of relativism is that no transboundary legal or moral standards exist against which human rights practices may be judged acceptable or unacceptable. Thus, relativists claim that substantive human rights standards vary among different cultures and necessarily reflect national idiosyncrasies. What may be regarded as a human rights violation in one society may properly be considered lawful in another, and Western ideas of human rights should not be imposed upon Third World societies. Tolerance and respect for self-determination preclude cross-cultural normative judgments. Alternatively, the relativist thesis holds that even if, as a matter of customary or conventional international law, a body of substantive human rights norms exists, its meaning varies substantially from culture to culture. . . .

The discussion here will be . . . circumscribed by two assumptions which have solid foundations in international law. The first assumption is that human rights are a substantive part of international law, not only as a matter of treaty, but also as part of customary law. It follows that arguments premised upon the exclusively municipal nature of human rights law are inconsistent with present international law. The cultural relativist may, but need not, disagree with this assumption. He need only hold that the various freedoms have different meanings when applied to different societies. Some relativists would even agree that a few basic human rights, such as the right to life and the freedom from torture, are absolute in the sense that even cultural traditions may not override them. But relativists do not regard other rights, such as the right to physical integrity, the right to participate in the election of one's government, the right to a fair trial, freedom of expression, freedom of

---

Virginia Journal of International Law 25 (1985): 869–898

association, freedom of movement, or the prohibition of discrimination, as required by international law. While I assume that the core meaning of international human rights law encompasses rights beyond the right to life and to freedom from torture, I do not attempt to prove this assumption. Rather, my main thesis can be condensed into the following two propositions:

a. If there is an international human rights standard—the exact scope of which it is admittedly difficult to ascertain—then its meaning remains uniform across borders.
b. Analogously, if there is a possibility of meaningful moral discourse about rights, then it is universal in nature and applies to all human beings despite cultural differences.

The second assumption made in this paper is that an obligation in international law indeed exists to respect the cultural identities of peoples, their local traditions, and customs. For example, the classical international law on the treatment of aliens has long recognized that Westerners cannot expect to enjoy Western judicial procedures in non-Western states. Arbitral tribunals have consistently refused to accept the claim that partially nonadversary criminal procedures violate the international minimum standard concerning the right to a fair trial.

However, to say that cultural identities should be respected does not mean that international human rights law lacks a substantive core. Such a core can be gleaned from international human rights treaties, both regional and universal, and diplomatic practice, including the relevant practices of international organizations. Indeed, human rights treaties offer a surprisingly uniform articulation of human rights law. They may safely be used as a reference, regardless of how many or which states are parties. The rights, *inter alia*, to life, to physical integrity, to a fair trial, freedom of expression, freedom of thought and religion, freedom of association, and the prohibition against discrimination are all rights upon which international instruments agree. Unless one wishes to give up the very notion of an international law of human rights altogether, these rights should have essentially the same meaning regardless of local traditions. . . .

Critique of normative relativism. As a moral theory, normative relativism cannot withstand scrutiny. First, its straightforward formulation reflects a fundamental incoherence. It affirms at the same time that (a) there are no universal moral principles; (b) one ought to act in accordance with the principles of one's own group; and (c), (b) is a universal moral principle. David Lyons demonstrated that the typical anthropologists' version of relativism ("an act is right if, and only if, it accords with the norms of the agent's group") does not validate conflicting moral judgments, because each group is regarded as a separate moral realm. Consequently, the incoherence attached to normative relativism springs from the fact that the very assertion of universal relativism is self-contradictory, not from the fact that it validates conflicting substantive moral judgments. If it is true that no universal moral principle exists, then the relativist engages in self-contradiction by stating the universality of the relativist principle. . . .

A second problem with normative relativism is that it overlooks an important feature of moral discourse, its *universalizability*. Independently of substantive morals, when we talk about right and wrong or rights and duties, and act accordingly, we are [according to Alan Gewirth] logically committed to "act in accordance with the generic rights of [our] recipients as well as [our] selves," on pain of self-contradiction. This not only means that we cannot make exceptions in our own favor, but also that individuals must be treated as equally entitled to basic rights regardless of contingent factors such as their cultural surroundings. The requirement of universalizability may be thought of as having a logical nature, or alternatively, as being a requirement of moral plausibility. If the first approach is correct, the relativist simply refuses to engage in meaningful moral discourse. Under the second approach, the relativist endorses the highly implausible position that in moral matters we can pass judgments containing proper names, and that consequently we may make exceptions in our own favor. . . .

Third, normative relativism runs counter to the principle that persons have moral worth *qua* persons and must be treated as ends in themselves, not as functions of the ends of others. . . . This principle of moral worth forbids the imposition upon individuals of cultural standards that impair human rights. Even if relativists could show that authoritarian practices are somehow required by a community—a claim which in many cases remains to be proven—they would still fail to explain why individuals should surrender their basic rights to the ends of the community. If women in Moslem countries are discriminated against, it is not enough to say that a tradition, no matter how old and venerable, requires such

discrimination. The only defense consistent with the principle of autonomy would be a showing that each subjugated woman consented to
waive her rights. However, because of the mystical and holistic assumptions underlying relativism, presumably the relativist would not regard
such a test as relevant or necessary.

Quite apart from the moral implausibility of normative relativism, it
is worth noting the extreme conservatism of the doctrine. Normative
relativism tells us that if a particular society has always had authoritarian practices, it is morally defensible that it continue to have them. It
works as a typical argument of authority: it has always been like this,
this is our culture, so we need not undertake any changes. . . . Not only
does positive international law fail to provide any basis for the relativist
doctrine, but the underlying philosophical structure of relativism also
reveals profound flaws.

Two by-products of relativism: elitism and conspiracy. In this part I will
briefly consider two doctrines closely associated with relativism. The
first theory asserts that one can appropriately honor human rights in
certain societies, usually the most sophisticated ones, but not in others,
on account, for example, of the latter's insufficient economic development. This doctrine, which can be called "elitism," necessarily follows
from relativism. The second theory states that the law of human rights
results from a conspiracy of the West to perpetuate imperialism. The
"conspiracy theory," by contrast, does not follow inevitably from, and is
not required by, cultural relativism. . . .

[The] elitist theory of human rights holds that human rights are good
for the West but not for much of the non-Western world. Surprisingly,
the elitist theory of human rights is very popular in the democratic West,
not only in conservative circles but also, and even more often, among
the liberal and radical groups. The right-wing version of elitism embodies the position, closely associated with colonialism, that backward
peoples cannot govern themselves and that democracy only works for
superior cultures. The left-wing version, often articulated by liberals who
stand for civil rights in Western countries but support leftist dictatorships
abroad, reflects a belief that we should be tolerant of and respect the
cultural identity and political self-determination of Third World countries (although, of course, it is seldom the people who choose to have
dictators; more often the dictators decide for them).

The position of relativist scholars who are human rights advocates illustrates an eloquent example of concealed elitism. Such persons find themselves in an impossible dilemma. On the one hand they are anxious to articulate an international human rights standard, while on the other they wish to respect the autonomy of individual cultures. The result is a vague warning against "ethnocentrism," and well-intentioned proposals that are deferential to tyrannical governments and insufficiently concerned with human suffering. Because the consequence of either version of elitism is that certain national or ethnic groups are somehow less entitled than others to the enjoyment of human rights, the theory is fundamentally immortal and replete with racist overtones.

The final aspect of relativism to be discussed is what Karl Popper might describe as "the conspiracy theory of human rights." This theory asserts that human rights are a Machiavellian creation of the West calculated to impair the economic development of the Third World. Starting from the Marxist assumption that civil and political rights are "formal" bourgeois freedoms that serve only the interests of the capitalists, the conspiracy theory holds that human rights serve the same purpose in the international arena. It sees them as instruments of domination because they are indissolubly tied to the right to property, and because in the field of international economic relations, the human rights movement fosters free and unrestricted trade which seriously hurts the economies of Third World nations. Furthermore, proponents of the conspiracy theory charge that human rights advocacy amounts to moral imperialism. . . .

The conspiracy theory, however, fails to justify the link between the support for human rights and support for particular property rights or trade policies—a fundamental flaw. The argument made in this paper does not presuppose or imply any position in this regard. Moreover, to claim that civil and political rights must be suppressed as a necessary condition for the improvement of Third World economies grossly distorts the facts. . . .

The contention that the West imposed human rights on the world and that "poor peoples" do not care about freedom is clearly a myth. First, it contradicts the plain fact that a growing awareness exists in the Third World about the need for reinforcing the respect for human rights. Second, even if, *gratia argumentandi*, some Western plot created human rights philosophy, that fact alone would not necessarily undermine its moral value. . . . [T]he circumstances surrounding the origin of human rights principles are irrelevant to their intrinsic value and cannot detract from their beneficial features.

Conclusion. The human rights movement has resisted the relativist attack by emphasizing that social institutions, including international law, are created by and for the individual. Consequently, as far as rights are concerned, governments serve as but the agents of the people. International norms aim to protect individuals, not governments, by creating concrete limits on how human beings may be treated.

I have suggested that cultural relativism is not, and ought not to be, the answer to human rights concerns. Supported neither by international law nor by independent moral analysis, cultural relativism exhibits strong discriminatory overtones and is to a large extent mistaken in its factual assumptions.

I also demonstrated that regardless of its historical origins, the international law of human rights cannot mean one thing to the West and another to the Third World. International human rights law embodies the imperfect yet inspired response of the international community to a growing awareness of the uniqueness of the human being and the unity of the human race. It also represents an eloquent body of norms condemning the effects of organized societal oppression of individuals. Fortunately, the Third World is now starting to play a role in the process of universalizing human rights. The significance of its new role will increase when governing elites cease to use authoritarian traditions as a shield against legitimate demands for basic human rights. ▲

CROSS-CULTURAL DIALOGUE

In stating his position against normative cultural relativism, Tesón repeatedly makes reference to international law and international agreements or accords, such as the UDHR. Rights theorists have often appealed to such laws or agreements with one of two emphases: universalism or internationalism. A universalist approach focuses on how human rights are applicable to all humans, regardless of when or where they live and their particular citizenship. The point is that human rights pertain to humans—all humans—as individuals. This is the understanding of human rights for Tesón, who, as we have seen, speaks explicitly of the universalizability of (some) moral discourse. Under such a view, international law does not necessarily create human rights but recognizes and codifies them in a global context. When nations sign on to, say, the UDHR, they are not granting human rights to their citizens; they are declaring their recognition of and commitment to upholding those universal human rights that their citizens have (as humans).

An internationalist approach to human rights, however, focuses on international politics and international law as establishing rights for their citizens, where those rights are in accord with international conceptions and practices regarding such rights. In large part, the universalist/internationalist distinction is like the legal/moral rights distinction discussed in Chapter 3, but in a global context with nation states as the primary players.

In the reading below, Sudanese legal scholar Abdullahi Ahmed An-Na'im argues for a third way of addressing human rights globally, which he refers to as a cross-cultural approach. This approach is not quite universalist because An-Na'im does not insist that the content of human rights is necessarily the same across different cultures, although he does not deny that individuals have some moral, or extralegal, rights. Nor is it quite an internationalist approach because he does not insist on the codification of laws with common content across nations. Instead, his cross-cultural approach is pragmatic, arguing that neither universal standards, which hold regardless of cultural context, nor international law, which imposes legal regulations and sanctions across borders, provide the best means of securing the flourishing and well-being of individuals. Rather than universalizing or internationalizing the moral regulation of behavior (which is what rights are meant to do), an internalizing of moral values and practices that will secure people's rights is most useful. For An-Na'im, such internalization occurs, or will occur, when there is cross-cultural dialogue that recognizes and appreciates differences among cultures (as opposed to universalism), while at the same time not imposing values (as internationalism does), but convincing people among different cultures that there exist moral rights that pertain to all humans. As he states at the outset, "[P]eople are more likely to observe normative propositions if they believe them to be sanctioned by their own cultural traditions." If people can be convinced, not told or directed, that certain regulations of behavior are good and consistent with their other values, then they are much more likely to embrace those regulations. If the goal is to enhance the well-being of persons, and rights are seen as a means of doing that, then the pragmatic emphasis of cross-cultural dialogue is to start with the views and values that people hold and then engage in respectful and thoughtful dialogue with them so that they internalize the importance of rights. This approach is a sort of bottom-up approach, as opposed to the top-down approach of passing legislation at the level of world bodies (internationalism) or insisting that there are commonalities that trump differences (universalism). Such an approach is not an abandonment of human rights, that is, rights pertaining to all humans; it is merely, for An-Na'im, the most fruitful and realistic approach to take in trying to secure them. As he puts it, "I believe not only that universal cultural legitimacy is necessary, but also that it is possible to develop it retrospectively in relation to fundamental human rights through enlightened interpretations of cultural norms."

As part of his argument in favor of a cross-cultural dialogue approach to human rights, An-Na'im discusses the particular example of the right to be free of cruel, inhuman, and degrading treatment or punishment. If anything is a human right, he says, this would be an ideal example, and it is one that is included in numerous international rights accords. One issue connected to this basic human right, however, is the understanding of what exactly counts as cruel, inhuman, or degrading treatment or punishment. For An-Na'im, it is simply a nonstarter to try to give an interpretation of this right in the absence of people's cultural traditions and values. For example, most Muslims would approach the interpretation of this right (and any other one) from the perspective of Shari'ah (religious Islamic law, which An-Na'im explains below). Most Muslims and Muslim regimes will simply not take seriously an account of cruel, inhuman, or degrading treatment or punishment that is not consistent with Shari'ah, just as many Americans would not take seriously an account of it that was not consistent with the U.S. Constitution. This is not obstinacy; rather it is just the factual background and starting point for both groups. Returning to the broad issue of cultural relativism, such a cross-cultural dialogue approach recognizes, for An-Na'im, the obvious fact of such relativism, while not conflating descriptive and normative cultural relativism. This approach begins from the assumption that, in fact, different cultural traditions regulate behavior in different ways, to attain different goals, for different reasons. However, the approach sees this as the starting point, not necessarily the ending point. Through dialogue, cross-cultural consensus could well be attained, possibly even international or universal consensus. These types of consensus are more likely to be attained via this approach, he claims, and if they are, they will be the result of internalization by people in different cultures, so they will more likely be truly adopted and embraced. Here is An-Na'im in his own words:

ABDULLAHI AHMED AN-NA'IM, "TOWARD A CROSS-CULTURAL APPROACH TO DEFINING INTERNATIONAL STANDARDS OF HUMAN RIGHTS"*

The general thesis of my approach is that, since people are more likely to observe normative propositions if they believe them to be sanctioned by their own cultural traditions, observance of human rights standards can be improved through the enhancement of the cultural legitimacy of those standards. The claim that all the existing human rights standards already enjoy universal cultural legitimacy may be weak from a historical point of view in the sense that many cultural traditions in the world have had little say in the formulation of those standards. Nevertheless, I believe not only that universal cultural legitimacy is necessary, but also that it is possible to develop it retrospectively in relation to fundamental human rights through enlightened interpretations of cultural norms.

Given the extreme cultural diversity of the world community, it can be argued that human rights should be founded on the existing least common denominator among these cultural traditions. On the other hand, restricting international human rights to those accepted by prevailing perceptions of the values and norms of the major cultural traditions of the world would not only limit these rights and reduce their scope, but also exclude extremely vital rights. Therefore, expanding the area and quality of agreement among the cultural traditions of the world may be necessary to provide the foundation for the widest possible range and scope of human rights. I believe this can be accomplished through the proposed approach to universal cultural legitimacy of human rights.

The cultural legitimacy thesis accepts the existing international standards while seeking to enhance their cultural legitimacy within the major traditions of the world through internal dialogue and struggle to establish enlightened perceptions and interpretations of cultural values and norms. Having achieved an adequate level of legitimacy *within* each tradition, through this internal stage, human rights scholars and

---

*In *Human Rights in Cross-Cultural Perspectives: A Quest for Consensus*, ed. Abdullahi Ahmed An-Na'im (Philadelphia: University of Pennsylvania Press, 1992), 19–43.

advocates should work for *cross-cultural* legitimacy, so that peoples of diverse cultural traditions can agree on the meaning, scope, and methods of implementing these rights. Instead of being content with the existing least common denominator, I propose to broaden and deepen universal consensus on the formulation and implementation of human rights through internal reinterpretation of, and cross-cultural dialogue about, the meaning and implications of basic human values and norms. . . .

Culture is . . . the source of the individual and communal world view: it provides both the individual and the community with the values and interests to be pursued in life, as well as the legitimate means for pursuing them. It stipulates the norms and values that contribute to people's perception of their self-interest and the goals and methods of individual and collective struggles for power within a society and between societies. As such, culture is a primary force in the socialization of individuals and a major determinant of the consciousness and experience of the community. The impact of culture on human behavior is often underestimated precisely because it is so powerful and deeply embedded in our self-identity and consciousness.

Our culture is so much a part of our personality that we normally take for granted that our behavior patterns and relationships to other persons and to society become the ideal norm. The subtlety of the impact of culture on personality and character may be explained by the analogy of the eye: we tend to take the world to be what our eyes convey to us without "seeing" the eye and appreciating its role. In this case, the information conveyed by the eye is filtered and interpreted by the mind without the individual's conscious awareness of this fact. Culture influences, first, the way we see the world and, further, how we interpret and react to the information we receive.

The analogy may also explain our ethnocentricity, the tendency to regard one's own race or social group as the model of human experience. Ethnocentricity does not mean that there is no conflict and tension between a person and his or her own culture, or between various classes and groups within a society. It rather incorporates such conflict and tension in the ideal model, leading us to perceive the conflict and tension we have within our own culture as part of the norm. For example, some feminists in one cultural tradition may assume that women in other cultures have (or ought to have) the same conflicts and tensions with their societies and are seeking (or ought to seek) the same answers. . . .

Cultural relativism has been charged with neutralizing moral judgment and thereby impairing action against injustice. According to one author [I. C. Jarvie], "It has these objectionable consequences: namely, that by limiting critical assessment of human works it disarms us, dehumanizes us, leaves us unable to enter into communicative interaction; that is to say, unable to criticize cross-culturally, cross-sub-culturally; intimately, relativism leaves no room for criticism at all . . . behind relativism nihilism looms." Some writers on human rights are suspicious of a cultural relativism that denies to individuals the moral right to make comparisons and to insist on universal standards of right and wrong. . . .

In my view, the merits of a reasonable degree of cultural relativism are obvious, especially when compared to claims of universalism that are in fact based on the claimant's rigid and exclusive ethnocentricity. The charge that it may breed tolerance of injustice is a serious one, however. . . . Morality may be universal in the sense that all cultures have it, but that does not in any way indicate the *content* of that morality, or provide criteria for judgment or for action by members of that culture or other cultures. The least common denominator of the universality of morality must include some of its basic precepts and not be confined to the mere existence of some form of morality. Moreover, in accordance with the logic of cultural relativism, the shared moral values must be authentic and not imposed from the outside. As indicated earlier, the existing least common denominator may not be enough to accommodate certain human rights. This fact would suggest the need to broaden and deepen common values to support these human rights. This process, however, must be culturally legitimate with reference to the norms and mechanisms of change within a particular culture. . . .

I would emphasize that, in this age of self-determination, sensitivity to cultural relativity is vital for the international protection and promotion of human rights. This point does not preclude cross-cultural moral judgment and action, but it prescribes the best ways of formulating and expressing judgment and of undertaking action. As [anthropologist Clifford] Geertz states, morality and knowledge cannot be placed beyond culture. In intercultural relations, morality and knowledge cannot be the exclusive product of some cultures but not of others. The validity of cross-cultural moral judgment increases with the degree of universality of the values upon which it is based; further, the efficacy of action increases with the degree of the actor's sensitivity to the internal logic and frame of reference of other cultures. . . .

Although human rights require action within each country for their implementation, the present international human rights regime has been conceived and is intended to operate within the framework of international relations. . . . As applied to cooperation in the protection and promotion of human rights . . . developing cross-cultural consensus in support of treaties and compacts is desirable. Cultural diversity, however, is unavoidable as the product of significant past and present economic, social, and environmental differences. It is also desirable as the expression of the right to self-determination and as the manifestation of distinctive self-identity. Nevertheless, I believe that a sufficient degree of cultural consensus regarding the goals and methods of cooperation in the protection and promotion of human rights can be achieved through internal cultural discourse and cross-cultural dialogue. Internal discourse relates to the struggle to establish enlightened perceptions and interpretations of cultural values and norms. Cross-cultural dialogue should be aimed at broadening and deepening international (or rather intercultural) consensus. This direction may include support for the proponents of enlightened perceptions and interpretations within a culture. This effort, however, must be sensitive to the internal nature of the struggle, endeavoring to emphasize internal values and norms rather than external ones. . . .

The object of internal discourse and cross-cultural dialogue is to agree on a body of beliefs to guide action in support of human rights in spite of disagreement on the justification of those beliefs. . . . Total agreement on the interpretation and application of . . . practical conclusions may not be possible, however, because disagreement about their justification will probably be reflected in the way they are interpreted and applied. We should therefore be realistic in our expectations and pursue the maximum possible degree of agreement at whatever level it can be achieved. This approach can be illustrated by the following case study of the meaning of the human right "not to be subjected to cruel, inhuman or degrading treatment or punishment."

Some international human rights instruments stipulate that "no one shall be subjected to torture or to cruel, inhuman or degrading treatment or punishment." There is obvious overlap between the two main parts of this right, that is to say, between protection against torture and protection against inhuman or degrading treatment or punishment. For example, torture has been described as constituting "an aggravated and deliberate form of cruel, inhuman or degrading treatment or punishment." Nevertheless, there are differences between the two parts of the right. According to the definition of torture adopted in United Nations instruments, it "does not include pain or suffering arising from, inherent in or incidental to lawful sanctions." As explained below, this qualification is not supposed to apply to the second part of the right. In other words, lawful sanctions can constitute "cruel, inhuman or degrading treatment or punishment."

The following discussion will focus on the meaning of the second part of the right, that is to say, the meaning of the right not to be subjected to cruel, inhuman or degrading treatment or punishment. In particular, I will address the question of how to identify the criteria by which lawful sanctions can be held to violate the prohibition of cruel, inhuman or degrading treatment or punishment. The case of the Islamic punishments will be used to illustrate the application of the cross-cultural perspective to this question. . . .

Some predominantly Muslim countries, such as Afghanistan and Egypt, have already ratified the 1984 Convention [Against Torture, and Other Cruel, Inhuman or Degrading Treatment or Punishment]; others may wish to do so in the future. The meaning of cruel, inhuman, or degrading treatment or punishment in Islamic cultures, however, may be significantly, if not radically, different from the perceptions of the meaning in the clause in other parts of the world.

Islamic law, commonly known as Shari'ah, is based on the Qur'an, which Muslims believe to be the literal and final word of God, and on Sunna, or traditions of the Prophet Muhammad. Using these sources, as well as pre-Islamic customary practices of the Middle East which were not explicitly repudiated by Qur'an and Sunna, Muslim jurists developed Shari'ah as a comprehensive ethical and legal system between the seventh and ninth centuries AD. To Muslim communities, however, the Qur'an and Sunna were always believed to be absolutely binding as a matter of faith and were applied in individual and communal practice from the very beginning. Shari'ah codes were never formally enacted, but the jurists systematized and rationalized what was already accepted as the will of God, and developed techniques for interpreting divine sources and for supplementing their provisions where they were silent.

Due to the religious nature of Shari'ah, Muslim jurists did not distinguish among devotional, ethical, social, and legal aspects of the law, let alone among various types of legal norms. The equivalent of penal or criminal law would therefore have to be extracted from a wide range of primary sources. For the purposes of this discussion, Islamic criminal law may be briefly explained as follows. Criminal offenses are classified into three main categories: *hudud, jinayat,* and *ta'zir. Hudud* are a very limited group of offenses which are strictly defined and punished by the express terms of the Qur'an and/or Sunna. These include *sariqa,* or theft, which is punishable by the amputation of the right hand, and *zina,* or fornication, which is punishable by whipping of one hundred lashes for an unmarried offender and stoning to death for a married offender. *Jinayat* are homicide and causing bodily harm, which are punishable by *qisas,* or exact retribution (an eye for an eye) or payment of monetary compensation. The term *ta'zir* means to reform or rectify. *Ta'zir* offenses are those created and punished by the ruler in exercising his power to protect private and public interests.

It is important to emphasize that the following discussion addresses this question in a purely theoretical sense and should not be taken to condone the application of these punishments by any government in the Muslim world today. The question being raised is: Are Muslims likely to accept the repudiation of these punishments *as a matter of Islamic law* or the ground that they are cruel, inhuman, or degrading? This question should not be confused with the very important but distinct issue of whether these punishments have been or are being applied legitimately and in accordance with all the general and specific requirements of Islamic law. . . .

The basic question here is one of interpretation and application of a universally accepted human right. In terms of the principle . . . —agreement on "practical conclusions" in spite of disagreement on their justification—Muslims would accept the human right not to be subjected to cruel, inhuman, or degrading treatment or punishment. Their Islamic culture may indicate to them a different interpretation of this human right, however.

From a secular or humanist point of view, inflicting such a severe permanent punishment for any offense, especially for theft, is obviously cruel and inhuman, and probably also degrading. This may well be the private intuitive reaction of many educated modernized Muslims. However, to the vast majority of Muslims, the matter is settled by the categorical will of God as expressed in the Qur'an and, as such, is not open to question by human beings. Even the educated modernized Muslim, who may be privately repelled by this punishment, cannot risk the consequences of openly questioning the will of God. In addition to the danger of losing his or her faith and the probability of severe social chastisement, a Muslim who disputes the binding authority of the Qur'an is liable to the death penalty for apostasy (heresy) under Shari'ah.

Thus, in all Muslim societies, the possibility of human judgment regarding the appropriateness or cruelty of a punishment decreed by God is simply out of the question. Furthermore, this belief is supported by what Muslims accept as rational arguments. From the religious point of view, human life does not end at death, but extends beyond that to the next life. In fact, religious sources strongly emphasize that the next life is the true and ultimate reality, to which this life is merely a prelude. In the next *eternal* life, every human being will stand judgment and suffer the consequences of his or her actions in this life. A religiously sanctioned punishment, however, will absolve an offender from punishment in the next life because God does not punish twice for the same offense. . . .

Neither internal Islamic reinterpretation nor cross-cultural dialogue is likely to lead to the total abolition of this punishment as a matter of Islamic law. Much can be done, however, to restrict its implementation in practice. For example, there is room for developing stronger general social and economic prerequisites and stricter procedural requirements for the enforcement of the punishment. Islamic religious texts emphasize extreme caution in inflicting any criminal punishment. The Prophet said that if there is any doubt (*shubba*), the Qur'anic punishments should not be imposed. He also said that it is better to err on the side of refraining from imposing the punishment than to err on the side of imposing it in a doubtful case. Although these directives have already been incorporated into definitions of the offenses and the applicable rules of evidence and procedure, it is still possible to develop a broader concept of *shubba* to include, for example, psychological disorders as a defense against criminal responsibility. For instance, kleptomania may be taken as *shubba* barring punishment for theft. Economic need may also be a defense against a charge of theft. . . .

I believe that in the final analysis, the interpretation and practical application of the protection against cruel, inhuman, or degrading treatment or punishment in the context of a particular society should be determined by the moral standards of that society. I also believe that there are many legitimate ways of influencing and informing the moral standards of a society. To dictate to a society is both unacceptable as a matter of principle and unlikely to succeed in practice. Cross-cultural dialogue and mutual influence, however, is acceptable in principle and continuously occurring in practice. To harness the power of cultural legitimacy in support of human rights, we need to develop techniques for internal cultural discourse and cross-cultural dialogue, and to work toward establishing general conditions conducive to constructive discourse and dialogue. . . .

I have deliberately chosen the question of whether lawful sanctions can be condemned as cruel, inhuman, or degrading punishment or treatment in order to illustrate both the need for a cross-cultural approach to defining human rights standards and the difficulty of implementing this approach. The question presents human rights advocates with a serious dilemma. On the one hand, it is necessary to safeguard the personal integrity and human dignity of the individual against excessive or harsh punishments. The fundamental objective of the modern human rights movement is to protect citizens from the brutality and excesses of their own governments. On the other hand, it is extremely important to be sensitive to the dangers of cultural imperialism, whether it is a product of colonialism, a tool of international economic exploitation and political subjugation, or simply a product of extreme ethnocentricity. Since we would not accept others' imposing their moral standards on us, we should not impose our own moral standards on them. In any case, external imposition is normally counterproductive and unlikely to succeed in changing the practice in question. External imposition is not the only option available to human rights advocates, however. Greater consensus on international standards for the protection of the individual against cruel, inhuman, or degrading treatment or punishment can be achieved through internal cultural discourse and cross-cultural dialogue. ▲

Questions for Discussion

1. Lee claims that attempts by agents outside of a particular cultural tradition to change its values and practices constitute cultural imperialism. Is this correct? Does this view imply that any unwelcome influence by outside cultures constitutes cultural imperialism? To whom would it need to be unwelcome to constitute imperialism: the ruling regime, all citizens? Would this justify, say, a government's blocking Internet sites because the regime in office thinks they constitute an unwelcome cultural presence?

2. Tesón argues that there is an important distinction between descriptive and prescriptive (or normative) cultural relativism. Is he correct? If, as he claims, there are universal human rights, and they are violated by a particular regime in some culture, would other nations, then, be justified in taking action to enforce the recognition and protection of those rights in that culture?

3. An-Na'im says that cross-cultural dialogue is a genuine third approach to human rights (as opposed to universalism and internationalism). In what meaningful ways is it actually an alternative? Is he correct to say that his approach is more effective in promoting human rights than either universalism or internationalism? If not, why? If so, why do so many countries and regimes sign off on international rights accords? Also, how would implementation of human rights agreements be effected under a cross-cultural dialogue approach, especially if there is not much consensus across cultures on the content of rights?

4. Do the concerns raised about group rights, particularly groups as rights holders, also apply to cultures as rights holders? Indeed, can cultures be rights holders? If not, why? If so, can they also be rights audiences and bear duties to other rights-holding agents? If they cannot, why? If they can, how are the rights of cultures and of other rights-holding agents balanced (especially if they conflict)?

5. Chapter 6 raises a number of concerns communitarians have about the strident nature of rights talk and the overreliance on rights in addressing moral matters and conflicts. Do those concerns apply with respect to global rights discourse? Why or why not?

6. Do any conceptions of the nature of rights from Chapter 1 seem particularly relevant or irrelevant to concerns about global rights discourse? For example, Martha Nussbaum claims that rights are related to basic capabilities.

Are those capabilities culturally varied? Are they culturally determined? Or, in Chapter 2, Alan Dershowitz claims that the acts that count as injustices are clear and obvious, even if the nature of rights is not. Are injustices culturally relative?

7. Which perspectives for justifying rights covered in Chapter 2 best make sense of universal human rights? Which make most sense with the internationalist approach to human rights across boundaries or the adoption and implementation of international law as human rights instruments? Which seem more consistent with Lee's cultural relativist position? Which are more consistent with An-Na'im's cross-cultural dialogue view?

Further Reading

An-Na'im, Abdullahi Ahmed, ed. *Human Rights in Cross-Cultural Perspectives.* Philadelphia: University of Pennsylvania Press, 1995. A fine collection of essays on rights from multiple cultural perspectives.

Brysk, Alison, ed. *Globalization and Human Rights.* Berkeley: University of California Press, 2002. A collection of essays focusing on specific aspects of the globalization of rights, such as citizenship, cooperation, and communication.

Claude, Richard Pierre, and Burns H. Weston, eds. *Human Rights in the World Community: Issues and Action.* Philadelphia: University of Pennsylvania Press, 1992. A collection of essays focusing on global and international approaches and implementation of rights.

Donnelly, Jack. *International Human Rights.* Boulder, CO: Westview, 1993. A sustained analysis of rights, with an emphasis on political implementation and policies.

———. *Universal Human Rights in Theory and Practice.* 2nd ed. Ithaca, NY: Cornell University Press, 2002. An analysis of the nature of human rights, with particular emphasis on the issues of cultural relativism and international practices.

Evans, Robert, and Alice Frazer Evans, eds. *Human Rights: A Dialogue Between the First and Third Worlds.* Maryknoll, NY: Orbis Books, 1983. A collection of essays and commentaries on specific rights issues and cases in particular countries.

Forsythe, David P. *The Internationalization of Human Rights.* Lexington, KY: Lexington Books, 1991. An analysis of human rights within international law and practice.

Hsiung, James C., ed. *Human Rights in East Asia: A Cultural Perspective.* New York: Paragon House, 1985. A collection of essays focusing on the understanding and implementation of human rights in East Asian countries.

Lauren, Paul Gordon. *The Evolution of International Human Rights: Visions Seen.* Philadelphia: University of Pennsylvania Press, 2003. A sustained historical analysis of the emergence and transformation of human rights in global contexts.

Rouner, Leroy S., ed. *Human Rights and the World's Religions.* Notre Dame, IN: University of Notre Dame Press, 1988. A collection of essays analyzing rights from the perspectives of major world religions.

CHAPTER 8

RIGHT TO FREE EXPRESSION

In 1984, Gregory Lee Johnson burned an American flag in front of the Dallas, Texas, city hall, as a means of protest against the policies of Ronald Reagan's administration. Tried and convicted under a Texas law outlawing flag desecration, Johnson was sentenced to one year in jail and assessed a $2,000 fine. After the Texas Court of Criminal Appeals reversed the conviction, the state of Texas then appealed the case again, and in 1989 it went to the U.S. Supreme Court. The question put to the Court was whether desecration of the U.S. flag (by burning or some other method) was a matter of free speech, hence protected by the First Amendment to the U.S. Constitution. In a 5–4 vote, the Court ruled that Johnson's actions fell into the category of expressive conduct and had a distinctively political nature. The fact that an audience finds certain ideas or expression offensive, the Court found, does not justify prohibitions of speech. The Court also held that state officials did not have the authority to designate symbols to communicate only limited sets of messages: "If there is a bedrock principle underlying the First Amendment, it is that the Government may not prohibit the expression of an idea simply because society finds the idea itself offensive or disagreeable." In direct response to this case (*Texas v. Johnson*), the U.S. Congress passed the Flag Protection Act of 1989. The following year, however, the Supreme Court, in the case of *United States v. Eichman*, also struck down that law, on the same grounds that it violated the First Amendment.

During 2005 and 2006 a group of individuals from the Westboro Baptist Church, located in Topeka, Kansas, traveled the country, shouting at grieving family members at the funerals of soldiers and displaying such signs as "Thank God for Dead Soldiers," "God Blew Up the Troops," and "God Hates Fag Enablers." They were protesting what they saw as the corruption of morals in the United States, particularly regarding a tolerant attitude toward homosexuality, including the military's "Don't Ask, Don't Tell" policy. After such a protest at the funeral of Lance Corporal Matthew Snyder in Westminster, Maryland, the family of the deceased soldier sued Fred Phelps, founder and leader of the Westboro Baptist Church. An initial verdict supporting the Snyder family was overturned by an appeals court, which even required the Snyder family to pay Phelps's court costs. The appeals decision was based on the First Amendment protection of free speech.

In early 2010, the Oregon House of Representatives repealed a 1923 state law banning public school teachers from wearing headscarves and other religious dress in school. While the original state law was designed to keep Catholic nuns from teaching in public schools in Oregon, the spark that led to the repeal of this law came from a female Muslim math teacher, who wore a headscarf. The debate in the Oregon House focused as much on free expression as it did on religious freedom, with supporters of the repeal citing language in the state constitution declaring, "No law shall be passed restraining the free expression of opinion."

Clearly, these three cases all have in common their relevance to the right to free speech, or, more accurately, free expression. Most people take the right to free expression as fundamental, a social given, as it were. They do so not only because it is built into the U.S. Constitution—which, of course, it is, in the First Amendment—that is, because it is a legal right, but also because it is taken as a basic human right. Without such a right, they say, many other rights could not be exercised or enjoyed. Nonetheless, as everyone recognizes, the right to free expression is not absolute; there are constraints and limitations on this right—again, not only in a legal but also in a moral sense. That is, everyone recognizes that there are appropriate constraints and limitations on the right to free expression. For example, we understand why you cannot yell "Fire!" in a crowded theater; that is, it is appropriate to constrain a person's freedom of expression if exercising that freedom creates a "clear and present danger." In addition, most everyone recognizes the legitimacy of restricting a person's freedom of expression in cases of libel or slander. (Libel is a matter of issuing false statements about an individual to a third party, in written or broadcast form, that harm the individual's personal or business reputation and go beyond being offensive, objectionable, and insulting. Slander, on the other hand, is defamation by spoken communication.) Although people recognize and embrace some constraints and limitations on free expression, the important question is, What justifies such constraints and limitations? Perhaps libel should not be a ground for constraining speech! Perhaps the freedom to express moral outrage at someone's funeral should be trumped by other moral values or by some other basic right. (Indeed, in the Snyder case above, the family argued that the religious protesters had violated their privacy rights.) What, then, does justify not only constraints and limitations on free expression but also the very right of free expression itself?

Before we address this question head on, some preliminary points must be made. The right to free expression includes, but is actually broader than, the right to free speech. People can and do express themselves nonverbally, that is, in ways other than through words. Wearing a religious symbol, for example, can be a form of nonverbal expression, as is silently burning a flag. Burning a cross in one's yard or wearing a Nazi armband is a form of nonverbal expression. The point is that, although the First Amendment explicitly refers to "free speech," it is really the broader notion of freedom of expression that people understand as valuable and in need of protection.

Philosophers often call one aspect of the relationship between expression and speech "speech acts," referring to the notion that there are various types and levels of meaning. Basically, people often perform an action with speech that is beyond the simple act of speaking. For example, in normal contexts, when someone says, "I promise to take you to the airport on Monday," that person has done something more than simply say some words—that person has performed the act of promising. Or if a teacher remarks, "I suggest you look very closely at the material on pages five to fifteen in chapter one of our textbook," that teacher has more than issued an utterance—she has made a suggestion. She has performed a speech act. This common phenomenon is the basis for our ability to, say, praise or insult someone. We all recognize that the same words—such as, "That's a nice shirt"—can be said sincerely or sarcastically. We also recognize that language has different types of meaning. Consider the following case: You are late to class, and as you race into the classroom, you stumble and fall on the floor. Someone says, "Nice play, Shakespeare!" This situation involves various types of meaning. One is the literal meaning of the words: "Nice play, Shakespeare" means something different from "Today is cloudy." Besides the literal meaning of those words, there is the speaker's meaning, that is, what the person meant by those words. In this case, perhaps the person was trying to be funny and tease you about your clumsiness. What the *person* means might well differ from what the *words* mean. (This is why sarcasm works; the words mean one thing, but the person means quite the opposite.) In addition, there is the meaning of the utterance for the receiver of the words. In this case, even if the person meant only to tease you, you might be so embarrassed that you feel insulted and angry; you do not take the remark as teasing. The meaning for you is (perhaps) quite different from that intended by the speaker. So, in this situation, if someone asked, "What was just expressed?" various responses would be appropriate: the meaning literally expressed, that intended, and that received.

Now, the important point regarding this case, and speech acts in general, is that many philosophers argue that no sharp division exists between speech and conduct. Expression—what is expressed—blends, or is a middle ground between, pure speech and pure action (if there is such a thing as pure speech or pure action). If this is so, then when considering what would justify constraints and limitations on free expression, we should treat speech as a form of conduct and consider what would justify constraints and limitations on a person's behavior (or actions). We turn to this issue now. However, first we must note that many people reject this blending of speech and conduct, claiming there is an important distinction between the two, even if there is no "bright line" or sharp division between them. By way of analogy, although there is no sharp division between night and day, but a gradual blending from one to the other, it does not follow that there is no distinction. After all, midnight is very different from noon, even if it is not clear or obvious whether dusk is night or day. This issue is crucial to the regulation of speech, and we consider it more fully later in this chapter when we turn to the issue of hate speech. For now, we consider arguments that have been given to justify either protecting free expression or constraining it.

MARKETPLACE OF IDEAS

Probably the most common argument given to justify the importance of free expression cites the "marketplace of ideas." The claim is that allowing free expression is the best means to get at truth. If people are free to express themselves, then those expressions with the greatest credibility will over time "win" in the marketplace of ideas. On the other hand, if ideas are stifled, then the truth is less likely to be recognized and attained. So, even if allowing people freedom of expression results in offensive, unwise, or downright crazy expressions of belief, people will be in a position to decide among those various expressions. The assumption is that if certain views are simply silly, they will be recognized as such and seen to be untrue. Stifling or censoring expression, however, will not lead to truth; indeed, one of the first efforts by people or governments to constrain freedom of action is to stifle and censor free expression.

Supporters of the claim that the marketplace of ideas will yield truth also say that the social exchange of ideas is the best means toward self-development. If exposed to different ideas and expressions, people are in a better position to learn for themselves how to assess and evaluate different claims. Freedom of expression, then, is important both for individuals and for society at large. Nothing is more fundamental to democracy, supporters argue, than freedom of expression. After all, if we cannot assume that people are able to assess and evaluate different ideas and claims, then how can we assume they are able to choose their representatives or political leaders?

Nonetheless, some people have rejected the marketplace-of-ideas view. It is not obvious, they claim, that truth (or even beneficial outcomes) will necessarily result from unconstrained freedom of expression. As they sometimes remark, the result can be market failure. The marketplace of ideas, they say, might only result in acceptance of the most comfortable beliefs, rather than true ones. The ideas that "win" in the marketplace might simply be those broadcast the loudest and most often. They point to political campaigns and commercial advertisements as examples that support this view. Politicians want your vote and will say whatever they think will get it! Instead of raising the difficult and unpleasant issues that must be faced, they will use empty slogans, catchwords, and sound bites to persuade you to vote for them. Likewise, commercial advertisements will say whatever will get you to buy a certain product, not necessarily providing full disclosure about it. So, say these critics, freedom of expression is of course important and extremely valuable, but unconstrained freedom of expression does not necessarily lead to truth or self-development. Some ideas are simply harmful, and those need oversight. In a democracy, such oversight can be achieved via the laws enacted and via the courts.

RESTRICTIONS ON EXPRESSION

Even the strongest advocates of freedom of expression acknowledge that some restrictions are appropriate and justified. The most common (proposed) justification for such restriction is the "harm principle," which, simply put, says that one person's freedoms may legitimately be restrained in order to prevent harm to others. People should be free to do or say whatever they want as long as what they do or say does not harm someone else. In the language of rights, you can do or say whatever you want as long as you do not infringe on the rights of others (i.e., harm them in the sense of infringing on their rights).

Although the harm principle seems straightforward and reasonable, it raises a number of questions and concerns. First, there is the question of what "harm" means. There is the obvious sense of physical harm. So, people do not get to kill, beat, or in some other way physically harm others. However, what about other forms of harm? Is psychological harm covered by the harm principle? For example, if one person stalks or verbally harasses or abuses, but never physically touches, another person, is that behavior covered under the harm principle? (The section below on hate speech focuses on this issue.) It is not enough simply to say that there are laws in place to prevent or restrict harassing behavior, because the issue is whether there is a justification for limiting such behavior (and for having such laws). Pointing to laws that exist only moves the question back, because then the question becomes whether those laws are justified in limiting someone's liberty. So, the first question about the harm principle entails what exactly "harm" means (and what cases of people's behavior would come under the label of "harm")?

Another concern with the harm principle is whether it is meant to cover only *actual* harm caused or it is also meant to prevent *potential* harm. For example, speed-limit laws that regulate driving are set up not simply to limit actual harm but to prevent it. That is, a person can have his liberty limited—for instance, by getting a fine or a ticket or losing his driver's license—not because he has actually harmed someone by speeding or driving recklessly but because his actions were potentially harmful. The point of such laws as speed-limit laws is to prevent actual harm before it happens, and people's liberty is limited on the basis of merely potential harm. The problem here is that it is extremely difficult to identify potential harm and which potential harms may be appropriately limited, since just about anything could be potentially harmful or used in a potentially harmful way. There is the potential for harm any time anyone gets in a car, not just when someone is speeding.

A third concern about the harm principle has to do with harm that results not because someone does something (such as hitting someone) but because someone does *not* do something. These are said to be cases of omission. For example, if one person sees a second person drowning and could easily help or rescue that drowning person, but simply chooses not to, has that first person harmed the second one?

These various questions about the harm principle focus on whether it is a good basis for legitimately limiting the freedom of persons, including their freedom of expression. Many people have claimed that even if these questions can be answered acceptably, other concerns and principles should be used to limit liberty. One such principle, called the "offense principle," states that in some situations the offense to others is justification enough for limiting someone else's liberty. For example, if a man stalking a woman is not literally harming her, at the minimum his behavior is annoying and offensive (and perhaps even threatening). Likewise, it is said, people who are being extremely loud or shrill in some situations should have their liberty limited, which is exactly what the Snyder family claimed with respect to the funeral protesters mentioned at the beginning of this chapter.

As already noted, even the strongest supporters of free expression recognize that there are some legitimate constraints and limitations to it. You might have the right to express your views, but you do not have the (legal) right to force your way into my home to do so. Nor do you have the legal right to stand in the middle of a grocery store, which is private property, and shout them. In legal terms, such restrictions are referred to as "time, manner, and place" restrictions. For instance, time restrictions might permit a local government to ban public demonstrations during rush hour within city limits. Courts have used place restrictions to limit how close protesters can be to, say, an abortion clinic. Manner restrictions focus on the mode of expression. For example, protesting in the nude in a public park could be restricted.

With respect to the content of expression, there is a long legal history of constraints and limitations on what people are allowed to express. One type of content that is legally (if not morally) constrained is speech that poses a threat to national security. In the early twentieth century, the U.S. Congress passed the Sedition Act of 1918, which severely limited certain forms of speech involving national-security interests. While this act was later repealed, the broad issue of using national security as a basis for restricting and limiting speech has persisted. This is even more the case in many other countries.

Another broad form of expression that is limited, at least to some extent, is obscenity. This involves, of course, not just speech but images as well. Numerous court cases and laws have dealt with the issue of obscenity—not only materials that are sexual in nature but also "foul" language, such as comedian George Carlin's famous seven dirty words that may not be said on the airwaves.

Another form of "constraint" on free expression has involved not prohibiting but requiring it. For instance, the issue of "equal time" and the "fairness doctrine" involved legal requirements for broadcasters to provide the time and opportunity for different points of view to be transmitted on specific controversial issues deemed to be of public importance. While the "fairness doctrine" in its original form was later repealed, other forms of regulation are still in place. For instance, some commercial products, such as cigarettes, are required to post warning labels on their packages. The broad point here is that freedom of expression has in fact been constrained and limited in a number of ways; it is not, in legal practice, an absolute right.

THE CASE OF HATE SPEECH

A particular form of expression at the forefront of social and legal concern recently has been hate speech. In a legal sense, an act of hate speech is not the same thing as a hate crime. Hate crimes are acts that are already defined as crimes (e.g., property crimes, such as destroying someone's house) but in addition are motivated by bias against some group or individual due to characteristics such as race, gender, sexual orientation, or the like. In a word, they are said to be motivated by hatred. Hate speech, on the other hand, does not in itself involve an already-recognized crime. Proponents of hate speech legislation claim that hate speech should be prohibited and, in effect, treated as a criminal act. If there is no sharp division between speech and conduct, both being forms of expression, then hate speech, like hate crimes, should be constrained. Indeed, the kinds of expression referred to when people speak of hate speech include not only direct verbal attacks (such as "You filthy fag!") but also cross burnings, public displays or marches (such as the famous pro-Nazi march in Jewish areas of Skokie, Illinois), mock slave auctions on college campuses, and so forth.

On moral and rights grounds, proponents of hate speech curtailment argue that hate speech violates the harm principle. It harms people whether there is a direct, immediate target (as in cases where someone, say, yells a racist epithet at another person) or an indirect "group" target (as in cases where someone publishes sexist or antigay pamphlets). Not only does it cause emotional and psychological harm, say these proponents, but also it causes broad social harm because it perpetuates intolerance and lessens restraint on hate crimes. On legal grounds, these proponents claim that hate speech violates the Fourteenth Amendment of the U.S. Constitution, which guarantees equal protection of the law. These proponents say that this equal protection clause actually means equal citizenship and that hate speech, because it is targeted at specific individuals or groups, denies equal citizenship. Simply put, they say, hate speech violates civil rights.

Those who oppose hate speech regulation do so on several grounds. First, they insist that an act of hate speech is not the same thing as a hate crime. It is completely appropriate, they say, to regulate criminal action, but speech—regardless of how offensive it might be—is not a crime. In addition, they claim, it is not obvious that hate speech violates the harm principle. Some people can and do simply shrug off offensive hate speech. This is the attitude of "sticks and stones may break my bones, but words can never hurt me." Different sensibilities cannot be the basis for legislation, they say, especially legislation of such a fundamental right as free expression. Beyond that, say these supporters of free expression, curtailing hate speech puts everyone on a slippery slope toward government censorship of citizens and their right to free expression. Hate speech, they claim, might be offensive and repugnant, but the "cure" of censorship is worse. Social condemnation of hate speech, not governmental regulation, is what is needed.

In terms of broad legal actions related to hate speech, the first case that went to the U.S. Supreme Court was 1952's *Beauharnais v. Illinois*. Joseph Beauharnais was arrested for distributing racist (white supremacist) materials, violating a state law. The Supreme Court ruled that this constituted libel, not against any specific individual but against a group, and upheld Beauharnais's conviction. (While this particular case was never overturned by later Supreme Court rulings, it was, in effect, rendered invalid, as later rulings held that libel can only be applied to legal individuals, not to groups.)

A more famous case was 1992's *R.A.V. v. City of Saint Paul*, in which a group of teenagers had burned a cross on the lawn of a black neighbor, an action that violated a city ordinance. The city argued that this law appropriately banned such actions because they were, in effect, like "fighting words," that is, words (or expressions) likely to bring about a breach of peace. The U.S. Supreme Court ruled otherwise; the Court decided unanimously that the ordinance was discriminatory because it banned, say, offensive symbols such as Nazi swastikas only when they were used by proponents of racial and religious hatred, but not if or when they were used as part of a protest against Nazism. Obnoxious and offensive expression, as opposed to threatening expression, the Court said, is protected by the First Amendment.

Regardless of actual legal rulings, many people have argued that hate speech should be regulated. These rulings against such regulation, they say, are wrong; they fail to protect the security rights of persons by overemphasizing the freedom of expression. In the reading below, legal counsel and scholar Alexander Tsesis argues that hate speech should not be protected by the First Amendment. He claims that hate speech in itself harms the individuals and groups to whom it is addressed, as well as society as a whole. It is also, he says, a precursor to violent conduct. It has no redeeming value, as the intent of hate speech is to marginalize what he calls "outgroups." Because the intent of hate speech is to marginalize and degrade, its effect is not to add to the marketplace of ideas but rather to silence its targets. To that extent, it is anti-democratic. As Tsesis remarks, "A society cannot simultaneously cultivate discriminatory attitudes and be committed to protecting personal rights." Recognizing the general value of free speech requires, then, "narrowly tailored" laws that prohibit certain kinds of speech.

ALEXANDER TSESIS, *DESTRUCTIVE MESSAGES: HOW HATE SPEECH PAVES THE WAY FOR HARMFUL SOCIAL MOVEMENTS**

. . . [Representative] democracy should protect minority civil rights by enacting narrowly tailored laws prohibiting instigatory speech that substantially increases the likelihood of discrimination. Lawmakers should be cognizant of historically persecuted groups' concerns about messages that are purposefully spread to harm them, their families, and friends. It is naïve, or at least dismissive of historical realities, to believe that all propagandists who spread messages of hate and destruction, except those calling for immediate action, will be content with words.

The premises of hate speech contravene universal fair treatment; they are meant to mark certain persons as unworthy of sympathy; these persons become expendable means to advancing the interests of those holding power. This process seeks to invalidate minority aspirations and preferences. Outgroups are viewed as merely instrumental for others, their goals are considered unimportant. Hate speech is intolerant and therefore could never be part of a universal rule of reciprocal action.

Stereotypes do not reflect the truth even when they emerge victorious in the marketplace of ideas, as pro-slavery thought did in postimperial

*(New York: New York University Press, 2002), 169–179.

Germany. Since persons join societies to protect their fundamental rights and to reap the benefits of basic rights, a better test of truth is the extent to which speech seeks, discovers, and establishes institutions conducive for human rights to thrive. Bigots use derogatory cultural stereotypes to deny outgroups the very rights they find essential and which they expect others to honor. The right to self-expression does not trump other people's dignitary rights.

Destructive messages deny the personhood of minorities. They establish paradigms of thought that are meant to solicit a group's adherents to act inhumanely. Hate speech poses a threat to social stability and individual safety. Infringements of an individual's personhood are intrinsically unjust. The value of such denigrating speech is so low that it pales in comparison to the interests in life, liberty, and self-preservation which it tries to incite others to violate. While hate speech is shrouded in the democratic mantle of freedom of expression, it seeks to undermine a designated group's sense of personal integrity and civic assurance.

To illustrate this point, suppose that some people burn a cross in their community, set up a sign informing Jews they are unwelcome, or design an Internet site to instigate a race war. All of these acts, explicitly or subtly, let people know that they are unwelcome, that the acts are designed to terrorize them, and that other community members plan to shun and exclude them. With the added voice of charismatic leaders, devotees of misethnicity [institutionalized hatred of certain ethnic groups] become further entrenched in cultural ideologies. Once any social problem—for example, unemployment—is ideologically linked to a particular outgroup, demagogues can offer solutions whose fierceness is commensurate with how entrenched in a culture the evoked stereotypes are. . . .

A society cannot simultaneously cultivate discriminatory attitudes and be committed to protecting personal rights. Human integrity is guaranteed only by states where each individual's liberty is viewed as equally precious, no matter how powerful or powerless his or her race and ethnic group may be. Persons living in an organized society with formal laws and rules owe one another a reciprocal duty of humanitarian treatment. This cannot be achieved where persons treat others in ways they would find unfair if treated so themselves, and where hate propaganda is allowed to influence the development of social institutions. The quest for justice entails using reason to arrive at empathic and tolerant customs, rules, and regulations. The libertarian argument that minority rights can best be protected by uninhibited and unrestricted hate propaganda is counterintuitive given the long-term dangers associated with hate speech. Hate messages are opposed to the spirit of social contract theory, which requires respect for the rights of the contractees. Only when everyone's liberty interests are recognized is there hope of ending the sometimes deadly blights of racism and ethnocentrism. Identification with other people's dignity derives best from a cosmopolitan conception of human consciousness and the expression of empathy toward diverse individuals. . . .

Free speech is not an absolute right. It is constrained by the rights of others to enjoy their lives and liberties without fear of hate groups expostulating on their inferiority and advocating their enslavement, extinction, or disenfranchisement.

Recognizing ethnic differences is not, of course, in and of itself detrimental. In fact, celebrating diversity facilitates civil interactions. The danger arises when individuals disseminate legitimizing discourse in order to organize exclusionary movements.

Placing no limits on speech—not even on expressions blatantly intended to make life miserable for minorities—preserves the rights of speakers at the expense of targeted groups. One person's right of expression should not infringe on other people's rights. This is a chief principle behind limits on speech via defamation statutes, zoning regulations, and obscenity laws. Everyone's right to develop personally is equally important both to individuals and to society. Successful hate speech, which gains a broad following, has the potential to inhibit the targets from full self-realization and reduces the total available talents in the social pool of abilities. Spain, for instance, hurt itself culturally and economically by expelling its Jewish population in 1492. The Expulsion came after years of Inquisition propaganda, and hurt both the exiled Jews and the remaining Spanish population. Teachings by zealous preachers like Vincent Ferrer, a later-canonized Dominican monk, in the late fourteenth and early fifteenth centuries, brought on a nationwide anti-Jewish hysteria. By ridding the country of Jews, the Spanish monarchs, Ferdinand and Isabella, were carrying out the religious doctrines of the Inquisition. The economic consequences were grave. Many commercial enterprises in Seville and Barcelona, for instance, were ruined. . . . Anti-Jewish preaching in Spain influenced a wide social segment of the population, and the result was devastating both for the Jews who fled and for the country that renounced them on dogmatic grounds.

The composite good of a society is reduced by the publication of material intent upon instigating pain and suffering for a particular group. Adopting an unrestrictive point of view on free speech assumes the character of dogma, taking a right as an ultimate duty and ignoring the ultimate end of constitutional government, which is the well-being of all social members. Thus, when the speech of some social contractees interferes with the right of others to live contented lives, it is speech, and not the essential rights necessary for well-being, that must be limited.

Speech is not the end of social justice. The First Amendment does not protect all expressions. It is designed to maintain an open dialogue about individual rights and overall welfare. In and of itself, speech is a neutral mechanism that can just as easily promote fascism as democracy, or justify genocide as civil rights. Ideological declarations that create irrational prejudices will not protect other rights. Hate messages can sway attitudes by their congruity with accepted exclusionary social schemas and linguistic paradigms. They can impress themselves on avowed supremacists and can also recruit young neophytes who, when they become adults, will carry on the tradition of vertical racial and ethnic hierarchies. Misethnic speech increases the reaches and continuity of racism and ethnocentrism in society. The hatreds underlying traditional scapegoating will not always burgeon into action. For that, social strains have to be at a peak. But they will lie dormant until the season is right for the noxious ideas to bud into violence.

Harboring hate speakers poses a threat to personal liberties. It enervates the very democratic ideals from which free speech arises. The overindulging of demagogues, therefore, deteriorates the commitment to fundamental rights that lies at the heart of people's decisions to join together and reside in communities. The risks that misethnic propaganda poses to social well-being are enormous. They significantly increase the likelihood that violence will be perpetrated against minorities and that their safety will be jeopardized. Further, propaganda is subversive to social order because it infuses stress into inter-group relations. . . .

Hate Speech Stifles Debate

The argument that hate speech furthers democracy is difficult to fathom, given that its very intent is to stifle political debate on the issues and replace it with false accusations and brutal solutions. It presents no ideas of any worth in improving people's lives, increasing people's knowledge, or furthering the human quest for social justice. Laws and regulations designed to protect democratic mainstays, like procedural and substantive justice, contain counter-majoritarian safeguards. The purveyors of hatred, on the other hand, seek to rationalize why out-groups should not have an equal share of rights in the democratic com-munity. Representative democracies are devoted to protecting the civil rights of their populations; therefore, hate speech, which argues that identifiable outgroups should not equally participate in social institu-tions and privileges, is incompatible with democracy.

Speech that purposefully tries to undermine minority well-being is contrary to the reciprocal duty of humanity; it rejects the ethical duty to treat others empathically and act for the increase of overall contentment. Instead of developing inclusive institutions, hate propaganda furthers in-justices by drawing on a cultural vocabulary that places minority rights below ingroup interests.

Outgroups suffer at the hands of bigots advocating supremacist doc-trines. Minorities are impeded in their cultural and social development because of daily uncertainties resulting from their relative political im-potence and inability to fully participate in formulating substantive policies. Their safety is compromised by the real potential for violence imbedded in the cultural attitudes that give rise to hate propaganda. Misethnic speech is more than merely offensive to particular people; it carries a historical significance of exclusion and subjugation. Its over-tones, therefore, are more sweeping and harmful to the life prospects of whole groups of people than mere defamation. The function that free speech plays in opening the political gates to all social contractees is also eviscerated by the constant bombardment of derogatory images which degrade minority political candidates based on irrelevant criteria and elevating persons because of their opposition to equal rights. . . .

Without constitutional and legislative checks on power, the majority can run roughshod over the minority's fundamental and basic rights. An unregulated system of speech, in which more powerful forces have greater access and control over informational distribution systems, might produce what Justice [Oliver Wendell] Holmes called a "proletarian dic-tatorship." But it is an abuse of representative democracy to manipulate its institutions to destroy the foundations on which it is established.

Hate groups pose a threat, though not always an immediate one, to representative democracy. They use slogans that have been successfully employed to recruit and incite crowds against outgroups. Through repeated exposure to bigotry, the populace is likely to become so desensitized that it will accept oppression as a matter of course, as has happened in the past.

Violent hate speech not only advocates antidemocratic ideals, it is an intrinsic part of an overall scheme to weaken democratic institutions by attacking pluralism and inciting injustices. Unrestricted transmission of these messages threatens to undermine the political influence of diverse groups whose participation is critical to the popular-input aspect of the democratic process. The very purpose of bigotry is to exclude weaker groups from political debate. Aspersions are intended to reduce participation in governmental discourse, and destructive messages are meant to intimidate and injure. Racial hierarchies, working to the disadvantage and detriment of the less powerful, are maintained, reinforced, and revivified by a state that legitimates the use of racist and ethnocentric dialogue, especially when that dialogue makes no secret about its ultimate goal to victimize outgroups.

Representative governments are obligated to prevent incitement against a whole group of people. The legislature should act before hate propaganda endears itself into the popular culture. Tolerance and egalitarianism should not be sacrificed at the altar of an absolutist free speech doctrine. Herd mentality is best avoided by strong laws, making clear society's disapprobation of inequality and injustice. Legislation can help assure that minorities will not be tyrannized and exploited by powerful interests. Hate speech statutes will display social disapprobation for hate speech and distinguish it from legitimate forms of political dialogue. Hate speech does not further political discourse; instead, it escalates the threat to law and order. ◣

Finally, law professor Nicholas Wolfson, in the reading below, argues that—as repugnant as hate speech is—it must be protected by the First Amendment. Wolfson acknowledges that hate speech has no redeeming value, that it causes suffering and humiliation to its targets, and that it has no (or, at best, minimal) ideational content or value. Nevertheless, he claims, prohibiting such speech would have worse consequences than allowing it.

For one thing, he says, many sorts and cases of speech are directed at specific targets and intended to be negative, even humiliating. For instance, academics frequently berate one another in pointed and even vicious language. In addition, there is such a wide disparity in responses to hate speech that there is no objective basis for prohibiting it. Prohibiting hate speech because of its intent or its effects, Wolfson says, would put us on a slippery slope toward prohibiting a great deal of critical expression—which would entail too great a cost and require vast government oversight, resulting in serious curtailment of democracy. This does not mean, he says, that hate speech can never be regulated. As in the case of clear and present danger, "physical harm, the proximity of words to immediate violence, is another matter and properly to be regulated."

NICHOLAS WOLFSON, *HATE SPEECH, SEX SPEECH, FREE SPEECH**

A considerable body of persuasive legal literature supports the thesis that racist or sexist hate speech should receive reduced, or even no, protection under the First Amendment. . . . The person who is called "kike," "nigger," or "fag" suffers emotional humiliation and personal loss of dignity. The victim feels threatened, humiliated, and diminished. It is asserted that he or she may suffer temporary or permanent psychological harm. Further, such expression, it is again argued, tears the weave of the community in which the speech is made, breaks down civil discourse, and incites weak-minded onlookers to similar thoughts and words. Finally, ideational content of the utterance is minimal.

The traditional civil-libertarian response is predictable. The First Amendment is designed to protect disgusting speech from the censorship of government. The offensiveness of the speech in question is never a reason for removing it from protection of the First Amendment. There are the usual exceptions—e.g., fighting words, obscenity, defamation, speech too closely "brigaded" with forbidden conduct—but otherwise the government must be viewpoint neutral. At this point, critics of the traditional

---

*(Westport, CT: Praeger Publishers, 1997), 47–53, 56–57, 59–63.

discourse ask the cogent question, Why should racist speech, which all enlightened men and women will admit is based upon false premises, be permitted? The factual assumptions underlying hate speech are to the effect that blacks, Jews, or women are inferior, stupid, greedy, or inherently violent. Both critics and traditionalists in the civil liberties community agree that the assumptions are false. The bigotry expressed in such racist remarks is based on "facts" on a par with the assumption that the world is flat. Moreover, traditionalists and critics, I submit, agree that the hatred expressed by such speech serves no socially redeeming value. . . . [Here] we consider . . . arguments for protecting such speech from censorship.

The arguments are somewhat complex, and so we summarize them. To begin with, we point out that it is difficult if not impossible to limit censorship to the four-letter epithet. There is an expansive body of highbrow, fancy literature and philosophy that denigrates minorities, women, and gays; yet censorship of such works as [Shakespeare's] *The Merchant of Venice* would be a draconian step few would endorse. However, if we limit censorship to the epithet, we create a two-tier approach: chilling of blue-collar muck and preservation of upper-crust mud. Second, much of what passes for debate in the intellectual and political community is redolent with emotion, insult, imagery, ridicule, and passion. (Remember the day when Patrick Buchanan presented a stuffed parrot to his audience to illustrate his contempt for then-Senator Bob Dole's alleged borrowing of his ideas?) The model of a free market of ideas limited to bloodless, cerebral cogitation is too limited to encompass the reality of discourse. Hence, to complain about racial and sexist speech because it is emotionally charged and low in ideational content is not very convincing.

Third, we address the contention that hate speech causes emotional, societal, and psychological harm and therefore should be censored. We argue that the purpose of free speech protection is to safeguard speech that the government views as harmful. Any other approach would permit the government to be the arbiter of what ideas are safe. Fourth, we consider the position that one-on-one hate speech—as it were, "in-your-face" hate speech—is in a different category from hate speech directed to the public, such as offensive books and television. We reject that distinction, short of the Brandenburg doctrine that permits regulation of speech that reasonably threatens imminent physical harm. . . .

Blue-Collar Epithet Vs. Learned Smear

The new critics argue that racial and sexist epithets are not only based upon false assumptions of fact about race and sexuality but are also (1) devoid of ideational content and (2) emotionally harmful to the victim. Let us take up the assertion that the insult is relatively free of ideational content, hence should not be protected by the First Amendment. The pejorative "Get lost nigger, kike, queer, etc.," is arguably a mere profane grunt, not an idea or opinion. It is also designed to intimidate rather than rationally communicate. Since the grunt is based upon factually false premises about the minority group and is an expression of anger or fear, not a rational idea, why not ban it without fear of compromising the First Amendment? . . .

Assume that the reference to "kike" was replaced by something like "you are a Jew." From my reading of the New Testament, I have concluded that Jews are responsible for the death of Christ. From my perusal of that great classic, *The Merchant of Venice*, I have concluded that Jews are greedy. From my study of Marx's work on the Jews, I have decided that they are inherently purveyors of the worst excesses of the capitalist system. . . . From my reading of Richard Wagner and the writer Ludwig Feuerbach, I have determined that Jews are depraved elements in the body politic. Hence, please leave this school or, better yet, leave the country.

The last paragraph is considered but nasty. It is intellectual (in the sense of references to learned sources) but false in its assertions. It threatens Jews and expresses anger and fear. Do we permit this kind of anti-Semitic statement, because it is clothed in the garments of rational thought, but ban the "Jew is kike" epithet? If we do, it appears that we are expressing a kind of elitist theory of permissible racist speech. Street vernacular won't cut it, but the racism of the academy will. . . . My gut reaction is to ban the popular version as well as the more "learned." But that cannot be done without fatally compromising the First Amendment.

Ideational and Emotional Content of Hate Speech

. . . Criticism of hate speech *because* of its emotional content is weak. Much of so-called intellectual debate is vitriolic, hateful, and derisive. Any cursory reading of book reviews or commentaries upon other thinkers will reveal the biting, often vicious, cut and parry of the members of the academy. Intellectuals cringe when reading reviews of their work, and, and, no doubt, realize that the victims of their own biting reviews will suffer emotional harm. . . .

The New Yorker, in a brief review of the movie *The Miser*, called it "tiresome, simpleminded, infantile." In the *National Review*'s December 31, 1990, issue, movie reviewer John Simon called the movie *Reversal of Fortune* "thoroughly offensive" and found parts of it "ineffably tasteless, almost sacrilegious." Simon, in the same issue, called the Broadway musical *Shogun* an "unqualified disaster—a bloated nightmare of stylistic miscegenation." This is emotional warfare, likely to inflict serious emotional harm upon the authors, producers, and performers. Do we ban it? . . .

A fine example of the use of action, emotion, and derision is the cinematic treatment of American fundamentalists. It is no secret that screenwriters and directors have not been overly kind to this minority group, who are forever depicted as ignorant, hypocritical boobs. On the silver screen they are pictured as religious frauds who mouth the words of piety while lusting for money and sex. The pictures wound the fundamentalist; it is clear that the directors intend the injury, and the intellectual content (as in many movies) may be thin. The movies are the pictorial equivalent of the epithet, "Fundamentalists are lying hypocritical frauds." I surmise the new critics of the First Amendment are not proposing the censorship of the cinema. They would argue, I suspect, that racism is without question evil, but anti-fundamentalism is widely and wisely supported in the enlightened culture. It is therefore not emotion, diatribe, or hatred that disqualifies speech, but rather lack of truthfulness. . . . Speech is to be treated in the way commercial speech is now treated by the Court: the government is to have the power to ban false speech or correct misleading speech.

Causal Relationship, or from Words to Harm

I personally believe that racist and sexist insults and epithets harm the listener, but I confess I do not know the amount or permanence of the alleged harm with scientific certitude. Social scientists attempt to quantify the harm, but their "science" is notoriously inexact. As pointed out above, much vigorous debate and controversy "harms" the recipient of the verbal attack. If discomfort of the listener is to be the test, however, censorship will always be justified. If in the final analysis harm, as perceived by judge or jury, is the measure by which we regulate speech, there will be nothing left of the First Amendment. There will be no difference in the treatment of words as contrasted to deeds. When societies choose to censor, they do so because of perceived potential for harm as defined by the interests in positions of power. Speech that government considers harmless will not be censored, and there is obviously no need for a First Amendment for that kind of speech. If we deed to government the power to define what is harmful and to censor speech that in its opinion will cause harm, we open the way to government thought-control. As Judge Easterbrook put it, "[a]ny other answer leaves the government in control of all the institutions of culture, the great censor and director of which thoughts are good for us." . . .

Once we begin to censure speech on major issues because of its perceived societal harm, we have rationalized pervasive censorship. For example, censors may allege the following: television violence causes violent behavior; communist speech causes totalitarian overthrow of democratic government; criticism of religion creates a societal breakdown of the nuclear family; deconstructionism is the ruination of literary studies. In all of these and other great disputes, the protagonists, pro and con, of causality are able to quote their favorite social science research papers. However, sociological research is a notoriously inexact science. If we permit legislatures to pass censorship laws based upon such uncertain science, we will in effect justify a weak rational-basis test for the validity of such legislation. That is, a statute will pass muster if the legislature has a fairly reasonable basis for the censorship. Such a test is not much different from that for the validity of legislation regarding conduct. The First Amendment will be a much-weakened doctrine.

Direct Insults Versus Public Assault

. . . But should we distinguish the infliction of emotional harm on private figures from the infliction of such harm on public figures, or from racist remarks not directed at any individual? The difference, for example, is between the hate speech directed at an individual and generalized hate speech set forth in a book. . . .

I have the following problems with private-vs.-public distinctions in the area of alleged racist or sexist speech. First, it is an opening wedge to permitting excessive state regulation of private speech. That is a potentially momentous intrusion. If the state can regulate the civility of private discourse in matters of race or sex, there is no rational reason for preventing the state from requiring civility across the entire range of private conversations and speech—and the definer will be the state. My examples of literary and scholarly savagery toward opponents are an example of the kind of discourse that could be regulated under cover of diminishing emotional harm and softening the edge of argument. A characteristic of totalitarian societies has been the state's often successful effort to censor and chill private speech. . . .

[Further,] it is impossible to limit the ban to statements only of the nature of "X, you are a kike." People differ radically in their definition of what is racist or sexist. Indeed the terms are used sometimes with careless abandon. To some, for example, the advocacy of anti-quota policies is racist, and in the context of a private argument, a racist epithet. In the domain of private speech, the courts would enter a thicket of the usual interpretation and development that would inevitably act as a chill and deterrent to face-to-face, private speech. . . .

Perhaps the most important is another point, however. The argument that racist speech directed at a private individual is more deserving of censorship than that directed at the world in general is based on a dangerous premise. It supposes that the private epithet creates more harm than a published racist philosophical tract. This proposition is empirically dubious. Television broadcasts or books aimed at creating general racist sentiments against a group or a class are more dangerous to society than the personal insult. The latter hurts an individual, but the former can influence vast groups, mold public opinion, and create a racist environment. Of course, this merely reflects the truism that books and television have consequences, which is why, absent the First Amendment, society always attempts to censor what it considers dangerous speech. But this distinction underlines the danger of using harm as an argument for limiting speech: the end result is pervasive censorship. Of course, physical harm, the proximity of words to immediate violence, is another matter and properly to be regulated. ◣

Questions for Discussion

1. Tsesis seems to suggest that unless there is hate speech regulation, there is more likely to be a tyranny of the majority over minorities. Is that correct?

2. Is Wolfson right that there is no substantive difference between a "face-to-face" case of hate speech and a published pamphlet that is directed at a group generally?

3. Is there indeed an important distinction between speech and conduct, or are they, as advocates of speech acts say, both simply forms of expression that blend into each other? If there are legitimate grounds for regulating and limiting speech (such as libel), and those grounds involve the harm principle, then does hate speech harm? Why or why not?

4. Given the claims about the justification of rights from Chapter 2, what ultimately justifies a right to free expression?

5. Hate speech (and hate crimes) seem necessarily to involve groups; even if the target is a particular individual, it seems to be an individual as an instance of some group (based on race, gender, sexual orientation, and so forth) rather than simply as a person. If this is so, are proponents of the regulation of hate speech therefore committed to embracing group rights? Are the concerns raised about group rights in Chapter 4 relevant to this issue?

Further Reading

Fish, Stanley. *There's No Such Thing As Free Speech . . . and It's a Good Thing, Too.* Oxford: Oxford University Press, 1994. A spirited critique of unrestrained free speech.

Haiman, Franklyn Saul. *"Speech Acts" and the First Amendment.* Carbondale: Southern Illinois University Press, 1993. A brief survey of types of speech acts and defense of free expression against restraints on it.

Harer, John B., and Jeanne Harrell. *People For and Against Restricted or Unrestricted Expression.* Westport, CT: Greenwood Press, 2002. A compilation of various views on free speech from academicians and public figures.

Schauer, Frederick. *Free Speech: A Philosophical Inquiry.* Cambridge: Cambridge University Press, 1982. A substantive and sophisticated analysis of issues related to free speech.

Walker, Samuel. *Hate Speech: The History of an American Controversy.* Lincoln: University of Nebraska Press, 1994. A survey of legal and philosophical issues, practices, and policies involving hate speech and freedom of expression.

CHAPTER 9

EMPLOYMENT RIGHTS

The Second Amendment of the U.S. Constitution guarantees the legal right to bear arms. In 2007, Shirley Katz, a high school teacher in southern Oregon, went to court to challenge her school's policy that prevented her from bringing her legally owned pistol to her workplace. She had a concealed-weapons permit and claimed that she needed to bring her weapon to school because she feared for her personal safety; she had taken out several restraining orders against her former husband, and she feared that if he appeared at her workplace, she would be in danger. Besides this practical reason, she claimed that she had a constitutional right to bear arms. (After two years of litigation, the Oregon Court of Appeals eventually ruled against her request and in favor of the school district's prohibition against allowing weapons at the school.)

In 2009, Chad Carlson, the head football coach at a different high school in Oregon, was fired after refusing to resign over an incident that had taken place away from work. The school district's punishment culminated an internal review launched after Carlson, along with two other coaches, pled guilty to charges that they had interfered with police after attending an Ultimate Fighting Competition match. The coaches had interfered when another assistant coach was accused of groping a woman on a train platform. The assistant coach denied the allegations, and the woman did not pursue charges. Carlson appealed his termination by the school district but was not reinstated.

Do teachers have the right to bring legally owned weapons to their place of employment? Does an employer have the right to discipline (including up to the point of firing) an employee for that employee's conduct away from the workplace? These questions are not simply about a person's legal rights—that is, what the law says may or may not occur—but about a person's moral or human rights. Should there be laws that allow an employer to fire an employee for alleged misconduct away from the workplace (whether or not there actually are such laws)? If such a dismissal takes place, does it violate some moral or human right of the employee? Many such questions are connected to employment rights, that is, rights associated with one's relationship to others in the context of the workplace. Do workers *as workers* have certain rights? Do employers *as employers* have certain rights? With respect to relevant third parties, such as shareholders who own stock in certain companies, do they have certain rights?

Relevant important questions about rights related to employment concern not only who (or what parties) might have rights but also the broader issue of rights as they pertain to people's lives in the context of employment. Much of a person's adult life (and, for some people, even their preadult lives) is spent in the context of a job. Even limiting the focus to a typical eight-hour workday, those eight hours comprise one-third of a day. Assuming a person sleeps eight hours per day, the eight hours spent at work constitute half of a person's waking life. Surely, say many, if rights are relevant to a person's well-being, they are relevant to this half of her waking life! Surely, since the need to be employed and earn a living is universal across humanity, human rights should apply to the types of interactions that involve one's relationships with others in this area of life. And, indeed, growing legislation (usually framed as business law or employment law) involving economic rights and responsibilities appears to reveal the recognition that employment rights are significant. Given this recognition, there are two broad areas of concern with respect to employment rights: a right *to* employment and rights *within* employment.

RIGHT TO EMPLOYMENT

One broad concern about employment rights is the issue of whether people have a right to be employed. Is there a right to work, a right to a job? Article 23 of the Universal Declaration of Human Rights (see Part III) states,

1. Everyone has the right to work, to free choice of employment, to just and favorable conditions of work and to protection against unemployment.
2. Everyone, without any discrimination, has the right to equal pay for equal work.

3. Everyone who works has the right to just and favorable remuneration ensuring for himself and his family an existence worthy of human dignity, and supplemented, if necessary, by other means of social protection.

4. Everyone has the right to form and to join trade unions for the protection of his interests.

As noted in previous chapters, interpretations differ as to what exactly is meant when a right is claimed. To say that everyone has a right to work or to free choice of employment might mean that everyone is entitled to seek employment and has the freedom of opportunity to try to find a job. Or it might mean that everyone has the right to actually be employed in some job or other (and is not merely entitled to seek work). While almost no one actually claims that everyone has the right to an actual job, as we will see below, many people understand a right to work or to employment to mean more than just a right to look for work. In particular, people have raised questions about discrimination in the acquisition of a job. Are a person's rights violated, for instance, if a prospective employer requires a background check? Does such a check violate that person's right to privacy (assuming there is such a right)? Many people think it would depend on what information the employer was seeking. Is access to a person's previous work history appropriate information for a prospective employer to require? What about information on a person's criminal record, voting record, marriage status, or sexual orientation? While people have varying opinions about what sorts of information a prospective employer has legitimate access to, the broad question is, Does a prospective employer have a right to personal information about a prospective employee? If a person does not grant access to certain personal information and does not get the job, has there been any violation of some right of that person (and, if so, what right)?

These sorts of questions have arisen especially in the context of what is sometimes called "preferential treatment" and, more specifically, in terms of "affirmative action." These are more often spoken of in the context of justice and fairness rather than directly in terms of rights, but they can easily be couched as a matter of rights. Discrimination in itself is not necessarily unjust or unfair. We discriminate, in the sense that we make evaluative decisions and choices, all the time. We discriminate between different restaurants when we want to go out to eat or between different teachers when we choose which classes to take. To be discriminating can mean to have fine judgment (as having a discriminating taste in, say, wines). However, some cases of discrimination, we say, are unjust or unfair. We tend to think that discriminating against (or for!) a person strictly on the basis of, say, race or gender is, in certain contexts, inappropriate. (In some contexts, discrimination on the basis of race or gender might be appropriate.) In the context of employment, we normally think that matters of race or sexual orientation are irrelevant to being considered for a job. So, if someone is denied a job strictly on the basis of race or sexual orientation, we might well deem this a case of unjust discrimination and a violation of the person's right to equal treatment. And, indeed, much civil rights legislation and policy is based on this very claim. In such a situation, then, we might very well say that, although a person does not have a right to some particular job, being excluded from that job on the basis of irrelevant criteria violated that person's right to equal treatment. (Again, not all such acts of discrimination on the basis of, say, race, are necessarily unjust. Legally, there exist "bona fide occupational qualifications" that are considered appropriate grounds for discrimination. For example, the owner of a small, local Asian restaurant might want to hire only Asian waiters because he believes this will enhance the "genuine" Asian ambiance of the restaurant.) Nevertheless, when prospective employees have complained about unfair hiring practices, they have done so on the basis of a violation of their right to equal treatment.

RIGHTS WITHIN EMPLOYMENT

Far more than the right *to* employment, rights *within* employment are the focus of rights theorists and the enactment of legal rights. People frame issues regarding a variety of aspects of employment in the language of rights. These aspects include rights to safe and healthy working conditions, fair compensation, due process in workplace rewards and punishments, collective bargaining, privacy, and others. These various concerns often overlap; for example, the right to fair compensation can overlap with the right to due process if there is, say, gender discrimination at play in terms of wages (so, women being paid less than men for performing the same job is relevant to both fair compensation and due process).

With respect to safe and healthy working conditions, what rights, if any, are relevant? To approach answering this question, it would be relevant first to ask what constitutes safe and healthy working conditions. Every job has associated risks, some of which are much more evident than others; a firefighter or police officer faces rather obvious risks on the job. Office workers might not run the risks associated with fighting fires or dealing with bad guys, but nonetheless these types of jobs still entail risks as well. At a legal level in the

United States, the federal Occupational Health and Safety Act regulates businesses in a variety of ways involving workplace safety. These include requiring, for example, clean and sanitary work spaces, guardrails on stairwells, clearly marked and unobstructed exits from buildings, and so forth. Such things are required by law and therefore constitute legal rights, but if these laws were not in place, would there be a violation of anyone's moral or human rights? The argument that indeed there would be relies on the notion of moral responsibility with respect to omissions (i.e., not doing something one is supposed to do). This is different from cases such as requiring a smoke-free workplace. In the case of allowing workers to smoke in the workplace, sufficient medical evidence shows that secondhand smoke can injure people. In this instance, a person's right not to be harmed entails that an employer must prohibit smoking in the workplace, at least where smoking could result in harm to other workers. An employer who allowed employees to smoke at work would be guilty of allowing an employee to be harmed while on the job because there would be a direct causal connection between allowing the act of smoking and the harm that resulted from secondhand smoke. However, by not posting exit signs in a building, an employer has not directly caused harm to anyone. Instead, in such a case, the claim is that this omission, that is, this failure to act, has led (or might lead) to a subsequent harm, hence violation of a person's right not to be harmed.

Closely related to issues of a right to safe and healthy working conditions are issues of—for lack of a better word—a right to "nonoppressive" working conditions. One specific aspect would include employees being free from harassment and hostility in the workplace. The claim is not simply that it would be a good idea and good business practice to prevent and forbid personal harassment of employees in the workplace but that such acts of harassment or hostile work environments violate a person's rights. This is usually stated in terms of violations to a person's well-being, either in the sense of that person's dignity or that person's safety.

Another type of "nonoppressive" working condition often handled in the context and language of rights is the right of an employee to engage in whistle-blowing without fear of punishment by the employer. Whistle-blowing refers to an employee's publicly disclosing some (perceived) wrongdoing by the employer or business. The question pertaining to rights is whether an employee's rights have been violated (and, if so, what specific rights) if she is punished by her employer because she has blown the whistle on some policy or practice by the employer or business. Does a person have a moral or human right to keep her current job even after having publicly disclosed damaging information about the employer or business? Libertarians, who have argued for negative political rights, have fairly universally claimed that no rights are violated if an employer punishes an employee in such a case. They might acknowledge that good business practices should, of course, be followed so that whistle-blowing will not become an issue, but this is separate from whether punishing an employee violates her rights. Civil rights advocates and those who tend to defend the notion of positive economic rights would see such punishment as a violation of the employee's rights, in particular her right to a "nonoppressive" workplace.

Yet another specific issue that has arisen with respect to working conditions is the right of an employer to relevant information about employees and the right of employees to privacy. Two aspects of this issue have been especially highlighted in recent years. One aspect is the issue of drug testing of employees. The issue, of course, concerns whether employers have a legitimate right to information about an employee's status vis-à-vis drugs. This concern has actually been expanded even more to include broader concerns about health requirements for employees. For instance, some employers have begun to demand a no-smoking policy for their employees not only within but outside the workplace. They claim that they lose productivity when workers are absent or ill (because of their personal lifestyle choices). In addition, they pay health-care costs for their employees, and certain lifestyle choices (such as smoking) affect these costs. As a result, they argue, they have a right not only to access such information about their employees but also to require certain standards and criteria from them. Furthermore, they say, if employees have a right to safe and healthy working conditions, then the status of their fellow employees, say, vis-à-vis drugs, is relevant; for the safety of other employees, employers should have access to such information and should be able to implement certain standards and criteria of employment. Critics have argued that employers do not have a right to such information or to impose such requirements because, although the desire for such information and requirements is understandable, it is trumped by an employee's right to privacy.

The second aspect of this issue that has become especially prominent in recent years is the issue of electronic performance monitoring. Given the fact that more and more work is now done electronically, employers can and do monitor employees' work via modern technology. In many workplaces, employers have access to whatever online work employees do. Employers can access the content of e-mails and electronic messages, as well as discover whatever

Internet sites an employee visits. There are also other forms of monitoring and surveillance. For instance, devices can be installed on company cars that allow employers to know exactly where those cars are driven. Advocates of electronic performance monitoring claim that employers have a legitimate right to information about the activities of employees. If employees are engaging in non-work-related activities while on the job, then this is relevant for the employer to know. This is not oppressive or a violation of employees' privacy, they say, because employers are simply making sure employees are working appropriately. If employees are on task and doing what they are supposed to be doing, rather than shopping online or visiting websites irrelevant to their work assignments, then they have nothing to be concerned about if the employer monitors them. Critics, of course, disagree and claim that such monitoring—at least, some such monitoring—creates an oppressive work environment.

The issue of monitoring and employers' rights to information versus employees' privacy rights has extended beyond the workplace to questions about employees' non-workplace activities. The case of the high school football coach presented at the beginning of this chapter serves as an example. The coach was involved in an altercation away from his workplace. There was no evidence that his actions did, or even would, negatively affect his performance while at work. Nonetheless, his employer found his actions away from the workplace to be grounds for punishment with respect to his job. In this particular case, the employer acted reactively, that is, imposed a punishment after the employee had engaged in an action. In addition, the coach's actions involved questions about his legal conduct. If an employee were to engage in some action that was legal but still disturbing to her employer— say she engaged very visibly in a pro–Al Qaeda demonstration—would this be legitimate grounds for the employer to punish that employee? Many advocates of employee rights say no; what employees do away from the workplace that does not directly affect their work negatively is a matter of their right to liberty and self-determination. Beyond cases such as these, there are cases in which the employer acts not reactively—only after an employee has done something—but proactively, that is, to ensure that the employee does not do certain things. Some employers, for instance, have monitored the personal activities of employees in legally acceptable ways, such as going past the employee's home at different times of the day or speaking with neighbors and known acquaintances about the employee's activities. These cases and scenarios speak to the broad issue of employers' rights to information about employees and employees' rights to liberty and privacy. All of these cases, and the relevant rights that pertain to them, are especially salient because they arise in the context of employment relationships. To the extent that fundamental human rights, such as a right to information or a right to privacy, have content that is meaningful to people's actual lives, these employment relationships—in which people spend a large part of their lives—are particularly important.

EMPLOYMENT AT WILL

One issue that straddles the distinction between rights to and within employment is the issue of employment at will (EAW), also sometimes called "contract at will." EAW is the doctrine (and practice) that sees an employment relationship as voluntary, based on the consent of the two parties involved, the employer and the employee, each of whom is said to enter into the employment relationship willingly. In addition, each is free to end or opt out of that relationship at any time. So, an employee can quit whenever he chooses; on the other hand, the employer can also fire the employee whenever he chooses. Neither party is required to give any justification for ending the relationship, although the other party might want and appreciate it. This is a different sort of employment relationship than one covered by a contract. In a contractual relationship, each party agrees to certain specified terms of employment and cannot simply end that relationship (break the contract) without the consent of the other party. A vast number of workers both in the United States and around the world are "at-will" employees; they are in an EAW relationship.

Employment at will is said to leave both employers and employees somewhat vulnerable to each other's whims. An employee might be passed over for promotion or demoted or even fired for no good reason at all; at the same time, an employer might have a worker simply walk off the job for no good reason in the middle of an important phase of work. Nonetheless, the common practice of employment at will has been defended on basic grounds of the rights of each party. From the perspective of the employee, a person should have the right to quit a job if she wants. One's very fundamental right to liberty includes not being forced into slavery! Outside of a contract, requiring someone to work in a job that she does not want would be, in effect, a form of slavery. From the perspective of the employer, a person should have the right to operate her business however she pleases (assuming no violations of other rights). After all, the business is her private property. If she no longer wants someone to work for her, she has the right to not be forced to employ that person. Outside of a contract, requiring someone to employ another person would be, in effect, a form of slavery. An employment relationship, then, is often interpreted in terms of people's rights to liberty and to private property. Even so, some people have argued that employment at will is fraught with potential and actual violations of people's rights, as the case below illustrates.

In 1980, the American Greetings Corporation hired Howard Smith III as a materials handler at the plant in Osceola, Arkansas. He was promoted to forklift driver and held that job until 1989, when he became involved in a dispute with his shift leader. According to Smith, the dispute occurred at work, and when he tried to discuss the matter after work, the shift leader hit him. The next day Smith was fired.

Smith was an "at-will" employee. He neither belonged to nor was protected by any union or union agreement. He had no special legal protection, for there was no apparent question of discrimination based on age, gender, race, or disability. And he was not alleging a problem with worker safety on the job. The *American Greetings Employee Handbook* stated, "We believe in working and thinking and planning to provide a stable and growing business, to give such service to our customers that we may provide maximum job security for our employees." It did not state that employees could not be fired without due process or reasonable cause. According to the common-law EAW principle, Smith's job at American Greetings could therefore legitimately be terminated without cause at any time by either Smith or his employer, as long as that termination did not violate any law, agreement, or public policy.

Smith challenged his firing in the Arkansas court system as a "tort of outrage." A tort of outrage occurs when an employer engages in "extreme or outrageous conduct" or intentionally inflicts terrible emotional stress. If such a tort is found to have occurred, the action—in this case, the dismissal—can be overturned.

Smith's case went to the Arkansas Supreme Court in 1991. In court the management of American Greetings argued that Smith was fired for provoking management into a fight. The court held that the firing was not in violation of law or a public policy, that the employee handbook did not specify restrictions on at-will termination, and that the alleged altercation between Smith and his shift leader "did not come close to meeting" criteria for a tort of outrage. Howard Smith lost his case and his job.

In the first reading below, law professor Richard Epstein defends the doctrine and practice of employment at will (which he calls "contract at will"), claiming that it is both fair and beneficial to both employers and employees. It is fair because, he says, it protects *both* employers and employees, and it is beneficial because it *protects* both employers and employees. While he acknowledges that sometimes each party could be harmed by the other, in the vast majority of cases and situations, at-will employment works well for, and indeed benefits, both parties. Furthermore, employment at will is based on the presumption of both private property (businesses belong to employers) and individual liberty (people can choose whether to be employees). Of course, cases of unjust and wrongful discharge occur, but these should not be the focus of sweeping public policy, and the notion of having government interfere with and regulate at-will relationships is flawed at best.

RICHARD EPSTEIN, "IN DEFENSE OF THE CONTRACT AT WILL"*

The Fairness of the Contract at Will

The first way to argue for the contract at will is to insist upon the importance of freedom of contract as an end in itself. Freedom of contract is an aspect of individual liberty, every bit as much as freedom of speech, or freedom in the selection of marriage partners or in the adoption of religious beliefs or affiliations. Just as it is regarded as prima facie unjust to abridge these liberties, so too is it presumptively unjust to abridge the economic liberties of individuals. The desire to make one's own choices about employment may be as strong as it is with respect to marriage or participation in religious activities, and it is doubtless more pervasive than the desire to participate in political activity. Indeed for most people, their own health and comfort, and that of their families, depend critically upon their ability to earn a living by entering the employment market. If government regulation is inappropriate for personal, religious, or political activities, then what makes it intrinsically desirable for employment relations?

It is one thing to set aside the occasional transaction that reflects only the momentary aberrations of particular parties who are overwhelmed

---

University of Chicago Law Review 51 (1984): 947–982.

by major personal and social dislocations. It is quite another to announce that a rule to which vast numbers of individuals adhere is so fundamentally corrupt that it does not deserve the minimum respect of the law. With employment contracts we are not dealing with the widow who has sold her inheritance for a song to a man with a thin moustache. Instead we are dealing with the routine stuff of ordinary life; people who are competent enough to marry, vote, and pray are not unable to protect themselves in their day-to-day business transactions.

Courts and legislatures have intervened so often in private contractual relations that it may seem almost quixotic to insist that they bear a heavy burden of justification every time they wish to substitute their own judgment for that of the immediate parties to the transactions. Yet it is hardly likely that remote public bodies have better information about individual preferences than the parties who hold them. This basic principle of autonomy, moreover, is not limited to some areas of individual conduct and wholly inapplicable to others. It covers all these activities as a piece and admits no ad hoc exceptions, but only principled limitations.

This general proposition applies to the particular contract in question. Any attack on the contract at will in the name of individual freedom is fundamentally misguided. . . . [T]he contract at will is sought by both parties. Any limitation upon the freedom to enter into such contracts limits the power of workers as well as employers and must therefore be justified before it can be accepted. In this context the appeal is often to an image of employer coercion. To be sure, freedom of contract is not an absolute in the employment context, any more than it is elsewhere. Thus the principle must be understood against a backdrop that prohibits the use of private contracts to trench upon third-party rights, including uses that interfere with some clear mandate of public policy, as in cases of contracts to commit murder or perjury.

In addition, the principle of freedom of contract also rules out the use of force or fraud in obtaining advantages during contractual negotiations; and it limits taking advantage of the young, the feeble-minded, and the insane. But the recent wrongful discharge cases do not purport to deal with the delicate situations where contracts have been formed by improper means or where individual defects of capacity or will are involved. Fraud is not a frequent occurrence in employment contracts, especially where workers and employers engage in repeat transactions. Nor is there any reason to believe that such contracts are marred by misapprehensions, since employers and employees know the footing on which they have contracted: the phrase "at will" is two words long and has the convenient virtue of meaning just what it says, no more and no less.

An employee who knows that he can quit at will understands what it means to be fired at will, even though he may not like it after the fact. So long as it is accepted that the employer is the full owner of his capital and the employee is the full owner of his labor, the two are free to exchange on whatever terms and conditions they see fit, within the limited constraints just noted. If the arrangement turns out to be disastrous to one side, that is his problem; and once cautioned, he probably will not make the same mistake a second time. More to the point, employers and employees are unlikely to make the same mistake more than once. It is hardly plausible that contracts at will could be so pervasive in all businesses and at all levels if they did not serve the interests of employees as well as employers. The argument from fairness then is very simple, but not for that reason unpersuasive.

The Utility of the Contract at Will

The strong fairness argument in favor of freedom of contract makes short work of the various for-cause and good-faith restrictions upon private contracts. Yet the argument is incomplete in several respects. In particular, it does not explain why the presumption in the case of silence should be in favor of the contract at will. Nor does it give a descriptive account of *why* the contract at will is so commonly found in all trades and professions. Nor does the argument meet on their own terms the concerns voiced most frequently by the critics of the contract at will. Thus, the commonplace belief today (at least outside the actual world of business) is that the contract at will is so unfair and one-sided that it cannot be the outcome of a rational set of bargaining processes any more than, to take the extreme case, a contract for total slavery. While we may not, the criticism continues, be able to observe them, defects in capacity at contract formation nonetheless must be present: the ban upon the contract at will is an effective way to reach abuses that are pervasive but difficult to detect, so that modest government interference only strengthens the operation of market forces.

In order to rebut this charge, it is necessary to do more than insist that individuals as a general matter know how to govern their own lives. It is also necessary to display the structural strengths of the contract at will that explain why rational people would enter into such a contract, if not all the time, then at least most of it. The implicit assumption in this argument is that contracts are typically for the mutual benefit of both parties. Yet it is hard to see what other assumption makes any sense in analyzing institutional arrangements (arguably in contradistinction to idiosyncratic, nonrepetitive transactions). To be sure, there are occasional cases of regret after the fact, especially after an infrequent, but costly, contingency comes to pass. There will be cases in which parties are naïve, befuddled, or worse. Yet in framing either a rule of policy or a rule of construction, the focus cannot be on that biased set of cases in which the contract aborts and litigation ensues. Instead, attention must be directed to standard repetitive transactions, where the centralizing tendency powerfully promotes expected mutual gain. It is simply incredible to postulate that either employers or employees, motivated as they are by self-interest, would enter routinely into a transaction that leaves them worse off than they were before, or even worse off than their next best alternative.

From this perspective, then, the task is to explain how and why the at-will contracting arrangement (in sharp contrast to slavery) typically works to the mutual advantage of the parties. Here, as is common in economic matters, it does not matter that the parties themselves cannot articulate the reasons that render their judgment sound and breathe life into legal arrangements that are fragile in form but durable in practice. The inquiry into mutual benefit in turn requires an examination of the full range of costs and benefits that arise from collaborative ventures. It is just at this point that the nineteenth-century view is superior to the emerging modern conception. The modern view tends to lay heavy emphasis on the need to control employer abuse. Yet . . . the rights under the contract at will are fully bilateral, so that the employee can use the contract as a means to control the firm, just as the firm uses it to control the worker. . . .

[Under contract at will] the worker can quit whenever the net value of the employment contract turns negative. As with the employer's power to fire or demote, the threat to quit (or at a lower level to come late or leave early) is one that can be exercised without resort to litigation. Furthermore, that threat turns out to be most effective when the employer's opportunistic behavior is the greatest because the situation is one in which the worker has least to lose. To be sure, the worker will not necessarily make a threat whenever the employer insists that the worker accept a less favorable set of contractual terms, for sometimes the changes may be accepted as an uneventful adjustment in the total compensation level attributable to a change in the market price of labor. This point counts, however, only as an additional strength of the contract at will, which allows for small adjustments *in both directions* in ongoing contractual arrangements with a minimum of bother and confusion. . . .

Another reason why employees are often willing to enter into at-will employment contracts stems from the asymmetry of reputational losses. Any party who cheats may well obtain a bad reputation that will induce others to avoid dealing with him. The size of these losses tends to differ systematically between employers and employees—to the advantage of the employee. Thus in the usual situation there are many workers and a single employer. The disparity in number is apt to be greatest in large industrial concerns, where the at-will contract is commonly, if mistakenly, thought to be most unsatisfactory because of the supposed inequality of bargaining power. The employer who decides for bad reason or no reason at all may not face any legal liability under the classical common law rule. But he faces very powerful adverse economic consequences. If coworkers perceive the dismissal as arbitrary, they will take fresh stock of their own prospects, for they can no longer be certain that their faithful performance will ensure their security and advancement. The uncertain prospects created by arbitrary employer behavior is functionally indistinguishable from a reduction in wages unilaterally imposed by the employer. At the margin some workers will look elsewhere, and typically the best workers will have the greatest opportunities. By the same token the large employer has more to gain if he dismisses undesirable employees, for this ordinarily acts as an implicit increase in wages to the other employees, who are no longer burdened with uncooperative or obtuse coworkers. . . .

The contract at will also helps workers deal with the problem of risk diversification. . . . Ordinarily, employees cannot work more than one, or perhaps two, jobs at the same time. . . . The contract at will is designed in part to offset the concentration of individual investment in a single job by allowing diversification among employers *over time*. The employee is not locked into an unfortunate contract if he finds better opportunities elsewhere or if he detects some weakness in the internal structure of the firm. A similar analysis applies on the employer's side where he is a sole proprietor, though ordinary diversification is possible when ownership of the firm is widely held in publicly traded shares. . . .

Conclusion

The recent trend toward expanding the legal remedies for wrongful discharge has been greeted with wide approval in judicial, academic, and popular circles. In this paper, I have argued that the modern trend rests in large measure upon a misunderstanding of the contractual processes and the ends served by the contract at will. No system of regulation can hope to match the benefits that the contract at will affords in employment relations. The flexibility afforded by the contract at will permits the ceaseless marginal adjustments that are necessary in any ongoing productive activity conducted, as all activities are, in conditions of technological and business change. The strength of the contract at will should not be judged by the occasional cases in which it is said to produce unfortunate results, but rather by the vast run of cases where it provides a sensible private response to the many and varied problems in labor contracting. . . . The doctrine of wrongful discharge is the problem and not the solution. This is one of the many situations in which the courts and legislatures should leave well enough alone. ▶

In this chapter's final reading below, philosophers Patricia Werhane and Tara Radin argue that there should be definite and specific limitations on the doctrine and practice of employment at will. Their primary concern is that employment at will (often) runs afoul of a basic right to due process. For them, employers and employees are not equal partners in a relationship; rather, employers hold a much more powerful position. Of course, in an EAW relationship, an employee is free to quit at any time, but, they say, in situations in which demand for jobs is greater than supply, an employee is not on an equal footing with an employer. In such a case, if an employee does not like, say, the working conditions, the employer can much more easily find another worker than the employee can find another job. Werhane and Radin claim that employees as *persons* deserve respect; they are not merely packages of labor but people, and due process means treating them as such, that is, as ends in themselves and not merely as means to the employer's ends. (One note: In the reading below, the authors mention "proprietary rights." This simply means rights of ownership. So, a business owner has proprietary rights over her business, and an employee has proprietary rights over her labor.)

PATRICIA H. WERHANE AND TARA J. RADIN, "EMPLOYMENT AT WILL AND DUE PROCESS"*

The principle of EAW is a common-law doctrine that states that, in the absence of law of contract, employers have the right to hire, promote, demote, and fire whomever and whenever they please. . . .

In the United States, EAW has been interpreted as the rule that, when employees are not specifically covered by union agreement, legal statute, public policy, or contract, employers "may dismiss their employees at will . . . for good cause, for no cause, *or even for causes morally wrong*, without being thereby guilty of a legal wrong" [quoted from the case of *Payne v. Western*, 81 Tenn. 507 (1884)]. At the same time, "at-will" employees enjoy rights parallel to employer prerogatives, because employees may quit their jobs for any reason whatsoever (or for no reason) without having to give any notice to their employers. "At-will" employees range from part-time contract workers to CEOs, including all those workers and managers in the private sector of the economy not covered by agreements, statutes, or contracts. Today at least 60 percent of all employees in the private sector in the United States are "at-will" employees. These employees have no rights to due process or to appeal employment decisions, and the employer does not have any obligation to give reasons for demotions, transfers, or dismissals. Interestingly, while employees in the *private* sector of the economy tend to be regarded as "at-will" employees, *public*-sector employees have guaranteed rights, including due process, and are protected from demotion, transfer, or firing without cause.

Due process is a means by which a person can appeal a decision in order to get an explanation of that action and an opportunity to argue

---

*In *Ethical Theory and Business*, ed. Tom L. Beauchamp and Norman E. Bowie, 6th ed. (Upper Saddle River, NJ: Prentice Hall, 2001), 267–274.

against it. Procedural due process is the right to a hearing, trial, grievance procedure, or appeal when a decision is made concerning oneself. Due process is also substantive. It is the demand for rationality and fairness: for good reasons for decisions. EAW has been widely interpreted as allowing employees to be demoted, transferred, or dismissed without due process, that is, without having a hearing and without requirement of good reasons or "cause" for the employment decision. This is not to say that employers do not have reasons, usually good reasons, for their decisions. But there is no moral or legal obligation to state or defend them. EAW thus sidesteps the requirement of procedural and substantive due process in the workplace, but it does not preclude the institution of such procedures or the existence of good reasons for employment decisions. . . .

In what follows we shall present a series of arguments defending the claim that the right to procedural and substantive due process should be extended to all employees in the private sector of the economy. We will defend this claim partly on the basis of human rights. We shall also argue that the public/private distinction that precludes application of constitutional guarantees in the private sector has sufficiently broken down so that the absence of a due process requirement in the workplace is an anomaly.

EAW is often justified for one or more of the following reasons:

1. The proprietary rights of the employers guarantee that they may employ or dismiss whomever and whenever they wish.
2. EAW defends employee and employer rights equally, in particular the right to freedom of contract, because an employee voluntarily contracts to be hired and can quit at any time.
3. In choosing to take a job, an employee voluntarily commits herself to certain responsibilities and company loyalty, including the knowledge that she is an "at-will" employee.
4. Extending due process rights in the workplace often interferes with the efficiency and productivity of the business organization.
5. Legislation and/or regulation of employment relationships further undermine an already overregulated economy.

Let us examine each of these arguments in more detail. [Discussion of the fourth argument is not included in this reading.] The principle of

EAW is sometimes maintained purely on the basis of proprietary rights of employers and corporations. In dismissing or demoting employees, the employer is not denying rights to *persons*. Rather, the employer is simply excluding that person's *labor* from the organization.

This is not a bad argument. Nevertheless, accepting it necessitates consideration of the proprietary rights of employees as well. To understand what is meant by "proprietary rights of employees" it is useful to consider first what is meant by the term "labor." "Labor" is sometimes used collectively to refer to the workforce as a whole. It also refers to the activity of working. Other times it refers to the productivity or "fruits" of that activity. Productivity, labor in the third sense, might be thought of as a form of property, or at least as something convertible into property, because the productivity of working is what is traded for remuneration in employee-employer work agreements. For example, suppose an advertising agency hires an expert known for her creativity in developing new commercials. This person trades her ideas, the product of her work (thinking), for pay. The ideas are not literally property, but they are tradable items because, when presented on paper or on television, they are sellable by their creator and generate income. But the activity of working (thinking in this case) cannot be sold or transferred.

Caution is necessary, though, in relating productivity to tangible property, because there is an obvious difference between productivity and material property. Productivity requires the past or present activity of working, and thus the presence of the person performing the activity. Person, property, labor, and productivity are all different in this important sense. A person can be distinguished from his possessions, a distinction that allows for the creation of legally fictional persons such as corporations or trusts that can "own" property. Persons cannot, however, be distinguished from their working, and this activity is necessary for creating productivity, a tradable product of one's working.

In dismissing an employee, a well-intentioned employer aims to rid the corporation of the costs of generating that employee's work products. In ordinary employment situations, however, terminating that cost entails terminating that employee. In those cases the justification for the "at-will" firing is presumably proprietary. But treating an employee "at will" is analogous to considering her a piece of property at the disposal of the employer or corporation. Arbitrary firings treat people as things. When I "fire" a robot, I do not have to give reasons, because a robot is not a rational being. It has no use for reasons. On the other hand, if I fire a person arbitrarily, I am making the assumption that she does not need reasons either. If I have hired people, then, in firing them, I should treat them as such, with respect, throughout the termination process. This does not preclude firing. It merely asks employers to give reasons for their actions, because reasons are appropriate when people are dealing with other people.

This reasoning leads to a second defense and critique of EAW. It is contended that EAW defends employee and employer rights equally. An employer's right to hire and fire "at will" is balanced by a worker's right to accept or reject employment. The institution of any employee right that restricts "at-will" hiring and firing would be unfair unless this restriction were balanced by a similar restriction controlling employee job choice in the workplace. Either program would do irreparable damage by preventing both employees and employers from continuing in voluntary employment arrangements. These arrangements are guaranteed by "freedom of contract," the right of persons or organizations to enter into any voluntary agreement with which all parties of the agreement are in accord. Limiting EAW practices or requiring due process would negatively affect freedom of contract. Both are thus clearly coercive, because in either case persons and organizations are forced to accept behavioral restraints that place unnecessary constraints on voluntary employment agreements.

This second line of reasoning defending EAW, like the first, presents some solid arguments. A basic presupposition upon which EAW is grounded is that of protecting equal freedoms of employees and employers. The purpose of EAW is to provide a guaranteed balance of these freedoms. But arbitrary treatment of employees extends prerogatives to managers that are not equally available to employees, and such treatment may unduly interfere with a fired employee's prospects for future employment if that employee has no avenue for defense or appeal. This is also sometimes true when an employee quits without notice or good reason. Arbitrary treatment of employees *or* employers therefore violates the spirit of EAW—that of protecting the freedoms of both the employees and employers.

The third justification of EAW defends the voluntariness of employment contracts. If these are agreements between moral agents, however, such agreements imply reciprocal obligations between the parties in question for which both are accountable. It is obvious that, in an employment contract, people are rewarded for their performance. What is seldom noticed is that, if part of that employment contract is an expectation of loyalty, trust, and respect on the part of the employee, the employer must, in return, treat the employee with respect as well. The obligations required by employment agreements, if these are free and noncoercive agreements, must be equally obligatory and mutually restrictive on both parties. Otherwise one party cannot expect—morally expect—loyalty, trust, or respect from the other. . . .

The strongest reasons for allowing the abuses of EAW and for not instituting a full set of employee rights in the workplace, at least in the private sector of the economy, have to do with the nature of business in a free society. Businesses are privately owned voluntary organizations of all sizes from small entrepreneurships to large corporations. As such, they are not subject to the restrictions governing public and political institutions. Political procedures such as due process, needed to safeguard the public against the arbitrary exercise of power by the state, do not apply to private organizations. Guaranteeing such rights in the workplace would require restrictive legislation and regulation. Voluntary market arrangements, so vital to free enterprise and guaranteed by freedom of contract, would be sacrificed for the alleged public interest of employee claims. . . .

[There is] a tradition in Western thinking that distinguishes between the public and private spheres of life. The public sphere contains that part of a person's life that lies within the bounds of government regulation, whereas the private sphere lies outside those bounds. . . . Because entrepreneurships and corporations are privately owned, and since employees are free to make or break employment contracts of their choice, employee-employer relationships, like family relationships, are treated as "private." . . .

There are some questions, however, with the justification of the absence of due process with regard to the public/private distinction. Our economic system is allegedly based on private property, but it is unclear where "private" property and ownership end and "public" property and ownership begin. In the workplace, ownership and control is often divided. Corporate assets are held by an ever-changing group of individuals and institutional shareholders. It is no longer true that owners exercise any real sense of control over their property and its management. Some do, but many do not. Moreover, such complex property relationships are spelled out and guaranteed by the state. . . .

There are similarities between government-owned, public institutions and privately owned organizations. . . . [B]oth private and public institutions run transportation, control banks, and own property. While the goals of private and public institutions differ in that public institutions are allegedly supposed to place the public good ahead of profitability, the simultaneous call for business to become socially responsible and the demand for governmental organizations to become efficient and accountable further question the dichotomy between "public" and "private." . . .

The expansion of employee protections to what we would consider just claims to due process gives to the state and the courts more opportunity to interfere with the private economy and might thus further skew what is seen by some as a precarious but delicate balance between the private economic sector and public policy. We agree. But if the distinction between public and private institutions is no longer clear-cut, and the traditional separation of the public and private spheres is no longer in place, might it not then be better to recognize and extend constitutional guarantees so as to protect all citizens equally? If due process is crucial to political relationships between the individual and the state, why is it not central in relationships between employees and corporations since at least some of the companies in question are as large and powerful as small nations? Is it not in fact inconsistent with our democratic tradition *not* to mandate such rights? ◣

Questions for Discussion

1. Epstein says that employment at will is fair to both employers and employees because, for one thing, each could harm the other by ending the relationship on a whim. This seems to presuppose that the employer and employee are on an equal footing with each other, that is, that they have "equal power." Is this so?

2. Werhane and Radin claim that "the right to procedural and substantive due process should be extended to all employees in the private sector of the economy" and that the doctrine and practice of employment at will can and does violate such due process. Is this so? Would any employer who simply said that an employee was annoying and could be replaced

with someone less annoying be guilty of violating due process? This might be rude (even if true), but is it a violation of a human right?

3. Are the concerns raised in Chapter 4 about the very notion of group rights relevant to employment rights? Are employers *as employers* legitimate rights holders?

4. Do any conceptions of the nature of rights from Chapter 1 seem particularly relevant or irrelevant to concerns about employment rights? For example, is Ronald Dworkin's claim that rights are trumps particularly applicable to employment rights? Or is John Hospers's claim from Chapter 2 that rights are justified because humans need them to survive particularly applicable to employment rights?

5. Are rights, as opposed to other moral concerns such as duties or goals, necessary for treating employment relationships? What, if anything, is more effectively or more justly handled by framing employment relations (including perceived wrongs) in terms of rights?

Further Reading

Fleischer, Charles H. *Employer's Rights*. Naperville, IL: Sphinx Publishing, 2004. A thorough compilation of legal rights enjoyed by employers in the United States.

Gross, James A., and Lance Compa, eds. *Human Rights in Labor and Employment Relations: International and Domestic Perspectives*. Champagne, IL: Labor and Employment Relations Association, 2009. A collection of essays emphasizing the role of human rights, particularly from the perspective of employees, in labor contexts.

Werhane, Patricia H., and Tara J. Radin (with Norman E. Bowie). *Employment and Employee Rights*. Malden, MA: Blackwell, 2004. An excellent introduction to issues related to human and legal rights of employees.

Westin, Alan F., and Stephan Salisbury, eds. *Individual Rights in the Corporation: A Reader on Employee Rights*. New York: Pantheon Books, 1980. A very substantive compilation of readings on various issues related to employment rights.

Wolkinson, Benjamin W., and Richard N. Block. *Employment Law: The Workplace Rights of Employees and Employers*. Cambridge: Blackwell, 1996. An accessible, broad survey of legal rights pertaining to both employers and employees.

CHAPTER 10

RIGHT TO PRIVACY

In the 1965 case of *Griswold v. Connecticut*, the U.S. Supreme Court voted 7–2 to strike down a Connecticut state law that made it a crime to use, or to counsel anyone in the use of, contraceptives. Much of the ruling's focus, and certainly its enduring legacy, had to do with the Court's making its decision in the name of "the right to privacy." Arguing for the majority, Justice William O. Douglas claimed that, although no right to privacy is explicitly stated in the U.S. Constitution, it is a penumbral right—meaning, in this context, that the right is understood and implied by other rights as well as by previous court rulings. Douglas remarked,

> The right of freedom of speech and press includes not only the right to utter or to print, but the right to distribute, the right to receive, the right to read (*Martin v. Struthers*, 319 U.S. 141, 143) and freedom of inquiry, freedom of thought, and freedom to teach (*see Wiemann v. Updegraff*, 344 U.S. 183, 195)—indeed, the freedom of the entire university community. . . . Without those peripheral rights, the specific rights would be less secure. . . .
>
> In *NAACP v. Alabama*, 375 U.S. 449, 462, we protected the "freedom to associate and privacy in one's associations," noting that freedom of association was a peripheral First Amendment right. Disclosure of membership lists of a constitutionally valid association, we held, was invalid as entailing the likelihood of a substantial restraint upon the exercise by petitioner's members of their right to freedom of association. . . . In other

words, the First Amendment has a penumbra where privacy is protected from governmental intrusion. . . .

The present case, then, concerns a relationship lying within the zone of privacy created by several fundamental constitutional guarantees. And it concerns a law which, in forbidding the use of contraceptives, rather than regulating their manufacture or sale, seeks to achieve its goals by means having a maximum destructive impact upon that relationship. Such a law cannot stand in light of the familiar principle, so often applied by this Court, that a governmental purpose to control or prevent activities constitutionally subject to state regulation may not be achieved by means which sweep unnecessarily broadly and thereby invade the area of protected freedoms. . . .

We deal with a right of privacy older than the Bill of Rights—older than our political parties, older than our school system. Marriage is a coming together for better or for worse, hopefully enduring, and intimate to the degree of being sacred. It is an association that promotes a way of life, not causes; a harmony in living, not political faiths; a bilateral loyalty, not commercial or social projects. Yet it is an association for as noble a purpose as any involved in our prior decisions.

The two justices who dissented from the majority's ruling, Hugo Black and Potter Stewart, both agreed that the Connecticut law was a bad law, but both also insisted that there is no constitutionally guaranteed right to privacy. In addition, both rejected the claim that such a right is penumbral. Black commented,

One of the most effective ways of diluting or expanding a constitutionally guaranteed right is to substitute for the crucial word or words of a constitutional guarantee another word or words, more or less flexible and more or less restricted in meaning. This fact is well illustrated by the use of the term *right of privacy* as a comprehensive substitute for the Fourth Amendment's guarantee against "unreasonable searches and seizures." "Privacy" is a broad, abstract and ambiguous concept which can easily be shrunken in meaning but which can also, on the other hand, easily be interpreted as a constitutional ban against many things other than searches and seizures. I have expressed the view many times that First Amendment freedoms, for example, have suffered from a failure of the courts to stick to the simple language of the First Amendment in construing it, instead of invoking multitudes of words substituted for those the Framers used. . . .

For these reasons, I get nowhere in this case by talk about a constitutional "right of privacy" as an emanation from one or more constitutional provisions. I like my privacy as well as the next one, but I am nevertheless compelled to admit that government has a right to invade it unless prohibited by some specific constitutional provision. For these reasons, I cannot agree with the Court's judgment and the reasons it gives for holding this Connecticut law unconstitutional.

Stewart added,

Since 1879, Connecticut has had on its books a law which forbids the use of contraceptives by anyone. I think this is an uncommonly silly law. As a practical matter, the law is obviously unenforceable, except in the oblique context of the present case. As a philosophical matter, I believe the use of contraceptives in the relationship of marriage should be left to personal and private choice, based upon each individual's moral, ethical, and religious beliefs. As a matter of social policy, I think professional counsel about methods of birth control should be available to all, so that each individual's choice can be meaningfully made. But we are not asked in this case to say whether we think this law is unwise, or even asinine. We are asked to hold that it violates the United States Constitution. And that I cannot do. . . .

What provision of the Constitution, then, does make this state law invalid? The Court says it is the right of privacy "created by several fundamental constitutional guarantees." With all deference, I can find no such general right of privacy in the Bill of Rights, in any other part of the Constitution, or in any case ever before decided by this Court.

Regardless of its legal status, a great many people certainly claim that there is a moral or human right to privacy. Minimally, most people have a strong sense that it is important to protect privacy and that when it is not protected (or when it is violated), a definite wrong or injustice has occurred. One area of concern with respect to privacy includes intrusion into one's personal affairs by the government or official agencies. For example, following the events of September 11, 2001, and the subsequent passage of the USA PATRIOT Act, many people grew concerned about the level and types of electronic surveillance of individuals by the government. Many acts of law enforcement, such as strip searches and telephone wiretaps, have been criticized as intrusions into individuals' personal affairs. Of course, some have also criticized surveillance by nongovernmental entities, such as employers monitoring employees' e-mails and Internet use, as an invasion of privacy (and violation of privacy rights). Besides surveillance, many hold other forms of nonconsensual viewing, such as the photographing or videotaping of a person without his or her permission or even simple unpermitted voyeurism, as violations of privacy (rights). Some people have even argued that violations of privacy can occur when information is "forced" on someone, especially after that person has averred not to want access to it (such as when a person is told the whereabouts of birth parents even after insisting on not desiring to know). Although such a case might seem an unlikely violation of privacy, it relates to the access and control of information about a person, which, as we will see below, is a primary focus of privacy concerns and privacy rights.

In addressing the relationship between privacy and rights, the first issue is the distinction between a *right to privacy* and *privacy rights*. The former emphasizes the notion that there is something of value, namely, privacy, with coherent features or characteristics, and this thing of value is not reducible to other values or things of value. There might well be reasons why privacy is a value—for example, it is a matter of dignity and respect or has social, utilitarian worth—but privacy is not the same thing as dignity or utility. Privacy, under this notion, might be justified by, but is not reducible to, other values. The term *privacy rights*, on the other hand, places the emphasis on rights that involve some particular (set of) concerns, namely, those concerns about privacy. This term is more often the focus of legal matters, both in terms of litigation and legislation. The difference between these two notions is subtle, and throughout this chapter they are used interchangeably, but the difference is worth mentioning because different authors and rights theorists use one or other of the two expressions (and do not always enunciate a distinction).

The primary conceptual issue about a right to privacy asks, What is a right to privacy a right to? This question can be understood in two ways: First, what is privacy? Second, what specific content and scope does privacy have so as to entail specific regulations of behavior?

The first concern—what is privacy such that there is a right to it?—not surprisingly, turns out to be rather complicated. It seems that an array of concerns relate to what people mean by "privacy." Sometimes people mean concealment or secrecy, such as what is written in my diary is intended for me alone and is no one else's business. Sometimes people mean seclusion, such as being by oneself, away from everyone else. Sometimes people mean restriction, such as limiting what others may know with respect to me. In these ways, privacy is strongly connected to confidentiality and anonymity. These fairly straightforward intuitions about what constitutes privacy are sometimes grouped under the definition of privacy as a state of being left alone. However, being left alone is not the same thing as privacy, and it definitely does not capture the kinds of concerns raised with respect to a right to privacy. Besides being left alone, sometimes privacy means or entails a lack of disclosure of information about a person. So, it would be a violation of a person's privacy, say, if another person told others details about the first person's life (e.g., sexual past, history of cosmetic surgery, or personal phobias). Also, privacy is often understood as an individual's control over information about him- or herself. Not only the disclosure but also perhaps the collection of information about a person might constitute a violation of his or her privacy. For example, the local grocery store can (and does) collect and store information about one's purchasing habits, which is recorded via the "club card" that one uses in that store. A new breed of coupons even has bar codes loaded with data, including, if printed from the Internet or one's cell phone, the customer's identity, Internet address, Facebook information, and even the search terms used to find the coupon. In addition, privacy is sometimes understood as a matter of exclusive access to a person or his or her possessions or to information about that person. For instance, taking pictures of a person without his or her permission (e.g., journalists doing investigative reporting) or even digging through someone's trash is a violation of privacy. Another aspect of privacy sometimes entails respect for an individual's autonomy, that is, acknowledging or abiding by his or her wishes with regard to personal information. This last aspect of privacy concerns the person's dignity and independence rather than the content of the information about the person that is, say, disclosed or collected; this includes cases in which information is "forced" on a person, as mentioned above. All of these ways in which privacy can be violated point to a broad conception of what privacy is: An agent's privacy is a matter of control over information about, access to, and the agency of that person.

The notion of privacy as the control by a particular person of information about him- or herself raises some immediate questions. For example, the content of that information could regard the person's actions (e.g., I tell you that I saw so-and-so do such and such yesterday), statements (e.g., I tell you that so-and-so said such and such), thoughts, feelings, motivations, and so forth. It could also concern the person's possessions (e.g., I tell you that so-and-so owns such and such). So, your privacy can be violated when someone else has control over information regarding you. Again, that control could take the form of disclosure or distribution of such information to others or the collection and perhaps storage (probably for future disclosure or distribution) of such information.

In addition, a violation of privacy might occur when access to a person or to information about a person is out of that person's control. If you wiretap my phone, you have access to me and information about me; assuming this is done without my knowledge and consent, this violates my privacy. This aspect of privacy is somewhat controversial because, given the "public" information available to so many people today (e.g., personal information about where a person lives that is accessible via public records), many avenues of such access are outside of an individual's control.

Also, a violation of privacy could occur when someone else has control over one's agency, that is, one's ability to act. For example, many people argue that public humiliation reduces one's ability to take charge of one's personal decisions, as does being stalked or hounded by others (e.g., celebrities being followed everywhere by paparazzi). Such situations are often viewed as violations of an individual's privacy.

All of these issues just raised speak to the complexity of the very notion of privacy. When we ask what a right to privacy is a right to, these considerations are meant to answer that question. However, these dimensions of privacy are not as obvious or clear as they might seem at first. That is to say, there are uncertainties about the scope and content of control over information about, access to, and the agency of persons; as a result, there are uncertainties about what exactly a right to privacy is a right to. These uncertainties can be presented in the form of questions about competing interests and perhaps even competing rights. There is often at least a prima facie conflict between one agent's interest in (and perhaps right to) privacy versus another agent's interest in (and perhaps right to) information. For example, an insurance company that pays for someone's health-care costs might have an interest in (and perhaps right to) information about that person even if that person does not want such information disclosed. Or voters might have an interest in (and perhaps right to) information about the moral character of a political candidate and, so, have an interest in (and perhaps right to) information about private activities of that candidate. Or a business might have an interest in (and perhaps right to) protecting its goods and, so, installs surveillance cameras in its stores even though they record the movements of persons in those stores without their permission and, possibly, knowledge. The point here is that, at least on the surface, there is reason to claim that one agent's purported right to privacy might very well conflict with another agent's purported right to information, and it is not self-evident that the right to privacy trumps the right to information in such contexts and cases.

Another concern that has been raised about the right to privacy, especially with respect to control over information about oneself, is whether all violations of privacy are also violations of a right to privacy. Someone might engage in annoying or otherwise indecorous behavior that infringes on someone else's perceived privacy, but such annoying behavior might not necessarily violate the other person's rights. For instance, paparazzi might follow a celebrity around wherever he or she goes in public (or they might loiter outside a celebrity's home), but in itself such behavior might not necessarily violate any rights that the celebrity has.

Critics of the right to privacy also claim that collection and distribution of information about a person, even without that person's consent, is not necessarily a violation of any right, even if it could be construed as a violation of privacy. For example, the infamous case of Rodney King, who was being beaten in 1991 by some Los Angeles police officers, became well known because a bystander videotaped the incident at the scene. This bystander both collected and distributed this information about Rodney King without King's consent. Given that the incident occurred in public—that is, outside—critics claim that this did not violate King's privacy (so it was a case of an agent not having control over information about himself) and certainly did not violate King's right to privacy.

One final issue regarding a right to privacy: Many commentators have raised concerns about the distinction between what is public and what is private. While the *Griswold* case noted above is often cited as showing that no one, including the government, may legitimately infringe on people's private lives and activities, critics have claimed that the line between what is private and what is public is neither sharp nor clear. In fact, they have claimed, maintaining a sharp division between the public and private can be used to justify abuses within the private sphere, whether of children by their parents, wives or husbands by their spouses, employees by their employers, or citizens by their government.

Advocates of a right to privacy have responded to these various concerns and criticisms. They have argued that, although it might be difficult to state necessary and sufficient conditions for what constitutes privacy or legitimate control over information about oneself, this difficulty does not negate the fundamental interest in maintaining the dignity and well-being provided by the protective bubble of privacy. Especially with modern information technology, it might be difficult to identify and enunciate exactly the appropriate boundaries that constitute one's private realm, but this only means that more sustained and focused attention must be paid to addressing what is private and what a right to privacy is a right to.

Of the two readings that follow, the first is a classic statement of the right to privacy written by Samuel Warren and Louis Brandeis. Although now more than a century old, this statement is seen as a definitive defense of the notion of such a right. Warren and Brandeis argue that changing technologies (in their case, the advent of photography) entail new rights and protections, since such technologies can and do lead to new wrongs and injustices. In some respects, a right to privacy is analogous to a right to property, they say, but the analogy is not an identity. That is, the protection of one's thoughts, sentiments, emotions, and so forth—or, as they put it at one point, one's personality—is akin to, but not the same as, protection of one's material property. Actual, and even potential, infringements on someone's privacy require, they claim, a new set of rights, ones focused on control of one's personality; such rights should be understood as the right to be left alone. Here is what Warren and Brandeis say:

SAMUEL WARREN AND LOUIS BRANDEIS, "THE RIGHT TO PRIVACY"*

That the individual shall have full protection in person and in property is a principle as old as the common law; but it has been found necessary from time to time to define anew the exact nature and extent of such protection. Political, social, and economic changes entail the recognition of new rights, and the common law, in its eternal youth, grows to meet the new demands of society. Thus, in very early times, the law gave a remedy only for physical interference with life and property, for trespasses *vi et armis* [with force of arms]. Then the "right to life" served only to protect the subject from battery in its various forms; liberty meant freedom from actual restraint; and the right to property secured to the individual his lands and his cattle. Later, there came a recognition of man's spiritual nature, of his feelings and his intellect.

*Harvard Law Review 4 (1890): 193–220.

Gradually the scope of these legal rights broadened; and now the right to life has come to mean the right to enjoy life,—the right to be let alone; the right to liberty secures the exercise of extensive civil privileges; and the term "property" has grown to comprise every form of possession—intangible, as well as tangible. . . .

This development of the law was inevitable. The intense intellectual and emotional life, and the heightening of sensations which came with the advance of civilization, made it clear to men that only a part of the pain, pleasure, and profit of life lay in physical things. Thoughts, emotions, and sensations demanded legal recognition, and the beautiful capacity for growth which characterizes the common law enabled the judges to afford the requisite protection, without the interposition of the legislature.

Recent inventions and business methods call attention to the next step which must be taken for the protection of the person, and for securing to the individual what Judge Cooley calls the right "to be let alone." Instantaneous photographs and newspaper enterprise have invaded the sacred precincts of private and domestic life; and numerous mechanical devices threaten to make good the prediction that "what is whispered in the closet shall be proclaimed from the house-tops." For years there has been a feeling that the law must afford some remedy for the unauthorized circulation of portraits of private persons; and the evil of invasion of privacy by the newspapers, long keenly felt, has been but recently discussed by an able writer. The alleged facts of a somewhat notorious case brought before an inferior tribunal in New York a few months ago, directly involved the consideration of the right of circulating portraits; and the question whether our law will recognize and protect the right to privacy in this and in other respects must soon come before our courts for consideration.

Of the desirability—indeed of the necessity—of some such protection, there can, it is believed, be no doubt. The press is overstepping in every direction the obvious bounds of propriety and of decency. Gossip is no longer the resource of the idle and of the vicious, but has become a trade, which is pursued with industry as well as effrontery. To satisfy a prurient taste the details of sexual relations are spread broadcast in the columns of the daily papers. To occupy the indolent, column upon column is filled with idle gossip, which can only be procured by intrusion upon the domestic circle. The intensity and complexity of life, attendant upon advancing civilization, have rendered necessary some retreat from the world, and man, under the refining influence of culture, has become more sensitive to publicity, so that solitude and privacy have become more essential to the individual; but modern enterprise and invention have, through invasions upon his privacy, subjected him to mental pain and distress, far greater than could be inflicted by mere bodily injury. . . .

It is our purpose to consider whether the existing law affords a principle which can properly be invoked to protect the privacy of the individual; and, if it does, what the nature and extent of such protection is.

Owing to the nature of the instruments by which privacy is invaded, the injury inflicted bears a superficial resemblance to the wrongs dealt with by the law of slander and of libel, while a legal remedy for such injury seems to involve the treatment of mere wounded feelings, as a substantive cause of action. The principle on which the law of defamation rests, covers, however, a radically different class of effects from those for which attention is now asked. It deals only with damage to reputation, with the injury done to the individual in his external relations to the community, by lowering him in the estimation of his fellows. The matter published of him, however widely circulated, and however unsuited to publicity, must, in order to be actionable, have a direct tendency to injure him in his intercourse with others, and even if in writing or in print, must subject him to the hatred, ridicule, or contempt of his fellowmen,—the effect of the publication upon his estimate of himself and upon his own feelings not forming an essential element in the cause of action. In short, the wrongs and correlative rights recognized by the law of slander and libel are in their nature material rather than spiritual. . . .

The common law secures to each individual the right of determining, ordinarily, to what extent his thoughts, sentiments, and emotions shall be communicated to others. Under our system of government, he can never be compelled to express them (except when upon the witness stand); and even if he has chosen to give them expression, he generally retains the power to fix the limits of the publicity which shall be given them. The existence of this right does not depend upon the particular method of expression adopted. It is immaterial whether it be by word or by signs, in painting, by sculpture, or in music. Neither does the existence of the right depend upon the nature or value of the thought or emotions, nor upon the excellence of the means of expression. The same protection is accorded to a casual letter or an entry in a diary and to the most valuable poem or essay, to a botch or daub and to a masterpiece. In every such case the individual is entitled to decide whether that which is his shall be given to the public. No other has the right to publish his productions in any form, without his consent. This right is wholly independent of the material on which the thought, sentiment, or emotions is expressed. It may exist independently of any corporeal being, as in words spoken, a song sung, a drama acted. Or if expressed on any material, as in a poem in writing, the author may have parted with the paper, without forfeiting any proprietary right in the composition itself. The right is lost only when the author himself communicates his production to the public,—in other words, publishes it. It is entirely independent of the copyright laws, and their extension into the domain of art. The aim of those statutes is to secure to the author, composer, or artist the entire profits arising from publication; but the common-law protection enables him to control absolutely the act of publication, and in the exercise of his own discretion, to decide whether there shall be any publication at all. The statutory right is of no value, unless there is a publication; the common-law right is lost as soon as there is a publication. . . .

That this protection cannot rest upon the right to literary or artistic property in any exact sense, appears the more clearly when the subject-matter for which protection is invoked is not even in the form of intellectual property, but has the attributes of ordinary tangible property. Suppose a man has a collection of gems or curiosities which he keeps private: it would hardly be contended that any person could publish a catalogue of them, and yet the articles enumerated are certainly not intellectual property in the legal sense, any more than a collection of stoves or of chairs.

The belief that the idea of property in its narrow sense was the basis of the protection of unpublished manuscripts led an able court to refuse, in several cases, injunctions against the publication of private letters, on the ground that "letters not possessing the attributes of literary compositions are not property entitled to protection;" and that it was "evident the plaintiff could not have considered the letters as of any value whatever as literary productions, for a letter cannot be considered of value to the author which he never would consent to have published." But those decisions have not been followed, and it may not be considered settled that the protection afforded by the common law to the author of any writing is entirely independent of its pecuniary value, its intrinsic merits, or of any intention to publish the same and, of course, also, wholly independent of the material, if any, upon which, or the mode in which, the thought or sentiment was expressed.

These considerations lead to the conclusion that the protection afforded to thoughts, sentiments, and emotions, expressed through the medium of writing or of the arts, so far as it consists in preventing publication, is merely an instance of the enforcement of the more general right of the individual to be let alone. It is like the right not to be assaulted or beaten, the right not to be imprisoned, the right not to be maliciously prosecuted, the right not to be defamed. In each of these rights, as indeed in all other rights recognized by the law, there inheres the quality of being owned or possessed—and (as that is the distinguishing attribute of property) there may be some propriety in speaking of those rights as property. But, obviously, they bear little resemblance to what is ordinarily comprehended under that term. The principle which protects personal writings and all other personal productions, not against theft and physical appropriation, but against publication in any form, is in reality not the principle of private property, but that of an inviolate personality.

If we are correct in this conclusion, the existing law affords a principle from which may be invoked to protect the privacy of the individual from invasion either by the too enterprising press, the photographer, or the possessor of any other modern device for rewording or reproducing scenes or sounds. For the protection afforded is not confined by the authorities to those cases where any particular medium or form of expression has been adopted, not to products of the intellect. The same protection is afforded to emotions and sensations expressed in a musical composition or other work of art as to a literary composition; and words spoken, a pantomime acted, a sonata performed, is no less entitled to protection than if each had been reduced to writing. The circumstance that a thought or emotion has been recorded in a permanent form renders its identification easier, and hence may be important from the point of view of evidence, but it has no significance as a matter of substantive right. If, then, the decisions indicate a general right to privacy for thoughts, emotions, and sensations, these should receive the same protection, whether expressed in writing, or in conduct, in conversation, in attitudes, or in facial expression.

It may be urged that a distinction should be taken between the deliberate expression of thoughts and emotions in literary or artistic compositions and the casual and often involuntary expression given to them in the ordinary conduct of life. In other words, it may be contended that the protection afforded is granted to the conscious products of labor, perhaps as an encouragement to effort. This contention, however plausible, has, in fact, little to recommend it. If the amount of labor involved be adopted as the test, we might well find that the effort to conduct one's self properly in business and in domestic relations had been far greater than that involved in painting a picture or writing a book; one would find that it was far easier to express lofty sentiments in a diary than in the conduct of a noble life. If the test of deliberateness of the act be adopted, much casual correspondence which is now accorded full protection would be excluded from the beneficent operation of existing rules. After the decisions denying the distinction attempted to be made between those literary productions which it was intended to publish and those which it was not, all considerations of the amount of labor involved, the degree of deliberation, the value of the product, and the intention of publishing must be abandoned, and no basis is discerned upon which the right to restrain publication and reproduction of such so-called literary and artistic works can be rested, except the right to privacy, as a part of the more general right to the immunity of the person,—the right to one's personality. . . .

We must therefore conclude that the rights, so protected, whatever their exact nature, are not rights arising from contract or from special trust, but are rights as against the world; and, as above stated, the principle which has been applied to protect these rights is in reality not the principle of private property, unless that word be used in an extended and unusual sense. The principle which protects personal writings and any other productions of the intellect or of the emotions, is the right to privacy, and the law has no new principle to formulate when it extends this protection to the personal appearance, sayings, acts, and to personal relation, domestic or otherwise.

If the invasion of privacy constitutes a legal *injuria*, the elements for demanding redress exist, since already the value of mental suffering, caused by an act wrongful in itself, is recognized as a basis for compensation.

The right of one who has remained a private individual, to prevent his public portraiture, presents the simplest case for such extension; the right to protect one's self from pen portraiture, from a discussion by the press of one's private affairs, would be a more important and far-reaching one. If casual and unimportant statements in a letter, if handiwork, however inartistic and valueless, if possessions of all sorts are protected not only against reproduction, but also against description and enumeration, how much more should the acts and sayings of a man in his social and domestic relations be guarded from ruthless publicity. If you may not reproduce a woman's face photographically without her consent, how much less should be tolerated the reproduction of her face, her form, and her actions, by graphic descriptions colored to suit a gross and depraved imagination. . . .

It would doubtless be desirable that the privacy of the individual should receive the added protection of the criminal law, but for this, legislation would be required. Perhaps it would be deemed proper to bring the criminal liability for such publication within narrower limits; but that the community has an interest in preventing such invasions of privacy, sufficiently strong to justify the introduction of such a remedy, cannot be doubted. Still, the protection of society must come mainly through a recognition of the rights of the individual. Each man is responsible for his own acts and omissions only. If he condones what he reprobates, with a weapon at hand equal to his defense, he is responsible for the results. If he resists, public opinion will rally to his support. Has he then such a weapon? It is believed that the common law provides him with one, forged in the slow fire of the centuries, and today fitly tempered to his hand. The common law has always recognized a man's house as his castle, impregnable, often, even to his own officers engaged in the execution of its command. Shall the courts thus close the front entrance to constituted authority, and open wide the back door to idle or prurient curiosity? ◣

Writing more than a century after Warren and Brandeis, law professor Lloyd Weinreb asks whether there is any nonutilitarian justification for a right to privacy. He ends up by saying no; the best argument for any reasonable sense of a right to privacy turns out to be utilitarian and contextual, which is to say, a matter of social good in given contexts. Along the way to this conclusion, he states that an interest in privacy, which agents might have for many reasons, does not entail a right to privacy. So, for example, I might engage in illegal or immoral activities and have an interest in keeping them private; this, in itself, does not imply that I have a right to privacy. Indeed, there might be very good reasons for the collection and distribution of information about agents without, or even contrary to, their consent. But, for Weinreb, even if we acknowledge the important interest in privacy, it might be that such legitimate interest—for instance, the protection of one's autonomy—could be justified and covered under a right to liberty and self-determination, without having also to raise a further issue of a right to privacy. In the end, then, there is good reason, says Weinreb, minimally to be skeptical about a right to privacy and perhaps even to reject such a right.

LLOYD L. WEINREB, "THE RIGHT TO PRIVACY"*

The question that I address in this paper is whether there is a right to privacy. It is not the question whether in the United States there is a legal right to privacy or, more particularly, a constitutional right to privacy. There are any number of ordinary legal rights and specific constitutional rights that might be so described, and the U.S. Supreme Court has referred also to a generic "right to privacy" that is implicit in the U.S. Constitution. Nor is the question that I address whether persons have a moral claim to privacy that others ought to respect. I assume that in many circumstances, respecting a person's claim to privacy is productive of the good, and, if so, that the claim ought to be respected. Rather, my question is whether persons have a right to privacy not dependent on positive law, such that it ought ordinarily to be respected without regard to the consequences, good or bad, simply because it is a right. . . .

The question is more than a matter of conceptual clarity. What is at stake, at bottom, is the ground or grounds on which the various claims to privacy, those that are recognized as legal rights as well as those that are not, are based: whether it is more than convention, or one side of the imponderable distinction between self- and other-regarding conduct, or, more narrowly focused, a common human desire to conceal or withhold from others certain information that they have some reason to

Social Philosophy and Policy 17 (2000): 25–44.

want. An interest in privacy may rest on any of those grounds and may be a sufficient ground of a legal right, as a matter of social policy. A legal right so justified, however, is vulnerable to opposing arguments: that the convention is otiose and ought to be discarded, or that significant other-regarding aspects of conduct have been overlooked or undervalued, or that information obtained by methods that are not themselves objectionable is generally available to all for their use. Even if the legal right withstands such arguments, it may fall short of the privacy that is claimed. Conventions are stretched by novel practices unknown when the conventions took shape and require justification for their extension. Changing technology and new information alter the balance between what is self-regarding and what is not. Information that previously was confidential as a practical matter is generated, collected, and disseminated with an efficiency that shatters old compromises, and to those who want to use the information, can implies ought. One way or another, the contingency of a merely legal right seems less than we need if privacy is to be preserved. . . .

Not the least of the difficulties about privacy is that it is so elusive. Just about anything may be private: persons, places, things, actions, words, thoughts, emotions—"whatever," as Seinfeld likes to say. It is not apparent what might join, say, a retired schoolteacher, a family cottage, a monkey wrench, singing in the shower, an expletive, speculation about the quality of mercy, and a suppressed rage, under the common umbrella of privacy. Evidently it has to do with a connection to some definite person; for whatever it is that is private, the privacy at stake attaches not to it but to someone. It is far from clear, however, what that connection is, unless it is privacy itself. Privacy largely conceived readily encompasses the argument against regulation of self-regarding conduct that Mill made the cornerstone of his defense of liberty. But it is just as easy to think of privacy as an aspect of liberty; efforts of the government to collect personal data are often decried as an attack on liberty. Privacy may include shelter from the presence of others. Yet privacy is not solitude, and it becomes an issue only in relation to others. Certain activities, mostly sexual or bodily functions, which are anything but secret or unusual, are private if anything is, but in this instance, privacy is as much an obligation as a privilege or right. Included prominently within this hodgepodge is informational privacy, having to do with a person's control over what is known about him, which itself takes various forms.

An invasion of informational privacy may involve observing or listening to a person without his consent, in which case the notion of privacy as shelter also may be involved. Much more generally, the invasion of informational privacy includes any manner, unauthorized by the person himself, of obtaining information about him or collecting or distributing it, even if there is no actual intrusion on him personally. The mere fact that a person prefer that information be unknown to others does not make it private. It is neither necessary nor sufficient that the information be secret, or embarrassing, or out of the ordinary, or, indeed, anything except private. But what makes it private is not evident. . . .

It is scarcely surprising that the right to privacy is problematic, if it is so uncertain what it is a right *to*. The matter is complicated further because the notion of privacy has a resonance that informs many of its particular concrete forms. With rare exceptions, we think of privacy as a *good* that *belongs* to someone. Unsurprisingly, those two characteristics, without more, are easily translated into a right. The aura of a right may surround any aspect of privacy, a tendency of thought that is encouraged by a distinct, wholly abstract conception of privacy, which has not to do with any particular form of privacy but is only a reflection, as it were, of personal autonomy. . . .

When people speak of a right to privacy, they mostly have in mind informational privacy, a person's control over others' acquisition and distribution of information about himself. That is what the Supreme Court had in mind, for example, when it said that the Fourth Amendment protects a person's "legitimate expectation of privacy," whether or not there was a trespass in the ordinary sense. Some other aspect of privacy, like shelter from the presence of others or the exclusion of others from some space, may also be involved, but the core of informational privacy and what the right to privacy most often concerns is simply a person's right to determine the distribution of personal information. . . . Not all information, nor even all personal information, is private, however. Not the least of the difficulties confronting a defense of the right to privacy is specifying without circularity what information it shields.

A person may resist the disclosure of information because of its consequences. Although the Supreme Court has separated the right to privacy protected by the Fourth Amendment from the remedy for a violation of a right, the reason for asserting the right is almost invariably to avoid the incriminating consequences of the violation. But an invasion of privacy is thought to be wrong—an injury—in itself, even if there is no harmful consequence. Insofar as persons have a desire for privacy, whatever their reasons, satisfying the desire contributes to the social good. Insofar as persons want to have information or would be pleased if they had it, however, satisfying their desire would also contribute to the social good. One may have little impulse to relieve the curiosity, prurient or otherwise, of readers of the tabloids, but calculations of the good do not discriminate. For most purposes, furthermore, in the absence of a special need for secrecy, the possession of information is regarded as empowering and its distribution, therefore, is desirable.

Seeking a foundation for the right to privacy that is not subject to variable and changing practices of a community and its assessment of the good, defenders of the right have looked to personal autonomy as a quality of personhood itself, not dependent on local convention. Because privacy in all its forms attaches uniquely to persons and because the abstract notion of privacy, discussed above, is scarcely more than a reflection of autonomy, the connection of informational privacy in particular with autonomy has seemed attractive. . . .

[There are arguments that show] how privacy can enhance one's sense of his own potency as an autonomous actor living in community with others like himself. None of them, however, makes the case for a right to privacy independent of its value as a social good. At bottom, the case fails because in each instance it *directly* concerns only what *others* know. Although the context in which he acts has changed, the person whose privacy is invaded is, *qua* actor, the same after the invasion as before; or if he is not, it is because of *his own* reaction to the fact that others have acquired the information in question about him. Although there are certain conditions of autonomy that are conditions of personhood and attach as rights to all human beings, they do not qualify the contingent, determinate circumstances in which persons act. . . .

In a large number of familiar situations, information about a person that would ordinarily be regarded as private is not so regarded, because, in the circumstances, its disclosure is thought to serve the proper interests of others or the public generally. The assertion that some information has significant other-regarding consequences, if accepted, is ordinarily a full response to a claim of informational privacy. So, for example, if a woman asked her would-be lover or fiancé whether he was HIV-positive or had been promiscuous without protection in the past (or if, as is not uncommon, she insisted that he be tested for the AIDS virus), it would be odd indeed to berate her for invading his privacy. On the contrary, even if he were not asked, he would be criticized if he failed to disclose such information. . . . Likewise in the public arena, debate about the disclosure of facts about the "private life" of a candidate for public office focuses on their relevance to his ability to perform his duties; if it is agreed that the facts are relevant—that is, have other-regarding significance—objections to their disclosure fade. So long as the conclusion that information is generally not other-regarding is accepted, a person's privacy with respect to that information may have the aspect of a right, because the possibility of harmful consequences to others is not in issue. Once that possibility is raised, however, and is seriously in issue, privacy loses its quality as a right and is decided as a matter of the good.

In ordinary discourse, there is no need for a sharp distinction between the right and the good; all that needs to be said is that, in view of the circumstances, the person's privacy is not a barrier to disclosure. If the kind of information that is at stake generally is regarded as private, the situation may be described as one in which the person does indeed have a right to privacy but has waived it—by becoming engaged or running for office—or his right is overcome by the good of disclosure, rather than as one in which he has no right to waive or to be overcome in the first place. The so-called "waiver," however, which rarely is explicit, consists of nothing but the fact that the information is not, in the circumstances, regarded as private. Although a rare departure from a right in especially exigent circumstances need not defeat its quality as a right, it is the very essence of a right that it does not depend on a calculation of the good and ordinarily prevails despite the harm that its exercise may cause others. "I have a right to . . . " is not an assertion that the contemplated course of action is morally correct or will not have unfortunate consequences; rather, it is an assertion that even if it be otherwise, it does not matter.

The recognition of a person's privacy is not, as is the application of a right, independent of circumstances. On the contrary, it is freighted with assumptions about circumstances and varies accordingly. The particular circumstances may be disregarded if there is a rule favoring privacy in some category of cases to which the instance in question belongs. Nevertheless, the justification for privacy in that instance is not the person's right but the social good. One who believed that privacy ought not be respected would argue, on grounds of the good, either that the rule was not applicable in that instance or that if it was, the rule was mistaken in that respect or generally. If his argument prevailed, there would be no residue of a personal right.

If it is correct that informational privacy is conventional only, grounded in the practices and normative understandings of the community and variable from one community to another, then it is reasonable to suppose that within a community as well, it may depend on circumstances. To think of informational privacy in this way gives up the rhetorical advantage of associating it with rights generally and with the demands of individual autonomy or liberty in particular, in exchange for a sharper, clearer understanding of its true value. In an age when, as we are told, information is the key to social well-being and wealth, insistence on privacy will look increasingly like Luddism. The march of technology creates uses for information that was previously random data or makes available information that was unknown or even unknowable—in a sense, therefore, inviolably private. A response that does no more than assert a right to privacy may prevail for a time, but only so long as the benefits that it opposes are small. Eventually the debate will be about the good. That does not mean that privacy must always be the loser. It does mean that those who would defend privacy as we know it will have to provide a convincing account of the human good that overshadows the material rewards that are offered in its place. It will not be easy. ◣

Questions for Discussion

1. Warren and Brandeis claim that a unique right, namely, a right to privacy, is necessary because other rights, such as property or autonomy rights, do not (cannot?) provide the necessary protection of agents. A "right to be left alone," then, is not equivalent or reducible to any other rights. Is this correct? What protections or empowerments does a right to be left alone give that other rights do not (or cannot)?

2. Weinreb seems to argue that the only real justification for a right to privacy is a utilitarian one. Is this correct? As with many negative rights, is the right to privacy not a protection for an agent against the majority? Would Weinreb's view justify government surveillance without an agent's

knowledge or consent? He also claims that an interest in privacy does not entail a right to it. But if such an interest does not, what could? Is the interest in privacy not simply an interest in the well-being and autonomy of an agent?

3. Chapter 6 raises a number of concerns communitarians have about the strident nature of rights talk and the overreliance on rights in addressing moral matters and conflicts. Do those concerns apply with respect to privacy rights discourse? Why or why not?

4. Do any conceptions of the nature of rights from Chapter 1 seem particularly relevant or irrelevant to concerns about privacy rights? For example, is Martha Nussbaum's claim that rights are related to agents' capabilities particularly applicable to privacy rights? Or is John Stuart Mill's claim from Chapter 2 that rights are justified by their utilitarian function particularly applicable to privacy rights?

5. Chapter 7 notes that many people see much of rights discourse as framed by Western cultural concerns and assumptions. Are privacy rights legitimately subject to such a claim? That is, is the right to privacy based mostly on Western values?

Further Reading

Etzioni, Amitai. *The Limits of Privacy*. New York: Basic Books, 2000. A communitarian perspective, including a critique, on privacy and claims to privacy rights.

Glenn, Richard A. *The Right to Privacy: Rights and Liberties Under the Law*. Santa Clara, CA: ABC-CLIO, 2003. A historical overview of the emergence of a right to privacy in American culture and law.

Mills, Jon. *Privacy: The Lost Right*. Oxford: Oxford University Press, 2008. An argument defending privacy rights via an analysis of privacy and specific legal cases.

Paul, Ellen Frankel, Fred D. Miller Jr., and Jeffrey Paul, eds. *The Right to Privacy*. Cambridge: Cambridge University Press, 2000. A collection of essays covering a wide range of philosophical issues related to rights and privacy.

Solove, Daniel. *Understanding Privacy*. Cambridge, MA: Harvard University Press, 2008. An overview of issues and difficulties related to privacy and information technology.

CHAPTER 11

INTELLECTUAL PROPERTY RIGHTS

In 1813, Thomas Jefferson wrote a letter to Isaac McPherson Monticello, which included the following remarks against the notion that there could be a patent on ideas:

> It has been pretended by some, (and in England especially,) that inventors have a natural and exclusive right to their inventions, and not merely for their own lives, but inheritable to their heirs. But while it is a moot question whether the origin of any kind of property is derived from nature at all, it would be singular to admit a natural and even an hereditary right to inventors. It is agreed by those who have seriously considered the subject, that no individual has, of natural right, a separate property in an acre of land, for instance. By an universal law, indeed, whatever, whether fixed or movable, belongs to all men equally and in common, is the property for the moment of him who occupies it; but when he relinquishes the occupation, the property goes with it. Stable ownership is the gift of social law, and is given late in the progress of society. It would be curious then, if an idea, the fugitive fermentation of an individual brain, could, of natural right, be claimed in exclusive and stable property. If nature has made any one thing less susceptible than all others of exclusive property, it is the action of the thinking power called an idea, which an individual may exclusively possess as long as he keeps it to himself; but the moment it is divulged, it forces itself into the possession of every one, and the receiver

303

cannot dispossess himself of it. Its peculiar character, too, is that no one possesses the less, because every other possesses the whole of it. He who receives an idea from me, receives instruction himself without lessening mine; as he who lights his taper [i.e., candle] at mine, receives light without darkening me. That ideas should freely spread from one to another over the globe, for the moral and mutual instruction of man, and improvement of his condition, seems to have been peculiarly and benevolently designed by nature, when she made them, like fire, expansible over all space, without lessening their density in any point, and like the air in which we breathe, move, and have our physical being, incapable of confinement or exclusive appropriation. Inventions then cannot, in nature, be a subject of property. Society may give an exclusive right to the profits arising from them, as an encouragement to men to pursue ideas which may produce utility, but this may or may not be done, according to the will and convenience of the society, without claim or complaint from any body. Accordingly, it is a fact, as far as I am informed, that England was, until we copied her, the only country on earth which ever, by a general law, gave a legal right to the exclusive use of an idea. In some other countries it is sometimes done, in a great case, and by a special and personal act, but, generally speaking, other nations have thought that these monopolies produce more embarrassment than advantage to society; and it may be observed that the nations which refuse monopolies of invention, are as fruitful as England in new and useful devices.

This letter shows that Jefferson, although often cited by many classical liberals and libertarians as a defender of natural rights, including property rights, did not consider matters of intellect (at least some of them), such as ideas, to be property in the same sense as material property, deserving of the kinds of protections that material property had. On the other hand, in the previous chapter, we saw Samuel Warren and Louis Brandeis argue that the right to privacy includes such things—indeed, especially such things—as thoughts, sentiments, and so forth. These sorts of mental creations—ideas, inventions, designs—are often referred to as "intellectual property." More precisely, the copyrights, patents, trademarks, and so forth, assigned to such mental creations are said to be intellectual property. Given the claim that today we live in a world of information, itself an abstract entity, the notion of intellectual property is even more prevalent and important than it was in Jefferson's time. It leads, of course, to the issue of intellectual property rights. As with the right to privacy, the question is, How, if at all, can the notion of intellectual property rights best be understood and justified?

Among the concerns connected to this question is the issue of what constitutes intellectual property. First, there is the matter of property. What makes something property? There are all sorts of things in the world (where the word "things" includes, of course, objects but also events and processes). What makes these things property, and, in particular, what makes them the property of some particular agent? One claim is that something becomes someone's property by virtue of first possession. Something becomes my property if I come to possess it before anyone else does. Such a claim is rather difficult to maintain, however, because it is difficult (at best) to say what constitutes first possession, or even that possession is clear and uncontroversial. If—and this is a big *if*—I am the first person to stumble upon, say, some hidden lake deep in a forest, what makes that a first possession? Is my assertion that I am the finder of this lake (even assuming that, indeed, I am the first agent to find it) sufficient for me to possess it? Or what would it mean to say that I am the first possessor of the new car that I bought? I am certainly not the first possessor of the multitude of materials that went into the making of the car. There are social structures in place that identify me as the legal owner of this new car, but that is not the issue here, since those social structures have to do with legal ownership, not with a natural right. In addition, it is not clear how that elucidates what it even means to say that I possess it (first).

A second, and more endorsed, conception of property has to do with one's labor as the criterion of ownership. This notion holds that what makes something property, and, in particular, my property, is that I possess it or have exclusive control over it because of my actions and activities that led to me having control over it—in a word, my labor. So, this new car is (my) property because I did such and such, resulting in my having control over this object; in normal social contexts today, I worked, got paid, and gave someone else my money (which itself was my property) in exchange for the car and exclusive control over it. An enormous volume of writing and debate has focused on this conception of property as the result of one's labor, and a full discussion of it is far beyond the scope of the present chapter. Suffice it to say that this labor conception of property is endorsed by a great many theorists—but also rejected by many.

Another notion and justification given concerning property is utilitarian: The possession and control of (certain) things is a social good and has utility in promoting the well-being both of the possessor/controller of those things and of society in general. An additional conception is sometimes referred to as the "personality" view of property, which basically holds that having possession and control over (certain) things is fundamental to an agent's personality and agency. Without such property, agents would not be able to function in ways that promoted their own well-being or agency or the well-being or agency of others. (Imagine what life would be like if you could not call a great many things your own; it would be difficult to conduct normal daily activities.)

With respect to intellectual property, it is not so much external but mental things that are possessed or controlled. By their nature, such mental things are abstract, not material. They are "things" like ideas, designs, and thoughts. They have content; for example, if I create a new song, there is content, namely, a (structured) collection of sounds or rhythms. Or if I write a book, there is a (structured) collection of words and other linguistic entities. However, these creations are, at least on the surface, quite different from material objects. For one thing, such mental things are said to be nonrivalrous, which simply means that one agent is not a rival of another agent in terms of the use of that thing. While a car is rivalrous—that is, if I use it, you cannot use it at the same time— an idea is not. My use of an idea does not preclude your use of the same idea. As Jefferson said in his letter above, "[H]e who lights his taper at mine, receives light without darkening me." In other words, my possession or control of light is unaffected, or at least not negatively affected, by your possession or control of light. Or if I possess and control a copy of some song, your possessing and controlling another copy of that same song does not preclude me from fully using my copy. So, we are not rivals with respect to the song.

On the other hand, proponents of intellectual property and intellectual property rights have argued that one's mental creations are still the result of an agent's labor and, as such and for the same reasons, are the property of that agent. If it is correct to say that my car is my property, and therefore I have possession and control of it, then my song is also my property, and I legitimately have possession and control of it. If I choose to allow you to use my car, it is still my car, and if I allow you to use my song (i.e., have a copy of it or sing it), it is still my song. The point is that, as it is my property, I have control over it. Yes, you can steal my car or steal my song (at least, a copy of it), but that does not mean that it is not my property. If you do steal my car, then you have violated my rights, and I have legitimate recourse to getting it back. If you steal my song (i.e., obtain a copy of it without my consent), then, likewise, you have violated my rights, and I have legitimate recourse to getting it back—which, in the case of the song, would mean regaining control of it (since no material object has been lost).

A common view, then, is that intellectual property, even though it is nonmaterial and nonrivalrous, is nonetheless the product of one's labor and, so, a piece of property such that the owner—or, in the case of intellectual property, the creator—has appropriate and legitimate possession and control of it. A classic defender of intellectual property and intellectual property rights is Lysander Spooner. Writing in the late 1800s, Spooner stated in clear and uncompromising terms the case for intellectual property rights. In the reading below, he argues that whatever contributes to or constitutes the well-being of an agent is wealth and, as wealth, is or can become property. All labor for Spooner is ultimately mental labor, since whatever work one does is a matter of mentality (even lifting bricks requires thought). Property is possessed wealth, and possession is, in his word, dominion (i.e., control). Intellectual property, then, is no different in its nature as property from material property and is just as governed by natural rights of dominion.

LYSANDER SPOONER, "THE LAW OF INTELLECTUAL PROPERTY—THE LAW OF NATURE"*

The Right of Property in Ideas to Be Proved by Analogy

In order to understand the law of nature in regard to intellectual property, it is necessary to understand the principles of that law in regard to property in general. We shall then see that the right to property in *ideas*, is at least as strong as—and in many cases identical with—the right of property in material things.

To understand the law of nature, relative to property in *general*, it is necessary, in the first place, that we understand the distinction between *wealth* and *property*; and, in the second place, that we understand how and when wealth becomes property. . . .

What is wealth? Wealth is any thing, that is, or can be made, valuable to man, or available for his use. The term *wealth* properly includes every

*In *The Collected Works of Lysander Spooner*, ed. Charles Shively, vol. 3 (Weston, MA: M&S Press, 1971), 9–12, 15–21, 28–30.

conceivable object, idea, and sensation, that can either contribute to, or constitute, the physical, intellectual, moral, or emotional well-being of man. Light, air, water, earth, vegetation, minerals, animals, every material thing, living or dead, animate or inanimate, that can aid, *in any way*, the comfort, happiness, or welfare of man, are wealth.

Things intangible and imperceptible by our physical organs, and perceptible only by the intellect, or felt only by the affections, are wealth. Thus liberty is wealth; opportunity is wealth; motion or labor is wealth; rest is wealth; reputation is wealth; love is wealth; sympathy is wealth; hope is wealth; knowledge is wealth; truth is wealth; for the simple reason that they all contribute to, or constitute in part, a man's well-being. . . .

Another reason why tangibility and perceptibility by our physical organs are no criteria of wealth is that it really is not our physical organs, but the *mind, and only the mind*, that takes cognizance even of material objects. We are in the habit of saying that the eye sees any *material* object. But, in reality, it is only the *mind* that sees it. The mind sees *through the eye*. It uses the eye merely as an instrumentality for seeing it. An eye, without a mind, could see nothing. . . . And every thing, of which the mind does take cognizance, is equally wealth, whether it be material or immaterial; whether it be tangible or perceptible, through the instrumentality of our physical organs, or not. It would be absurd to say that one thing was wealth, because the mind was obliged to use such material instruments as the hand, or the eye, to perceive it and that another thing, as an *idea*, for example, was not *wealth*, simply because the mind could perceive it *without using* any *material instruments*.

It is plain, therefore, that an *idea*, which the mind perceives, without the instrumentality of our physical organs, is as clearly wealth, as is a house, or a horse, or any *material thing*, which the mind sees by the aid of the eye, or touches through the instrumentality of the hand. The capacity of the thing, whether it be a horse, a house, or an idea, to contribute to, or constitute, the well-being of man, is the only criterion by which to determine whether or not it be wealth; and not its tangibility or perceptibility, through the agency of our physical organs.

An *idea*, then, is wealth. It is equally wealth, whether it be regarded, as some ideas may be, simply as, in itself, an object of enjoyment, reflection, meditation, and thus a *direct* source of happiness; or whether it be regarded, as other ideas may be, simply as a means to be used for acquiring other wealth, intellectual, moral, affectional, or material. . . .

What is property? Property is simply wealth, *that is possessed*—*that has an owner*; in contradistinction to wealth, that has no owner, but lies exposed, *unpossessed*, and ready to be converted into property, by whomsoever chooses to make it his own.

All property is wealth; but all wealth is not property. A very small portion of the wealth in the world has any owner. It is mostly unpossessed. Of the wealth in the ocean, for example, an infinitesimal part ever becomes property. And occasionally one takes possession of a fish, or a shell, leaving all the rest of the ocean's wealth without an owner. . . . Of intellectual wealth, too, doubtless a very minute portion of all that is susceptible of acquisition, and possession, has ever been acquired— that is, has ever become property. Of all the truths, and of all the knowledge, which will doubtless sometime be possessed, how little is now possessed.

What Is the Right of Property?

The right of property is simply *the right of dominion*. It is the right— which one man has, *as against all other men*, to the exclusive control, dominion, use, and enjoyment of any particular thing. The principle of property is, that a thing belongs to one man, and not to another; *mine*, and *thine*, and *his*, are the terms that convey the idea of property. . . . The *right* of property is one's *right* of ownership, enjoyment, control, and domination, of and over any object, idea, or sensation. . . .

What Things Are Subjects of Property?

Every conceivable thing, whether intellectual, moral, or material, of which the *mind* can take cognizance, and which can be possessed, held, used, controlled, and enjoyed, by one person, and not, *at the same instant of time*, by another person, is rightfully a subject of property. . . .

The air that a man inhales is his, *while it is inhaled*. When he has exhaled it, it is no longer his. The air that he may enclose in a bottle, or in his dwelling, is his, *while it is so enclosed*. When he has discharged it, it is no longer his. The sunlight that falls upon a man, or upon his land, or that comes into his dwelling, is his; and no other man has a right to forbid his enjoyment of it, or compel him to pay for it.

A man's *body* is his own. It is the propriety of his mind. (It is the mind that owns every thing, that is property. Bodies own nothing; but are themselves subjects of property—that is, of dominion. Each body is the property—that is, is under the dominion—of the mind that inhabits it.) And no man has a right, as being the proprietor, to take another man's body out of the control of his mind. In other words, no man can own another man's body.

All a man's enjoyments, all his feelings, all his happiness, *are his property*. They are his, and not another man's. They belong to him, and not to others. And no other man has the right to forbid him to enjoy them or to compel him to pay for them. Other men may have enjoyments, feelings, happiness, *similar* in their nature, to his. But they cannot own *his* feelings, *his* enjoyments, or *his* happiness. They cannot, therefore, rightfully require him to pay them for them, as if they were theirs, and not his own. . . .

Because all men *give* more or less of their thoughts gratuitously to their fellow men, in conversation, or otherwise, it does not follow at all that their thoughts are not their property, which they have a natural *right* to set their own price upon, and to withhold from other men, unless the price be paid. Their thoughts are thus given gratuitously, or in exchange for other men's thoughts, (as in conversation) either for the reason that they would bring nothing more in the market, or would bring too little to compensate for the time and labor of putting them in a marketable form, and selling them. Their market value is too small to make it *profitable* to sell them. Such thoughts men give away gratuitously, or in exchange for such thoughts as other men voluntarily give in return—just as men give to each other material commodities of small value, as nuts, and apples, a piece of bread, a cup of water, a meal of victuals, from motives of complaisance and friendship, or in expectation of receiving similar favors in return; and not because these articles are not as much property as are the most valuable commodities that men ever buy or sell. But for nearly all information that is specially valuable, or valuable enough to command any price worth demanding—though it be given in one's private ear, as legal or medical advice, for example—a pecuniary compensation is demanded, with nearly the same uniformity as for a material commodity. And no one doubts that such information is a legitimate and lawful consideration for the equivalent paid. Courts of justice uniformly recognize them as such, as in the case of legal, medical, and various other kinds of information. One man can sue for and recover pay for ideas, which, as lawyer, physician, teacher, or editor, he has sold to another man, just as he can for land, food, clothing, or fuel.

What Is the Foundation of the Right of Property?

The right of property has its foundation, first, in the natural right of each man to provide for his own subsistence; and, secondly, in his right to provide for his general happiness and well-being, in addition to a mere subsistence.

The right to live includes the right to accumulate the means of living; and the right to obtain happiness in general, includes the right to accumulate such commodities as minister to one's happiness. These rights, then, to live, and to obtain happiness, are the foundations of the right to property. Such being the case, it is evident that no other human right has a deeper foundation in the nature and necessities of man, than the right of property. If, when one man has dipped a cup of water from the stream, to slake his own thirst, or gathered food, to satisfy his own hunger, or made a garment, to protect his own body, other men can rightfully tell him that these commodities are not *his*, but *theirs*, and can rightfully take them from him, without his consent, [then] his right to provide for the preservation of his own life, and for the enjoyment of happiness, are extinct.

The right of property in intellectual wealth has manifestly the same foundation as the right of property in material wealth. Without intellectual wealth—that is, without ideas—material wealth could neither be accumulated nor fitted to contribute, nor made to constitute, to the sustenance or happiness of man. Intellectual wealth, therefore, is indispensable to the acquisition and use of other wealth. It is also, of itself, a direct source of happiness, in a great variety of ways. Furthermore, it is not only a thing of value, for the owner's uses, but, as has before been said, like material wealth, it is a merchantable commodity; has a value in the market; and will purchase, for its proprietor, other wealth in exchange. On every ground, therefore, the right of property in ideas has as deep a foundation in the nature and necessities of man, as has the right of property in material things.

How Is the Right of Property Transferred?

From the very nature of the right of property, that right can be transferred, from the proprietor, only by his own consent. What is the right of property? It is, as has before been explained, a right of control, of dominion. If, then, a man's property be taken from him without his consent, his right of control, or dominion over it, is necessarily infringed; in other words, his right of property is necessarily violated. Even to *use* another's property, without his consent, is to violate his right to property; because it is for the time being assuming a dominion over wealth, the rightful dominion over which belongs solely to the owner.

These are the principles of the law of nature, relative to all property. They are as applicable to intellectual, as to material, property. The *consent*, or *will*, of the owner alone, can transfer the right of property in either, or give to another the right to use either. . . .

Conclusions from the Preceding Principles

The conclusions that follow from the principles now established, obviously are, that a man has a natural and absolute right—and if a natural and absolute, then necessarily a *perpetual*, right—of property, in the ideas, of which he is the discoverer or creator; that his right of property, *in ideas*, is intrinsically the same as, and stands on identically the same grounds with, his right of property in material things; that no distinction, *of principle*, exists between the two cases. ◣

Given Spooner's claims and what is, certainly for many, a commonsense case that intellectual property is legitimate—after all, if I create a design for some instrument, does that design not belong to me as much as my car belongs to me?—what kinds of objections have been raised to the notion of intellectual property and to intellectual property rights?

While for Spooner and many others the nonmaterial and nonrivalrous nature of intellectual property is irrelevant, for many others it is not. That is, critics have claimed that ideas cannot be possessed or controlled. At most, they say, specific instances of mental entities can be possessed or controlled. For example, the ideas in this book are not possessed or controlled by me, although perhaps their particular expression in this book are. At most, then, I might be able to claim their particular expression as my property (and perhaps not even that). Further, how can ideas be individuated and identified as belonging to a specific agent, even a particular expression of ideas? After all, a songwriter does not possess or control the notes, rhythms, or tempos that constitute a particular song; nor does an author possess or control the words that constitute a particular book.

Besides questions about the very nature of intellectual objects as property, concerns have been raised about the forms of intellectual property and their corresponding rights. Included under the notion of intellectual property are copyrights, patents, trademarks, designs, trade secrets, and others. With these various forms of intellectual property, the question arises of what exactly an intellectual property right is a right to. As I have said many times throughout this chapter, the notion of property rights is addressed as the possession and control of something. But are property rights, especially intellectual property rights, well understood in terms of possession and control? For example, do possession and control entail only "first use" of the object, or do they entail what is often called "monopolistic use" of the object? "First use" means that the creator of the object controls it only at its inception; after that, it becomes a public entity. "Monopolistic use" means that the creator of the object controls all subsequent uses (or, say, copies) of it. For example, if one purchases a copy of a computer program (say, Microsoft Word), Microsoft Corporation receives payment since it created that program. Now that one has purchased it, and it—that is, that particular copy—has become the property of the purchaser, does that agent now possess and control that particular copy? If so, then the creator has first-use property rights. However, if the purchaser may not subsequently make further copies and sell them or give them away (i.e., if the purchaser does not have possession and control), then the creator has monopolistic property rights. Many critics of intellectual property rights claim that monopolistic use is entailed by the view of Spooner and those who agree with him. However, they argue, such rights are illegitimate because the social utility of access to ideas outweighs such monopolistic control. Indeed, they argue, the notion of fair use of ideas clearly indicates that this is how intellectual objects are best understood and treated (e.g., the fair use practice of allowing individuals to make copies of written works so that the ideas can be disseminated and valued).

In the reading below, Edwin Hettinger argues that two broad justifications for intellectual property rights are mistaken. The first justification is the labor view discussed earlier. Hettinger claims that there are a number of concerns about this purported justification. For one thing, he says, such a view might justify only the value added by the creator of an intellectual object, not its to-tal value. Since it is difficult, at best, to identify the value added, it is even more difficult to determine such value. A usual claim is that the value (and the value added) is the market value. So, what people are willing to pay for a computer program or a new book or the design of some new instrument—that is, the market value—is the determinant of its value. But, says Hettinger, the market value is not what the creator of the product produces; in addition, markets work only after property rights have already been established. Fur-thermore, he says, it is not obvious that the market value of an intellectual ob-ject is the same thing as the freedom of exchange of that object (i.e., control over the use of the object).

In addition to objecting to the labor view of justification of intellectual property, Hettinger rejects the dignity/agency argument for intellectual prop-erty rights. Owning the fruits of one's labor, including having control of them in the marketplace, is not obviously necessary, he says, for one's dignity, secu-rity, privacy, or agency. Consequently, he claims, the case for intellectual prop-erty rights has not been made.

EDWIN C. HETTINGER, "JUSTIFYING INTELLECTUAL PROPERTY"*

Labor, Natural Intellectual Property Rights, and Market Value

Perhaps the most powerful intuition supporting property rights is that people are entitled to the fruits of their labor. What a person produces with her own intelligence, effort, and perseverance ought to belong to her and to no one else. "Why is it mine? Well, it's mine because I made it, that's why. It wouldn't have existed but for me."

John Locke's version of this labor justification for property derives property rights in the product of labor from prior property rights in one's body. A person owns her body and hence she owns what it does, namely, its labor. A person's labor and its product are inseparable, and so ownership of one can be secured only by owning the other. Hence,

*Philosophy and Public Affairs 18 (1989): 31–52.

if a person is to own her body and thus its labor, she must also own what she joins her labor with—namely, the product of her labor.

This formulation is not without problems. For example, Robert Nozick wonders why a person should gain what she mixes her labor with instead of losing her labor. (He imagines pouring a can of tomato juice into the ocean and asks whether he thereby ought to gain the ocean or lose his tomato juice.) More importantly, assuming that labor's fruits are valuable, and that laboring gives the laborer a property right in this value, this would entitle the laborer only to the value she added, and not to the total value of the resulting product. Though exceedingly difficult to measure, these two components of value (that attributable to the object labored on and that attributable to the labor) need to be distinguished. . . .

What portion of the value of writings, inventions, and business information is attributable to the intellectual laborer? Clearly authorship, discovery, or development is necessary if intellectual products are to have value for us: we could not use or appreciate them without this labor. But it does not follow from this that all of their value is attributable to that labor. Consider, for example, the wheel, the entire human value of which is not appropriately attributable to its original inventor.

The value added by the laborer and any value the object has on its own are by no means the only components of the value of an intellectual object. Invention, writing, and thought in general do not operate in a vacuum; intellectual activity is not creation ex nihilo. Given this vital dependence of a person's thoughts on the ideas of those who came before her, intellectual products are fundamentally social products. Thus even if one assumes that the value of these products is entirely the result of human labor, this value is not entirely attributable to any particular laborer (or small group of laborers).

Separating out the individual contribution of the inventor, writer, or manager from this historical/social component is no easy task. Simply identifying the value a laborer's labor adds to the world with the market value of the resulting product ignores the vast contributions of others. A person who relies on human intellectual history and makes a small modification to produce something of great value should no more receive what the market will bear than should the last person needed to lift a car receive full credit for lifting it. If laboring gives the laborer the right to receive the market value of the resulting product, this market value should be shared by all those whose ideas contributed to the origin of the product. The fact that most of these contributors are no longer present to receive their fair share is not a reason to give the entire market value to the last contributor.

Thus an appeal to the market value of a laborer's product cannot help us here. Markets work only after property rights have been established and enforced, and our question is what sorts of property rights an inventor, writer, or manager should have, given that the result of her labor is a joint product of human intellectual history.

Even if one could separate out the laborer's own contribution and determine its market value, it is still not clear that the laborer's right to the fruits of her labor naturally entitles her to receive this. Market value is a socially created phenomenon, depending on the activity (or non-activity) of other producers, the monetary demand of purchasers, and the kinds of property rights, contracts, and markets the state has established and enforced. The market value of the same fruits of labor will differ greatly with variations in these social factors.

Consider the market value of a new drug formula. This depends on the length and the extent of the patent monopoly the state grants and enforces, on the level of affluence of those who need the drug, and on the availability and price of substitutes. The laborer did not produce these. The intuitive appeal behind the labor argument—"I made it, hence it's mine"—loses its force when it is used to try to justify owning something others are responsible for (namely, the market value). The claim that a laborer, in virtue of her labor, has a "natural right" to this socially created phenomenon is problematic at best.

Thus, there are two different reasons why the market value of the product of labor is not what a laborer's labor naturally entitles her to. First, market value is not something that is produced by those who produce a product, and the labor argument entitles laborers only to the products of their labor. Second, even if we ignore this point and equate the fruits of labor with the market value of those fruits, intellectual products result from the labor of many people besides the latest contributor, and they have claims on the market value as well. . . .

Having a moral right to the fruits of one's labor might also mean having a right to possess and personally use what one develops. This version of the labor theory has some force. On this interpretation, creating something through labor gives the laborer a prima facie right to possess and personally use it for her own benefit. The value of protecting individual freedom guarantees this right as long as the creative labor, and the possession and use of its product, does not harm others.

But the freedom to exchange a product in a market and receive its full market value is again something quite different. To show that people have a right to this, one must argue about how best to balance the conflicts in freedoms which arise when people interact. One must determine what sorts of property rights and markets are morally legitimate. One must also decide when society should enforce the results of market interaction and when it should alter those results (for example, with tax policy). There is a gap—requiring extensive argumentative filler—between the claim that one has a natural right to possess and personally use the fruits of one's labor and the claim that one ought to receive for one's product whatever the market will bear.

Such a gap exists as well between the natural right to possess and personally use one's intellectual creations and the rights protected by copyrights, patents, and trade secrets. The natural right of an author to personally use her writings is distinct from the right, protected by copyright, to make her work public, sell it in a market, and then prevent others from making copies. An inventor's natural right to use the invention for her own benefit is not the same as the right, protected by patent, to sell this invention in a market and exclude others (including independent inventors) from using it. An entrepreneur's natural right to use valuable business information or techniques that she develops is not the same as the right, protected by trade secret, to prevent her employees from using these techniques in another job.

In short, a laborer has a prima facie natural right to possess and personally use the fruits of her labor. But a right to profit by selling a product in the market is something quite different. This liberty is largely a socially created phenomenon. The "right" to receive what the market will bear is a socially created privilege, and not a natural right at all. The natural right to possess and personally use what one has produced is relevant to the justifiability of such a privilege, but by itself it is hardly sufficient to justify that privilege.

Deserving Property Rights Because of Labor

The above argument that people are naturally entitled to the fruits of their labor is distinct from the argument that a person has a claim to labor's fruits based on desert. If a person has a natural right to something—say her athletic ability—and someone takes it from her, the return of it is something she is owed and can rightfully demand. Whether or not she deserves this athletic ability is a separate issue. Similarly, insofar as people have natural property rights in the fruits of their labor, these rights are something they are owed, and not something they necessarily deserve.

The desert argument suggests that the laborer deserves to benefit from her labor, at least if it is an attempt to do something worthwhile. This proposal is convincing, but does not show that what the laborer deserves is property rights in the object labored on. The mistake is to conflate the created object which makes a person deserving of a reward with what that reward should be. Property rights in the created object are not the only possible reward. Alternatives include fees, awards, acknowledgment, gratitude, praise, security, power, status, and public financial support.

Many considerations affect whether property rights in the created object are what the laborer deserves. This may depend, for example, on what is created by labor. If property rights in the very things created were always an appropriate reward for labor, then as Lawrence Becker notes, parents would deserve property rights in their children. Many intellectual objects (scientific laws, religious and ethical insights, and so on) are also the sort of thing that should not be owned by anyone. . . .

Property rights in the thing produced are also not a fitting reward if the value of these rights is disproportional to the effort expended by the laborer. "Effort" includes (1) how hard someone tries to achieve a result, (2) the amount of risk voluntarily incurred in seeking this result, and (3) the degree to which moral considerations played a role in choosing the result intended. The harder one tries, the more one is willing to sacrifice, and the worthier the goal, the greater are one's deserts.

Becker's claim that the amount deserved is proportional to the value one's labor produces is mistaken. The value of labor's results is often significantly affected by factors outside a person's control, and no one deserves to be rewarded for being lucky. Voluntary past action is the only valid basis for determining desert. Here only a person's effort (in the sense defined) is relevant. Her knowledge, skills, and achievements insofar as they are based on natural talent and luck, rather than effort expended, are not. A person who is born with extraordinary natural talents, or who is extremely lucky, deserves nothing on the basis of these characteristics. If such a person puts forward no greater effort than another, she deserves no greater reward. Thus, two laborers who expend equal amounts of effort deserve the same reward, even when the value of the resulting products is vastly different. Giving more to workers whose products have greater social value might be justified if it is needed as an incentive. But this has nothing to do with giving the laborer what she deserves. . . .

Giving an inventor exclusive rights to make and sell her invention (for seventeen years) may provide either a greater or a lesser reward than she deserves. Some inventions of extraordinary market value result from flashes of genius, while others with little market value (and yet great social value) require significant efforts.

The proportionality requirement may also be frequently violated by granting copyright. Consider a five-hundred-dollar computer program. Granted, its initial development costs (read "efforts") were high. But once it has been developed, the cost of each additional program is the cost of the disk it is on—approximately a dollar. After the program has been on the market several years and the price remains at three or four hundred dollars, one begins to suspect that the company is receiving far more than it deserves. Perhaps this is another reason so much illegal copying of software goes on: the proportionality requirement is not being met, and people sense the unfairness of the price. Frequently, trade secrets (which are held indefinitely) also provide their owners with benefits disproportional to the effort expended in developing them.

Sovereignty, Security, and Privacy

Private property can be justified as a means to sovereignty. Dominion over certain objects is important for individual autonomy. Ronald Dworkin's liberal is right in saying that "some sovereignty over a range of personal possessions is essential to dignity." Not having to share one's personal possessions or borrow them from others is essential to the kind of autonomy our society values. Using or consuming certain objects is also necessary for survival. Allowing ownership of these things places control of the means of survival in the hands of individuals, and this promotes independence and security (at least for those who own enough of them). Private ownership of life's necessities lessens dependence between individuals, and takes power from the group and gives it to the individual. Private property also promotes privacy. It constitutes a sphere of privacy within which the individual is sovereign and less accountable for her actions. Owning one's own home is an example of all of these: it provides privacy, security, and a limited range of autonomy.

But copyrights and patents are neither necessary nor important for achieving these goals. The right to exclude others from using one's invention or copying one's work of authorship is not essential to one's sovereignty. Preventing a person from personally using her own invention or writing, on the other hand, would seriously threaten her sovereignty. An author's or inventor's sense of worth and dignity requires public acknowledgment by those who use the writing or discovery, but here again, giving the author or inventor the exclusive right to copy or use her intellectual product is not necessary to protect this.

Though patents and copyrights are not directly necessary for survival (as are food and shelter), one could argue that they are indirectly necessary for an individual's security and survival when selling her inventions or writings is a person's sole means of income. In our society, however, most patents and copyrights are owned by institutions (businesses, universities, or governments). Except in unusual cases where individuals have extraordinary bargaining power, prospective employees are required to give the rights to their inventions and works of authorship to their employers as a condition of employment. Independent authors or inventors who earn their living by selling their writings or inventions to others are increasingly rare. Thus arguing that intellectual property promotes individual security makes sense only in a minority of cases. Additionally, there are other ways to ensure the independent intellectual laborer's security and survival besides copyrights and patents (such as public funding of intellectual workers and public domain property status for the results).

Controlling who uses one's invention or writing is not important to one's privacy. As long as there is no requirement to divulge privately created intellectual products (and as long as laws exist to protect people from others taking information they choose not to divulge—as with trade secret laws), the creator's privacy will not be infringed. Trying to justify copyrights and patents on grounds of privacy is highly implausible given that these property rights give the author or inventor control over certain uses of writings and inventions only after they have been publicly disclosed.

Trade secrets are not defensible on grounds of privacy either. A corporation is not an individual and hence does not have the personal features privacy is intended to protect. Concern for sovereignty counts against trade secrets, for they often directly limit individual autonomy by preventing employees from changing jobs. Through employment contracts, by means of gentlemen's agreements among firms to respect trade secrets by refusing to hire competitors' employees, or simply because of the threat of lawsuits, trade secrets often prevent employees from using their skills and knowledge with other companies in the industry.

Some trade secrets, however, are important to a company's security and survival. If competitors could legally obtain the secret formula for Coke, for example, the Coca-Cola Company would be severely threatened. Similar points hold for copyrights and patents. Without some copyright protection, companies in the publishing, record, and movie industries would be severely threatened by competitors who copy and sell their works at lower prices (which need not reflect development costs). Without patent protection, companies with high research and development costs could be underpriced and driven out of business by competitors who simply mimicked the already developed products. This unfair competition could significantly weaken incentives to invest in innovative techniques and to develop new products. . . . Notice, however, that the concern here is with the security and survival of private companies, not of individuals. ▰

Questions for Discussion

1. Spooner claims that possession of something means that the thing possessed is one's property, even the air that one breathes "while it is inhaled." Is this correct? Is this a version of the "first-possession" justification of property? If not, why? If so, is it subject to the objections raised against the first-possession view?

2. Hettinger argues that the labor view does not provide a justification for intellectual property rights. In particular, he says that market value is not indicative of the creator's labor and, so, of what the creator is entitled to. Why

not? What else, other than market value, could indicate the value of the creator's labor? In addition, would Hettinger's argument apply to material property? That is, does his view entail that the market value of, say, a car is not reflective of the value added by a person's labor and, so, is not indicative of what a person deserves for that property? Again, if not market value, what else could possibly be the appropriate measure? And would it follow from his view that material objects also cannot be legitimately considered one's property?

3. Chapter 6 raises a number of concerns communitarians have about the strident nature of rights talk and the overreliance on rights in addressing moral matters and conflicts. Do those concerns apply with respect to intellectual property rights discourse? Why or why not?

4. Do any conceptions of the nature of rights from Chapter 1 seem particularly relevant or irrelevant to concerns about intellectual property rights discourse? For example, is Joseph Raz's claim that rights are basically the social manifestation of significant interests particularly applicable to intellectual property rights? Or is John Hospers's claim from Chapter 2 that rights are justified by their necessity for human action particularly applicable to intellectual property rights?

5. Chapter 7 notes that many people see much of rights discourse as framed by Western cultural concerns and assumptions. Are intellectual property rights legitimately subject to such a claim? That is, is the right to intellectual property based mostly on Western values?

Further Reading

Drahos, Peter, and Ruth Mayne, ed. *Global Intellectual Property Rights: Knowledge, Access and Development.* New York: Palgrave Macmillan, 2002. A collection of essays on rights as they relate to innovation, development, access, and ownership of technology, including information technology.

Moore, Adam D., ed. *Information Ethics: Privacy, Property, and Power.* Seattle: University of Washington Press, 2005. A fine collection of essays focusing on information control, including aspects of privacy and intellectual property rights.

Spinello, Richard, and Herman T. Tavani, eds. *Intellectual Property Rights in a Networked World: Theory and Practice.* Hershey, PA: Information Science Publishing, 2005. A collection of various philosophical perspectives on intellectual property rights, both theoretical and practical.

Stichler, Richard N., and Robert Hauptman, eds. *Ethics, Information and Technology: Readings.* Jefferson, NC: McFarland, 1998. A collection of essays related to various aspects of information, particularly ethical concerns, including rights and social justice.

Torremans, Paul L. C. *Copyright and Human Rights: Freedom of Expression, Intellectual Property, Privacy.* London: Kluwer Law International, 2004. A collection of essays focusing on aspects of information technology, law, and rights, especially as they relate to privacy and intellectual property.

CHAPTER 12

VICTIMS' RIGHTS

The decision in the case of *Payne v. Tennessee* (501 U.S. 808), heard by the U.S. Supreme Court in 1991, upheld the constitutionality of admitting victim impact evidence during the penalty phase of capital cases. Pervis Tyrone Payne was convicted by a jury of the murders of Charisse Christopher and her two-year-old daughter, as well as of first-degree assault on her three-year-old son. The defendant committed the crimes after Christopher refused his sexual advances. The stabbings were so numerous and widespread that blood covered the floors and walls of the victims' apartment. During the penalty phase of the trial, Payne called his mother and father, his girlfriend, and a clinical psychologist as witnesses, all of whom testified to various mitigating factors in his character and background. The state called the grandmother of the surviving son, Nicholas. She testified that the child continued to cry out for his mother and sister and that the experience had had a marked effect on the little boy and other family members. In his argument for the death penalty, the prosecutor commented upon the continuing effects of the episode on Nicholas and other relatives. The Tennessee Supreme Court affirmed the imposition of the death penalty and rejected Payne's contention that the grandmother's testimony and the prosecutor's comments violated his Eighth Amendment rights (against cruel and unusual punishment) under previous U.S. Supreme Court decisions. Payne then sought review by the U.S. Supreme Court. In delivering the Court's majority opinion, Chief Justice William Rehnquist remarked,

Payne echoes the concern voiced in Booth's case [*Booth v. Maryland*, 482 U.S. 496] that the admission of victim impact evidence permits a jury to find that defendants whose victims were assets to their community are more deserving of punishment than those whose victims are perceived to be worthless. . . . As a general matter, however, victim impact evidence is not offered to encourage comparative judgments of this kind—for instance, that the killer of a hardworking, devoted parent deserves the death penalty, but that the murderer of a reprobate does not. It is designed to show instead *each* victim's "uniqueness as an individual human being," whatever the jury might think the loss to the community resulting from his death might be. . . . Victim impact evidence is simply another form or method of informing the sentencing authority about the specific harm caused by the crime in question, evidence of a general type long considered by sentencing authorities.

In his dissenting opinion, Justice John Paul Stevens, joined by Justice Harry Blackmun, stated,

Evidence that serves no purpose other than to appeal to the sympathies or emotions of the jurors has never been considered admissible. Thus, if a defendant, who had murdered a convenience store clerk in cold blood in the course of an armed robbery, offered evidence unknown to him at the time of the crime about the immoral character of his victim, all would recognize immediately that the evidence was irrelevant and inadmissible. Evenhanded justice requires that the same constraint be imposed on the advocate of the death penalty. . . . The premise that a criminal prosecution requires an evenhanded balance between the State and the defendant is . . . incorrect. The Constitution grants certain rights to the criminal defendant and imposes certain limitations on the State designed to protect the individual from overreaching by the disproportionately powerful State. Thus, the State must prove a defendant's guilt beyond a reasonable doubt.

Payne was not the first time the Court wrestled with victim impact evidence or with victims' rights more broadly, but it pointed, at the highest legal levels, to several important issues connected to victims' rights. For example, Rehnquist claimed that allowing victim impact evidence does not violate the Eighth Amendment and that such evidence is simply one kind among others that sentencing authorities may (and do) use in relating sentencing to the harm caused by a crime (or criminal act). For his part, Stevens claimed that in the context of legal proceedings, the burden of proof must lie with the state. As just mentioned, advocacy for victims' rights did not begin or end with *Payne*. Indeed, for well over thirty years, citizens' groups, such as the National Organization for Victim Assistance, have advocated for victims, and numerous state legislatures have passed statutes related to victims' rights. At the beginning of 2003, two-thirds of U.S. states had passed constitutional amendments recognizing and identifying specific rights of crime victims. In addition to amendments to many state constitutions, a bill had been proposed (several times) in the U.S. Senate to amend the U.S. Constitution with a Victims' Rights Amendment. The primary sponsors of this bill were Diane Feinstein (D-CA) and John Kyl (R-AZ). This bill, in its various editions, was supported by Presidents Bill Clinton and George W. Bush but, as of 2010, had not passed in the Senate. Although it has not become law, the bill does address a concern felt by many that the legal criminal justice system has long emphasized the rights of the accused over those of victims, a concern echoed in the remarks above made about *Payne*. For example, while a person accused of a crime has the legal right to a speedy trial by a jury of peers and to be present throughout that trial, the victim of the crime has no legal right to either. The issue of victims' rights, then, falls under the larger issues of retributive justice (concerned with relevant punishment of a criminal) and restorative justice (concerned with restoring something to or compensating a victim).

Why would anyone not support victims' rights? The recognition of, or failure to recognize, victims' rights shapes in part which legal proceedings are affected by victim testimony and when. Supporters of victims' rights maintain that such recognition helps balance the legal and moral concerns of victims with those of offenders. For critics of victims' rights, such recognition contaminates the presumption of innocence and due legal process.

A preliminary point to make is that some opposition to victims' rights legislation is not based on philosophical or conceptual grounds but takes into account more practical legal and political matters. For example, during a debate over a federal Victims' Rights Amendment in the late 1990s, Beth Wilkinson, a federal prosecutor from the Oklahoma City bombing case, argued against such an amendment. She contended that had victims of the bombing been able to block the plea agreement of Michael Fortier, who was granted leniency in return for significant testimony against other defendants, Timothy McVeigh and Terry Nichols might not have been convicted. While such matters are relevant to the passage of statutes and to the role of victim impact evidence in specific cases, they are not the focus in this chapter. Rather, here we look at concerns over three aspects of victims' rights: who the victim is, what he or she has rights to, and why legal rights as opposed to some other mode of legal response.

One issue within the scope of victims' rights is who exactly counts as the victim of a crime. Though it is obvious that the person directly harmed is a victim, other people, such as a murder victim's family, can be—and often are—indirectly harmed. This becomes especially important when a victim impact statement (VIS) is allowed into the legal proceedings. A VIS is a written or verbal statement of a victim's views concerning the impact a crime has had on him or her. In cases in which the direct victim cannot give a VIS, other relevant persons (such as family members) can give one. These statements are usually offered during sentencing or release hearings and provide not only the victims' opinions about the impact of the crime on their lives but also their recommendations as to an appropriate sentence—and even about the risks they perceive to themselves if the accused or convicted defendant is released or given a lesser sentence.

This question of who counts as a victim is not simply an academic exercise in determining a set of necessary and sufficient conditions for such. Rather, it points to a fundamental understanding of the relevant parties involved in a case. For example, in Sections 42 and 43 of the Oregon state constitution, "victim" is defined as follows:

> "Victim" means any person determined by the prosecuting attorney to have suffered direct financial, psychological or physical harm as a result of a crime and, in the case of a victim who is a minor, the legal guardian of the minor. In the event that no person has been determined to be a victim of a crime, the people of Oregon, represented by the prosecuting attorney, are considered to be the victims. In no event is it intended that the criminal defendant be considered the victim.

Now, this definition of "victim" raises two concerns. First, there is the problem of developing a clear and useful working concept of just who falls within the scope of the term. As noted above, indirect victims, such as family members, are usually included as sufferers of the crime, thus as victims. This extension of the scope of "victim" to include indirect victims is made explicit by victim impact statements. One difficulty entails drawing a nonarbitrary line between indirect victims and others. For example, if a person's home is burgled, and the next-door neighbor then purchases a home security system in order to avoid also being burgled, is the neighbor an indirect victim, hence entitled to some form of compensation from the defendant? The difficulty here is not that we have not yet done a good enough job of enunciating who is a victim; the difficulty, say critics, is that the concept of victim is vague to the point of being legally unwieldy, given that there are direct and indirect victims, actual and virtual victims, manifest and latent victims, primary and secondary victims, and so on. Who, then, would and should be given relevant legal status? Who would and should be awarded relevant legal rights? Who would and should qualify for relevant restitution and compensation?

The second concern about who counts as a victim is highlighted by Oregon's language that "the people of Oregon," represented by the prosecuting attorney, are considered victims in the event that no person is so determined. The point here is that this identifies the victim as the state that prosecutes. The legal process is between the state and the defendant. Because it is the state, and not an individual person, who prosecutes, Justice Stevens emphasized that due process requires that the power of the state must be limited and balanced by the presumption of innocence, by the insistence that guilt be shown beyond a reasonable doubt. To enhance the power of the state in legal proceedings by augmenting the role of individual persons, identified as victims, would be to challenge a fundamental and foundational conception of limiting the power of the state.

Besides the broad issue of who counts as a victim, there also is the issue of just what victims do or would have rights to. Speaking descriptively, the answers vary from state to state, but they generally fall into several categories: (1) a right to information about numerous concerns, such as the status and location of the offender as well as programs for victim assistance, compensation, protection, and safety; (2) a right to participation in the different stages of legal proceedings, such as attending relevant hearings, providing statements (including a VIS) in the context of the proceedings, designating and conferring with a lawful representative, and contesting any postconviction release of the offender; and (3) a right to restitution or compensation, that is, to have the prosecutor ask the judge to order the offender to reimburse the victim for expenses incurred as a result of the crime or to access educational or employment services for victims who, because of the crime, cannot continue in their past careers.

This issue of what victims have a right to raises a second sort of concern: Does allowing victims' views and interests to be heard before a judge or jury has returned a verdict contaminate the legal deliberation process and run counter to the idea that the accused is innocent until proven guilty? Such victim testimony violates due process during two phases, say critics: first, prior to decision making about conviction and, second, during sentencing after a conviction. For the determination of guilt or innocence, the burden of proof must lie with the state; victim impact statements are not criminal evidence and so should not be allowed at this stage of legal proceedings. Once guilt is determined, victim statements can only inject emotion, perhaps desire for revenge, into the process. In addition, critics claim, VISs run counter to equal justice under the law since the offender is being sentenced not according to objective, common standards of punishment but at least in part based on how well victims make their case for suffering. So, for example, two similar or legally identical crimes might result in very dissimilar sentences because of the varying eloquence of victims or other interested parties.

How do victims' rights advocates respond to these concerns? They claim that victims, by definition, have been harmed or wronged in some way. Our basic sense of fairness, couched as restorative justice, demands that something be done to compensate or, if possible, restore to some prior state those who have unjustly suffered. In addition, they may want protection from further harms and wrongs and so may demand, say, to be informed of future dealings with the perpetrator of those harms and wrongs. Any vagueness as to an exact determination of just who counts as a relevant victim does not undo the very clear determination of some victims (e.g., the person assaulted or robbed). As with determining what exactly counts as cruel and unusual punishment, any vagueness can and will be dealt with via specific legal language and court decisions. Victims' rights, as legal rights written into statutes and state constitutions, will, with time, be assessed in terms of their efficacy in promoting and protecting the welfare of persons who have been victimized. Likewise, just what victims have a right to, say advocates, is often quite clear and obvious; in any case, like the issue of vagueness, this, too, will become clearer over time via statutes and court decisions. These sorts of objections, say advocates, do not negate the fact that agents have rights—rights because they are victims, not because they are persons or citizens or members of some other category— and it is appropriate to regulate behavior on that basis.

In the first reading below, law professor Paul Cassell argues in favor of victims' rights. In particular, he argues in favor of amending the U.S. Constitution to add specific language enunciating the rights of victims. Cassell claims that the Constitution guarantees the public and interested parties "appropriate participation" in criminal procedures—for example, the right of the media to attend trials and to access certain relevant documentation is so guaranteed. Since the interests of the press and the public are legitimate in such contexts, then, surely, the interests of victims are also legitimate and should be constitutionally guaranteed. Justice demands that victims have a right to be heard. Cassell rejects the objection that the eloquence or emotional impact of victims' input could (and would?) contaminate due process; the same objection could be raised regarding the relative eloquence or emotional impact of the varying skills of different attorneys, yet we do not question or deny their legitimacy. As Cassell puts it, there must be equal justice not only between cases but also within cases. Here, then, is Cassell:

PAUL G. CASSELL, "BARBARIANS AT THE GATES? A REPLY TO CRITICS OF THE VICTIMS' RIGHTS AMENDMENT"*

The Victims' Rights Amendment will likely be the next amendment to our Constitution. Currently pending before Congress, the Amendment establishes a bill of rights for crime victims, protecting their basic interests in the criminal justice process. Under the Amendment, victims of violent crimes would have the rights to receive notice about court hearings, to attend those hearings, to speak at appropriate points in the process, to receive notification if an offender is released or escapes, to obtain an order of restitution from a convicted offender, and to require the court's consideration of their interest in a trial free from unreasonable delay. The Amendment has attracted considerable bipartisan support, as evidenced by its endorsement by the President and strong approval in the Senate Judiciary Committee at the end of the 104th Congress. Based on this vote, the widely respected *Congressional Quarterly* has identified the Amendment as perhaps the "pending constitutional amendment with the best chance of being approved by Congress in the foreseeable future."

Utah Law Review 2 (1999): 479–544.

As the Victims' Rights Amendment has moved closer to passage, defenders of the old order have manned the barricades against its adoption. In Congress, the popular press, and the law reviews, they have raised a series of philosophical and practical objections to protecting victims' rights in the Constitution. These objections run the gamut, from the structural (the Amendment will change "basic principles that have been followed throughout American history"), to the pragmatic ("it will lay waste to the criminal justice system"), to the aesthetic (it will "trivialize" the Constitution). In some sense, such objections are predictable. The prosecutors, defense attorneys, and judges who labor daily in the criminal justice vineyards have long struggled to hold the balance true between the State and the defendant. To suddenly find third parties—rather, third persons who are not even parties—threatening to storm the courthouse gates provokes, at least from some, an understandable defensiveness. If nothing else, victims promise to complicate life in the criminal justice system. But more fundamentally, if these victims' pleas for recognition are legitimate, what does that say about how the system has treated them for so many years? . . .

The most basic level at which the Victims' Rights Amendment could be disputed is the normative one: victims' rights are simply undesirable. Few of the objections to the Amendment, however, start from this premise. Instead, the vast bulk of the opponents flatly concede the need for victim participation in the criminal justice system. For example, the senators on the Senate Judiciary Committee who dissented from supporting the Amendment began by agreeing that "[t]he treatment of crime victims certainly is of central importance to a civilized society, and we must never simply 'pass by on the other side.'" Additionally, various law professors who sent a letter to Congress opposing the Amendment similarly begin by explaining that they "commend and share the desire to help crime victims" and that "[c]rime victims deserve protection." Further, [Duke University law] Professor [Robert] Mosteller agrees that "every sensible person can and should support victims of crime" and that the idea of "guarantee[ing] participatory rights to victims in judicial proceedings . . . is salutary."

The principal critics of the Amendment agree not only with the general sentiments of victims' rights advocates but also with many of their specific policy proposals. Striking evidence of this agreement comes from the federal statute proposed by the dissenting senators, which would extend to victims in the federal system most of the same rights provided in the Amendment. Other critics, too, have suggested protection for victims in statutory rather than constitutional terms. In parsing through the relevant congressional hearings and academic literature, many of the important provisions of the Amendment appear to garner wide acceptance. Few disagree, for example, that victims of violent crime should receive notice that the offender has escaped from custody and should receive restitution from an offender. What is most striking, then, about debates over the Amendment is not the scattered points of disagreement, but rather the abundant points of *agreement*. This harmony suggests that the Amendment satisfies a basic requirement for a constitutional amendment—that it reflect values widely shared throughout society. There is, to be sure, normative disagreement about some of the proposed provisions in the Amendment, disagreements analyzed below. But the natural tendency to focus on points of conflict should not obscure the substantial points of widespread agreement. . . .

Some opponents of the Amendment object that the victim's right to be heard will interfere with a defendant's efforts to mount a defense. At least some of these objections refute straw men, not the arguments for the Amendment. For example, to prove that a victim's right to be heard is undesirable, objectors sometimes claim (as was done in the Senate Judiciary Committee minority report) that "[t]he proposed Amendment gives victims [a] constitutional right to be heard, if present, and to submit a statement at *all* stages of the criminal proceeding." From this premise, the objectors then postulate that the Amendment would make it "much more difficult for judges to limit testimony by victims *at trial*" and elsewhere to the detriment of defendants. This constitutes an almost breathtaking misapprehension of the scope of the rights at issue. Far from extending victims the right to be heard at "all" stages of a criminal case including the trial, the Amendment explicitly limits the right to public "proceedings to determine a conditional release from custody, an acceptance of a negotiated plea, or a sentence." At these three kinds of hearings—bail, plea, and sentencing—victims have compelling reasons to be heard and can be heard without adversely affecting the defendant's rights. Proof that victims can properly be heard at these points comes from what appears to be a substantial inconsistency by the dissenting senators. While criticizing the right to be heard in the Amendment, these senators simultaneously sponsored federal legislation to extend to victims in the federal system precisely the same rights. They urged their colleagues to pass their statute in lieu of the Amendment because "our bill provides the very same rights to victims as the proposed constitutional amendment." In defending their bill, they saw no difficulty in giving victims a chance to be heard, a right that already exists in many states. . . .

[DePaul University law professor Susan] Bandes and other critics argue that victim impact statements result in unequal justice. Justice [Lewis] Powell made this claim in his since-overturned decision in *Booth v. Maryland*, arguing that "in some cases the victim will not leave behind a family, or the family members may be less articulate in describing their feelings even though their sense of loss is equally severe." This kind of difference, however, is hardly unique to victim impact evidence. To provide one obvious example, current rulings from the Court invite defense mitigation evidence from a defendant's family and friends, despite the fact that some defendants may have more or less articulate acquaintances. In *Payne*, for example, the defendant's parents testified that he was "a good son" and his girlfriend testified that he "was affectionate, caring, and kind to her children." In another case, a defendant introduced evidence of having won a dance choreography award while in prison. Surely this kind of testimony, no less than victim impact statements, can vary in persuasiveness in ways not directly connected to a defendant's culpability; yet, it is routinely allowed. One obvious reason is that if varying persuasiveness were grounds for an inequality attack, then it is hard to see how the criminal justice system could survive at all. Justice [Byron] White's powerful dissenting argument in *Booth* went unanswered, and remains unanswerable: "No two prosecutors have exactly the same ability to present their arguments to the jury; no two witnesses have exactly the same ability to communicate the facts; but there is no requirement . . . [that] the evidence and argument be reduced to the lowest common denominator." Given that our current system allows almost unlimited mitigation evidence on the part of the defendant, an argument for equal justice requires, if anything, that victim statements be allowed. Equality demands fairness not only *between* cases, but also *within* cases. Victims and the public generally perceive great unfairness in a sentencing system with "one side muted." The Tennessee Supreme Court stated the point bluntly in its decision in *Payne*, explaining that "[i]t is an affront to the civilized members of the human race to say that at sentencing in a capital case, a parade of witnesses may praise the background, character and good deeds of Defendant . . . without limitation as to relevancy, but nothing may be said that bears upon the character of, or the harm imposed, upon the victims." With simplicity but haunting eloquence, a father whose ten-year-old daughter, Staci, was murdered, made the same point. Before the sentencing phase began, Marvin Weinstein asked the prosecutor for the opportunity to speak to the jury because the defendant's mother would have the chance to do so. The prosecutor replied that Florida law did not permit this. Here was Weinstein's response to the prosecutor:

> What? I'm not getting a chance to talk to the jury? He's not a defendant anymore. He's a murderer! A convicted murderer! The jury's made its decision. . . . His mother's had her chance all through the trial to sit there and let the jury see her cry for him while I was barred. . . . Now she's getting another chance? Now she's going to sit there in that witness chair and cry for her son, that murderer, that murderer who killed my little girl!
>
> Who will cry for Staci? Tell me that, who will cry for Staci?

There is no good answer to this question, a fact that has led to a change in the law in Florida and, indeed, all around the country. Today the laws of the overwhelming majority of states admit victim impact statements in capital and other cases. These prevailing views lend strong support to the conclusion that equal justice demands the inclusion of victim impact statements, not their exclusion. . . .

Perhaps the most basic challenge to the Victims' Rights Amendment is that victims' rights simply do not belong in the Constitution. The most fervent exponent of this view may be constitutional scholar Bruce Fein, who has testified before Congress that the Amendment is improper because it does not address "the political architecture of the nation." Putting victims' rights into the Constitution, the argument runs, is akin to constitutionalizing provisions of the National Labor Relations Act or other statutes, and thus would "trivialize" the Constitution. Indeed, the argument concludes, to do so would "detract from the sacredness of the covenant." . . .

Indeed, our Constitution has been amended a number of times to protect participatory rights of citizens. For example, the Fourteenth and Fifteenth Amendments were added, in part, to guarantee that the newly freed slaves could participate on equal terms in the judicial and electoral processes, the Seventeenth Amendment to allow citizens to elect their own Senators, and the Nineteenth and Twenty-Sixth Amendments to provide voting rights for women and eighteen-year-olds. The Victims' Rights Amendment continues in that venerable tradition by recognizing that citizens have the right to appropriate participation in the state procedures for punishing crime.

Confirmation of the constitutional worthiness of victims' rights comes from the judicial treatment of an analogous right: the claim of the media to a constitutionally protected interest in attending trials. In *Richmond Newspapers, Inc. v. Virginia*, the Court agreed that the First Amendment guaranteed the right of the public and the press to attend criminal trials. Since that decision, few have argued that the media's right to attend trials is somehow unworthy of constitutional protection, suggesting a national consensus that attendance rights to criminal trials are properly the subject of constitutional law. Yet, the current doctrine produces what must be regarded as a stunning disparity in the way courts handle claims of access to court proceedings. Consider, for example, two issues actually litigated in the Oklahoma City bombing case. The first was the request of an Oklahoma City television station for access to subpoenas for documents issued through the court. The second was the request of various family members of the murdered victims to attend the trial, discussed previously. My sense is that the victims' request should be entitled to at least as much respect as the media request. However, under the law that exists today, the television station has a First Amendment interest in access to the documents, while the victims' families have no constitutional interest in challenging their exclusion from the trial. The point here is not to argue that victims deserve greater constitutional protection than the press, but simply that if press interests can be read into the Constitution without somehow violating the "sacredness of the covenant," the same can be done for victims.

[Law professor Lynne] Henderson has advanced a variant on the victims'-rights-doesn't-belong-in-the-Constitution argument with her claim that "a theoretical constitutional ground for victim's rights" has yet to be provided. Law professors, myself included, enjoy dwelling on theory at the expense of real-world issues, but even on this plane, the objection lacks merit. Henderson seems to concede, if I read her correctly, that new constitutional rights can be justified on grounds that they support individual dignity and autonomy. In her view, then, the question becomes one of discovering which policies society should support as properly reflecting individual dignity and autonomy. On this score, there is little doubt that society currently believes that a victim's right to participate in the criminal process is a fundamental one deserving protection. . . .

A further variant on the unworthiness objection is that our Constitution protects only "negative" rights against governmental abuse. Professor Henderson writes here, for example, that the Amendment's rights differ from others in the Constitution, which "tend to be individual rights *against* government." Setting aside the possible response that the Constitution ought to recognize affirmative duties of government, the fact remains that the Amendment's thrust is to check governmental power, not expand it. Again, the Oklahoma City case serves as a useful illustration. When the victims filed a challenge to a sequestration order directed at them, they sought the liberty to attend court hearings. In other words, they were challenging the exercise of government power deployed against them, a conventional subject for constitutional protection. The other rights in the Amendment fit this pattern, as they restrain government actors, rather than extract benefits for victims. Thus, the State must give notice before it proceeds with a criminal trial; the State must respect a victim's right to attend that trial; and the State must consider the interests of victims at sentencing and other proceedings. These are the standard fare of constitutional protections, and indeed defendants already possess comparable constitutional rights. Thus, extending these rights to victims is no novel creation of affirmative government entitlements. ◤

Toward the beginning of this chapter, I asked, Why would anyone not support victims' rights? I have already noted that there are questions about such rights, especially concerning the fairness of allowing victims to play a "third-party" role in criminal proceedings. Since the state tries defendants, the legal standing of the latter must be jealously guarded against the overwhelming power of the former, which is why so many structural and procedural safeguards are in place. One person who has argued against victims rights—or, at least, against augmenting them at the federal level via an amendment to the U.S. Constitution—is University of Utah law professor Lynne Henderson, herself the victim of a brutal rape in which she was nearly killed. As she notes at the beginning of the reading below, it is difficult to take a principled stand against victims' rights (or against incorporating them into federal constitutional law) because, on the surface, it looks as if doing so is antivictim. Nonetheless, she does oppose such rights legislation. She argues, in part, that an amendment to the U.S. Constitution is not the appropriate venue for establishing victims' rights; rather this should be done—and, indeed, is being done—at the state level. Furthermore, she claims, criminal justice should not necessarily focus on the harm done, since some crimes result in minimal, if any, actual (physical) harm. The breaking of the law or the wrongfulness of a defendant's actions is the same whether a victim suffers little or, in two like cases, one victim suffers less than another; therefore, punishment should be a function of law breaking or wrongness of action, not necessarily of harm done. Finally, and perhaps most importantly, for Henderson, if the emphasis with respect to victims should be on their recovery and, where possible, restoration, then perhaps combative rights are not the best vehicle for achieving this goal. Opposition to victims' rights, then, and to certain victims' rights legislation does not indicate a lack of caring about victims, for Henderson. Rather, such opposition is a matter of balancing the power of the state with that of accused individuals and of the best social mechanisms to employ in helping victims as well as ensuring fairness and due process. Although the bulk of Henderson's remarks below focus on the wisdom of enshrining victims' rights in the U.S. Constitution, underlying those specific concerns are the deeper issues of equal justice and the role of rights in securing and protecting it.

LYNNE H. HENDERSON, "REVISITING VICTIM'S RIGHTS"*

Against an appealing plea from a victim of a horribly violent crime or a grief-stricken family, finding a good sound bite to justify opposition to an amendment *is* difficult. Those who do oppose such an amendment are accused of being anti-victim, pro-status-quo, unimaginative, or pro-criminal. This is not necessarily the case, however, as many victim organizations are coming to recognize. For example, Victim Services, the

*Utah Law Review 2 (1999): 383–442.

largest victim assistance agency in the country, indicated in a letter to Senator Orrin Hatch, Chair of the Senate Judiciary Committee, "We believe the proposed amendment is premature and inappropriate at this time when existing [state and federal] provisions that aim to address victims' interests have not been evaluated. Rather, what we need is research, discussion and debate." Empirical research and theoretical and practical considerations argue against adoption of a victim's rights amendment at this time. I am not urging caution because no one cares about crime victims, but rather because critical distance is essential before we embrace such a change in our fundamental charter of government. . . .

While proponents tend to focus their argument in the context of particular provisions of the Bill of Rights dealing with the rights of the accused, a theoretical constitutional ground for victim's rights has yet to be developed. Because the victim's rights amendment seems more related to criminal procedure than constitutional law, no serious scholarly consideration of the implications of the amendment in terms of constitutional law has appeared in law reviews—an omission that I believe is a mistake. . . .

The Constitution of the United States is a basic charter of government. It contains an allocation of rights and responsibilities among branches of government and among the national and state governments, as well as substantive and procedural provisions relating to the rights and relations of government to individual citizens. While the victim's rights amendment raises important concerns regarding federal and state relations, my purpose here is to examine the issue of federal relations to individuals. The Constitution has largely been interpreted as determining the relationship of the individual to the State, not the relationship of the individual to other individuals. Although there are good arguments that the Thirteenth and Fourteenth Amendments apply to the acts of individuals—despite the Court's adoption of the "state action" doctrine—the focus has been on the relation of the individual to the government. The relationship of the individual to the State is largely defined in terms of participation in democratic processes, but it also includes certain rights of the individual against the State. Even the Constitution's participation and process allocations cannot be divorced from substantive normative choice about whose participation matters and why. The Bill of Rights and the Fourteenth Amendment appear to contain both substantive and procedural commitments to and restraints on the State's power over individuals.

These constitutional rights for individuals are primarily "negative" rights or liberties that limit the State's power to interfere with the activities of citizens. Constitutional theory and law have tended to emphasize textual rights and negative liberties over positive rights despite arguments by progressive and liberal constitutional scholars that positive liberties and claims against the government are also part of our constitutional theory and order. These arguments have mostly failed to convince the courts. Only in rare instances have the courts found that positive entitlements or claims on the government ensure meaningful exercise of rights. For example, in *Gideon v. Wainwright*, the Supreme Court determined that the right to counsel and notions of fairness required states to pay for counsel for indigent criminal defendants. Occasionally, the Court has affirmed positive entitlements via procedural due process when the government seeks to deprive citizens of other liberty or property rights. In *Goldberg v. Kelly*, for example, the Court held that an individual was entitled to a hearing before the government could deprive him of welfare payments. In *Boddie v. Connecticut*, the Court held that a state could not charge indigent persons a fee before allowing them to file for divorce, finding that individuals have a fundamental interest in making choices about marriage and family. However, most of these rulings have involved states trying to deprive an individual of a specific constitutional or statutory right or entitlement rather than individual claims that the government must provide a benefit or assistance. Indeed, the Court has been extremely reluctant to expand the duties of government to provide positive rights or entitlements, no matter how sympathetic the claim, perhaps because the Court is loath to encroach on decisions involving allocation of resources better left to the political branches.

The victim's rights amendment would be unique in requiring the government to involve private parties in court proceedings that are not aimed at depriving these persons of life, liberty, or property. In the instance of victims who are not witnesses to the offense, primarily survivors of a homicide victim, the amendment gives victims, upon whom the government makes no demands whatsoever, the right to participate and attempt to influence the outcome of the government's case. At first this may seem quite progressive, humane, and unobjectionable, but upon closer examination, it presents a number of problems. Inconsistent with victim's rights arguments in constitutional practice, the government has no constitutional duty to protect citizens against private violence. Victims of war, whether soldiers killed in battle, soldiers injured and traumatized by war, or civilians wrongly interred or injured by government, have no recognized constitutional claims, although the government has caused the injury. Victims of racism and prejudice have no constitutional claims if those who injure them are private parties, despite the injurious effects of these practices. Thus, there must be some very special justification for privileging crime victims by giving them constitutional rights. . . .

[An] argument based on dignity is that victims have some sort of fundamental right that ought to be enshrined in the Constitution. The interest of the individual is never defined in terms of a grounding for the right, other than a rather vague Kantian notion that all are entitled to equal dignity and respect in their interactions with the government and its courts. But such an argument fails to distinguish crime victims from other victims of wrongs committed by private parties or anyone else who interacts with the government and courts; it states too much. Obviously, everyone should be given equal dignity and respect.

[Harvard law] Professor Laurence Tribe, who has long advocated various expansions of rights, has touched upon a kind of fundamental rights concern in his writings in support of an amendment. After initially opposing a victim's rights amendment, Tribe determined that a constitutional amendment granting rights to crime victims ought to be adopted. To my knowledge, however, Tribe has not yet developed a coherent statement identifying the specific source or nature of these fundamental rights, nor has he clarified the theoretical basis for them. Rather, he has framed his claims on some unarticulated notion of human dignity to argue for rights to participate in criminal proceedings, without identifying why there is an autonomy or dignitary interest unique or strong enough to be recognized by the Constitution, or what that interest actually is.

Doctrinally and historically, fundamental rights involve an individual's liberty and autonomy to make choices that are rooted in the constitutional text (freedom of speech or religion), structure (the right to travel), American history and practice, or in terms of human dignity, autonomy, and personhood (the right to contraceptives). Again, however, fundamental rights, whether explicitly in the constitution's text or implied from that text, tend to be rights against government.

One doctrinal touchstone for determining fundamental rights is whether such rights are fundamental to the concept of ordered liberty or grounded in our history and traditions. This approach does not justify finding crime victim's rights, as such rights are neither part of our history and traditions nor fundamental to ordered liberty. A more expansive view that advocates recognition of new rights is often based on questions of individual autonomy and principles of "equal concern and respect." Although the courts have frequently been hostile to expanding the meaning of fundamental rights based on dignity and autonomy arguments, the cases and principles within constitutional jurisprudence might provide a theoretical basis for an argument for victim's rights. Tribe apparently adopts the position that victims ought to have positive rights because criminal cases involve some kind of basic human right that people widely agree deserves serious and permanent respect. At one point, Tribe characterizes the relevant right as the "right not to be victimized yet again through the process by which governmental bodies and officials prosecute, punish, and release the accused or convicted offender," which he sees as "indisputably basic human rights against government, rights that any civilized system of justice *would aspire to protect* and strive never to violate." However, if the concern is with honoring individual concerns about the positive law, it is hard to see why crime victims alone ought to have special rights in litigation when victims of other wrongs do not.

Tribe also makes a strong substantive statement in asserting that "[t]he ultimate concern of the criminal justice system ought to be with the victim." Tribe's argument requires a justification as to why the victim's individual interests should trump the community's concerns with crime, including fair process for those accused, equality in the application of the law, and the goals of the criminal sanction—deterrence, retribution, rehabilitation, and protection. If the trump is some right of the victim, it remains to be determined what core right is relevant and why. . . .

Some of Tribe's concerns, as well as those of other advocates of the amendment, are with the appearance of fairness and due process for victims. Victims have been harmed and ought to have some special participatory rights that enable them to tell courts what they think and how they feel about their cases. Professor [Robert] Mosteller has labeled this the "participatory" rationale for creating constitutional rights for victims. Puzzlingly, if victims have a fundamental right to participate, they ought to have a right not to participate as well. Tribe nowhere addresses a right not to be coerced into cooperating. A victim can be traumatized and denied autonomy and choice when forced to prosecute, which, under current law, can and does occur. . . .

In terms of participation in the formation and adoption of laws, including legal rights and remedies, victims are hardly in need of special constitutional protection. The success of victim interest groups in changing law through the democratic process cannot be denied: No one can argue with a straight face that legislatures and representatives have been deaf to victims' concerns about sentencing, probation, parole, and defining substantive offenses. Victims are hardly a persecuted group or a discrete and insular minority whose participation in the process has been blocked. . . .

Assuming that we can properly identify who is a victim and who is not for purposes of legal claims, surely those identified victims can assert a right to corrective justice. Victims have been harmed in some way by an offense, and the person who harmed them ought to be held accountable. The tort system is designed to accomplish this result. The tort process requires proof of harm and proof that the defendant caused the harm. The victim controls the litigation and the trial as the plaintiff; her story, injuries, and damages are the focus. Perhaps because such litigation is expensive and few have the resources to sue their assailants, together with the fact that many—but hardly all—who are guilty of criminal offenses are essentially judgment-proof, the focus has become centered on the criminal process. While understandable, these practical realities do not necessarily justify victim participation in prosecution under current theory and practice in the United States.

There are many differences between the concerns of tort and those of the criminal process. The State and the community are negatively affected by crime, and the criminal law is the community's response. In criminal cases, it is the State and the community that bear the burden and expense of identifying, prosecuting, punishing, imprisoning, and executing offenders. Individuals do not bear these expenses, beyond their contributions as taxpayers to the funds that support all prosecutions. The individual victim or victims may, however, bear the costs of missed work, child care, and transportation to attend court or meet with authorities. The criminal process is more concerned with whether a defendant ought to be held culpable for committing the offense, and the reason for that emphasis is largely one involving moral calibrations of blameworthiness and concerns with rationales for inflicting pain or punishment on the offender. These moral considerations have little to do with the actual effects on the victim.

Although the public, and perhaps many victim advocates, focus on the harm caused by a criminal defendant's conduct, harm is not necessarily the basis for punishment. Generalized concerns of deterrence, retribution, incapacitation, and rehabilitation are not necessarily tied to actual harm to victims. The criminal process is concerned with harm only insofar as the definition of the crime includes a harm; we punish many offenders even when the substantive crime does not involve physical harm to a victim, and even though the crime might entail an emotional harm such as fear and might further be classified as a violent crime. For example, the crime of robbery generally does not depend on the use of force, but the threat of force that places a victim in fear. In other crimes, the force may not be aimed at the victim at all—picking pockets is forcible, but only in the sense that physical action is required to take the wallet from the unsuspecting victim. The current amendment's term, "crime of violence," would probably include attempted murder or other attempted violent crimes; yet, attempts do not require that any harm occur. Assault with a deadly weapon does not require a resulting physical harm. Burglary requires no harm whatsoever, although it is traditionally considered a very serious crime.

The effect of a serious crime on an individual often ought not be used to determine the degree of punishment. For example, the fact that a rape survivor copes well with her experience and suffers little or no post-traumatic stress is not a reason to say that the crime is not among one of the most serious offenses against the person and ought to be punished accordingly. Similarly, a robbery victim may not be physically injured and may be quite resilient emotionally, but that does not mean that robbery is a trivial offense, or that the victim is less a victim than one who suffers from post-traumatic stress disorder as a result. . . .

No general law or legal system can sensitively address or provide nuanced responses to all the issues raised by extreme trauma. Rather than adopting a constitutional amendment dealing with a very narrow category of victims and situations—those in which someone is labeled a relevant victim, someone is charged with the crime, and someone is convicted of the crime—to deal with victims compassionately, we need to concentrate on things that aid recovery. ◣

Questions for Discussion

1. Cassell claims that everyone acknowledges that victims have suffered injustice by the fact of being victimized, and, as victims, they've experienced a violation of their rights. Does that fact suffice to legitimate an amendment to the U.S. Constitution? One concern about victims' rights is that they could contaminate the presumption of innocence of the defendant and, hence, corrupt fairness in the proceedings of criminal justice. Does Cassell provide a sufficient response to this concern?

2. Henderson acknowledges that victims' rights have been incorporated into state statutes. If that is appropriate, then why should such rights not be guaranteed at the federal level, particularly as constitutional guarantees? She also claims that due process, in the sense of equal fairness, is not served by allowing the effect of a crime on a victim to be weighed. That is, the eloquence or emotional impact of victims' testimony should not (in part) determine legal justice. But if the eloquence and emotional impact of the participating attorneys' statements are allowable, then why should those of victims not be? Finally, if rights are not the appropriate basis for determining the outcome of sentencing, then what is the appropriate basis? Is it social utility?

3. Should the concerns raised in Chapter 4 about group rights, particularly groups as rights holders, also apply to victims as rights holders? If victims as victims can be rights holders, can they also be rights addressees and bear duties to other rights-holding agents? If not, why not? If they can, how are the rights of victims and other rights-holding agents balanced (especially if they conflict)?

4. Chapter 6 raises a number of concerns communitarians have about the strident nature of rights talk and the overreliance on rights in addressing moral matters and conflicts. Do those concerns apply with respect to victims' rights discourse? Why or why not?

5. Do any conceptions of the nature of rights from Chapter 1 seem particularly relevant or irrelevant to concerns about victims' rights discourse? For

example, is Joel Feinberg's assertion that rights are valid claims particularly applicable to victims' rights? Or is John Stuart Mill's claim from Chapter 2 that social utility justifies rights particularly applicable to victims' rights?

Further Reading

Carrington, Frank. *Victims' Rights: Law and Litigation.* New York: M. Bender, 1989. A strong defense of victims' rights, including an argument for expanding and codifying them into law.

Fletcher, George P. *With Justice for Some: Victims' Rights in Criminal Trials.* Reading, MA: Addison-Wesley, 1995. A strong defense of victims' rights.

Jasper, Margaret. *Victims' Rights Law.* Dobbs Ferry, NY: Oceana, 1997. An overview of victims' rights within the American legal system.

Sebba, Leslie. *Third Parties: Victims and the Criminal Justice System.* Columbus: Ohio State University Press, 1996. An analysis of the role and status of victims within the American legal system, including an overview of reforms, legislation, and policy reviews.

Stark, James H., and Howard W. Goldstein. *The Rights of Crime Victims.* Carbondale: Southern Illinois University Press, 1985. An overview of various aspects of victims' rights, detailing numerous specific rights and laws.

CHAPTER 13

CHILDREN'S RIGHTS

The issue of who or what can be the holder of rights has come up various times throughout this book. Chapter 4 looks at whether groups *as groups* are legitimate rights holders as well as whether nonhuman animals are legitimate rights holders. Chapter 6 presents a list of numerous claims to rights, including many types of agents said to have rights (e.g., women's rights, prisoners' rights, fetuses' rights, gay rights, parents' rights, and so forth). Sometimes contention about such rights, or about who has rights, gets framed differently, depending on whether those purported rights are supported or opposed. For example, supporters often label gay rights as "equal rights," but opponents label them as "special rights." Those who label them as special rights do so because they claim that such rights apply only to a particular group of individuals. The same claim, of course, would hold for disability rights (they apply only to particular individuals, namely, those who are disabled) or student rights (they apply only to particular individuals, namely, those who are students), and so forth. Such rights are also sometimes labeled as special rights because their content applies only to particular individuals. That is, the specific content of the rights (or what certain persons have a right to) applies only to particular persons, so here the emphasis is on the content, not the bearer. For instance, disabled persons have a legal right to park in particular areas, and no one else has a legal right to park there. So, some argue, this is a special right, one that applies only to particular people, not to everyone equally.

Chapter 12 considers the issue of victims' rights, rights that pertain to people *as victims*. Among all of those who, both potentially and actually, fall victim to wrongs and injustice, many are children. We all are aware of the countless acts of child abuse that occur. One particularly infamous case that went all the way to the U.S. Supreme Court (decided in 1989) was *DeShaney v. Winnebago County Department of Social Services.* As the Court records state explicitly, "[T]he facts of this case are undeniably tragic." The parents of Joshua DeShaney (born in 1979) were divorced soon after he was born, and the father, Randy DeShaney, was awarded custody of Joshua. Randy and Joshua soon moved to Winnebago County in Wisconsin. County authorities learned in early 1982 that Joshua might be the victim of child abuse at the hands of his father. The father denied the allegations, and the Winnebago County Department of Social Services did not pursue them further at that point. A year later Joshua was admitted to a local hospital with evident signs of physical abuse. The county convened a child-protection team, which subsequently determined that there was insufficient evidence of child abuse to retain Joshua in the custody of the court. After consultation with the father, and based on the recommendation of the child-protection team, the juvenile court dismissed the child-protection case and returned Joshua to Randy's custody. A month later emergency room personnel called the Department of Social Services caseworker who was handling Joshua's case to report that once again Joshua was being treated for suspicious injuries. After investigating, the caseworker concluded that there was no basis for action. In November 1983 the emergency room once again notified the Department of Social Services of injuries to Joshua and suspected child abuse. Finally, in March 1984 Randy DeShaney beat four-year-old Joshua so severely that the boy fell into a life-threatening coma. Although Joshua did not die, he suffered brain damage so severe that he has remained profoundly retarded and confined to state care.

Randy DeShaney was subsequently tried and convicted of child abuse (and served less than two years in jail before being released). Joshua's mother and Joshua (via proxy, of course) brought a legal complaint against the Winnebago County Department of Social Services, claiming that they deprived Joshua of his liberty without due process of law, in violation of his rights under the Fourteenth Amendment of the U.S. Constitution, by failing to intervene to protect him against a risk of violence at his father's hands, of which they knew or should have known.

Various lower courts dismissed the suit, which was then appealed all the way to the U.S. Supreme Court, which, in early 1989, ruled 6–3 against Joshua and his mother. The majority of the Court held that a state or county

agency does not have an obligation under the due process clause of the Fourteenth Amendment to prevent child abuse when the child is (1) in parental,
not agency, custody, and (2) the state did not create the danger of abuse or increase the child's vulnerability to it. The due process clause (adopted in 1868)
reads, "No State shall make or enforce any law which shall abridge the privileges or immunities of citizens of the United States; nor shall any State deprive any person of life, liberty, or property, without due process of law; nor
deny to any person within its jurisdiction the equal protection of the laws." In
his ruling, then chief justice William Rehnquist stated,

> [The purpose of the due process clause] was to protect the people from the
> State, not to ensure that the State protected them from each other. The
> Framers [of the U.S. Constitution] were content to leave the extent of gov-
> ernmental obligation in the latter area to the democratic political process.
> Consistent with these principles, our cases have recognized that the Due
> Process Clauses generally confer no affirmative right to governmental aid,
> even where such aid may be necessary to secure life, liberty, or property in-
> terests of which the government itself may not deprive the individual. . . .
> If the Due Process Clause does not require the State to provide its citizens
> with particular protective services, it follows that the State cannot be held
> liable under the Clause for injuries that could have been averted had it
> chosen to provide them. As a general matter, then, we conclude that a
> State's failure to protect an individual against private violence simply does
> not constitute a violation of the Due Process Clause.

The three justices who opposed this ruling—William Brennan, Thur-
good Marshall, and Harry Blackmun—claimed that Rehnquist and his supporters were being unconscionably formalistic in their reading of the due
process clause and in their interpretation of the case. They replied,

> "The most that can be said of the state functionaries in this case," the
> Court today concludes, "is that they stood by and did nothing when sus-
> picious circumstances dictated a more active role for them." . . . It may
> well be, as the Court decides . . . that the Due Process Clause, as con-
> strued by our prior cases, creates no general right to basic governmental
> services. That, however, is not the question presented here. . . . No one, in
> short, has asked the Court to proclaim that, as a general matter, the Con-
> stitution safeguards positive as well as negative liberties. . . .

The Court's baseline is the absence of positive rights in the Constitution and a concomitant suspicion of any claim that seems to depend on such rights. From this perspective, the DeShaneys' claim is first and foremost about inaction (the failure, here, of respondents to take steps to protect Joshua), and only tangentially about action (the establishment of a state program specifically designed to help children like Joshua). And from this perspective, holding these Wisconsin officials liable—where the only difference between this case and one involving a general claim to protective services is Wisconsin's establishment and operation of a program to protect children—would seem to punish an effort that we should seek to promote.

I would begin from the opposite direction. I would focus on the action that Wisconsin has taken with respect to Joshua and children like him, rather than on actions that the State failed to take. . . .

It simply belies reality, therefore, to contend that the State "stood by and did nothing" with respect to Joshua. . . . Through its child protection program, the State actively intervened in Joshua's life and, by virtue of this intervention, acquired ever more certain knowledge that Joshua was in grave danger. . . . Because of the posture of this case, we do not know why respondents did not take steps to protect Joshua; the Court, however, tells us that their reason is irrelevant, so long as their inaction was not the product of invidious discrimination. . . .

My disagreement with the Court arises from its failure to see that inaction can be every bit as abusive of power as action, that oppression can result when a State undertakes a vital duty and then ignores it. Today's opinion construes the Due Process Clause to permit a State to displace private sources of protection and then, at the critical moment, to shrug its shoulders and turn away from the harm that it has promised to try to prevent.

Whatever one thinks about the ruling in this case or about the Court majority's focus on how to properly interpret the due process clause of the Fourteenth Amendment, it is clear that child abuse is a horrific wrong. Many people claim this abuse is wrong because it violates a person's rights. Such abuse is a violation of *any*one's rights, but it is even more repugnant because children, as opposed to adults, are particularly vulnerable and helpless.

While most people would acknowledge that children have rights, at least some rights, as individuals—so, a one-year-old child has the same right to life as a fifty-one-year-old adult—there is less agreement that there are specific children's rights (i.e., rights held by children as children that nonchildren do not have). (Of course, when people speak of such rights, they mean them as moral rights, not simply as legal rights.)

Given the vulnerable and dependent nature of children, such rights would not merely be negative rights. As University of Pennsylvania law professor Barbara Bennett Woodhouse has noted, "From the infant's perspective, the right to be 'left alone' would constitute a death sentence." Children, especially very young children, need to be provided with goods and services by others in order to survive, so their right to life cannot reasonably be understood as simply entitlement to noninterference by others. Most people believe also that children, again because of their special vulnerable and dependent nature, have a right to protection against neglect. In recognition of the special moral status of children, the UN General Assembly adopted the Convention on the Rights of the Child in 1990, which included many "standard" human rights (e.g., right to life, freedom of expression, freedom from attack and abuse, right to education, right to health care) as well as rights specific to children (e.g., the right not to be separated from their parents against their will unless such separation is in their best interests). By the end of the twentieth century, more than 130 countries were signatories to this convention.

As with victims' rights, why would anyone oppose children's rights? As it turns out, a number of concerns have been raised about children's rights, some of them focused on general issues and others on specific rights claims made in the name of children's rights. One seemingly minor concern is exactly who counts as a "child." This is not a tiresome semantic quibble. There is an enormous difference between a typical one-year-old person and a seventeen-year-old person, even though neither is legally considered an adult. The level of vulnerability and helplessness of a seventeen-year-old is obviously vastly less than that of a one-year-old; hence, the claim of rights to provisions and protection is much less salient for the seventeen-year-old. But the issue is not simply about chronological age. There are clear reasons why, say, a five-year-old child does not have the right to vote or to drive, sign contracts, or enjoy many of the rights that adults do; a five-year-old child simply does not have the developmental capacities to make such rights reasonable or meaningful. But what about a developmentally disabled person who is deemed to have a "mental" age of five, even though the person is chronologically thirty-five years old? Should this person enjoy all the rights that most thirty-five-year-old people enjoy—for example, signing a legal contract—even though this person is developmentally a five-year-old? In a related manner, while the parents of a five-year-old child are usually allowed and expected to make decisions on behalf of that child, should the parents of this "developmental" five-year-old similarly be allowed and expected to make such decisions? Or, to put it another way, what rights does this thirty-five-year-old person enjoy, and what duties—flowing from this person's rights—do the parents bear? Are these duties indeed the same as if the person were chronologically five years old?

This point speaks to broader issues related to children's rights. Rights theorists usually cash out these concerns in terms of a *protectionist* or *liberationist* view. The protectionist view holds that children, by their nature as children, need protection and rearing. They are incapable of looking after their own well-being and, hence, need protection and guidance. Normally, the parents will provide these, but if they do not, then the state is expected to do so. In either case, the child has certain rights based on its developmental status. In addition, the parents have certain rights as well as duties. Under the liberationist view, children are as fully persons as are adults. Although children might function as moral patients early in life, they are also moral agents, and their agency must not be inappropriately constrained or violated. Liberationists claim that, while children are not as fully developed as adults, they are not without rights, including rights held against their own parents. Rather than thinking of children as "belonging to" parents, as though children are a form of property, we must think of children as legitimate moral agents with rights commensurate with their capacities.

Both groups (the protectionists and liberationists) claim that most important are the child's interests, and any rights held by children must be understood in those terms. Agreement on this, however, merely raises more questions. Who decides what is in the best interests of the child? Who "implements" what is in the child's best interests? How should immediate versus long-term interests be weighed? Such questions relate directly to specific rights claimed for children. For example, numerous cases brought to the courts involve parents refusing certain (sometimes any) medical treatment for their children. In many such cases, the parents' refusal is based on religious beliefs (e.g., the child's life is in God's hands). These parents are concerned not only with their child's immediate physical well-being but with his or her soul and eternal well-being. Both the parents and the state claim to be concerned with the interests and well-being of the child. What rights, then, does the child have in such a case, and what rights do the parents have (and what rights does the state have)?

Less dramatically, we all know of cases in which parents have objected to material being taught to their children in school. A rather well-publicized case involved the presence in an elementary school library of the book *Heather Has Two Mommies*, which some parents found objectionable (because it seemed to embrace, or at least not condemn, lesbian relationships). These parents claimed that they had the right to disallow their children's exposure to this book. Did their children have a right to access to this book? Those who oppose the liberationist view claim that it is parents' responsibility and right to make decisions for their children. To the extent that children's rights place constraints on parental authority, such rights are illegitimate, they claim. Often this argument is made in the name of privacy and against state intervention in the private lives of citizens. If the state can dictate decisions regarding children's education, health care, and rearing, they argue, then the rights of parents are clearly violated. This does not mean, of course, that parents can do anything to or with their children. Even the most ardent protectionist advocates would condemn the actions of Randy DeShaney. But, they claim, spanking or grounding a child (with the goal of socializing him or her to become a well-functioning adult in the future) is a far cry from child abuse, and placing restrictions on a child's access to information, freedom of expression, or freedom of association is not a violation of rights but responsible parenting.

Liberationists respond to these claims not by insisting that the state take over the role of parents or place unreasonable demands and controls on them. Instead, relative to a child's developmental capacities, the state must act for children's well-being when parents do not. Such action, they say, should be not only reactive (e.g., removing a child from an abusive home) but also proactive (e.g., requiring a school curriculum that will serve the child in the long run). Children, they argue, do have rights because of their status as children, and, yes, they do hold those rights even against their parents, should their parents violate them.

The following two readings present both positions. In the first, Margaret Coady argues in favor of children's rights, that is, special rights belonging to children as children. The final reading, by Martin Guggenheim, presents a rejection of children's rights. First, Coady argues that children do not merely have welfare (or positive) rights of provision and protection; in addition, they have autonomy rights indicative of their status as independent agents. Denying autonomy rights to children is, says Coady, a throwback to treating them merely as units in a family and functionally as property of the parents. Not only does such a status for children have no moral basis, but it also fails to promote the long-term interest of children, which is to become autonomous adults. Allowing them to be actively involved, in relevant ways given their capacities, enhances their development. This is not merely a utilitarian justification; instead, for Coady, it is the proper recognition of children's rights as persons.

MARGARET M. COADY, "THE CONTINUING IMPORTANCE OF THINKING THAT CHILDREN HAVE RIGHTS"*

The argument in this article is that it is important to continue thinking that children have rights and, in particular, that they have what have been called autonomy rights. . . . The first part of this article looks at a brief history of children's rights in the twentieth century in order to bring out what is meant by autonomy rights. The second part examines and counters the arguments of some philosophers who either would prefer not to talk about rights as far as children are concerned, or would grant children only much more restricted rights.

The first international declaration of children's rights occurred in 1924 with the Declaration of the Rights of the Child promulgated by the League of Nations. This Declaration is primarily concerned with the child receiving the material and spiritual necessities for its well-being and development. Many of the provisions are similar to later declarations of children's rights. The provisions cover protection of children from poverty, hunger and exploitation. One provision, that which states that the "delinquent child must be reclaimed," is very much the product of the time, reflecting the "child saving" attitudes of the day.

As a statement of rights the 1924 Declaration is unusual in that it is not directed at governments, but rather more generally at all adults who should recognize children's needs. The declaration does not allow children to make claims; instead it exhorts all adults to recognize their duty to children. The statements in this declaration are far removed from acknowledging autonomy rights of children.

The United Nations Declaration of the Rights of the Child, proclaimed in 1959, was even further from acknowledging autonomy rights. This Declaration has many similarities to the earlier declaration covering chil-

---

*Australian Journal of Professional and Applied Ethics 7 (2005): 47–57.

dren's need for protection, adequate nutrition, housing and medical services. But it also included added rights to education and to recreation. An influential addition is the reference to the "best interests of the child" as the guiding consideration for those making decisions for children. But there is no acknowledgment of children themselves making decisions or even being involved in making decisions in matters that affect them. There is still no reference to civil or political rights; and in one aspect, namely employment, the 1959 Declaration is even more protective than the earlier Declaration. Principle 9 of the 1959 Declaration states, "The child shall not be admitted to employment before an appropriate minimum age." The 1924 principle 4 states, "The child must be put in a position to earn a livelihood, and must be protected against every form of exploitation."

The obsession with protection in the Declaration meant that the idea of rights as providing freedoms and powers was ignored. As might have been expected, there was a reaction against this view of childhood by theorists who had a different view of children and rights. In the 1970s writers such as John Holt and Richard Farson argued that rights for children would only be achieved if children were allowed to be self-determining. For these child liberationists, children were similar to other groups seeking recognition of their rights. They argued that calls for the protection of women had covered up endemic exploitation of women and similarly in the case of children, appeals to protective rights in fact meant that children were deprived of many of the rights held by adults. In *Escape from Childhood* Holt went as far as demanding that all children should have the right to vote, arguing that any group which does not have representation on law-making bodies will inevitably be exploited. Holt also argued that children should have the right to work for money, and in this element, is closer to the 1924 Declaration than the 1959 Declaration. Other child liberationists argued that the child's right to self-determination was fundamental to any understanding of children's rights. In the spectrum which exists between rights understood as the free exercise of autonomy and rights understood as paternalist provision of the necessities of life, the liberationists were on the side of the free exercise of autonomy. . . .

The 1989 United Nations Convention on the Rights of the Child went beyond protective rights and included some civil and political rights for children. The "right to be heard" guaranteed in Article 12 has been seen by some writers (e.g., Geraldine Van Bueren, in her book *The International Law on the Rights of the Child*) as the most significant Article in the Convention. It reads:

> 12 (1) States parties shall assure to the child who is capable of forming his or her own views the right to express those views freely in all matters affecting the child, the views of the child being given due weight in accordance with the age and maturity of the child. (2) For this purpose, the child shall in particular be provided the opportunity to be heard in any judicial and administrative proceedings affecting the child, either directly or through a representative or an appropriate body, in a manner consistent with the procedural rules of national law.

Van Bueren points out that recognition of this right means that the child must be consulted in all matters which affect him or her. It disaggregates the child's interests from those of the family as a whole, and in doing this is revolutionary in international law. However, Van Bueren also points out that, while children must be consulted in all decisions that affect them, their views are not necessarily determinative.

Articles 13 to 16 acknowledge the child's right to freedom of expression, freedom of thought, conscience and religion, right to peaceful assembly, and right to privacy. Most of these freedoms are qualified by reference to parental guidance and the developing capacities of the child. Nevertheless they do mark a dramatic change in official United Nations understanding of children's rights. These are rights which recognize the child as a human agent who can and does consider reasons for actions and whose interests are separable from those of his or her family. Some of the critics (e.g., Bruce Hafen and Jonathan Hafen) of these rights have called them "autonomy rights." They could equally be called freedom rights or claim rights. While these autonomy rights granted to children move beyond protection in recognizing the separate interests of children, they are not incompatible with protection.

Although the UN Convention on the Rights of the Child has received wide international recognition, it was also the cause of much heated criticism. There are even attempts to persuade some countries which have already ratified the Convention to withdraw or modify their support for it. One example of this occurred in Australia in 1997 when a Senate Committee of the Parliament of the Commonwealth of Australia was reexamining Australia's commitment to the UN Convention on the Rights of the Child.

A long term U.S. opponent of the Convention, Professor Bruce Hafen, put a submission and gave evidence to the Senate committee claiming that "avant-garde thinkers about liberation ideology" in the U.S. had failed in the courts in that country, and so had gone to the international human rights forum where those rights had been gullibly accepted by countries which did not realize the Convention contained these "autonomy rights." It is these autonomy rights which have been at the heart of most criticisms of the Convention (Joint Standing Committee 1998), and it is these autonomy rights which I want to defend. I do this here by looking at [a line] of argument against rights for children [proffered] by Barbara Arneil. . . .

Arneil sees rights talk as too much connected with its origins in liberal theory. She traces the development of liberal theory from its beginnings in the seventeenth century and sees it as mainly concerned to "create citizens of a state rather than subjects of a king." Central to the idea of liberal citizenship was the idea that the citizen freely consented to join the association which governed him. This was the key difference from the absolute rule of a monarch. But as with the Greek polis there were criteria which excluded many from becoming citizens. The main criterion which excluded children from being liberal citizens was their lack of rationality and therefore of capacity to give informed consent. Much of the advocacy of children's right to vote adopted the premises of this argument and gave evidence of children's, particularly older children's, rationality, and rationality was often construed in very narrow cognitive terms. Arneil rightly points out that one of the effects of adopting the terms of the debate and accepting rationality as the criterion for citizenship, is that while including some older children often referred to as mature minors, the citizenship rights of younger children are ignored or assumed to be meaningless. "The infant's or preschooler's interests have very little bearing on any discussion of autonomy rights. In both cases, the focus on rationality and adult rights allows a single sentence dismissal of early childhood."

Arneil is unhappy for a number of reasons with the idea of autonomy rights for children. She wants a view of community which included children from birth rather than waiting for them to develop rationality. She quotes with approval the communitarian critics of liberalism who criticize rights discourse claiming that the dimension of sociality is missing from it. These critics of liberalism argue that people are in important ways constituted by their social ties, and that the rights discourse, in depicting an isolated individual who may have interests opposed to the social groupings to which she belongs, heightens tensions within and between these social groupings. Arneil believes that the communitarian view is a particularly realistic view of community as far as children are concerned. "If the 'unencumbered' individual is difficult to sustain when talking about adults, it is even more problematic when applied to a child. For children are even less detachable, even more in need of affective commitments, and affected in a more profound way by the context and culture within which they live and mature." Rather than an ethic which stresses rights, Arneil believes that the relationships between adults and children are better encapsulated in an ethic of care which looks not at what rights children should have but at how adults ought to treat children. Onora O'Neill may be seen to have a similar view. She wonders why there is "so much current discussion of fundamental ethical issues (which focuses) on children's rights and not on obligations to children." She contrasts children's rights with the rights of other oppressed groups. "Children are more fundamentally but less permanently powerless; their main remedy is to grow up."

There are a number of objections to Arneil's approach. It is not clear whether she is arguing that the associational model of society is appropriate for adults but not for children. So adults can have autonomy rights, but children cannot. If this is her argument, that we can have one model of society for adults and a different one for children, then there seems no reason for it. Why should we make such a division? While children are certainly dependent and affected by the context and culture in which they live, so are adults. It is more a matter of degree and particular circumstance which determines who is able to make decisions.

Rather than suggesting two different models of society, one for adults and one for children, Arneil may be adopting the whole communitarian attack on the notion of rights and saying that we should forget all rights talk for adults and children because rights talk for either group assumes the unencumbered adult male. She would certainly differ from O'Neill if this is her reasoning. Supposing this is her concern, then it is too radical a criticism to counter here. . . .

A more serious concern is posed by Arneil's and O'Neill's return to the idea that the focus should be on responsibilities that adults owe to children, rather than rights possessed by children. It is of concern because in this view children are once again seen as beings who are treated, rather than people who have an internal life and who make decisions. One response to Arneil and O'Neill is to point out that children are more complex beings than has often been thought. This is not a version of the earlier rejected argument that children are more competent than has been thought, the argument that accepted the premise of the rationality criterion for voting rights. The complexity being referred to here is more to do with complexity of the inner life of a child, not with cognitive precocity. It is true that previous images of a child's moral understanding, promoted in the work of, for example, [Lawrence] Kohlberg and [Jean] Piaget, viewed the child as a less competent version of the liberal individual as characterized by Arneil and other critics of liberalism, that is, as the isolated thinker, but in the child's case as not yet having the cognitive abilities to make her own decisions. However child development work over the last few decades indicates that even very young children have a much richer inner life than that assumed in the work of some earlier child developmentalists. . . .

What I have attempted to do in this article is to give an idea of the kinds of autonomy rights which children should be accorded, namely the kinds described in the UN Convention on the Rights of the Child. I have then defended the idea of children's rights against some who are cynical about the idea of rights for children. In defending children's rights, particularly autonomy rights, there is some public relations work to be done since many adults are ambivalent about children's rights. As Katherine O'Donovan puts it, "Children are agents, do act and sometimes in ways that upset adults' conceptions of childhood. Laws are made by adults and legal uneasiness about children's agency can be seen in legislation in which beneficence towards children in civil law jostles with criminal responsibility." But it is not just public relations work but also philosophical work which is needed in order to determine how the idea of agency and autonomy rights can be reconciled with an idea about which most persons' intuition would agree. This idea is that there are many areas, not just the criminal law, where to hold children as entirely responsible for their actions and decisions is inhumane. ◄

In opposition to Coady and the liberationist position, Martin Guggenheim argues against children's rights, at least against what he sees as the content of the modern children's rights movement (especially in the United States). Guggenheim claims that children do not need to be liberated; they are not an oppressed group. He acknowledges that parents do not always act in the best interests of their children; indeed, as in the DeShaney case, they sometimes act against the well-being of their children. But, he claims, such cases do not justify removing parental control over their children. He states, "[I]t is not the condition of control that is wrong. It is the way it is being exercised." Control and guidance are exactly what children need, he says, not freedom. It would be irresponsible for parents to let children decide what they will eat or whether they will learn proper hygiene, for example. Finally, he says that the result of the children's rights movement has been (1) the expansion of state authority, which is the very opposite of enhancing the rights of individuals, and (2) the erosion of parental responsibility, in the sense that more and more parents are now "taking it to the judge" in order to make important and difficult parental and familial decisions.

MARTIN GUGGENHEIM, *WHAT'S WRONG WITH CHILDREN'S RIGHTS?**

What is a child's right . . . is often in the eyes of the beholder. Some children's rights advocates continue to draw upon the excess of rhetoric of the early days of the modern movement. Thus, a current leading children's rights advocate and law professor, Kathleen Federle, advocates for overcoming children's "subordination" and "oppression," connecting the way Americans treated slaves with the way the law limits the freedom of children. According to Federle, just as the "infantilization of African Americans was nothing more than an attempt to control and oppress an entire race," "[t]heories which cannot accommodate the rights of children perpetuate these traditions of power and dominance." Federle is only one of many current writers who have likened the legal status of children to that of slaves. One philosopher, writing in 2002, called the status of children in American law "a sort of moral nightmare" and "an evil and morally hideous" position.

---

*(Cambridge, MA: Harvard University Press, 2005), 8–16, 245–249, 264–266.

This has had unfortunate consequences for the children's rights movement. The call for freedom and an end to oppression, as applied to children, is received by many Americans as overheated nonsense. And for good reason. Most adults are unpersuaded that children, like other minorities, are an oppressed group, and that laws discriminating against them should be measured against a heightened standard to ensure children's rights are protected by the majority. Such arguments, in the words of the philosopher Onora O'Neill, have "neither theoretical nor political advantages."

There is no denying that law insists that children be subordinate to adults and subject to adult authority. But this subordination has virtually nothing to do with the oppression experienced by racial minorities or by women. It is false to suggest that adults are oppressing children by developing laws that restrict the liberties of children. In many contexts, children are in the control of adults for unassailable reasons. As most of us recognize, childhood is a stage of life that normally ends through the natural course of development. More pertinently, the rules created by adults for children are designed with the idea that children will emerge from childhood and enter adulthood.

This does not mean, of course, that everything adults do in the exercise of their control over children is appropriate. But it is not the condition of control that is wrong. It is the way it is being exercised. . . .

It is worse than misguided to speak of highly dependent children, such as newborns or toddlers, as needing or lacking "freedom." They need the opposite. Children need caring adults to ensure they will live and grow into independent adults. Children, at least for an important period of their lives, are dependent on adults for their very existence. In the language of an early nineteenth-century court, it would be an act of cruelty to deny (very young) children custody. . . .

[I]t is futile to separate children and their rights from the rest of society. To state the obvious, children live in a world of adults. As a result, most changes in law concerning children will impact adults (and vice versa). Rules concerning children simultaneously are rules concerning adults. The inverse sometimes, but not as often, is true: Rules concerning adults often are rules concerning children. . . .

The consequences of the inseparability of children and their interests from the rest of society's interests also has deeper implications. Virtually anything can be said to affect children. When the list ranges from minimum wage requirements; driving while intoxicated; same-sex marriages; resource fights over allocating money for defense, space exploration, health care, education, and child care; it is clear that an adult can credibly invoke children's rights into almost any debate of national import. . . .

[G]iving parents superior rights to the care and custody of their children over all others is the opposite of the denial of children's humanity. Instead, it should be seen as an affirmation of a sensible goal of providing children with their best chance to grow and be supported within a family, with an edifice of significant barriers to state control and intervention. . . .

An overarching characteristic of the children's rights movement is a distrust of parental authority. The basis for some of this distrust is undeniably well grounded. Parents do not always act in their children's interests. But the modern solution for children's rights advocates has been to fuel a movement that encourages litigation to protect and enforce children's rights. Only a fraction of the causes of action regularly pursued against parents, however, have anything to do with protecting children from extremes of parental misconduct.

The problem with how children's rights are used in modern family disputes is that they are used more often than not as an opportunity to "take it to the judge." One of the few palpable results of the children's rights movement over the last forty years is that more children are enmeshed in legal proceedings than would have been imaginable a generation ago. . . .

More children than ever are the subject of legal proceedings whose purpose is to terminate their parents' rights. More children than ever are in state-supervised foster care, denied the opportunity to live with their parents, and, even, to remain legally related to them. And more children than ever are embroiled in contentious custody and relocation cases. The enormous waste of resources engendered by this system should trouble us in itself, although there are far more grave consequences. . . .

"Rights" work best when they clearly delineate the power of a state official to act. In the topsy-turvy world of children's rights, "rights" have the opposite effect. Relying on them *expands* the power of state officials.

This unusual relationship between rights and state action is vastly underappreciated. A child's "right" to limit parental authority only to those decisions that further the child's best interests broadly authorizes state officials to oversee and control families. . . .

If children's rights were understood to include limiting state officials from overreaching, huge numbers of cases currently litigated in the name of children's rights would be barred. Fights between adults over children would almost certainly continue to be waged. But courts would not be permitted to decide those disputes based on the child's best interests. That standard only ensures greater intervention through protracted litigation and an almost boundless authority by the judge to regulate the family. . . .

Children's rights are generally served best by restricting the conditions under which their lives are subject to review by state officials. The rule that pregnant minors must obtain judicial permission to obtain an abortion is a violation of that principle. We may disagree about the wisdom of a rule that a parent's approval is needed, but there should be no disagreement that it is not a judge's proper business. . . .

Children do not need rights within the family. What they need are rules that work. Keeping families free from state oversight will do more for children than encouraging litigation and judicial intervention. Adults are the only ones who need and want children to have rights. Regrettably, many children's advocates have unintentionally encouraged adults who wish to rearrange power relationships in families. If children's rights did not work for these adults, the movement would be of far less consequence. . . .

The history of the modern children's rights movement proves, if nothing else, that reliance on children's rights is no guarantee against the enactment of policies that serve children poorly. Even more to the point, nothing within the rights lexicon can protect children from adults' insistence on treating children like adults.

Some will counter that this is but a variation on the now familiar claim that the civil rights movement has not proven sufficient to advance the plight of minorities in the United States. Many note, for example, that racism and discrimination continue in the United States despite the formal outlawing of discrimination. This suggests that rights invariably have a limited utility and that much more is needed to transform a society than the recognition that individuals or a class of people have rights. But it would be wrong to think these phenomena as being basically the same. They are radically different. . . .

Equal protection rights are a powerful means of preventing government from officially privileging one group over another. They provide minorities with the ability to demand equal treatment under the law. An ever-growing number of blacks are real beneficiaries of civil rights laws and live a materially better life because of these laws. That these laws do not reach far enough is not to say they do not reach far.

But equal protection rights are outside of most formulations of children's rights. Very often, however, children deserve to have rights that adults already have. For those interested in doing better for children, we should recognize that some arguments will be more persuasive than others. At least in the United States, the strongest arguments for treating children better, in almost every context, will stress their needs or interests. It is considerably more straightforward to argue against an adultlike sentence for children based on children's interests and needs. Much is gained by this. Just as important, little is lost.

The principle advantage to relying on rights in the first place is their capacity to require particular outcomes in legal disputes. Thus, courts and judges are said to be compelled to rule a certain way once particular rights are established. But, for reasons having nothing to do with children in the first place, we should expect courts to protect children only against the most egregious state acts. . . .

When rights come to mean little more than what adults should do to treat children appropriately, we really mean something different from rights in the first place. Rights are most coherent when enforcing legally recognized norms. Thus, rights are commonly pressed when one seeks to get something someone else already has. For this reason, it is often sensible to rely on them when arguing claims for treating children like adults. But when the claim is that children deserve to be treated *un*like adults, they need something other than rights upon which to depend.

If children's rights advocates could recast claims on behalf of children from rights to what is fair and just for children, perhaps we could recapture a time when adults would better accept their responsibilities toward children. However, inadvertently, our current emphasis on children's rights reduces the pressure on adults to do right by children.

We have reached the point in our history where perhaps the greatest goal for advancing children's rights should be a return to a time when we treated children like children: when the mistakes they made were understood to be part of the natural process of growing up; and when adults understood their obligations.

There is little doubt that a caring society would insist on carefully considering the needs and interests of its children when debating knotty social choices. What is doubtful is whether there is much use for considering children's rights, at least to the extent the term means anything beyond their needs and interests. One thing, however, is certain: unless children's rights include society's obligations to deal with children well, children don't need them. ◣

Questions for Discussion

1. Coady's view seems to be that rights of provision and protection are not sufficient for children because such rights reflect the view that children are at most moral patients. But, for her, they are also moral agents and, as such, have autonomy rights. What autonomy rights would a five-year-old child have? A ten-year-old? A fifteen-year-old? If the child's autonomy rights conflicted with those of his or her parents, which would have precedence and why? Moral agents, as rights holders, are also generally seen as duty holders. That is, if some agent can have rights, then it can also have duties (with respect to the rights of others). How, if at all, can children be duty holders, especially very young children? If they cannot, then how can they be rights holders?

2. Guggenheim seems to argue that children *as children* do not need special rights since they are not an oppressed group, at least not in the sense that women and minorities have been. However, children *as children* are vulnerable and dependent in ways that adults are not. Why would their status as vulnerable and dependent beings not justify them as having special rights, since that status seems to place special duties on others? Guggenheim also claims that the children's rights movement has led to greater state authority, but has he provided an account of why such enhanced authority is a problem?

3. Should the concerns raised in Chapter 4 about group rights, particularly groups as rights holders, also apply to children as rights holders? If children as children can be rights holders, can they also be rights addressees and bear duties to other rights-holding agents? If not, why not? If they can, how are the rights of children and other rights-holding agents balanced (especially if they conflict)?

4. Chapter 6 raises a number of concerns communitarians have about the strident nature of rights talk and the overreliance on rights in addressing moral matters and conflicts. Do those concerns apply with respect to children's rights discourse? Why or why not?

5. Do any conceptions of the nature of rights from Chapter 1 seem particularly relevant or irrelevant to concerns about children's rights discourse? For example, is Joseph Raz's claim that rights are significant interests particularly applicable to children's rights? Or is Gilbert Harman's claim from Chapter 2 that rights are justified by their value in the context of social bargaining particularly applicable to children's rights?

Further Reading

Archard, David. *Children: Rights and Childhood*. New York: Routledge, 2004. An analysis of conceptions of childhood, the relation of children to families, and a detailed statement of aspects of children's rights.

Hawes, Joseph M. *The Children's Rights Movement: A History of Advocacy and Protection*. Boston: Twayne Publishers, 1991. A sustained historical overview of social and legal attitudes and practices related to the promotion of children's rights.

Ladd, Rosalind Ekman, ed. *Children's Rights Re-visioned: Philosophical Readings*. Belmont, CA: Wadsworth, 1996. A collection of essays and cases involving rights related to children and families.

Mason, Mary Ann. *From Father's Property to Children's Rights*. New York: Columbia University Press, 1996. A historical analysis of the treatment of children in American society, with an emphasis on law and rights related to child custody.

Woodhouse, Barbara Bennett. *Hidden in Plain Sight: The Tragedy of Children's Rights from Ben Franklin to Lionel Tate (The Public Square)*. Princeton, NJ: Princeton University Press, 2008. A sustained analysis of child custody and rights, focusing on concepts of privacy, agency, equality, and protection.

PART III

SELECTED RIGHTS DOCUMENTS

The documents in Part III comprise a selection of important rights documents that have both reflected and shaped our notions of the nature, content, and value of rights. Spanning over two centuries, beginning with the U.S. Declaration of Independence and selected amendments to the U.S. Constitution in the late 1700s and going up to the Cairo Declaration of Human Rights in Islam in 1990, these documents speak to and reveal varying conceptions and views about rights. The historically earlier documents tend to emphasize political rights held by individuals against governments. Later documents, essentially those from the twentieth century, speak more to social and economic concerns, emphasizing not what governments may not do to people but what they need to guarantee for people. The most famous of the documents, the 1948 Universal Declaration of Human Rights, first formulates the notion of human rights, that is, rights pertaining to people on the basis of their humanity alone. The most recent of the documents, those from the late twentieth century, however, offer varying interpretations of the very notion of human rights and of the nature of rights.

As with the specific practice and application of rights from Part II, the documents included here can also serve as test cases for the theory and practice of rights. Are these various documents internally consistent? Are they coherent with the other rights documents, or do they contradict each other? What exactly is their function? Is it to protect and enhance the well-being of persons? Of citizens? Of governments? Can the various provisions of these documents actually be carried out in practice? If not, what value do they have? Are there rights that these documents do not enunciate or embrace? If so, does this degrade the purposes or value of the documents? If not, does this mean that those "rights" are not really rights after all? Are these various documents more or less consistent with certain conceptual views about the nature and content or justifications of rights? Do they help sustain or overcome criticisms that have been made about rights?

U.S. DECLARATION OF INDEPENDENCE (1776)

The U.S. Declaration of Independence of 1776 and subsequent Bill of Rights adopted in 1791 (with even more rights-focused amendments added later) were the direct result of a movement toward identifying natural rights—that is, rights that individuals had against their own governments purely by virtue of their status as persons. This view of natural rights had slowly grown in Western intellectual thought over the course of several centuries and, by the 1700s, had gained considerable legitimacy and respectability. It was championed by esteemed European intellectuals like John Locke, Jacques Rousseau, and Immanuel Kant. There were, of course, historical events that led up to the American colonies' declaring independence from the British Empire. Britain had incurred considerable debt as a result of several wars earlier in the century, with the result that British king George III had taxed the American colonies quite heavily. At the same time, many colonists believed that they did not have appropriate representation in Parliament, Britain's governing body. Over a number of years, these colonists questioned Parliament's authority over them. As these political tussles grew, British efforts escalated to suspend the increasingly rebellious attitudes of the colonists—not via negotiation but rather via coercion, such as by blocking American ports and declaring American ships as enemy vessels. Such political and historical events may have led to revolution on the part of the American colonists, but with respect to political philosophy, the content of the Declaration of Independence (and subsequent Bill of Rights) resulted from the advocacy of natural rights, a view that had grown over the course of several centuries but had fully and explicitly blossomed only with these documents.

> When in the Course of human events it becomes necessary for one people to dissolve the political bands which have connected them with another and to assume among the powers of the earth, the separate and equal station to which the Laws of Nature and of Nature's God entitle them, a decent respect to the opinions of mankind requires that they should declare the causes which impel them to the separation.

We hold these truths to be self-evident, that all men are created equal, that they are endowed by their Creator with certain unalienable Rights, that among these are Life, Liberty and the pursuit of Happiness.—That to secure these rights, Governments are instituted among Men, deriving their just powers from the consent of the governed,—That whenever any Form of Government becomes destructive of these ends, it is the Right of the People to alter or to abolish it, and to institute new Government, laying its foundation on such principles and organizing its powers in such form, as to them shall seem most likely to effect their Safety and Happiness. Prudence, indeed, will dictate that Governments long established should not be changed for light and transient causes; and accordingly all experience hath shown that mankind are more disposed to suffer, while evils are sufferable than to right themselves by abolishing the forms to which they are accustomed. But when a long train of abuses and usurpations, pursuing invariably the same Object evinces a design to reduce them under absolute Despotism, it is their right, it is their duty, to throw off such Government, and to provide new Guards for their future security.—Such has been the patient sufferance of these Colonies; and such is now the necessity which constrains them to alter their former Systems of Government. The history of the present King of Great Britain is a history of repeated injuries and usurpations, all having in direct object the establishment of an absolute Tyranny over these States. To prove this, let Facts be submitted to a candid world.

He has refused his Assent to Laws, the most wholesome and necessary for the public good. He has forbidden his Governors to pass Laws of immediate and pressing importance, unless suspended in their operation till his Assent should be obtained; and when so suspended, he has utterly neglected to attend to them. He has refused to pass other Laws for the accommodation of large districts of people, unless those people would relinquish the right of Representation in the Legislature, a right inestimable to them and formidable to tyrants only. He has called together legislative bodies at places unusual, uncomfortable, and distant from the depository of their Public Records, for the sole purpose of fatiguing them into compliance with his measures. He has dissolved Representative Houses repeatedly, for opposing with manly firmness his invasions on the rights of the people. He has refused for a long time, after such dissolutions, to cause others to be elected, whereby the Legislative Powers, incapable of Annihilation, have returned to the People at large for their exercise; the State remaining in the mean time exposed to all the dangers of invasion from without, and convulsions within. He has endeavored to prevent the population of these States; for that purpose obstructing the Laws for Naturalization of Foreigners; refusing to pass others to encourage their migrations hither, and raising the conditions of new Appropriations of Lands. He has obstructed the Administration of Justice by refusing his Assent to Laws for establishing Judiciary Powers. He has made Judges dependent on his Will alone for the tenure of their offices, and the amount and payment of their salaries. He has erected a multitude of New Offices, and sent hither swarms of Officers to harass our people and eat out their substance. He has kept among us, in times of peace, Standing Armies without the Consent of our legislatures. He has affected to render the Military independent of and superior to the Civil Power.

He has combined with others to subject us to a jurisdiction foreign to our constitution, and unacknowledged by our laws; giving his Assent to their Acts of pretended Legislation: For quartering large bodies of armed troops among us: For protecting them, by a mock Trial from punishment for any Murders which they should commit on the Inhabitants of these States: For cutting off our Trade with all parts of the world: For imposing Taxes on us without our Consent: For depriving us in many cases, of the benefit of Trial by Jury: For transporting us beyond Seas to be tried for pretended offences: For abolishing the free System of English Laws in a neighboring Province, establishing therein an Arbitrary government, and enlarging its Boundaries so as to render it at once an example and fit instrument for introducing the same absolute rule into these Colonies: For taking away our Charters, abolishing our most valuable Laws and altering fundamentally the Forms of our Governments: For suspending our own Legislatures, and declaring themselves invested with power to legislate for us in all cases whatsoever.

He has abdicated Government here, by declaring us out of his Protection and waging War against us. He has plundered our seas, ravaged our coasts, burnt our towns, and destroyed the lives of our people. He is at this time transporting large Armies of foreign Mercenaries to complete the works of death, desolation, and tyranny, already begun with circumstances of Cruelty and Perfidy scarcely paralleled in the most barbarous ages, and totally unworthy the Head of a civilized nation. He has constrained our fellow Citizens taken Captive on the high Seas to bear Arms against their Country, to become the executioners of their friends and Brethren, or to fall themselves by their Hands. He has excited domestic insurrections amongst us, and has endeavored to bring on the inhabitants of our frontiers, the merciless Indian Savages whose known rule of warfare, is an undistinguished destruction of all ages, sexes and conditions.

In every stage of these Oppressions We have Petitioned for Redress in the most humble terms: Our repeated Petitions have been answered only by repeated injury. A Prince, whose character is thus marked by every act which may define a Tyrant, is unfit to be the ruler of a free people. Nor have we been wanting in attentions to our British brethren. We have warned them from time to time of attempts by their legislature to extend an unwarrantable jurisdiction over us. We have reminded them of the circumstances of our emigration and settlement here. We have appealed to their native justice and magnanimity, and we have conjured them by the ties of our common kindred to disavow these usurpations, which would inevitably interrupt our connections and correspondence. They too have been deaf to the voice of justice and of consanguinity. We must, therefore, acquiesce in the necessity, which denounces our Separation, and hold them, as we hold the rest of mankind, Enemies in War, in Peace Friends.

We, therefore, the Representatives of the united States of America, in General Congress, Assembled, appealing to the Supreme Judge of the world for the rectitude of our intentions, do, in the Name, and by Authority of the good People of these Colonies, solemnly publish and declare, That these united Colonies are, and of Right ought to be Free and Independent States, that they are Absolved from all Allegiance to the British Crown, and that all political connection between them and the State of Great Britain, is and ought to be totally dissolved; and that as Free and Independent States, they have full Power to levy War, conclude Peace, contract Alliances, establish Commerce, and to do all other Acts and Things which Independent States may of right do.—And for the support of this Declaration, with a firm reliance on the protection of Divine Providence, we mutually pledge to each other our Lives, our Fortunes, and our sacred Honor.

U.S. BILL OF RIGHTS (1791) AND SELECTED LATER AMENDMENTS

Amendment I

Congress shall make no law respecting an establishment of religion, or prohibiting the free exercise thereof; or abridging the freedom of speech, or of the press; or the right of the people peaceably to assemble, and to petition the government for a redress of grievances.

Amendment II

A well-regulated militia, being necessary to the security of a free state, the right of the people to keep and bear arms, shall not be infringed.

Amendment III

No soldier shall, in time of peace be quartered in any house, without the consent of the owner, nor in time of war, but in a manner to be prescribed by law.

Amendment IV

The right of the people to be secure in their persons, houses, papers, and effects, against unreasonable searches and seizures, shall not be violated, and no warrants shall issue, but upon probable cause, supported by oath or affirmation, and particularly describing the place to be searched, and the persons or things to be seized.

Amendment V

No person shall be held to answer for a capital, or otherwise infamous crime, unless on a presentment or indictment of a grand jury, except in cases arising in the land or naval forces, or in the militia, when in actual service in time of war or public danger; nor shall any person be subject for the same offense to be twice put in jeopardy of life or limb; nor shall be compelled in any criminal case to be a witness against himself, nor be deprived of life, liberty, or property, without due process of law; nor shall private property be taken for public use, without just compensation.

Amendment VI

In all criminal prosecutions, the accused shall enjoy the right to a speedy and public trial, by an impartial jury of the state and district wherein the crime shall have been committed, which district shall have been previously ascertained by law, and to be informed of the nature and cause of the accusation; to be confronted with the witnesses against him; to have compulsory process for obtaining witnesses in his favor, and to have the assistance of counsel for his defense.

Amendment VII

In suits at common law, where the value in controversy shall exceed twenty dollars, the right of trial by jury shall be preserved, and no fact tried by a jury, shall be otherwise reexamined in any court of the United States, than according to the rules of the common law.

Amendment VIII

Excessive bail shall not be required, nor excessive fines imposed, nor cruel and unusual punishments inflicted.

Amendment IX

The enumeration in the Constitution, of certain rights, shall not be construed to deny or disparage others retained by the people.

Amendment X

The powers not delegated to the United States by the Constitution, nor prohibited by it to the states, are reserved to the states respectively, or to the people.

Amendment XIII (1865)

Section 1. Neither slavery nor involuntary servitude, except as a punishment for crime whereof the party shall have been duly convicted, shall exist within the United States, or any place subject to their jurisdiction.

Section 2. Congress shall have power to enforce this article by appropriate legislation.

Amendment XIV (1868)

Section 1. All persons born or naturalized in the United States, and subject to the jurisdiction thereof, are citizens of the United States and of the state wherein they reside. No state shall make or enforce any law which shall abridge the privileges or immunities of citizens of the United States; nor shall any state deprive any person of life, liberty, or property, without due process of law; nor deny to any person within its jurisdiction the equal protection of the laws.

Section 2. Representatives shall be apportioned among the several states according to their respective numbers, counting the whole number of persons in each state, excluding Indians not taxed. But when the right to vote at any election for the choice of electors for President and Vice President of the United States, Representatives in Congress, the executive and judicial officers of a state, or the members of the legislature thereof, is denied to any of the male inhabitants of such state, being twenty-one years of age, and citizens of the United States, or in any way abridged, except for participation in rebellion, or other crime, the basis of representation therein shall be reduced in the proportion which the number of such male citizens shall bear to the whole number of male citizens twenty-one years of age in such state.

Section 3. No person shall be a Senator or Representative in Congress, or elector of President and Vice President, or hold any office, civil or military, under the United States, or under any state, who, having previously taken an oath, as a member of Congress, or as an officer of the United States, or as a member of any state legislature, or as an executive or judicial officer of any state, to support the Constitution of the United States, shall have engaged in insurrection or rebellion against the same, or given aid or comfort to the enemies thereof. But Congress may by a vote of two-thirds of each House, remove such disability.

Section 4. The validity of the public debt of the United States, autho-
rized by law, including debts incurred for payment of pensions and
bounties for services in suppressing insurrection or rebellion, shall not
be questioned. But neither the United States nor any state shall assume
or pay any debt or obligation incurred in aid of insurrection or rebellion
against the United States, or any claim for the loss or emancipation of
any slave; but all such debts, obligations and claims shall be held illegal and void.

Section 5. The Congress shall have power to enforce, by appropriate
legislation, the provisions of this article.

Amendment XV (1870)

Section 1. The right of citizens of the United States to vote shall not be
denied or abridged by the United States or by any State on account of
race, color, or previous condition of servitude.

Section 2. The Congress shall have power to enforce this article by
appropriate legislation.

Amendment XIX (1920)

The right of citizens of the United States to vote shall not be denied or
abridged by the United States or by any State on account of sex. Congress shall have power to enforce this article by appropriate legislation.

FRENCH DECLARATION OF THE RIGHTS OF MAN AND CITIZEN (1789)

Although the U.S. Declaration of Independence and subsequent American Revolution took place thirteen years before the French Revolution, the latter was seen at the time as more significant. By 1789 the American nation had barely begun to exist as a political entity, while France was a world power with a long and storied history. A number of the intellectuals who inspired Thomas Jefferson and others to declare independence, largely on the basis of natural rights, were French (such as Jean-Jacques Rousseau). The French Declaration of the Rights of Man and Citizen responded not only to the Enlightenment view of natural rights but also to the harsh economic conditions that France suffered at the time as well as what was seen as the opulence and arrogance of the nobility and of the reign of King Louis XVI. By the end of the 1700s, France had incurred tremendous debt (in part because of its support of the Americans against the British in the American Revolution), and a very heavy tax burden was placed on the French citizenry. Although France was a monarchy, Louis XVI had permitted a body, called the Estates-General, to function somewhat as a legislative body. The Estates-General consisted of three groups: the clergy, the nobility, and "propertied" commoners (i.e., citizens who owned property). The Third Estate (i.e., the propertied citizens) quickly broke away from the Estates-General and convinced the First Estate (the clergy) to join them. They formed the National Constituent Assembly, one of whose first acts was to draft what came to be known as the French Declaration of the Rights of Man and Citizen. The primary author of the declaration was the Marquis de LaFayette, who had served alongside American troops in the American Revolution. In drafting the declaration, LaFayette collaborated directly with Thomas Jefferson. Following the French Revolution and the downfall of the French monarchy, the declaration became the preamble of the French Constitution of 1791.

The representatives of the French people, organized as a National Assembly, believing that the ignorance, neglect, or contempt of the rights of man are the sole cause of public calamities and of the corruption of governments, have determined to set forth in a solemn declaration the

natural, unalienable, and sacred rights of man, in order that this declaration, being constantly before all the members of the Social body, shall
remind them continually of their rights and duties; in order that the acts
of the legislative power, as well as those of the executive power, may be
compared at any moment with the objects and purposes of all political
institutions and may thus be more respected, and, lastly, in order that
the grievances of the citizens, based hereafter upon simple and incon-
testable principles, shall tend to the maintenance of the constitution
and redound to the happiness of all. Therefore the National Assembly
recognizes and proclaims, in the presence and under the auspices of
the Supreme Being, the following rights of man and of the citizen:

Articles

1. Men are born and remain free and equal in rights. Social distinctions
   may be founded only upon the general good.
2. The aim of all political association is the preservation of the natural
   and imprescriptible rights of man. These rights are liberty, property,
   security, and resistance to oppression.
3. The principle of all sovereignty resides essentially in the nation. No
   body nor individual may exercise any authority which does not proceed directly from the nation.
4. Liberty consists in the freedom to do everything which injures no one
   else; hence the exercise of the natural rights of each man has no limits except those which assure to the other members of the society the
   enjoyment of the same rights. These limits can only be determined
   by law.
5. Law can only prohibit such actions as are hurtful to society. Nothing
   may be prevented which is not forbidden by law, and no one may be
   forced to do anything not provided for by law.
6. Law is the expression of the general will. Every citizen has a right to
   participate personally, or through his representative, in its foundation.
   It must be the same for all, whether it protects or punishes. All citizens,
   being equal in the eyes of the law, are equally eligible to all dignities
   and to all public positions and occupations, according to their abilities, and without distinction except that of their virtues and talents.
7. No person shall be accused, arrested, or imprisoned except in the
   cases and according to the forms prescribed by law. Any one solicit-

ing, transmitting, executing, or causing to be executed, any arbitrary order, shall be punished. But any citizen summoned or arrested in virtue of the law shall submit without delay, as resistance constitutes an offense.

8. The law shall provide for such punishments only as are strictly and obviously necessary, and no one shall suffer punishment except it be legally inflicted in virtue of a law passed and promulgated before the commission of the offense.

9. As all persons are held innocent until they shall have been declared guilty, if arrest shall be deemed indispensable, all harshness not essential to the securing of the prisoner's person shall be severely repressed by law.

10. No one shall be disquieted on account of his opinions, including his religious views, provided their manifestation does not disturb the public order established by law.

11. The free communication of ideas and opinions is one of the most precious of the rights of man. Every citizen may, accordingly, speak, write, and print with freedom, but shall be responsible for such abuses of this freedom as shall be defined by law.

12. The security of the rights of man and of the citizen requires public military forces. These forces are, therefore, established for the good of all and not for the personal advantage of those to whom they shall be intrusted.

13. A common contribution is essential for the maintenance of the public forces and for the cost of administration. This should be equitably distributed among all the citizens in proportion to their means.

14. All the citizens have a right to decide, either personally or by their representatives, as to the necessity of the public contribution; to grant this freely; to know to what uses it is put; and to fix the proportion, the mode of assessment and of collection and the duration of the taxes.

15. Society has the right to require of every public agent an account of his administration.

16. A society in which the observance of the law is not assured, nor the separation of powers defined, has no constitution at all.

17. Since property is an inviolable and sacred right, no one shall be deprived thereof except where public necessity, legally determined, shall clearly demand it, and then only on condition that the owner shall have been previously and equitably indemnified.

UNIVERSAL DECLARATION OF HUMAN RIGHTS (1948)

The Universal Declaration of Human Rights (UDHR) was an immediate outcome of the creation of the United Nations. It was an international recognition and global response to sufferings and atrocities, such as the Holocaust, perpetuated by governments and regimes against individuals and peoples. This declaration made commonplace the concept of human rights—that is, rights pertaining to persons as humans and not merely as citizens of a particular country—and shaped later international law and treaties on that basis. Although the UDHR was not ratified until the end of 1948, three years after the formation of the United Nations, work on this declaration began with the drafting of the Charter of the United Nations in 1945, particularly with the establishment of the UN Commission on Human Rights, in 1946, and a mandate by the UN General Assembly to draft an international bill of rights. Social and political theorists had long spoken of the concept of natural rights to designate rights that individuals hold simply as individuals, as opposed to the concept of legal rights that individuals hold as citizens within some legal system. However, not until the middle of the twentieth century, following the Nuremberg and Tokyo war trials, was there an international political push to foster and implement rights in a more global context. The language of natural rights quickly transformed into that of human rights—rights possessed by all humans regardless of their citizenship—with a corresponding assertion of the international responsibility to respect and enforce these rights pertaining to all humans. Following ratification of the UDHR, the UN General Assembly passed numerous other documents promoting and extending human rights, as did many other governmental and nongovernmental bodies. The UDHR itself came to be referred to as the first component of the International Bill of Human Rights, with later components being the International Covenant on Civil and Political Rights and the International Covenant on Economic, Social, and Cultural Rights, both passed in 1966.

Preamble

Whereas recognition of the inherent dignity and of the equal and inalienable rights of all members of the human family is the foundation of freedom, justice and peace in the world,

Whereas disregard and contempt for human rights have resulted in barbarous acts which have outraged the conscience of mankind, and the advent of a world in which human beings shall enjoy freedom of speech and belief and freedom from fear and want has been proclaimed as the highest aspiration of the common people,

Whereas it is essential, if man is not to be compelled to have recourse, as a last resort, to rebellion against tyranny and oppression, that human rights should be protected by the rule of law,

Whereas it is essential to promote the development of friendly relations between nations,

Whereas the peoples of the United Nations have in the Charter reaffirmed their faith in fundamental human rights, in the dignity and worth of the human person and in the equal rights of men and women and have determined to promote social progress and better standards of life in larger freedom,

Whereas Member States have pledged themselves to achieve, in cooperation with the United Nations, the promotion of universal respect for and observance of human rights and fundamental freedoms,

Whereas a common understanding of these rights and freedoms is of the greatest importance for the full realization of this pledge,

Now, Therefore THE GENERAL ASSEMBLY proclaims THIS UNIVERSAL DECLARATION OF HUMAN RIGHTS as a common standard of achievement for all peoples and all nations, to the end that every individual and every organ of society, keeping this Declaration constantly in mind, shall strive by teaching and education to promote respect for these rights and freedoms and by progressive measures, national and international, to secure their universal and effective recognition and observance, both among the peoples of Member States themselves and among the peoples of territories under their jurisdiction.

Article 1

All human beings are born free and equal in dignity and rights. They are endowed with reason and conscience and should act towards one another in a spirit of brotherhood.

Article 2

Everyone is entitled to all the rights and freedoms set forth in this Declaration, without distinction of any kind, such as race, color, sex, language, religion, political or other opinion, national or social origin, property, birth or other status. Furthermore, no distinction shall be made on the basis of the political, jurisdictional or international status of the country or territory to which a person belongs, whether it be independent, trust, non-self-governing or under any other limitation of sovereignty.

Article 3

Everyone has the right to life, liberty and security of person.

Article 4

No one shall be held in slavery or servitude; slavery and the slave trade shall be prohibited in all their forms.

Article 5

No one shall be subjected to torture or to cruel, inhuman or degrading treatment or punishment.

Article 6

Everyone has the right to recognition everywhere as a person before the law.

Article 7

All are equal before the law and are entitled without any discrimination to equal protection of the law. All are entitled to equal protection against any discrimination in violation of this Declaration and against any incitement to such discrimination.

Article 8

Everyone has the right to an effective remedy by the competent national tribunals for acts violating the fundamental rights granted him by the constitution or by law.

Article 9

No one shall be subjected to arbitrary arrest, detention or exile.

Article 10

Everyone is entitled in full equality to a fair and public hearing by an independent and impartial tribunal, in the determination of his rights and obligations and of any criminal charge against him.

Article 11

1. Everyone charged with a penal offence has the right to be presumed innocent until proved guilty according to law in a public trial at which he has had all the guarantees necessary for his defense.
2. No one shall be held guilty of any penal offence on account of any act or omission which did not constitute a penal offence, under national or international law, at the time when it was committed. Nor shall a heavier penalty be imposed than the one that was applicable at the time the penal offence was committed.

Article 12

No one shall be subjected to arbitrary interference with his privacy, family, home or correspondence, nor to attacks upon his honor and reputation. Everyone has the right to the protection of the law against such interference or attacks.

Article 13

1. Everyone has the right to freedom of movement and residence within the borders of each state.
2. Everyone has the right to leave any country, including his own, and to return to his country.

Article 14

1. Everyone has the right to seek and to enjoy in other countries asylum from persecution.
2. This right may not be invoked in the case of prosecutions genuinely arising from non-political crimes or from acts contrary to the purposes and principles of the United Nations.

Article 15

1. Everyone has the right to a nationality.
2. No one shall be arbitrarily deprived of his nationality nor denied the right to change his nationality.

Article 16

1. Men and women of full age, without any limitation due to race, nationality or religion, have the right to marry and to found a family. They are entitled to equal rights as to marriage, during marriage and at its dissolution.
2. Marriage shall be entered into only with the free and full consent of the intending spouses.
3. The family is the natural and fundamental group unit of society and is entitled to protection by society and the State.

Article 17

1. Everyone has the right to own property alone as well as in association with others.
2. No one shall be arbitrarily deprived of his property.

Article 18

Everyone has the right to freedom of thought, conscience and religion; this right includes freedom to change his religion or belief, and freedom, either alone or in community with others and in public or private, to manifest his religion or belief in teaching, practice, worship and observance.

Article 19

Everyone has the right to freedom of opinion and expression; this right includes freedom to hold opinions without interference and to seek, receive and impart information and ideas through any media and regardless of frontiers.

Article 20

1. Everyone has the right to freedom of peaceful assembly and association.
2. No one may be compelled to belong to an association.

Article 21

1. Everyone has the right to take part in the government of his country, directly or through freely chosen representatives.
2. Everyone has the right of equal access to public service in his country.
3. The will of the people shall be the basis of the authority of government; this will shall be expressed in periodic and genuine elections which shall be by universal and equal suffrage and shall be held by secret vote or by equivalent free voting procedures.

Article 22

Everyone, as a member of society, has the right to social security and is entitled to realization, through national effort and international co-operation and in accordance with the organization and resources of each State, of the economic, social and cultural rights indispensable for his dignity and the free development of his personality.

Article 23

1. Everyone has the right to work, to free choice of employment, to just and favorable conditions of work and to protection against unemployment.
2. Everyone, without any discrimination, has the right to equal pay for equal work.
3. Everyone who works has the right to just and favorable remuneration ensuring for himself and his family an existence worthy of human dignity, and supplemented, if necessary, by other means of social protection.
4. Everyone has the right to form and to join trade unions for the protection of his interests.

Article 24

Everyone has the right to rest and leisure, including reasonable limitation of working hours and periodic holidays with pay.

Article 25

1. Everyone has the right to a standard of living adequate for the health and well-being of himself and of his family, including food, clothing, housing and medical care and necessary social services, and the right to security in the event of unemployment, sickness, disability, widowhood, old age or other lack of livelihood in circumstances beyond his control.
2. Motherhood and childhood are entitled to special care and assistance. All children, whether born in or out of wedlock, shall enjoy the same social protection.

Article 26

1. Everyone has the right to education. Education shall be free, at least in the elementary and fundamental stages. Elementary education shall be compulsory. Technical and professional education shall be made generally available and higher education shall be equally accessible to all on the basis of merit.
2. Education shall be directed to the full development of the human personality and to the strengthening of respect for human rights and fundamental freedoms. It shall promote understanding, tolerance and friendship among all nations, racial or religious groups, and shall further the activities of the United Nations for the maintenance of peace.
3. Parents have a prior right to choose the kind of education that shall be given to their children.

Article 27

1. Everyone has the right freely to participate in the cultural life of the community, to enjoy the arts and to share in scientific advancement and its benefits.
2. Everyone has the right to the protection of the moral and material interests resulting from any scientific, literary or artistic production of which he is the author.

Article 28

Everyone is entitled to a social and international order in which the rights and freedoms set forth in this Declaration can be fully realized.

Article 29

1. Everyone has duties to the community in which alone the free and full development of his personality is possible.
2. In the exercise of his rights and freedoms, everyone shall be subject only to such limitations as are determined by law solely for the purpose of securing due recognition and respect for the rights and freedoms of

others and of meeting the just requirements of morality, public order
and the general welfare in a democratic society.
3. These rights and freedoms may in no case be exercised contrary to
the purposes and principles of the United Nations.

Article 30

Nothing in this Declaration may be interpreted as implying for any
State, group or person any right to engage in any activity or to perform
any act aimed at the destruction of any of the rights and freedoms set
forth herein.

CONVENTION ON THE ELIMINATION OF ALL FORMS OF DISCRIMINATION AGAINST WOMEN (1979)

When the Commission on Human Rights was formed in 1946 as part of the United Nations, it included a subcommission, the Commission on the Status of Women (CSW). This commission began work on identifying and addressing discrimination and human rights violations that it saw as directed primarily toward women. Although the Universal Declaration of Human Rights speaks of "all human beings" and in almost every one of its articles speaks of "everyone," this commission claimed that some forms of discrimination were especially relevant to women—for example, forced marriages and limitations on active political participation. As early as 1952, the CSW was able to have resolutions passed by the UN General Assembly to address such concerns. During the 1960s and 1970s, an expansion of claims concerning discrimination against women resulted in the 1979 passage of the Convention on the Elimination of All Forms of Discrimination Against Women (CEDAW), which was adopted by near-unanimous consent (with ten countries abstaining, but no countries opposing). Since its original adoption, even more countries have signed on to CEDAW. A number of countries, however, have filed "reservations," stating that they are not bound by particular sections or articles contained in CEDAW (e.g., sections that run counter to certain domestic family laws within those countries). In addition, there have been more than forty "sessions" (held now by the high commissioner for human rights as part of the United Nations) focused on reviewing CEDAW and assessing its implementation.

The States Parties to the present Convention,

Noting that the Charter of the United Nations reaffirms faith in fundamental human rights, in the dignity and worth of the human person and in the equal rights of men and women,

Noting that the Universal Declaration of Human Rights affirms the principle of the inadmissibility of discrimination and proclaims that all human beings are born free and equal in dignity and rights and that everyone is entitled to all the rights and freedoms set forth therein, without distinction of any kind, including distinction based on sex,

Noting that the States Parties to the International Covenants on Human Rights have the obligation to ensure the equal rights of men and women to enjoy all economic, social, cultural, civil and political rights,

Considering the international conventions concluded under the auspices of the United Nations and the specialized agencies promoting equality of rights of men and women,

Noting also the resolutions, declarations and recommendations adopted by the United Nations and the specialized agencies promoting equality of rights of men and women,

Concerned, however, that despite these various instruments extensive discrimination against women continues to exist,

Recalling that discrimination against women violates the principles of equality of rights and respect for human dignity, is an obstacle to the participation of women, on equal terms with men, in the political, social, economic and cultural life of their countries, hampers the growth of the prosperity of society and the family and makes more difficult the full development of the potentialities of women in the service of their countries and of humanity,

Concerned that in situations of poverty women have the least access to food, health, education, training and opportunities for employment and other needs,

Convinced that the establishment of the new international economic order based on equity and justice will contribute significantly towards the promotion of equality between men and women,

Emphasizing that the eradication of apartheid, all forms of racism, racial discrimination, colonialism, neo-colonialism, aggression, foreign occupation and domination and interference in the internal affairs of States is essential to the full enjoyment of the rights of men and women,

Affirming that the strengthening of international peace and security, the relaxation of international tension, mutual co-operation among all States irrespective of their social and economic systems, general and complete disarmament, in particular nuclear disarmament under strict and effective international control, the affirmation of the principles of justice, equality and mutual benefit in relations among countries and the realization of the right of peoples under alien and colonial domination and foreign occupation to self-determination and independence, as well as respect for national sovereignty and territorial integrity, will promote social progress and development and as a consequence will contribute to the attainment of full equality between men and women,

Convinced that the full and complete development of a country, the welfare of the world and the cause of peace require the maximum participation of women on equal terms with men in all fields,

Bearing in mind the great contribution of women to the welfare of the family and to the development of society, so far not fully recognized, the social significance of maternity and the role of both parents in the family and in the upbringing of children, and aware that the role of women in procreation should not be a basis for discrimination but that the upbringing of children requires a sharing of responsibility between men and women and society as a whole,

Aware that a change in the traditional role of men as well as the role of women in society and in the family is needed to achieve full equality between men and women,

Determined to implement the principles set forth in the Declaration on the Elimination of Discrimination against Women and, for that purpose, to adopt the measures required for the elimination of such discrimination in all its forms and manifestations,

Have agreed on the following:

Part I

Article 1
For the purposes of the present Convention, the term "discrimination against women" shall mean any distinction, exclusion or restriction made on the basis of sex which has the effect or purpose of impairing or nullifying the recognition, enjoyment or exercise by women, irrespective of their marital status, on a basis of equality of men and women, of human rights and fundamental freedoms in the political, economic, social, cultural, civil or any other field.

Article 2
States Parties condemn discrimination against women in all its forms, agree to pursue by all appropriate means and without delay a policy of eliminating discrimination against women and, to this end, undertake:

a. To embody the principle of the equality of men and women in their national constitutions or other appropriate legislation if not yet incorporated therein and to ensure, through law and other appropriate means, the practical realization of this principle;

b. To adopt appropriate legislative and other measures, including sanctions where appropriate, prohibiting all discrimination against women;

c. To establish legal protection of the rights of women on an equal basis with men and to ensure through competent national tribunals and other public institutions the effective protection of women against any act of discrimination;

d. To refrain from engaging in any act or practice of discrimination against women and to ensure that public authorities and institutions shall act in conformity with this obligation;

e. To take all appropriate measures to eliminate discrimination against women by any person, organization or enterprise;

f. To take all appropriate measures, including legislation, to modify or abolish existing laws, regulations, customs and practices which constitute discrimination against women;

g. To repeal all national penal provisions which constitute discrimination against women.

Article 3

States Parties shall take in all fields, in particular in the political, social, economic and cultural fields, all appropriate measures, including legislation, to ensure the full development and advancement of women, for the purpose of guaranteeing them the exercise and enjoyment of human rights and fundamental freedoms on a basis of equality with men.

Article 4

1. Adoption by States Parties of temporary special measures aimed at accelerating de facto equality between men and women shall not be considered discrimination as defined in the present Convention, but shall in no way entail as a consequence the maintenance of unequal or separate standards; these measures shall be discontinued when the objectives of equality of opportunity and treatment have been achieved.

2. Adoption by States Parties of special measures, including those measures contained in the present Convention, aimed at protecting maternity shall not be considered discriminatory.

Article 5
States Parties shall take all appropriate measures:

a. To modify the social and cultural patterns of conduct of men and women, with a view to achieving the elimination of prejudices and customary and all other practices which are based on the idea of the inferiority or the superiority of either of the sexes or on stereotyped roles for men and women;
b. To ensure that family education includes a proper understanding of maternity as a social function and the recognition of the common responsibility of men and women in the upbringing and development of their children, it being understood that the interest of the children is the primordial consideration in all cases.

Article 6
States Parties shall take all appropriate measures, including legislation, to suppress all forms of traffic in women and exploitation of prostitution of women.

Part II

Article 7
States Parties shall take all appropriate measures to eliminate discrimination against women in the political and public life of the country and, in particular, shall ensure to women, on equal terms with men, the right:

a. To vote in all elections and public referenda and to be eligible for election to all publicly elected bodies;
b. To participate in the formulation of government policy and the implementation thereof and to hold public office and perform all public functions at all levels of government;
c. To participate in non-governmental organizations and associations concerned with the public and political life of the country.

Article 8

States Parties shall take all appropriate measures to ensure to women, on equal terms with men and without any discrimination, the opportunity to represent their Governments at the international level and to participate in the work of international organizations.

Article 9

1. States Parties shall grant women equal rights with men to acquire, change or retain their nationality. They shall ensure in particular that neither marriage to an alien nor change of nationality by the husband during marriage shall automatically change the nationality of the wife, render her stateless or force upon her the nationality of the husband.
2. States Parties shall grant women equal rights with men with respect to the nationality of their children.

Part III

Article 10

States Parties shall take all appropriate measures to eliminate discrimination against women in order to ensure to them equal rights with men in the field of education and in particular to ensure, on a basis of equality of men and women:

a. The same conditions for career and vocational guidance, for access to studies and for the achievement of diplomas in educational establishments of all categories in rural as well as in urban areas; this equality shall be ensured in pre-school, general, technical, professional and higher technical education, as well as in all types of vocational training;
b. Access to the same curricula, the same examinations, teaching staff with qualifications of the same standard and school premises and equipment of the same quality;
c. The elimination of any stereotyped concept of the roles of men and women at all levels and in all forms of education by encouraging co-education and other types of education which will help to achieve

this aim and, in particular, by the revision of textbooks and school programs and the adaptation of teaching methods;

d. The same opportunities to benefit from scholarships and other study grants;

e. The same opportunities for access to programs of continuing education, including adult and functional literacy programs, particularly those aimed at reducing, at the earliest possible time, any gap in education existing between men and women;

f. The reduction of female student drop-out rates and the organization of programs for girls and women who have left school prematurely;

g. The same opportunities to participate actively in sports and physical education;

h. Access to specific educational information to help to ensure the health and well-being of families, including information and advice on family planning.

Article 11

1. States Parties shall take all appropriate measures to eliminate discrimination against women in the field of employment in order to ensure, on a basis of equality of men and women, the same rights, in particular:

a. The right to work as an inalienable right of all human beings;

b. The right to the same employment opportunities, including the application of the same criteria for selection in matters of employment;

c. The right to free choice of profession and employment, the right to promotion, job security and all benefits and conditions of service and the right to receive vocational training and retraining, including apprenticeships, advanced vocational training and recurrent training;

d. The right to equal remuneration, including benefits, and to equal treatment in respect of work of equal value, as well as equality of treatment in the evaluation of the quality of work;

e. The right to social security, particularly in cases of retirement, unemployment, sickness, invalidity and old age and other incapacity to work, as well as the right to paid leave;

f. The right to protection of health and to safety in working conditions, including the safeguarding of the function of reproduction.

2. In order to prevent discrimination against women on the grounds of marriage or maternity and to ensure their effective right to work, States Parties shall take appropriate measures:
   a. To prohibit, subject to the imposition of sanctions, dismissal on the grounds of pregnancy or of maternity leave and discrimination in dismissals on the basis of marital status;
   b. To introduce maternity leave with pay or with comparable social benefits without loss of former employment, seniority or social allowances;
   c. To encourage the provision of the necessary supporting social services to enable parents to combine family obligations with work responsibilities and participation in public life, in particular through promoting the establishment and development of a network of child-care facilities;
   d. To provide special protection to women during pregnancy in types of work proved to be harmful to them.
3. Protective legislation relating to matters covered in this article shall be reviewed periodically in the light of scientific and technological knowledge and shall be revised, repealed or extended as necessary.

Article 12

1. States Parties shall take all appropriate measures to eliminate discrimination against women in the field of health care in order to ensure, on a basis of equality of men and women, access to health care services, including those related to family planning.
2. Notwithstanding the provisions of paragraph I of this article, States Parties shall ensure to women appropriate services in connection with pregnancy, confinement and the post-natal period, granting free services where necessary, as well as adequate nutrition during pregnancy and lactation.

Article 13

States Parties shall take all appropriate measures to eliminate discrimination against women in other areas of economic and social life in order to ensure, on a basis of equality of men and women, the same rights, in particular:

a. The right to family benefits;
b. The right to bank loans, mortgages and other forms of financial credit;
c. The right to participate in recreational activities, sports and all aspects of cultural life.

Article 14

1. States Parties shall take into account the particular problems faced by rural women and the significant roles which rural women play in the economic survival of their families, including their work in the non-monetized sectors of the economy, and shall take all appropriate measures to ensure the application of the provisions of the present Convention to women in rural areas.
2. States Parties shall take all appropriate measures to eliminate discrimination against women in rural areas in order to ensure, on a basis of equality of men and women, that they participate in and benefit from rural development and, in particular, shall ensure to such women the right:
   a. To participate in the elaboration and implementation of development planning at all levels;
   b. To have access to adequate health care facilities, including information, counseling and services in family planning;
   c. To benefit directly from social security programs;
   d. To obtain all types of training and education, formal and non-formal, including that relating to functional literacy, as well as, inter alia, the benefit of all community and extension services, in order to increase their technical proficiency;
   e. To organize self-help groups and co-operatives in order to obtain equal access to economic opportunities through employment or self-employment;
   f. To participate in all community activities;
   g. To have access to agricultural credit and loans, marketing facilities, appropriate technology and equal treatment in land and agrarian reform as well as in land resettlement schemes;
   h. To enjoy adequate living conditions, particularly in relation to housing, sanitation, electricity and water supply, transport and communications.

Part IV

Article 15

1. States Parties shall accord to women equality with men before the law.
2. States Parties shall accord to women, in civil matters, a legal capacity identical to that of men and the same opportunities to exercise that capacity. In particular, they shall give women equal rights to con- clude contracts and to administer property and shall treat them equally in all stages of procedure in courts and tribunals.
3. States Parties agree that all contracts and all other private instruments of any kind with a legal effect which is directed at restricting the legal capacity of women shall be deemed null and void.
4. States Parties shall accord to men and women the same rights with regard to the law relating to the movement of persons and the free- dom to choose their residence and domicile.

Article 16

1. States Parties shall take all appropriate measures to eliminate discrim- ination against women in all matters relating to marriage and family relations and in particular shall ensure, on a basis of equality of men and women:
   a. The same right to enter into marriage;
   b. The same right freely to choose a spouse and to enter into mar- riage only with their free and full consent;
   c. The same rights and responsibilities during marriage and at its dissolution;
   d. The same rights and responsibilities as parents, irrespective of their marital status, in matters relating to their children; in all cases the interests of the children shall be paramount;
   e. The same rights to decide freely and responsibly on the number and spacing of their children and to have access to the informa- tion, education and means to enable them to exercise these rights;
   f. The same rights and responsibilities with regard to guardianship, wardship, trusteeship and adoption of children, or similar institu- tions where these concepts exist in national legislation; in all cases the interests of the children shall be paramount;

   g. The same personal rights as husband and wife, including the right
      to choose a family name, a profession and an occupation;

   h. The same rights for both spouses in respect of the ownership, ac-
      quisition, management, administration, enjoyment and disposition
      of property, whether free of charge or for a valuable consideration.

2. The betrothal and the marriage of a child shall have no legal effect,
   and all necessary action, including legislation, shall be taken to
   specify a minimum age for marriage and to make the registration of
   marriages in an official registry compulsory.

Part V

Article 17

1. For the purpose of considering the progress made in the implementation of the present Convention, there shall be established a Committee on the Elimination of Discrimination Against Women (hereinafter
   referred to as the Committee) consisting, at the time of entry into
   force of the Convention, of eighteen and, after ratification of or accession to the Convention by the thirty-fifth State Party, of twenty-
   three experts of high moral standing and competence in the field
   covered by the Convention. The experts shall be elected by States
   Parties from among their nationals and shall serve in their personal
   capacity, consideration being given to equitable geographical distribution and to the representation of the different forms of civilization
   as well as the principal legal systems.

2. The members of the Committee shall be elected by secret ballot from
   a list of persons nominated by States Parties. Each State Party may
   nominate one person from among its own nationals.

3. The initial election shall be held six months after the date of the entry
   into force of the present Convention. At least three months before the
   date of each election the Secretary-General of the United Nations
   shall address a letter to the States Parties inviting them to submit their
   nominations within two months. The Secretary-General shall prepare
   a list in alphabetical order of all persons thus nominated, indicating
   the States Parties which have nominated them, and shall submit it to
   the States Parties.

4. Elections of the members of the Committee shall be held at a meeting of States Parties convened by the Secretary-General at United Nations Headquarters. At that meeting, for which two thirds of the States Parties shall constitute a quorum, the persons elected to the Committee shall be those nominees who obtain the largest number of votes and an absolute majority of the votes of the representatives of States Parties present and voting.

5. The members of the Committee shall be elected for a term of four years. However, the terms of nine of the members elected at the first election shall expire at the end of two years; immediately after the first election the names of these nine members shall be chosen by lot by the Chairman of the Committee.

6. The election of the five additional members of the Committee shall be held in accordance with the provisions of paragraphs 2, 3 and 4 of this article, following the thirty-fifth ratification or accession. The terms of two of the additional members elected on this occasion shall expire at the end of two years, the names of these two members having been chosen by lot by the Chairman of the Committee.

7. For the filling of casual vacancies, the State Party whose expert has ceased to function as a member of the Committee shall appoint another expert from among its nationals, subject to the approval of the Committee.

8. The members of the Committee shall, with the approval of the General Assembly, receive emoluments from United Nations resources on such terms and conditions as the Assembly may decide, having regard to the importance of the Committee's responsibilities.

9. The Secretary-General of the United Nations shall provide the necessary staff and facilities for the effective performance of the functions of the Committee under the present Convention.

Article 18

1. States Parties undertake to submit to the Secretary-General of the United Nations, for consideration by the Committee, a report on the legislative, judicial, administrative or other measures which they have adopted to give effect to the provisions of the present Convention and on the progress made in this respect:

   a. Within one year after the entry into force for the State concerned;

b. Thereafter at least every four years and further whenever the Committee so requests.
2. Reports may indicate factors and difficulties affecting the degree of fulfillment of obligations under the present Convention.

Article 19
1. The Committee shall adopt its own rules of procedure.
2. The Committee shall elect its officers for a term of two years.

Article 20
1. The Committee shall normally meet for a period of not more than two weeks annually in order to consider the reports submitted in accordance with article 18 of the present Convention.
2. The meetings of the Committee shall normally be held at United Nations Headquarters or at any other convenient place as determined by the Committee.

Article 21
1. The Committee shall, through the Economic and Social Council, report annually to the General Assembly of the United Nations on its activities and may make suggestions and general recommendations based on the examination of reports and information received from the States Parties. Such suggestions and general recommendations shall be included in the report of the Committee together with comments, if any, from States Parties.
2. The Secretary-General of the United Nations shall transmit the reports of the Committee to the Commission on the Status of Women for its information.

Article 22
The specialized agencies shall be entitled to be represented at the consideration of the implementation of such provisions of the present Convention as fall within the scope of their activities. The Committee may invite the specialized agencies to submit reports on the implementation of the Convention in areas falling within the scope of their activities.

Part VI

Article 23

Nothing in the present Convention shall affect any provisions that are more conducive to the achievement of equality between men and women which may be contained:

a. In the legislation of a State Party; or
b. In any other international convention, treaty or agreement in force for that State.

Article 24

States Parties undertake to adopt all necessary measures at the national level aimed at achieving the full realization of the rights recognized in the present Convention.

Article 25

1. The present Convention shall be open for signature by all States.
2. The Secretary-General of the United Nations is designated as the depositary of the present Convention.
3. The present Convention is subject to ratification. Instruments of ratification shall be deposited with the Secretary-General of the United Nations.
4. The present Convention shall be open to accession by all States. Accession shall be effected by the deposit of an instrument of accession with the Secretary-General of the United Nations.

Article 26

1. A request for the revision of the present Convention may be made at any time by any State Party by means of a notification in writing addressed to the Secretary-General of the United Nations.
2. The General Assembly of the United Nations shall decide upon the steps, if any, to be taken in respect of such a request.

Article 27

1. The present Convention shall enter into force on the thirtieth day after the date of deposit with the Secretary-General of the United Nations of the twentieth instrument of ratification or accession.

2. For each State ratifying the present Convention or acceding to it after the deposit of the twentieth instrument of ratification or accession, the Convention shall enter into force on the thirtieth day after the date of the deposit of its own instrument of ratification or accession.

Article 28

1. The Secretary-General of the United Nations shall receive and circulate to all States the text of reservations made by States at the time of ratification or accession.
2. A reservation incompatible with the object and purpose of the present Convention shall not be permitted.
3. Reservations may be withdrawn at any time by notification to this effect addressed to the Secretary-General of the United Nations, who shall then inform all States thereof. Such notification shall take effect on the date on which it is received.

Article 29

1. Any dispute between two or more States Parties concerning the interpretation or application of the present Convention which is not settled by negotiation shall, at the request of one of them, be submitted to arbitration. If within six months from the date of the request for arbitration the parties are unable to agree on the organization of the arbitration, any one of those parties may refer the dispute to the International Court of Justice by request in conformity with the Statute of the Court.
2. Each State Party may at the time of signature or ratification of the present Convention or accession thereto declare that it does not consider itself bound by paragraph 1 of this article. The other States Parties shall not be bound by that paragraph with respect to any State Party which has made such a reservation.
3. Any State Party which has made a reservation in accordance with paragraph 2 of this article may at any time withdraw that reservation by notification to the Secretary-General of the United Nations.

Article 30

The present Convention, the Arabic, Chinese, English, French, Russian and Spanish texts of which are equally authentic, shall be deposited with the Secretary-General of the United Nations.

AFRICAN CHARTER ON HUMAN AND PEOPLES' RIGHTS (PART I) (1981)

When the Universal Declaration of Human Rights (UDHR) was adopted in 1948, only three African nations voted in favor of it (Egypt, Ethiopia, and Liberia). This was not because there was widespread African opposition to it but because much of Africa was under colonial rule (i.e., rule by European countries). Over the next few decades this changed, with many struggles for the establishment of independent states. Part of this movement was the formation of the Organization of African Unity (OAU) in 1963. (The OAU lasted until 2002, when it was succeeded by the current African Union.) Immediately upon the enactment of the Charter of the OAU, work began on formulating an OAU document on human rights, which was finally completed and ratified in 1981. The African Charter on Human and Peoples' Rights (ACHPR) takes the basic view of the UDHR that rights are universal, but, largely because of the colonial legacy in Africa, it also claims that rights must be understood in social, cultural, and historical contexts. Two features of the ACHPR that distinguish it from previous international rights documents are (1) that it speaks to the rights not only of individuals but also of "peoples" (i.e., cultures and societies as such), and (2) that it speaks of duties as well as rights. Following the adoption of the ACHPR, the OAU later adopted other rights documents that focused even more specifically on rights related to elections, popular participation in government, and economic development, as well as the rights and welfare of children.

Preamble

The African States members of the Organization of African Unity, parties to the present convention entitled "African Charter on Human and Peoples' Rights,"

Recalling Decision 115 (XVI) of the Assembly of Heads of State and Government at its Sixteenth Ordinary Session held in Monrovia, Liberia, from 17 to 20 July 1979 on the preparation of a "preliminary draft on an African Charter on Human and Peoples' Rights providing inter alia for the establishment of bodies to promote and protect human and peoples' rights";

Considering the Charter of the Organization of African Unity, which stipulates that "freedom, equality, justice and dignity are essential objectives for the achievement of the legitimate aspirations of the African peoples";

Reaffirming the pledge they solemnly made in Article 2 of the said Charter to eradicate all forms of colonialism from Africa, to coordinate and intensify their cooperation and efforts to achieve a better life for the peoples of Africa and to promote international cooperation having due regard to the Charter of the United Nations and the Universal Declaration of Human Rights;

Taking into consideration the virtues of their historical tradition and the values of African civilization which should inspire and characterize their reflection on the concept of human and peoples' rights;

Recognizing on the one hand that fundamental human rights stem from the attributes of human beings which justifies their national and international protection and on the other hand that the reality and respect of peoples rights should necessarily guarantee human rights;

Considering that the enjoyment of rights and freedoms also implies the performance of duties on the part of everyone;

Convinced that it is henceforth essential to pay a particular attention to the right to development and that civil and political rights cannot be dissociated from economic, social and cultural rights in their conception as well as universality and that the satisfaction of economic, social and cultural rights is a guarantee for the enjoyment of civil and political rights;

Conscious of their duty to achieve the total liberation of Africa, the peoples of which are still struggling for their dignity and genuine independence, and undertaking to eliminate colonialism, neo-colonialism, apartheid, zionism and to dismantle aggressive foreign military bases and all forms of discrimination, particularly those based on race, ethnic group, color, sex, language, religion or political opinion;

Reaffirming their adherence to the principles of human and peoples' rights and freedoms contained in the declarations, conventions and other instrument adopted by the Organization of African Unity, the Movement of Non-Aligned Countries and the United Nations;

Firmly convinced of their duty to promote and protect human and peoples' rights and freedoms taking into account the importance traditionally attached to these rights and freedoms in Africa;

Have agreed as follows:

Part I: Rights and Duties

Chapter I—Human and Peoples' Rights

ARTICLE 1

The Member States of the Organization of African Unity parties to the present Charter shall recognize the rights, duties and freedoms enshrined in this Chapter and shall undertake to adopt legislative or other measures to give effect to them.

ARTICLE 2

Every individual shall be entitled to the enjoyment of the rights and freedoms recognized and guaranteed in the present Charter without distinction of any kind such as race, ethnic group, color, sex, language, religion, political or any other opinion, national and social origin, fortune, birth or other status.

ARTICLE 3

1. Every individual shall be equal before the law.
2. Every individual shall be entitled to equal protection of the law.

ARTICLE 4

Human beings are inviolable. Every human being shall be entitled to respect for his life and the integrity of his person. No one may be arbitrarily deprived of this right.

ARTICLE 5

Every individual shall have the right to the respect of the dignity inherent in a human being and to the recognition of his legal status. All forms of exploitation and degradation of man particularly slavery, slave trade, torture, cruel, inhuman or degrading punishment and treatment shall be prohibited.

ARTICLE 6

Every individual shall have the right to liberty and to the security of his person. No one may be deprived of his freedom except for reasons and conditions previously laid down by law. In particular, no one may be arbitrarily arrested or detained.

ARTICLE 7

1. Every individual shall have the right to have his cause heard. This comprises:
   a. the right to an appeal to competent national organs against acts of violating his fundamental rights as recognized and guaranteed by conventions, laws, regulations and customs in force;
   b. the right to be presumed innocent until proved guilty by a competent court or tribunal;
   c. the right to defense, including the right to be defended by counsel of his choice;
   d. the right to be tried within a reasonable time by an impartial court or tribunal.
2. No one may be condemned for an act or omission which did not constitute a legally punishable offence at the time it was committed. No penalty may be inflicted for an offence for which no provision was made at the time it was committed. Punishment is personal and can be imposed only on the offender.

ARTICLE 8

Freedom of conscience, the profession and free practice of religion shall be guaranteed. No one may, subject to law and order, be submitted to measures restricting the exercise of these freedoms.

ARTICLE 9

1. Every individual shall have the right to receive information.
2. Every individual shall have the right to express and disseminate his opinions within the law.

ARTICLE 10

1. Every individual shall have the right to free association provided that he abides by the law.
2. Subject to the obligation of solidarity provided for in 29 no one may be compelled to join an association.

ARTICLE 11

Every individual shall have the right to assemble freely with others. The exercise of this right shall be subject only to necessary restrictions provided for by law in particular those enacted in the interest of national security, the safety, health, ethics and rights and freedoms of others.

ARTICLE 12

1. Every individual shall have the right to freedom of movement and residence within the borders of a State provided he abides by the law.
2. Every individual shall have the right to leave any country including his own, and to return to his country. This right may only be subject to restrictions, provided for by law for the protection of national security, law and order, public health or morality.
3. Every individual shall have the right, when persecuted, to seek and obtain asylum in other countries in accordance with laws of those countries and international conventions.
4. A non-national legally admitted in a territory of a State Party to the present Charter, may only be expelled from it by virtue of a decision taken in accordance with the law.
5. The mass expulsion of non-nationals shall be prohibited. Mass expulsion shall be that which is aimed at national, racial, ethnic or religious groups.

ARTICLE 13

1. Every citizen shall have the right to participate freely in the government of his country, either directly or through freely chosen representatives in accordance with the provisions of the law.
2. Every citizen shall have the right of equal access to the public service of his country.
3. Every individual shall have the right of access to public property and services in strict equality of all persons before the law.

ARTICLE 14

The right to property shall be guaranteed. It may only be encroached upon in the interest of public need or in the general interest of the community and in accordance with the provisions of appropriate laws.

ARTICLE 15

Every individual shall have the right to work under equitable and satisfactory conditions, and shall receive equal pay for equal work.

ARTICLE 16

1. Every individual shall have the right to enjoy the best attainable state of physical and mental health.
2. States Parties to the present Charter shall take the necessary measures to protect the health of their people and to ensure that they receive medical attention when they are sick.

ARTICLE 17

1. Every individual shall have the right to education.
2. Every individual may freely take part in the cultural life of his community.
3. The promotion and protection of morals and traditional values recognized by the community shall be the duty of the State.

ARTICLE 18

1. The family shall be the natural unit and basis of society. It shall be protected by the State which shall take care of its physical health and moral.
2. The State shall have the duty to assist the family which is the custodian of morals and traditional values recognized by the community.
3. The State shall ensure the elimination of every discrimination against women and also ensure the protection of the rights of the woman and the child as stipulated in international declarations and conventions.
4. The aged and the disabled shall also have the right to special measures of protection in keeping with their physical or moral needs.

ARTICLE 19

All peoples shall be equal; they shall enjoy the same respect and shall have the same rights. Nothing shall justify the domination of a people by another.

ARTICLE 20

1. All peoples shall have the right to existence. They shall have the unquestionable and inalienable right to self-determination. They shall freely determine their political status and shall pursue their economic and social development according to the policy they have freely chosen.
2. Colonized or oppressed peoples shall have the right to free themselves from the bonds of domination by resorting to any means recognized by the international community.
3. All peoples shall have the right to the assistance of the States parties to the present Charter in their liberation struggle against foreign domination, be it political, economic or cultural.

ARTICLE 21

1. All peoples shall freely dispose of their wealth and natural resources. This right shall be exercised in the exclusive interest of the people. In no case shall a people be deprived of it.
2. In case of spoliation the dispossessed people shall have the right to the lawful recovery of its property as well as to an adequate compensation.
3. The free disposal of wealth and natural resources shall be exercised without prejudice to the obligation of promoting international economic cooperation based on mutual respect, equitable exchange and the principles of international law.
4. States parties to the present Charter shall individually and collectively exercise the right to free disposal of their wealth and natural resources with a view to strengthening African unity and solidarity.
5. States parties to the present Charter shall undertake to eliminate all forms of foreign economic exploitation particularly that practiced by international monopolies so as to enable their peoples to fully benefit from the advantages derived from their national resources.

ARTICLE 22

1. All peoples shall have the right to their economic, social and cultural development with due regard to their freedom and identity and in the equal enjoyment of the common heritage of mankind.
2. States shall have the duty, individually or collectively, to ensure the exercise of the right to development.

ARTICLE 23

1. All peoples shall have the right to national and international peace and security. The principles of solidarity and friendly relations implicitly affirmed by the Charter of the United Nations and reaffirmed by that of the Organization of African Unity shall govern relations between States.
2. For the purpose of strengthening peace, solidarity and friendly relations, States parties to the present Charter shall ensure that:
   a. any individual enjoying the right of asylum under 12 of the present Charter shall not engage in subversive activities against his country of origin or any other State party to the present Charter;
   b. their territories shall not be used as bases for subversive or terrorist activities against the people of any other State party to the present Charter.

ARTICLE 24

All peoples shall have the right to a general satisfactory environment favorable to their development.

ARTICLE 25

States parties to the present Charter shall have the duty to promote and ensure through teaching, education and publication, the respect of the rights and freedoms contained in the present Charter and to see to it that these freedoms and rights as well as corresponding obligations and duties are understood.

ARTICLE 26

States parties to the present Charter shall have the duty to guarantee the independence of the Courts and shall allow the establishment and improvement of appropriate national institutions entrusted with the promotion and protection of the rights and freedoms guaranteed by the present Charter.

Chapter II—Duties

ARTICLE 27

1. Every individual shall have duties towards his family and society, the State and other legally recognized communities and the international community.
2. The rights and freedoms of each individual shall be exercised with due regard to the rights of others, collective security, morality and common interest.

ARTICLE 28

Every individual shall have the duty to respect and consider his fellow beings without discrimination, and to maintain relations aimed at promoting, safeguarding and reinforcing mutual respect and tolerance.

ARTICLE 29

The individual shall also have the duty:

1. To preserve the harmonious development of the family and to work for the cohesion and respect of the family; to respect his parents at all times, to maintain them in case of need;
2. To serve his national community by placing his physical and intellectual abilities at its service;
3. Not to compromise the security of the State whose national or resident he is;
4. To preserve and strengthen social and national solidarity, particularly when the latter is threatened;
5. To preserve and strengthen the national independence and the territorial integrity of his country and to contribute to its defense in accordance with the law;
6. To work to the best of his abilities and competence, and to pay taxes imposed by law in the interest of the society;
7. To preserve and strengthen positive African cultural values in his relations with other members of the society, in the spirit of tolerance, dialogue and consultation and, in general, to contribute to the promotion of the moral well-being of society;
8. To contribute to the best of his abilities, at all times and at all levels, to the promotion and achievement of African unity.

CAIRO DECLARATION ON HUMAN RIGHTS IN ISLAM (1990)

The Cairo Declaration on Human Rights in Islam (CDHRI) was formulated and adopted by the Organization of the Islamic Conference largely as a response to what was seen as concerns about human rights as they were articulated in the Universal Declaration of Human Rights (UDHR). At the time of the UDHR's ratification in 1948, no Islamic countries voted against it. Saudi Arabia abstained, while Afghanistan, Egypt, Iran, Iraq, Lebanon, Pakistan, Syria, and Turkey all voted in favor of the UDHR. However, over the following several decades, political sensibilities and even regimes changed dramatically throughout much of the Islamic world. In particular, the Islamic Revolution in Iran in the late 1970s led to a broad resurgence of attention to Shari'ah, or Islamic law—that is, law (regulation of people's behavior) based on sacred Islamic scripture, with the result that civil law is understood as legitimate only to the extent that it conforms to (or at least does not contradict) sacred law. The UDHR, say many Islamic critics, essentially has a Western, and particularly Judeo-Christian, understanding of human rights. It fails to take into account religious, social, and cultural differences. Humans, hence human rights, are properly understood only in such contexts. More importantly, for these Islamic critics, Shari'ah represents the true word of God, and so, human relations—including human rights—must be understood relative to it. The fact that the political representatives from Islamic countries did not vote against the UDHR in 1948 does not negate these facts. They should have voted against it, say these critics, and to the extent that the UDHR is not consistent with Shari'ah, Islamic countries are under no obligation to support or abide by the UDHR. Instead, they say, the CDHRI represents the more appropriate view of human rights.

The Member States of the Organization of the Islamic Conference,
    Reaffirming the civilizing and historical role of the Islamic Ummah which God made the best nation that has given mankind a universal and well-balanced civilization in which harmony is established between this

life and the hereafter and knowledge is combined with faith; and the role that this Ummah should play to guide a humanity confused by competing trends and ideologies and to provide solutions to the chronic problems of this materialistic civilization;

Wishing to contribute to the efforts of mankind to assert human rights, to protect man from exploitation and persecution, and to affirm his freedom and right to a dignified life in accordance with the Islamic Shari'ah;

Convinced that mankind which has reached an advanced stage in materialistic science is still, and shall remain, in dire need of faith to support its civilization and of a self-motivating force to guard its rights;

Believing that fundamental rights and universal freedoms in Islam are an integral part of the Islamic religion and that no one as a matter of principle has the right to suspend them in whole or in part or violate or ignore them in as much as they are binding divine commandments, which are contained in the Revealed Books of God and were sent through the last of His Prophets to complete the preceding divine messages thereby making their observance an act of worship and their neglect or violation an abominable sin, and accordingly every person is individually responsible—and the Ummah collectively responsible—for their safeguard;

Proceeding from the above-mentioned principles,

Declare the following:

Article 1

a. All human beings form one family whose members are united by submission to God and descent from Adam. All men are equal in terms of basic human dignity and basic obligations and responsibilities, without any discrimination on the grounds of race, color, language, sex, religious belief, political affiliation, social status or other considerations. True faith is the guarantee for enhancing such dignity along the path to human perfection.

b. All human beings are God's subjects, and the most loved by him are those who are most useful to the rest of His subjects, and no one has superiority over another except on the basis of piety and good deeds.

Article 2

a. Life is a God-given gift and the right to life is guaranteed to every human being. It is the duty of individuals, societies and states to protect this right from any violation, and it is prohibited to take away life except for a Shari'ah-prescribed reason.

b. It is forbidden to resort to such means as may result in the genocidal annihilation of mankind.

c. The preservation of human life throughout the term of time willed by God is a duty prescribed by Shari'ah.

d. Safety from bodily harm is a guaranteed right. It is the duty of the state to safeguard it, and it is prohibited to breach it without a Shari'ah-prescribed reason.

Article 3

a. In the event of the use of force and in case of armed conflict, it is not permissible to kill non-belligerents such as old men, women and children. The wounded and the sick shall have the right to medical treatment; and prisoners of war shall have the right to be fed, sheltered and clothed. It is prohibited to mutilate dead bodies. It is a duty to exchange prisoners of war and to arrange visits or reunions of the families separated by the circumstances of war.

b. It is prohibited to fell trees, to damage crops or livestock, and to destroy the enemy's civilian buildings and installations by shelling, blasting or any other means.

Article 4

Every human being is entitled to inviolability and the protection of his good name and honor during his life and after his death. The state and society shall protect his remains and burial place.

Article 5

a. The family is the foundation of society, and marriage is the basis of its formation. Men and women have the right to marriage, and no restrictions stemming from race, color or nationality shall prevent them from enjoying this right.

b. Society and the State shall remove all obstacles to marriage and shall facilitate marital procedure. They shall ensure family protection and welfare.

Article 6

a. Woman is equal to man in human dignity, and has rights to enjoy as well as duties to perform; she has her own civil entity and financial independence, and the right to retain her name and lineage.

b. The husband is responsible for the support and welfare of the family.

Article 7

a. As of the moment of birth, every child has rights due from the parents, society and the state to be accorded proper nursing, education and material, hygienic and moral care. Both the fetus and the mother must be protected and accorded special care.

b. Parents and those in such like capacity have the right to choose the type of education they desire for their children, provided they take into consideration the interest and future of the children in accordance with ethical values and the principles of the Shari'ah.

c. Both parents are entitled to certain rights from their children, and relatives are entitled to rights from their kin, in accordance with the tenets of the Shari'ah.

Article 8

Every human being has the right to enjoy his legal capacity in terms of both obligation and commitment. Should this capacity be lost or impaired, he shall be represented by his guardian.

Article 9

a. The quest for knowledge is an obligation, and the provision of education is a duty for society and the State. The State shall ensure the

availability of ways and means to acquire education and shall guarantee educational diversity in the interest of society so as to enable
man to be acquainted with the religion of Islam and the facts of the
Universe for the benefit of mankind.

b. Every human being has the right to receive both religious and
worldly education from the various institutions of education and
guidance, including the family, the school, the university, the media,
etc., and in such an integrated and balanced manner as to develop
his personality, strengthen his faith in God and promote his respect
for and defense of both rights and obligations.

Article 10

Islam is the religion of unspoiled nature. It is prohibited to exercise any
form of compulsion on man or to exploit his poverty or ignorance in order to convert him to another religion or to atheism.

Article 11

a. Human beings are born free, and no one has the right to enslave, hu-
miliate, oppress or exploit them, and there can be no subjugation
but to God the Most-High.

b. Colonialism of all types being one of the most evil forms of enslavement is totally prohibited. Peoples suffering from colonialism have
the full right to freedom and self-determination. It is the duty of all
States and peoples to support the struggle of colonized peoples for
the liquidation of all forms of colonialism and occupation, and all
States and peoples have the right to preserve their independent identity and exercise control over their wealth and natural resources.

Article 12

Every man shall have the right, within the framework of Shari'ah, to free
movement and to select his place of residence whether inside or outside
his country and, if persecuted, is entitled to seek asylum in another country. The country of refuge shall ensure his protection until he reaches safety,
unless asylum is motivated by an act which Shari'ah regards as a crime.

Article 13

Work is a right guaranteed by the State and Society for each person able to work. Everyone shall be free to choose the work that suits him best and which serves his interests and those of society. The employee shall have the right to safety and security as well as to all other social guarantees. He may neither be assigned work beyond his capacity nor be subjected to compulsion or exploited or harmed in any way. He shall be entitled—without any discrimination between males and females—to fair wages for his work without delay, as well as to the holidays, allowances and promotions which he deserves. For his part, he shall be required to be dedicated and meticulous in his work. Should workers and employers disagree on any matter, the State shall intervene to settle the dispute and have the grievances redressed, the rights confirmed and justice enforced without bias.

Article 14

Everyone shall have the right to legitimate gains without monopolization, deceit or harm to oneself or to others. Usury (riba) is absolutely prohibited.

Article 15

a. Everyone shall have the right to own property acquired in a legitimate way, and shall be entitled to the rights of ownership, without prejudice to oneself, others or to society in general. Expropriation is not permissible except for the requirements of public interest and upon payment of immediate and fair compensation.
b. Confiscation and seizure of property is prohibited except for a necessity dictated by law.

Article 16

Everyone shall have the right to enjoy the fruits of his scientific, literary, artistic or technical production and the right to protect the moral and material interests stemming therefrom, provided that such production is not contrary to the principles of Shari'ah.

Article 17

a. Everyone shall have the right to live in a clean environment, away from vice and moral corruption, an environment that would foster his self-development; and it is incumbent upon the State and society in general to afford that right.
b. Everyone shall have the right to medical and social care, and to all public amenities provided by society and the State within the limits of their available resources.
c. The State shall ensure the right of the individual to a decent living which will enable him to meet all his requirements and those of his dependents, including food, clothing, housing, education, medical care and all other basic needs.

Article 18

a. Everyone shall have the right to live in security for himself, his religion, his dependents, his honor and his property.
b. Everyone shall have the right to privacy in the conduct of his private affairs, in his home, among his family, with regard to his property and his relationships. It is not permitted to spy on him, to place him under surveillance or to besmirch his good name. The State shall protect him from arbitrary interference.
c. A private residence is inviolable in all cases. It will not be entered without permission from its inhabitants or in any unlawful manner, nor shall it be demolished or confiscated and its dwellers evicted.

Article 19

a. All individuals are equal before the law, without distinction between the ruler and the ruled.
b. The right to resort to justice is guaranteed to everyone.
c. Liability is in essence personal.
d. There shall be no crime or punishment except as provided for in the Shari'ah.
e. A defendant is innocent until his guilt is proven in a fair trial in which he shall be given all the guarantees of defense.

Article 20

It is not permitted without legitimate reason to arrest an individual, or restrict his freedom, to exile or to punish him. It is not permitted to subject him to physical or psychological torture or to any form of humiliation, cruelty or indignity. Nor is it permitted to subject an individual to medical or scientific experimentation without his consent or at the risk of his health or of his life. Nor is it permitted to promulgate emergency laws that would provide executive authority for such actions.

Article 21

Taking hostages under any form or for any purpose is expressly forbidden.

Article 22

a. Everyone shall have the right to express his opinion freely in such manner as would not be contrary to the principles of the Shari'ah.
b. Everyone shall have the right to advocate what is right, and propagate what is good, and warn against what is wrong and evil according to the norms of Islamic Shari'ah.
c. Information is a vital necessity to society. It may not be exploited or misused in such a way as may violate sanctities and the dignity of Prophets, undermine moral and ethical values or disintegrate, corrupt or harm society or weaken its faith.
d. It is not permitted to arouse nationalistic or doctrinal hatred or to do anything that may be an incitement to any form of racial discrimination.

Article 23

a. Authority is a trust; and abuse or malicious exploitation thereof is absolutely prohibited, so that fundamental human rights may be guaranteed.
b. Everyone shall have the right to participate, directly or indirectly in the administration of his country's public affairs. He shall also have the right to assume public office in accordance with the provisions of Shari'ah.

Article 24

All the rights and freedoms stipulated in this Declaration are subject to the Islamic Shari'ah.

Article 25

The Islamic Shari'ah is the only source of reference for the explanation or clarification to any of the articles of this Declaration.

Credits

The following cites original publication information for readings included in the text. All excerpts are reprinted by permission.

CHAPTER 1

Dworkin, Ronald. "Rights As Trumps." In *Theories of Rights*, edited by Jeremy Waldron, 153–167. Oxford, UK: Oxford University Press, 1984. Also see Ronald Dworkin, *Taking Rights Seriously*. Cambridge, Mass.: The Belknap Press of Harvard University Press, pp. xi, 204–207, 268–269, 277. Reprinted by permission of the publisher. Copyright © 1977, 1978 by Ronald Dworkin.

Feinberg, Joel. "The Nature and Value of Rights." *Journal of Value Inquiry* 4 (1970): 243–251.

Nussbaum, Martha. "Capabilities and Human Rights." *Fordham Law Review* 66 (1997): 273–300.

Raz, Joseph. "On the Nature of Rights." *Mind* 93 (1984): 194–214. Reprinted by permission of Oxford University Press.

CHAPTER 2

Dershowitz, Alan. *Rights from Wrongs*. New York: Basic Books, 2004.

Harman, Gilbert. "Moral Relativism as a Foundation for Natural Rights." *Journal of Libertarian Studies* 4 (1980): 367–371.

Hospers, John. *Libertarianism*. Santa Barbara, CA: Reason Press, 1971.

Mill, John Stuart. "On the Connection Between Justice and Utility." In *Utilitarianism*, 41–53. Indianapolis: Hackett, 1979.

CHAPTER 3

Frey, R. G. "Moral Rights: Some Doubts." In *Interests and Rights: The Case Against Animals*, 4–17. Oxford, UK: Clarendon Press, 1980.

Hart, H. L. A. "Are There Any Natural Rights?" *Philosophical Review* 64, no. 2 (1955): 175–191. Courtesy of Duke University Press.

Machan, Tibor. "Between Positive and Negative Rights." In *Individuals and Their Rights*, 123–134. LaSalle, IL: Open Court, 1989. Reprinted by permission of Open Court Publishing Company, a division of Carus Publishing Company, Chicago, IL. Copyright © 1989 by Open Court Publishing.

Shue, Henry. *Basic Rights: Subsistence, Affluence, and U.S. Foreign Policy.* Princeton, NJ: Princeton University Press, 1980.

CHAPTER 4

Cohen, Carl. "In Defense of the Use of Animals." In *The Animal Rights Debate*, edited by Carl Cohen and Tom Regan, 3–124. Lanham, MD: Rowman & Littlefield, 2001.

Gould, Carol C. "Group Rights and Social Ontology." In *Groups and Group Rights*, edited by Christine Sistare, Larry May, and Leslie Francis, 43–57. Lawrence, KS: University of Kansas Press, 2001.

Regan, Tom. *The Case for Animal Rights.* Berkeley, CA: University of California Press, 1983.

Wall, Edmund. "Problems with the Group Rights Thesis." *American Philosophical Quarterly* 40 (2003): 269–285.

CHAPTER 5

D'Souza, Radha. "What's Wrong with Rights?" *Seedling* (October 2007): 2–3, accessed September 23, 2010, www.grain.org/seedling/?id=505#.

Husak, Douglas. "Why There Are No Human Rights." *Social Theory and Practice* 11 (1984): 125–141.

MacIntyre, Alasdair. *After Virtue: A Study in Moral Theory.* Notre Dame, IN: University of Notre Dame Press, 1981. Copyright © 1981, 1984, 2007 by

Alasdair MacIntyre. Reprinted with permission of the University of Notre Dame Press.

Wolgast, Elizabeth. "Wrong Rights." *Hypatia* 2, no. 1 (1987): 25–43. Copyright 1987 by Hypatia, Inc. Reprinted with permission of John Wiley & Sons, Inc.

CHAPTER 6

Bunger, Amy. "Rights Talk As a Form of Political Communication." In *Politics, Discourse, and American Society: New Agendas*, edited by Roderick P. Hart and Bartholomew H. Sparrow, 71–90. Lanham, MD: Rowman & Littlefield, 2001.

Glendon, Mary Ann. *Rights Talk: The Impoverishment of Political Discourse*. New York: Free Press, 1991.

Walker, Samuel. *The Rights Revolution*. Oxford, UK: Oxford University Press, 1998.

CHAPTER 7

An-Na'im, Abdullahi Ahmed. "Toward a Cross-Cultural Approach to Defining International Standards of Human Rights." In *Human Rights in Cross-Cultural Perspectives: A Quest for Consensus*, edited by Abdullahi Ahmed An-Na'im, 19–43. Philadelphia, PA: University of Pennsylvania Press, 1992.

Lee, Manwoo. "North Korea and the Western Notion of Human Rights." In *Human Rights in East Asia: A Cultural Perspective*, edited by James C. Hsiung, 129–151. New York: Paragon House, 1985.

Tesón, Fernando R. "International Human Rights and Cultural Relativism." *Virginia Journal of International Law* 25 (1985): 869–898.

CHAPTER 8

Tsesis, Alexander. *Destructive Messages: How Hate Speech Paves the Way for Harmful Social Movements*. New York: New York University Press, 2002.

Wolfson, Nicholas. *Hate Speech, Sex Speech, Free Speech*. Westport, CT: Praeger Publishers, 1997.

CHAPTER 9

Epstein, Richard. "In Defense of the Contract at Will." *University of Chicago Law Review* 51 (1984): 947–982.

Werhane, Patricia H., and Tara J. Radin. "Employment at Will and Due Process." In *Ethical Theory and Business*, edited by Tom L. Beauchamp and Norman E. Bowie, 267–274. 6th ed. Upper Saddle River, NJ: Prentice Hall, 2001.

CHAPTER 10

Warren, Samuel, and Louis Brandeis. "The Right to Privacy." *Harvard Law Review* 4 (1890): 193–220.
Weinreb, Lloyd L. "The Right to Privacy." *Social Philosophy and Policy* 17 (2000): 25–44.

CHAPTER 11

Hettinger, Edwin C. "Justifying Intellectual Property." *Philosophy and Public Affairs* 18 (1989): 31–52.
Spooner, Lysander. "The Law of Intellectual Property—the Law of Nature." In *The Collected Works of Lysander Spooner*, edited by Charles Shively, vol. 3, 9–12, 15–21, 28–30. Weston, MA: M&S Press, 1971.

CHAPTER 12

Boersema, David. "What's Wrong with Victims' Rights?" In *Remembrance and Reconciliation*, edited by Rob Gildert and Dennis Rothermel, 73–81. New York: Rodopi, 2011.
Cassell, Paul G. "Barbarians at the Gates? A Reply to Critics of the Victims' Rights Amendment." *Utah Law Review* 2 (1999): 479–544.
Henderson, Lynne H. "Revisiting Victim's Rights." *Utah Law Review* 2 (1999): 383–442.

CHAPTER 13

Coady, Margaret M. "The Continuing Importance of Thinking That Children Have Rights." *Australian Journal of Professional and Applied Ethics* 7 (2005): 47–57.
Guggenheim, Martin. *What's Wrong with Children's Rights?* Cambridge, MA: Harvard University Press, 2005, pp. 8–16, 245–249, 264–266. Copyright © 2005 by the President and Fellows of Harvard College.

Index

ormation can be obtained
sting.com
SA
91222
011B/44